In Victory, Magnanimity
In Peace, Goodwill

By the same author

The Community of Europe
The Recovery of Europe
The Europeans
Postwar
Federal Union: The Pioneers (with John Pinder)
The Language of Sailing

(Edited)
Europe Tomorrow
The New Atlantic Challenge
Western Europe: A Handbook

(Translated)
Memoirs by Jean Monnet
Europe: A History of Its Peoples by Jean-Baptiste Duroselle
Illustrated History of Europe
A History of Civilisations by Fernand Braudel

In Victory, Magnanimity
In Peace, Goodwill

A History of Wilton Park

RICHARD MAYNE

WHITEHALL HISTORY PUBLISHING
in association with
FRANK CASS
LONDON • PORTLAND, OR

First published in 2003 in Great Britain by
FRANK CASS PUBLISHERS
Crown House, 47 Chase Side, Southgate
London N14 5BP

and in the United States of America by
FRANK CASS PUBLISHERS
c/o ISBS, 5824 N.E. Hassalo Street
Portland, Oregon, 97213-3644

Website: www.frankcass.com

The author has been given free access to official documents.
He alone is responsible for the statements made and the views expressed.

British Library Cataloguing in Publication Data

Mayne, Richard, 1926–
    In victory, magnanimity, in peace, goodwill: a history of
    Wilton Park. – (Whitehall histories)
    1. Koeppler, Heinz 2. Wilton Park (Organisation) – History
    3. International relations 4. Democratization 5. Learned
    institutions and societies – Great Britain
    I. Title II. Great Britain. Foreign and Commonwealth Office
    327′ .06041

ISBN 0-7146-5433-7

Library of Congress Cataloging-in-Publication Data

A catalog record for this book is available
from the Library of Congress

Typeset in 11/13pt Ehrhardt by Frank Cass Publishers Ltd
Printed in Great Britain by MPG Books, Victoria Square, Bodmin, Cornwall

Contents

Illustrations

16. Wilton Park Academic Staff member George Roundell Greene (left) with Lord Beveridge (centre) at a conference in June 1956.
17. Dinner at Wilton Park during the 11th European Conference in March 1959.
18. Heinz Koeppler, 1960s.
19. HRH The Duke of Edinburgh arrives at Wilton Park for the 100th Conference in March 1968.
20. Heinz Koeppler addressing Wilton Park conference, 1970s.
21. Shirley Williams MP, at Wilton Park on the 25th Anniversary of its foundation, 12 January 1971. Assisting with the cutting of the cake are Chefs G. Gander and Mr Handerer.
22. The Right Hon. Edward Heath, Prime Minister, arriving by helicopter for the Jubilee Conference in June 1971.
23. Robert D. J. Gibson who retired from Wilton Park in 1976 at the end of 30 years' service.
24. Heinz Koeppler planting a memorial copper beech tree on his retirement 30 June 1977.
25. The last picture taken of Heinz Koeppler in Ashley Gardens, London, circa 1979.

Between pages 332 and 333:

26. Sir Robert Birley, Chairman of the Wilton Park Academic Council (1950–1982).
27. Dr Bruno Kreisky, Federal Chancellor of Austria, opened the 221st Wilton Park Conference in September 1980.
28. The Rt Hon. Sir Geoffrey Howe, British Foreign Secretary, attending the conference on USA and Europe in March 1984.
29. Alan Hughes, Deputy Director (1972–1984), in 1984.
30. Group photograph of the Employment Crisis conference in November 1986. Participants included Gordon Brown seated next to Geoffrey Denton, Director of Wilton Park (1983–1993).
31. Sir Geoffrey Howe and Geoffrey Denton admire the 1576 ceiling of Wiston House's Great Hall during the March 1984 conference.
32. Tim Slack, Director of Wilton Park (1977–1983).
33. Richard Langhorne, Director of Wilton Park (1993–1996).
34. HRH The Prince of Wales signing the Golden Book at Wilton Park's 50th Anniversary Conference 1996.
35. Harry Goring (right) welcomes the Prince of Wales to Wiston House with (left to right) John Knight (High Sheriff of

Foreword

Wilton Park changed my life. On that January day in 1948, the long trip from Hamburg to Beaconsfield was itself exciting enough. Armed with a Temporary Travel Document (no passport yet for Germans), an 'exit visa' and a 're-entry visa', the eighteen-year-old enjoyed the train journey to Hoek van Holland, suffered in the bowels of the ferry during the stormy night, nevertheless relished the English breakfast on the boat train, gazed with amazement at the great Metropolis, London, on the way from Liverpool Street to Marylebone, and ended up in the Buckinghamshire manor house that was then Wilton Park.

The following weeks opened both our eyes and our hearts. Along with the POWs, we, the free natives of Germany, were educated in English ways. Lord Pakenham came and patiently answered questions: 'Herr Mister Lord Pakenham, why do the English not respect their newspapers? Since we came, I have collected dozens of discarded papers.' The Minister for Germany answered with patience and good humour. Much later he, as Earl of Longford, was a very senior colleague of mine in the House of Lords. Lord Lindsay of Birker came and told us about democracy. The imposing figure of Heinz Koeppler was always present. And we ourselves formed a community within which lasting friendships could thrive.

Nowadays there is much discussion of citizenship and how it can be taught. I cannot think of a more painless and effective way than those weeks at Wilton Park. Diversity, leadership, practical information, examples were all there, and the mixture of fun and seriousness helped. No one returned home without a strong sense that democracy requires, beyond all institutions, democrats, and we had seen impressive examples.

Since then, Wilton Park has spread far and wide without ever abandoning its quality as a school of democratic citizenship. This is a story worth telling, and Richard Mayne – following in the footsteps of that great citizen of Britain and Europe, Robert Rhodes James – is splendidly qualified to tell it.

Ralf Dahrendorf
London, July 2002

Preface

This book is about an idea, not a house. Wilton Park *was* a house and *is* an institution; but its essence was always more. Its aim was and is to unite people: to bring together those who disagree, often violently, and by patient, outspoken discussion of their conflicting views and assumptions, to reconcile rivals and enemies in recognition of their common humanity, their shared problems, and their joint hopes of peace. The process began at the end of World War II with German prisoners-of-war. It continued with some of the civilians who were to build democratic Germany. It spread to involve other Europeans, Americans, and people from elsewhere, including the troubled Middle East. In today's strife-torn world, no task could be more urgent. For more than fifty years, Wilton Park has shown what can be done with care, tact, honesty, frankness and delicate hard work. The present book tells that story.

Its author should have been the late Sir Robert Rhodes James. He had long been a friend of Wilton Park and of its founder Heinz Koeppler. He had completed a great deal of preliminary research. But before he could write more than a few pages he was suddenly stricken by cancer. The Trustees of the Sir Heinz Koeppler Trust, which had commissioned the book, then asked me to take over. Having known Robert and admired his work, I felt both honoured and diffident. I am sure that his book would have been very different from mine. Happily, the beginning of his draft Preface survives, and deserves quotation here.

The histories of institutions are seldom exhilarating. The process is wearyingly familiar. As some anniversary approaches, the Directors, or Governors, Trustees or whatever, resolve to commission an official history of the great concern over which they preside. There is no question of it being objective, let alone critical, of anything or anyone concerned with the institution for at least the past fifty years. Dark moments in the institution's history will be ignored, or treated very cursorily. The Directors will keep a very close eye on the project.

The choice of author is handled with great care. He or she must be very sound – i.e. amenable to advice and pressure. The contract must make very plain who is the boss, and who is paying the piper. Only when the author cravenly agrees to

*these conditions will money – often a lot of it – change hands. The resultant prod-
uct, usually lavishly illustrated, is then treated as a Public Relations project, and
given away to clients and visitors, who express warm thanks and never read it.
Blessedly, there are exceptions to this dismal pattern ...*

There are. Robert instanced the forbearance of the Wellcome Trust,
which placed no such conditions on his biography of Sir Henry Wellcome
– and that of the Sir Heinz Koeppler Trust itself. I have enjoyed the same
freedom to portray Wilton Park 'warts and all'.

Like Robert, I have been allowed to see the relevant papers in the
Foreign and Commonwealth Office archive, very generously assisted both
by Heather Yasamee, Head of Records and Historical Department, and by
Dr Martin Longden. Other sources, beyond those of Wiston House itself,
have included the unpublished diaries of the late Sir Harold Nicolson and
his son Nigel; and the President and Fellows of Magdalen College, Oxford
– not to mention its Archivist, Dr Robin Darvall-Smith – have been as
immensely helpful to me as to Robert in illuminating the Oxford period of
Koeppler's life. His sister Hanni has also been an invaluable witness to
their childhood in Germany. His physician, Dr Alec Frank, gave me
notable personal insights; so did his former colleagues (especially Alan
Hughes) and his successors, including Tim Slack, Geoffrey Denton,
Richard Langhorne, and the present very hospitable incumbent, Colin
Jennings. Five members of the Wilton Park staff deserve particular thanks.
Dianne Guard undertook the mammoth technical task of adapting the
book from my disks to Wilton Park's system. Chris Langdon made extensive suggestions for keeping the text within manageable proportions.
Barbara Johnson painstakingly incorporated and re-formatted those that
we agreed. Lorraine Jones unearthed and helped select the illustrations.
And Janet Durrant held the whole project together, liaising with the FCO,
arranging meetings, making and distributing multiple copies of the type-
script, keeping everyone in the picture, and facilitating access to sources
both human and archival.

Published and other written sources have included Dexter M. Keezer's
pioneering 1973 volume *A Unique Contribution to International Relations:
The Story of Wilton Park*; Matthew Barry Sullivan's 1979 *Thresholds of
Peace: Four Hundred Thousand German Prisoners and the People of Britain
1944–1948*; Ortrud Honke's MA 1992 thesis at the Christian Albrechts
University, Kiel, *Wilton Park: An Anglo-German Conference Centre from
1946 to the mid-1950s* (translated by Oliver and Illa Hayward); David
Welch's chapter on 'Citizenship and Politics: The Legacy of Wilton Park
for Post-War Reconstruction' in *Contemporary European History*, 6, 2

(1997); John A. Ziegler's chapter on 'Wilton Park' in his 1998 book of essays; Philip Bauer's 1999 unpublished study at the Ludwig-Maximilians-Universität München, *Wilton Park 1946–48: Eine Bildungs-einrichting für Deutschland zwischen Selbsterziehung und Umerziehung*. My chapter on the history of Wiston House, in particular, is based almost entirely on the work of Janet Pennington, the leading local historian who wrote her Brighton University MA thesis on *The Wiston Estate: Crown Sequestration and its Effects, 1596–1634*, and who compiled a detailed history for Robert Rhodes James which I have shamelessly pillaged.

My own links with Wilton Park are three. I have attended (and addressed) meetings at Wiston House, where Wilton Park is now based. I knew Heinz Koeppler, who once sounded me out as a possible candidate to succeed him as Warden (it got no further than a lunch). And many years earlier, as a British Army subaltern, I was involved with German prisoners-of-war.

At the beginning of 1939, having successfully studied science in my first term at St Paul's School in London, I was given the option, like my classmates, of continuing with physics and chemistry or switching to German. I spoke French already, enjoyed languages, and knew that war was approaching – so German it was. In the army, which I joined in 1943, my life was probably saved by an attack of double pneumonia, which kept me out of action for many months. My first contact with 'the enemy', therefore, was after the War was over, and I was shipped out to Egypt to be Duty Signals Officer, Fayid. There in our desert camp were large numbers of German POWs – some of them from Rommel's Afrika Corps. Many had volunteered to work for the British, and relations with them were generally cordial, often marked by mutual respect. Three instances were typical. On one occasion, a British sergeant was killed by a local Egyptian: in the subsequent investigation, the POWs were helpful; but the greatest help came not from the most obsequious – a man I privately nicknamed 'Uriah Heep' – but from a defiant former U-boat captain, gruffly resentful of questions from a British pip-squeak. Another POW, a keen amateur sailor, had built himself a wooden racing dinghy; when I went out with him on the Great Bitter Lake, we far outpaced the steel-hulled converted air-sea rescue boats in which the rest of us sailed. He could easily have escaped. The third vignette came near to my repatriation. A concert had been planned in the camp, but at the last moment the expected orchestra failed to appear. The Germans had a camp choir, and offered to perform instead. They sang brilliantly. Their last number, 'Heimatland', evoked the return to home we were all longing for. British and Germans alike had lumps in their throats.

A number of POWs from Egypt later moved to Britain. Some of them attended Wilton Park. Experience in Fayid had shown that by no means all were rabid Nazis, and that dialogue was possible among people who a few years earlier had been strenuously trying to kill each other. It was something we rediscovered in the European Community. But Wilton Park got there first.

CHAPTER 1

Behind Barbed Wire

'My young comrades, I know that it is a sad thing to a soldier to have said to him "You have lost". But let me tell you this: It is better for Germany, better for us, that we have lost, because if we had won we should have lost ourselves.'

General Johann Theodor von Ravenstein,
Commander of the 21st Panzer Division, on May 8, 1945,
at Grande Ligne Camp, Quebec.

Pace revisionist historians, World War II was an ideological war. As early as September 1, 1939, the British Prime Minister, Neville Chamberlain, told the House of Commons that the Allies had no quarrel with the German people, only with the Nazi Government. In 1943, the future Poet Laureate Cecil Day Lewis, parodying official appeals in 'Where are the War Poets?', understated what many felt:

> It is the logic of our times,
> No subject for immortal verse –
> That we who lived by honest dreams
> Defend the bad against the worse.

A year later, the writer and critic V. S. (later Sir Victor) Pritchett, made the same point more confidently:

We have felt that our war is a war to defend civilization, even when we are not reading official propaganda; and we have felt this not because we are especially clear about what our civilization is, but because we have thought that this war and the kind of society that produced it, was a conspiracy against man.

1

In 1948, General Dwight D. Eisenhower, later to be US President, entitled his war memoirs *Crusade in Europe*.

But Crusades and Crusaders have been equivocal since 1095. War requires hatred, and breeds it. Field–Marshal Montgomery famously admitted that one of his tasks was to turn peaceable civilians into killers. Nor were civilians only peaceable. I remember actually exulting with my parents at the mass bomber raids on German cities. Did we imagine that they slaughtered only Nazis? Or that the whole population of Germany, including women and children, suffered from collective guilt? The answer is that we avoided the questions. Even Winston Churchill, in April 1940, confessed that he did not know how to distinguish between Nazis and Germans, Germans and Nazis. In desperate days, few people seemed to turn a hair at brutal sayings like 'The only good German's a dead German'.

It was understandable enough. For the British, this was the second time that Germany had plunged them into a war they had neither sought nor prepared; for the French, it was the third. Many were tempted to blame 'the German national character'. In 1941, Sir Robert Vansittart, who had been Permanent Under-Secretary at the Foreign Office from 1930 to 1938, published *Black Record*, arguing that 'Germany as a whole has always been hostile and unsuited to democracy.' While Vansittart's book was felt by many to be unBritish and in bad taste, and was disavowed by the Foreign Office, its assumptions were widely shared. As the historian D.C. Watt put it:

> The German people, it was argued, suffered from certain long-developed traits in their national character which had hitherto prevented any of the various experiments with democracy in the past from taking firm root and developing. One of these was an overwhelming regard for efficiency which led them to centralise for the sake of centralisation. Another was a sheep-like submissiveness to authority, and a worship of that authority as at the least a benevolent arbiter or, more often, as the source of orders, better qualified, in fact, to judge the needs of the nation than its constituent members … Nazi rule in this view represented simply the old spirit of Prussia, degraded to the level of the gutter and sullied by the beastliness and horrors inevitable to an administrative machine whose members had lost even the sense of honour and decency of the old Prussian aristocracy and been fouled by the racial theories of Nazi parlour fanaticism.

The recently ennobled Vansittart's views were contested in 1942 by Victor Gollancz in *Shall Our Children Live or Die? A Reply to Lord Vansittart on the German Problem*. Eloquent though Gollancz's pamphlet was, it had less impact than the original onslaught. And it became still more tempting to condemn the Germans *en masse* in the last months of the war, when Allied troops began to liberate the Nazi death camps. For the British the key date was April 15, 1945, when the first British tanks entered Bergen-Belsen – not designed as an extermination camp, but a charnel-house nonetheless. Its liberators found ten thousand unburied bodies and three hundred inmates dying every day. Brian Urquhart, whose company of the Parachute Regiment virtually blundered on the scene, described its effect on himself and his men.

> In 1945 little was generally known in the Army about concentration camps or even about the Nazi policy of exterminating the Jews and some other ethnic groups. We were thus almost totally unprepared for the horrors that we saw in Germany ... The Belsen experience had a stunning effect on all of us. British soldiers are by nature kindly, even about their enemies, and at this late stage of the war the Germans were still 'old Jerry' to them. After Belsen, the men never used that phrase again and treated the Germans they met with disgust and contempt.

Robert Rhodes James, just twelve at the time, was old enough to share the reaction:

> When newsreel films of the camps were shown in British cinemas many in the audiences were so shocked that they left before the main film, as I vividly remember in Oxford. Many left crying, others cursing ...
>
> In this context, the voices arguing for a humane long-term treatment of the German people did not lack courage, and there were not many of them.

One was George Orwell. In 1945 he visited a prisoner-of-war camp in southern Germany, and saw a former SS man savagely kicked:

> Quite apart from the scrubby, unfed, unshaven look that a newly captured man generally has, he was a disgusting specimen. But he did not look brutal or in any way frightening: merely neurotic and, in a low way, intellectual. His pale, shifty eyes were deformed by powerful spectacles. He could have been an unfrocked clergyman, an actor ruined by drink, or a spiritualist medium. I have seen very similar people in London common lodging houses, and also in the Reading Room of the British Museum. Quite obviously he was mentally unbalanced – indeed, only doubtfully sane, though at this moment sufficiently in his right mind to be frightened of getting another kick ... So the Nazi torturer of one's imagination, the monstrous figure against whom one had struggled for so many years, dwindled to this pitiful wretch, whose obvious need was not for punishment, but for some kind of psychological treatment.

3

The first attempts at such treatment had begun in 1940. At that time, there were few German prisoners-of-war in Britain; but the Political Warfare Executive (PWE), itself part of the Political Intelligence Department (PID) of the Foreign Office had begun a programme of 'screening and [with a touch of hubris] re-education'.

At the time, it had not got far. Before long, the bulk of the POWs had left Britain for Canada, Australia, and the United States. By early 1941, however, the British in North Africa had rounded up some 73,000 POWs, mostly Italians and Libyans. Many of the Italians were shipped back to Britain to meet the labour shortage on the land. Most German prisoners, regarded as more ideologically committed, continued to be sent across the Atlantic.

The year 1943 saw two dramatic changes. In Tunisia on May 13, the Axis 'Army Group Africa' capitulated to the Allies; and in Italy on September 3, Marshal Pietro Badoglio signed armistice terms. The Tunisian surrender brought some 250,000 German POWs into British and American camps. The Italian volte-face made it clear that supplies of Italian POW farmworkers in Britain were likely to dwindle and dry up. The British authorities hoped to send many German POWs back to Britain to replace the Italians.

The snag was a shortage of shipping. As a result, by June 1944, although 48,305 German POWs were in British hands, only 7,900 were in Britain itself. But as the war reached its climax the numbers rapidly increased, and fewer were shipped off to Canada and the United States, they included, as well as captured prisoners, 'Surrendered Enemy Personnel'.

Their growing numbers made more onerous their 'screening and re-education'. Screening, obviously enough, involved making distinctions that Churchill had refused in 1940. The wheat had to be winnowed from the chaff. But by now Churchill himself, like Orwell, had had a change of heart. He was still no apostle of appeasement. In 1943, at a private party, he asked for three encores of Noël Coward's fiercely ironical song 'Don't let's be beastly to the Germans'. It was clear, however, that he no longer failed to distinguish between Nazis and Germans in general; and to the latter he began to show greater humanity. Towards the end of the war, when the US Secretary of the Treasury Henry Morgenthau proposed a draconian regime for postwar Germany, including summary executions, group detention, labour battalions, the flooding of mines and the closing of factories to reduce the nation to 'pastoral' status, Churchill's immediate response was to refuse. 'Europe would be chained to a dead body,' he said. 'I agree with Burke. You cannot indict a whole nation.' And already in

1943 he circulated various Ministries asking for suggestions on how, after the war, co-operation with a democratic Germany could be promoted. This in turn raised the question of German 're-education'.

On March 10, 1943, the House of Lords debated the whole subject: Viscount Cecil of Chelwood declared that Britain should 'disarm Germany and give her the opportunity of re-educating herself'. R.A. Butler, the Minister of Education, made a similar point in the House of Commons on May 27, 1943 – shortly after the victory in North Africa that had so greatly swelled the numbers of POWs:

> In my opinion and that of my colleagues, the best way to start the re-education of Germany is to show the enemy what things she cannot do. That can best be done by the imposition of an overwhelming military defeat upon Germany so that she may learn once and for all that the evil doctrines which have inspired her philosophy and her leaders for so many years and have had such terrible results shall not be able to occur again ... We have to teach that nation that the philosophy of war, the philosophy of *Herrenvolk*, does not and never will pay. We have then to attempt to eliminate within the country the evil forces, evil doctrines and evil influences that have brought about that philosophy. We may then hope eventually to start such a leaven within the country that a real self-education and re-education arises.

On August 8, 1943, a War Cabinet paper laid down principles similar to those already stated by Cecil and Butler. Seeking from Germany 'a permanent change of heart and conversion to tolerable European behaviour', it declared:

> Efforts from without to convert the Germans will merely harden their unrepentant hearts. Germans alone can re-educate their fellow-countrymen, and Germans will make the attempt only if they are themselves convinced that the future of their country lies in cooperation with their neighbours.

Several months later, on December 9, 1943, representatives of the Foreign Office, the War Office, and the Ministry of Information met and approved a memorandum on 'The Re-education of Germany', which quoted the key passage from the War Cabinet's paper, and stressed that the control of re-education should be 'as indirect, invisible, and remote as is compatible with its being effective'. The memorandum was submitted to the War Cabinet on January 27, 1944. On February 24, 1944, at a meeting of the Ministerial Committee on Armistice Terms and Civil Administration, at which the memorandum was discussed, the Deputy Prime Minister Clement Attlee pointed out that it said nothing about 're-educating' prisoners-of-war. The Allied authorities in Germany itself faced forbidding responsibilities. Their most urgent task, in that lunar landscape, was still to help the country and its hungry, cold, ragged, exhausted inhabitants recover from devastation – clearing rubble, tracing refugees, housing 'displaced persons', feeding a population that lacked the barest essentials. 'Re-education' and 'denazification' there would take time. But in Britain it had begun in the POW camps, and could now be done more systematically. Accordingly, on September 18, 1944, the War Cabinet agreed 'that the Political Warfare Executive should undertake the re-education of German Prisoners of War and that all possible steps should be taken to facilitate their work'.

The Political Warfare Executive (PWE) worked closely with the Political Intelligence Department (PID) of the Foreign Office. The PID was headed by Major-General Kenneth Strong; its German section was led by Richard Crossman, the former Oxford don and future Cabinet Minister. To comply with the War Cabinet's directive, the PID and PWE set up a special Prisoners-of-War (Ps/W) Division to undertake 're-education', initially with a staff of only two. One, later to be named Controller, was Wing Commander F.H. Hitch, a former merchant banker who had proved his administrative ability as an assistant deputy director in the PWE. Hitch spoke no German; but his Chief Executive Officer, in charge of 're-education', was a proven expert, Cyrus Brooks. Quiet, pipe-smoking, and rather enigmatic, Brooks had been teaching English in Germany when World War I broke out in 1914: he had been interned for the duration. Later, he had translated Erich Kästner, author of *Emil and the Detectives*, and had written detective stories himself. One of his staff, previously an interrogator of prisoners-of-war, described him as 'an oriental-looking man who said little, smiled a lot, but with a definite twinkle: one's idea of a man in charge of spies.'

These two rapidly recruited a third. The 37-year-old Henry Faulk was tough, square-faced, shrewd, and energetic, with smiling, sharp, bespectacled eyes. A former grammar-school teacher from a farming family in Dundee, he had studied French and German at the University of Glasgow, and as part of his course there had had to spend a year in each country. So he had been in Berlin at the time of the elections in March 1933, and had seen Nazis beat up a teenage Jewish boy. In 1938 he was back in Germany, with a party of schoolboys, in Freiburg-im-Breisgau. Its Nazi Mayor told him that as a foreigner he could go to an *Arbeitsdienst* or Labour Service centre. He did so at Heidelberg, and experienced brainwashing at first hand. Although school-teaching was a reserved occupation, he joined up at the outbreak of World War II. After a time with the Cameron Highlanders, he was made an intelligence officer, and would have taken part in the 1944 D-Day landings had he not smashed his leg in a motorcycle accident late in 1943. Instead he became an interpreter in POW camps. Helped by 250 German other-rank volunteers, he had had spectacular success in dealing with 1,200 aggressively militant Nazi-led officers drafted in from another camp, where they had attempted a mass escape.

Faulk's fame reached Hitch and Brooks, who were looking hard – and with some difficulty – for German-speaking assistants to set up their 're-education' programme. Before long, he became Executive Field Officer in the Ps/W (Prisoners-of-War) Division, responsible for work in the camps, including practical 'screening' into three groups:

> the bulk of the prisoners fell into three main grades: 'A' (Whites) active socially and politically minded anti-Nazis and anti-militarists; 'B' (Greys) those with no deep social or political convictions, who often may be of a lower grade of intelligence but would appear amenable to instruction [sic]; and 'C' (Blacks) those who still maintained the Nazi and/or militarist outlook.

Of the 208,238 German POWs in Britain in November 1945, 19,448 had been categorised 'A', 85,380 'B', and 50,205 'C': 53,205 had yet to be screened. In an early study, Cyrus Brooks had been surprised to find how few fitted category 'A'. Of some 300 captured in 1940, only one had proved to be a confirmed anti-Nazi. Later surveys showed that most of the 'C' category prisoners were aged 26 to 35, and that those under 30 were twice as likely as their elders to trust Hitler, while half of those over thirty were likely to blame him for starting the war. But there was one fundamental point that many of their British captors tended to miss. For the Allies, Nazism meant what one historian, Matthew Barry Sullivan, called 'a policy of domination, militarism, conquest, oppression, persecution and sadistic cruelty'. But 'POWs valued National Socialism chiefly for its social and economic achievements, and laid twice as much stress on economic stability, social welfare and elimination of class conflict as on national power'. Clearly, 're-education' had to take account of underlying assumptions on both sides.

According to the Ps/W Division, it involved 'two main factors': 'eradication of the authoritarian and militarist outlook imbued in the Ps/W by upbringing and propaganda, and substituting the spirit of tolerance and the appreciation of the civic duties of a free individual within the framework of democracy.' In greater detail, official policy was defined as follows:

7

1. To eradicate from the minds of the prisoners belief in the German military tradition and the National Socialist ideology.

2. To impart to the prisoners an accurate understanding and a just appreciation of the principles of democratic government and their implications for the conduct of men and nations; in particular, to encourage the application of democratic principles to German conditions as a basis of the peaceful re-absorption of Germany into the European community [*sic*].

3. To present the British Commonwealth of Nations as an example of a democratic community in action, while avoiding the projection of Britain as a model to be slavishly copied.

4. To remove German misconceptions about European history of the last 50 years and especially about the origin, conduct and results of the two world wars.

This might have been better phrased. 'The German military tradition' was in many respects different from – and actively hostile to – 'the National Socialist ideology'; and 'the British Commonwealth of Nations' was not a 'community' in the sense that later became familiar in Europe.

Later, indeed, the whole notion of 're-education' was called in question. Henry Faulk defended it: 'Re-education wasn't meant to be *Hochnäsigkeit* [arrogance]. It was essentially the belief that Germans were better than Nazi doctrines that blinded them to morality by politics and was an attempt to give them the chance to see that.'

True. But the concept was more complex than it seemed; and it led to misunderstandings. The POWs, in their own distinguishing garb with scraps of old uniform, were sad, defeated, and often sullen, longing to be home. Many disliked the 'traitors' who toadied to their captors. Some were defiant, feeling saddled with guilt that belonged to others: a few were unregenerate, dreaming of revenge. To many of the British, they were a bewildering mixture: in some cases, fellow-soldiers now brought low; a burden to be housed, fed, and guarded; a resource to be used (or exploited) as volunteers for hard labour in building or on the land; and – still – the remnants of an enemy, to be subdued, tamed, converted, and if possible redeemed. When German resentment faced British reforming zeal, it was not a promising confrontation.

Nor did 're-education' always proceed smoothly. The Political Warfare Executive issued a camp newspaper, set up libraries, and installed radio

sets; but these were not always welcome or widely used. The camp newspaper, intended to inform its readers and foster a questioning spirit, was
often in the early days spurned or even destroyed in bulk by German camp
leaders. Extremist Nazis threw their weight about, intimidating fellow-
prisoners and several times attempting murder – not always unsuccessfully. Even in the United States, the future President of the European
Economic Commission, Walter Hallstein, narrowly escaped assassination
for running a 'Camp University'. It took time, as well as skill and discern-
ment, to recruit people willing to stand up to bullies and die-hards and
help change the minds of their fellow-prisoners. The Ps/W Division
added:

> These re-educationalists were mostly recruited from socially and politically
> active individuals, not necessarily always confined to anti-Nazis but includ-
> ing a certain number of Nazis as well, who, after careful re-vetting were
> found reliable as converts to the democratic outlook.

A major centre for such 'cells' of 'white' POWs was Ascot Park – one
of a number of interrogation and 'screening' establishments not far from
London. Another was in a converted hotel at Shap Wells in the
Westmorland fell country, where the German camp leader was the
Swabian nobleman Fürst von Urach and one of the inmates was the
Bavarian painter Karl-Josef Huber. As 'A' category of prisoners, they
formed an intellectual and social elite; and, as at other camps, they had
official visitors. In the summer of 1945 came one they did not easily forget.
As described by Matthew Barry Sullivan, he was known by his cover name
of 'Professor King':

> An extremely big man with abundant energy and brains, he stirred up'
> strong feelings, curiosity, and intense discussion wherever he went and
> obviously enjoyed doing this. A man with a mission, he resolutely refused
> to accept that a German officer was a gentleman just because he was an
> officer, which put not a few commandants immediately against him. He
> had strong, well-grounded views on recent German history on which he
> had lectured at Oxford. At any other officer camp his main contention was
> bound to rouse the maximum resentment. It was that German militarism
> was as much the enemy as Nazism; the Nationalist Party of the press baron
> Hugenberg, he held, had a special responsibility for bringing Hitler to
> power, as it hoped to use him to smash Weimar democracy and the Trade
> Union movement. This old ruling establishment, the 'Hugenbergs' ... had
> to go because they were basically anti-democratic, and there could be no
> sound new Germany unless they were powerless.

At Featherstone Park, the largest officer camp, he had called an open-air meeting. He was in his element – the 'Hugenbergs' were there in force before him – and he needled them relentlessly in his extraordinarily penetrating and powerful voice. He drew them out until, in the words of Dieter Frankel [a junior German officer],

> the older officers went on the barricades. Everything they said he contradicted and the provocation escalated. We younger ones held back while our seniors took him on. We were pretty certain, talking it over afterwards, that in spite of his English accent he wasn't English because of some of his phrases. We came to the conclusion he was sounding us out, discovering whose opinions warranted their being kept a watch on. Next time he comes, we thought, keep your mouths shut, or you'll be posted to a black camp, or stay an extra year. We discussed Professor King feverishly for days, and everyone was against him for stirring us up. But afterwards I thought how clever to penetrate under our skins like that and get us discussing matters we had avoided so far. He wanted to hear from us officers what got us keyed up. He succeeded magnificently!

Professor King inevitably turned up at Shap and confronted another all-officer audience, except this time there was scarcely a professional soldier among them. 'That night', says Huber dramatically, 'no one slept', and early next morning the Lagerfürst sent for the small fearless Bavarian as the only man who could confront the formidable King without being dominated by him. He was due to talk to the younger officers that morning. 'We must do something', said von Urach, 'or the camp will no longer be in my control'. Three of them, Urach, Muller and Huber, cornered the visitor in the well in the middle of the hotel and, sitting on the stairs, challenged what they felt was his wholesale condemnation of everything in Nazi Germany. King had been shown some of Huber's paintings. 'A painter like you couldn't make a living in Hitler's Germany!' 'On the contrary, we did manage to make ends meet. No one locked me up. Even people in the Party helped us.' King would not accept the implications of this and the conversation became heated, the other two gradually edging away from them on the stairs…Who was this imposing man with H.K. monogrammed on his handkerchief? Certainly not Professor King, the prisoners knew. Obviously a refugee and a German, for all the slight English accent with which he spoke; and at least partly Jewish.

The prisoners were right. 'Professor King' was not a professor, and his name was not 'King'. He was an intelligence officer, recruited in 1940 to the Political Intelligence Department (PID) of the Foreign Office. From 1941 to 1943 he had been the main liaison officer between the PID and the

BBC, concerned with broadcasts to Germany. He was now Assistant Director of the German and Austrian section of the PID, and deputy to Richard Crossman.

In this capacity, it was natural that he should have responded to Winston Churchill's 1943 circular asking for ideas about working with a democratic postwar Germany. In that year and again in 1944 he submitted proposals to the Joint Committee linking the Foreign Office, the Political Warfare Executive (PWE), the BBC, and the Ministry of Information. As he himself described them later,

> These proposals amounted to the setting up of an institution ... to provide an opportunity for men and women in the public life of Germany to overcome their isolation and to look at German problems from outside Germany, to gain a better understanding of British policy and by exchanging views on the basis of the running of a free society, to be stimulated into making efforts, or increasing their efforts, for the building up of German society in such a way that Germany could live in peace and friendship with her former enemies.

This was the germ of what became Wilton Park. And 'Professor King', its originator, was the extraordinary man who became its first Warden. His name was Heinz Koeppler. He had already had a remarkable career.

CHAPTER 2

A European Education

'It is as if ...German life were slowly ebbing away from contact with western Europe.'

D.H. Lawrence, *A Letter from Germany*, 1924

Heinz Koeppler's early experience made vivid the evils of nationalist excess. Prussian in territory disputed by Poland, Jewish in a Germany commandeered by Hitler, exiled in Britain and later a British citizen, he had what the Russian-French writer Romain Gary called, in the title of his novel about World War II air aces, '*Une éducation européenne*'.

He was born on June 30, 1912, in Wollstein, some 100 miles east of Berlin. As his sister Hanni, two years older, recalled, 'it was a small country town surrounded by flat agricultural country and woods, lying between two lakes. Its only claim to fame was that Robert Koch, the discoverer of the tuberculosis bacillus, who died in 1910, was its GP.'

Koch had made his discovery in 1882, following it in 1883 with the cholera bacillus. In the Franco-Prussian War of 1870-71 he had served briefly as a field surgeon. Afterwards, settling in Wollstein, he had built a small laboratory with a microscope, a microtome (for cutting thin slices of tissue), and a home-made incubator, where he began his study of algae, switching later to pathogenic organisms. In 1905 he won the Nobel Prize for the Physiology of Medicine.

A distinguished family doctor; but the Koeppler family, in its way, was distinguished too. Heinz Koeppler's grandfather Heinrich had married Johanna Caro, whose family had settled in Wollstein in the 1880s. His father Friedrich (Fritz), who had been born in Küstrin, had married Gertrud Bornstein, the youngest of a large family of five boys and three girls, in February 1909. In Hanni Koeppler's words, 'Fritz was a tall, good-looking, outgoing, successful young man. He drove about the country buying the cereal and potato harvest from the surrounding, mostly big, country estates, and was very popular with them.'

Fritz built a modern seven-bedroom house on the outskirts of the town. It was an imposing, stucco-faced building on a corner site behind a low white wooden fence, with tall windows, an alcoved entrance, and a balcony looking out on the street. As Hanni Koeppler recalled,

> On the ground floor, on the left side of the entrance were the offices, and on the right three reception rooms. The kitchen was in the cellar, and the food was pulled up in an elevator – to the delight of the children. On the left of the house were some rows of standard roses, divided by a path from the forecourt with a modern garage and storage buildings. The path led to the garden at the rear, and at the end of the path was a small garden-house with a flag on top which had 'Hanni and Heinz' printed on it. On the side of it was a drum in a cage which contained a red squirrel. The path divided the lawn from the vegetable garden and playground. At the back of the house was a veranda where we ate in the summer, and in front of it a large and very prolific walnut tree.

Here the Koeppler family led a comfortable, upper-middle-class life, with swimming in the lakes, where there were some wooden bathing cabins, and excursions in a red open touring car. Then came 1914, and World War I. Fritz Koeppler was conscripted into the German Army. He returned safely: but the Treaty of Versailles overturned the family's situation. Their home town, and the surrounding province of Posen, had been in the heart of Prussia since 1793, when the second partition of Poland had made it German territory. Now, at Versailles, Posen was returned to Poland, and Wollstein became Wolsztyn. The surrounding estates, with which Fritz Koeppler had traded, were now in the hands of Polish owners, and in the town itself, as Hanni remembered, 'the Poles with their red and white square caps took over. There was a very aggressive atmosphere, and most of the people, who thought of themselves as German, had to leave.' So, in November 1919, the Koepplers sold the family house and moved to Berlin. 'It was of course very hard to leave everything. But we children waved little black, red, and gold flags cheerfully when we boarded the train to Berlin. We moved to a splendid town flat in Charlottenburg, with its famous Palace [Schloss Charlottenburg] and Park.'

The flat was at number 111 on the Kaiserdamm, the long straight thoroughfare built to receive Kaiser Wilhelm I after his victory over France in 1871. It was not far, Koeppler's sister later discovered, from where Joseph Goebbels lived. 'At the front was a study and then a beautiful newly designed library and "salon", followed by a large dining-room, which you found in all houses – the "Berlin room" – which led to the bedroom wing.'

Here, the Koepplers settled once again into a happy and prosperous life. There was 'a huge family of uncles, aunts, and cousins, half of whom lived in Berlin. In spite of being a city of two million, theatres and entertainment were easily accessible and affordable. At the end of the Twenties, a new Opera House was built in Charlottenburg, and a cousin and we took turns at 7.00 a.m. on Sundays, queuing for tickets.' It was, after all, the time of the so-called Weimar Renaissance, in which Modernist architects like Walter Gropius, artists like George Grosz, and composers like Arnold Schoenberg broke with tradition as decisively as the film-makers of UFA, the *Universum Film Aktien Gesellschaft*.

In Berlin, Heinz Koeppler entered the *Schiller Realgymnasium*. This was, as Hanni recalled, 'quite a good walk away further into the town'. He settled down well, and was popular, but had no intimate friends. After two years it was suggested that he oversprang a class. In the school was a young teacher, Mr Sprague, who took an interest in Heinz and some other boys, and taught them 'Go' – quite a difficult Japanese game. 'In the corner of our dining-room there was a second big round table, where he spent many hours with friends building a crystal radio set; and, although he was not technically minded, they improved it and were glued to it for hours.'

Already, however, a week before his tenth birthday, Koeppler had been awakened to the dangers of right-wing fanaticism in Germany's peaceful, well-meaning, but fragile Weimar Republic. On June 24, 1922, the Foreign Minister Walther Rathenau was assassinated on his way to the office. Son of the Jewish industrialist Emil Rathenau, the founder of the giant *Allgemeine-Elektrizitäts-Gesellschaft* (AEG), Walther Rathenau had scrupulously respected Germany's obligations under the Versailles Treaty, which made him unpopular with some sections of German society. Then on April 16, 1922, he had signed the Treaty of Rapallo with the Soviet Union, re-establishing normal relations and strengthening trade ties. Although this offended the Western Allies, since it was the first instance of Germany's acting independently since World War I, it outraged the German Right, which accused Rathenau of 'creeping Communism'. His murder was one of many signs that the Weimar Republic was under serious threat. By the end of 1922, in fact, there had been nearly 400 political assassinations, most of them perpetrated by the extreme Right.

Meanwhile, inflation was growing. In January 1923, France and Belgium occupied the Ruhr, in retaliation for Germany's falling behind in its reparations payments. The German Government responded by urging closure of the factories. This helped turn inflation into hyperinflation. By

November 15, 1923, the mark had fallen to 4.2 trillion against the US dollar. Only then did the Government restabilise the currency and, in 1924, secure Allied agreement to ending occupation of the Ruhr, re-scheduling reparations payments, and granting substantial foreign loans of 800 million gold marks. By 1927 these had enabled German industrial production to return to its prewar 1913 peak.

Growing up amid such turbulence, it was impossible to ignore politics. In 1925, the Koeppler family reserved a table at a Berlin cafe from which they watched the funeral cortege of President Friedrich Ebert, whose successor was the 77-year-old Field-Marshal Paul von Hindenburg. 'In later years at school,' Koeppler's sister recalled, 'Heinz became involved in discussions and lectures at the *Hochschule für Politik*. Its director was Theodor Heuss, who became President of Germany in 1949. Heuss arranged a contest for public speaking for schoolboys, and Heinz got into it as the losing finalist, for best schoolboy orator of the country.' That was in Koeppler's final year at school. Schooling then, his sister added, was remarkably liberal for its time: among other things, she wrote an extended essay on the revolutionary Rosa Luxemburg, who with Karl Liebknecht formed the Spartacus League, forerunner of the German Communist Party.

In April 1930, Koeppler left school and began to study law at the University of Berlin. He stayed there a year. Then, it being easy to change universities, he moved on to Heidelburg. There he met a younger fellow-student, Hans Martin Goldberg, who was to be a lifelong friend. Looking back from a diplomatic career, Goldberg recalled:

> My choice of student organisation was predetermined, as both my elder brothers were 'Bundesbrüder' of the F.W.V., the 'Freie Wissenschaftliche Vereinigung', a liberal, non-denominational and non-colour-bearing student body with branches at most major German universities. We concerned ourselves with political and cultural discussions rather than the beer-swilling sessions of most student clubs – although as our one conces-sion to tradition we preserved one evening a week for communal drinking and singing. Organisationally the fraternity had three officers: chairman, vice-chairman, and secretary; and each new member (known as Fuchs or Fox) had to choose an older member (Bursch [fellow]) to guide him through the complexities of student life. That relationship was known as one of Leibfuchs to Leibbursch and was sealed by the exchange of a coloured ribbon, rather like a campaign ribbon. I chose Heinz Koeppler and our friendship lasted throughout life.

But fresh clouds were gathering around the Koeppler family. Hyper-inflation in the Weimar Republic had already hit the middle classes hard: a lifetime of savings would no longer buy a ticket on the U-Bahn. Fortunately, Fritz Koeppler had not had to live on savings alone: he had enjoyed the franchise for importing potatoes from Russia. But at the end of the 1920s, while the rest of Germany was recovering, the vital franchise expired. In Hanni's words, 'by the beginning of the 1930s there were no opportunities and no money'. Heinz, in the third semester of his Jurisprudence course at Heidelburg, now had no resources to pursue his studies. As Hanni put it, 'matters got quite desperate'.

However, there was a way out. Hans Martin Goldberg recalls: 'Of the few places in Germany giving grants to students, there was an institute of the University of Kiel which provided free places for students who were "of professorial potential", and Heinz was given a place, changing his studies from Law to Mediaeval History.' The change of subject was not, perhaps, unwelcome: Hanni remembers that Heinz had not been happy with his legal studies. What mattered was being accepted – 'really, a great honour', as Hanni said – at Christian Albert House, Kiel. This had originally been called 'Bergmann House' after its wealthy Swedish founder, who believed that promising students should know something of their contemporaries from other countries. It had been renamed Christian Albert House, after the Danish Prince who had founded Kiel University, when the founder's original endowment ran out and the University took over the costs. It offered fairly basic accommodation for some 40 students in a broad range of subjects, a third of them from outside Germany and all expected to achieve academic success.

At Kiel, Koeppler was elected president of the students' union; but student politics did not distract him from his studies. One of his teachers at Kiel, from 1929 to 1933, was the eminent jurist and mediaevalist Professor Hermann Kantorowicz, also from Posen. He described Koeppler as 'my favourite pupil' and 'one of the best students Germany has ever produced'. Armed with such testimonials – 'the likes of which,' said his friend Hans Martin Goldberg, 'I had never before or since seen' – Koeppler hoped to continue his studies in England.

In the meantime, however, fate had struck Koeppler's family a heavy blow. His father Fritz Koeppler had contracted a duodenal ulcer. In the late summer of 1932 the ulcer burst. Today, this might have been an incident, simply cured. Then, it provoked intestinal bleeding, and proved fatal. On September 3, 1932, Fritz Koeppler died. His daughter Hanni is convinced that his money worries were the cause.

This plunged the family into grief and crisis. It also threatened Heinz's last year at Kiel – and his future academic career. When the Kiel term ended in the summer of 1933, would he be able to afford to go to England?

Meanwhile, political clouds were gathering. On January 30, 1933, Adolf Hitler became Chancellor of Germany. In February came the Reichstag fire and the Nazi terror campaign. The March elections followed, which gave a majority to the Nazi NSDAP and the German National Peoples' Party (DNVP), led by Koeppler's pet hate, the press and movie baron Alfred Hugenberg.

The Nazi purge of democrats, Socialists, and Jews in the universities had not fully reached Kiel when Koeppler's term there came to an end. But Germany had become an uncomfortable place for a Jewish family. At first, it seemed only uncomfortable. 'We thought we just had to live with it', said Koeppler's sister Hanni. 'We bought everything in Jewish shops.' She herself took a job in a Jewish pharmacy. But she had one disturbing experience. She was staying with her aunt Julie when the Gestapo came to the door. She hid upstairs. The next day, her aunt professed to know nothing of what had happened. Before the defeat of the Nazi regime, a number of her aunts and uncles, as well as two cousins, had died in the camps.

One day in that fatal summer of 1933, Heinz Koeppler was walking down the Kurfürstendamm in Berlin when he met the father of his Heidelberg *Leibfuchs* Hans Martin Goldberg. 'Why are you still in Germany?' asked the father. 'It's no longer civilised, and not fit for a young Jew to live in.' Heinz answered that he couldn't emigrate: he had no money. Goldberg senior offered him a ticket to London, where he said he could stay with his son, who was studying there for the London University entrance examination. Overcome with gratitude, Koeppler accepted.

He arrived in London with his testimonials, a little luggage, a multi-buttoned German overcoat, and imperfect English. His friend Hans Martin Goldberg, at his lodgings at Chepstow Villas in Notting Hill, translated the testimonials, and Koeppler sent them to various possible sources of aid. Eventually, Goldberg remembered, he was 'supported by the Jewish Help Organisation for Academics at Woburn House and the International Organisation of Students [*sic*]'. With their help, he applied for an interview at Magdalen College, Oxford – and was accepted. Now he could continue his academic career.

Already in London he had informally shown his expertise. Goldberg had a cousin, Shimon Applebaum, who was studying archaeology. When they met in Notting Hill, they instantly took to each other. But Applebaum knew no German, and Koeppler's English was by no means fluent. So, as Goldberg remembered, 'Like the schoolmen of old they found mediaeval Latin a perfectly satisfactory vehicle of conversation.' Later, on a week's holiday with Goldberg in the Cotswolds, Koeppler showed that 'he viewed the world as a mediaeval history student. I still remember his remark when looking at one of the villages: 'The English built their villages in the valley, the continentals on top of hills. This shows that the main danger on the continent came from invaders; here, the main enemy was the weather.' Long years afterwards, looking back on Koeppler's life at his memorial service on May 24, 1979, Sir Robert Birley declared: 'I doubt whether he ever altogether lost his interest in the twelfth century.'

In October, 1933, Koeppler was admitted as a Commoner to Magdalen College, Oxford, and was given what its president called a 'modest room – a small set' in the College. A special decision of Congregation on October 24 gave him the status of Advanced Student. He also received a grant of £30 from the Magdalen Demyship Fund for the year 1933/34. Nor did the College's generosity stop there. On December 1, 1933, its Home Bursar was authorised to waive the usual requirement that he should pay Caution Money (then £20). On March 9, 1934, he was granted £30 from the Alex Varley Fund, and on February 20, 1935, a further £30 from the Tuition Fund. With this help, with casual earnings from translating and later teaching, and with aid from outside sources including the International Student Service and the Refugee Committee, Koeppler was able to spend the three years 1933–36 at Magdalen, working towards a D.Phil. degree. His subject was highly specialised: 'A study of the antecedents of *De claris iurisconsultis* of [Thomas] Diplovatatius (1468-1545)'. It was no accident that the first volume of Diplovatatius's treatise had been edited in 1919, with a colleague, by Koeppler's former Kiel professor Hermann Kantorowicz, who in 1933 had also fled from Nazi Germany.

'Heinz was completely in love with Oxford', says his sister. It was certainly a change after postwar Berlin and his widowed mother's now more modest apartment on Fritschestrasse in Charlottenburg. Koeppler kept – partly to contrast with his own spartan hospitality – the menu of a *Souper de Bal* at Magdalen on June 18, during Eights Week, 1934: it included trout, lobster, sole, salmon, prawns, foie gras, pigeon, lamb, asparagus, capon, pâté, tongue, ham, chicken, beef, strawberries, meringues, champagne jelly, and many other delicacies, all described in elegant *maître d'hôtel* French. What appealed to Koeppler, however, was not Oxford's spasmodic hedonism, but its intellectual vitality. Hanni again: 'With his outgoing personality he made innumerable friends of people who were later famous, and he was received with open arms.'

One of these friends was the classical scholar Gilbert Murray, who like Koeppler had come to Oxford as an immigrant – from Australia. 'In March 1935,' Hanni recalled, 'Heinz arranged for me to come to Oxford and stay in the flat of Richard Crossman, Fellow and Tutor of New

College, while Crossman was in Greece writing his book about Plato. Unfortunately, he was delayed for three days, so Gilbert and Lady Mary Murray asked me to stay with them … Professor Murray took me for walks and "listened" quite remarkably to a girl with no idea of English culture. I had not heard of Wales and the Irish troubles. I had however a great knowledge of English literature from Chaucer, Shakespeare, Milton, Carlyle, Eliot, Shaw, Galsworthy, etc. I was quite captured and grateful for his kindness. Heinz had some rooms in Magdalen College Tower at that time, and gave a party for me. It was only bottled water and French bread.' For this party, Koeppler annotated the previous year's *Souper de Bal* menu: 'June 18th, 1934 *is over and I don't offer you a* Souper de Bal *BUT I should like you to meet my sister in order to give her a glimpse of what Oxford is really like. Thursday Mar 14th. at 6 New Buildings, Magdalen. 5-7 R.S.V.P. H. Koeppler No Sherry (Bread and Water)*'.

The austerity was not feigned. Koeppler's family was still poor, and in 1934 he learned that funds promised by friends in Germany would not be forthcoming: his would-be benefactors were lawyers, and as Jews they had lost their jobs. Even if they had been able to help Koeppler, the Nazi Government in Germany blocked the export of currency. When this happened, Gilbert Murray's wife Mary and an Oxford Quaker friend, Arthur Gillett, guaranteed Koeppler's bank balance. But, as his sister Hanni confessed: 'We had no money at all, and Heinz had got an awful lot of debts.' Until the summer of 1935, when he moved out of College, he was paying between £50 and £60 a term in 'batells' – the charge made to undergraduates for board, lodging, etc. On July 22, 1935, Magdalen's Home Bursar was authorised to guarantee a loan that Koeppler had obtained from Barclays' Bank, on condition that he took out a life insurance policy for that amount in favour of the guarantors: the guarantee was to last for eleven years.

Now living out of College, in St Giles Street, Koeppler had to pay only some ten pounds a term in batells; but his debts, as Hanni said, 'took him quite some time to pay off'. They may even have cost him a bride. 'When he had finished studying, he had a girlfriend, Nancy – and he was going to marry. But he had debts. And she had a boyfriend, who was in the war. So they broke it off. It was a shame.'

Academically, nevertheless, Heinz Koeppler was flourishing. In January, 1936, *The Journal for Theological Studies* published part of his D.Phil. thesis under the title '*De viris illustribus* and Isidore of Seville'. In October of that year, Magdalen College elected him a Senior Demy – a foundation scholar with tutorial duties but not salaried as a full tutor. The post was annually renewable (and renewed) for a further two years. On

19

November 21, 1936, his thesis successfully completed, Koeppler was awarded his D.Phil. degree. On January 1, 1937, he took up his Senior Demyship, moving back into College.

His new field of research was ambitious, to say the least: 'A study of the Papacy as feudal overlord: some aspects of the constitutional history of the more important mediaeval city states and the influence of Teutonic and Roman Law on these constitutions.' 'This work,' said Koeppler, 'will be a preparation for a history of the Holy Roman Empire' – a book of 200,000 to 250,000 words which he hoped to write for Oxford's Clarendon Press. In undertaking it, he had the help and approval of the Regius Professor of Modern History, F.M. Powicke, who with A.B. Emden, Principal of St Edmund Hall, had recently published, in 1936, the revision of the late Hastings Rashdall's monumental history, *The Universities of Europe in the Middle Ages*. Koeppler had a striking testimonial from another distinguished historian, Vivian Hunter Galbraith, who from 1928 to 1937 had been a Fellow and Tutor in Modern History at Balliol College, Oxford, and University Reader in Diplomatic, and who in 1937 became Professor of History at Edinburgh. Koeppler, wrote Galbraith:

> is a scholar to his fingertips, yet human and alive, witty and disarming in conversation, yet with the firmness of character and perseverance to push through to the end a job he has begun. He has shown cheerfulness and dignity in rather difficult circumstances.

Already, in 1936, Heinz Koeppler had applied to the UK Home Secretary for naturalisation. The support of such illustrious colleagues, including no doubt Gilbert Murray, can have done his application no harm. In 1937, still aged only 25, Koeppler became a British citizen; and in 1938, to his great relief, his sister Hanni was also able to settle in England. That same year, with a £25 travel grant, Koeppler visited Italy, consulting archives in Perugia and the Vatican Library. Back in Oxford, he was appointed a Lecturer in History. His career as a mediaevalist was well and truly launched. As he surveyed the year 1939, he hoped to continue his work in Italy that summer, with a further travel grant awarded by the Council for Academic Studies. One fruit of his researches so far was his second printed article on mediaeval European history: 'Frederick Barbarossa and the Schools of Bologna'. This was published in the *English Historical Review*, No.216. Its date was October 1939.

Looking back, people in England remembered that summer of 1939 as one of long and golden days. But its political climate hardly matched its weather. It was a time of world crisis, a long uneasy interim after the false peace of Munich. Although equipped with a scholarship, Koeppler had to renounce his travel plans. Finally, on September 3, 1939, Britain declared war on Nazi Germany. The golden days were over. Everyone's future, including Koeppler's, was in suspense – 'for the duration', as that generation learned to say.

In his early years at Oxford, Heinz Koeppler had been puzzled by his colleagues' lack of concern about events in Germany. Long after World War II, he remembered what he called:

> the lamentable failure of well-meant efforts to improve Anglo-German understanding undertaken in Oxford in the mid-thirties. At that time neither dons nor undergraduates (graduate students hardly existed) were enamoured of the Third Reich, in fact they hated and despised it. Yet they hoped that if they accepted the many demands to receive as visitors German professors and students, they might possibly contribute to the prevention of a war which appeared more and more inevitable. Many of the German visitors were eager to discuss politics, to find out how the outside world regarded the Fuehrer. But Oxford was not at all eager. For to discuss political issues would have been awkward and might have led to lost tempers which to avoid has ever been one of the glories of *homo oxoniensis*. Thus our visitors were introduced to the mysteries of the game of cricket, were taken down to the river Isis – Thames to the plebeians – there to admire the picturesque if highly insanitary boat houses; they were shown the glorious architecture and the generous hospitality of Oxford Colleges. But Oxford refused resolutely to discuss the things that mattered. Looking back on this period, it is clear to me that I learned from it how not to enlarge international understanding, how it might be necessary, even if awkward, to tackle issues on which there existed a profound divergence, if one really desired progress in an exchange of views. The framework of discussion should be agreeable, the form friendly and polite but not at the cost of evading vital and critical topics of common concern.

One exception to the evasiveness was Koeppler's friend and patron Gilbert Murray. He had already spoken at the Oxford Union on behalf of a motion calling on the free nations 'to unite against German and Russian militarism'; and Koeppler later fondly remembered very fruitful talks with him. Nor did he talk only with Murray. In 1937, the President of Magdalen College, George Gordon, said to Koeppler: 'You're always talking about this fellow Hitler. Why don't you teach a course about him and his significance?' Not surprisingly, he did. He also joined the Royal Institute of International Affairs at Chatham House in London, and in Oxford was a member of the internationally oriented Bryce Club, of which he was briefly president. In these circles, like many others in those anxious years, he debated how the democracies could achieve the 'peace for our time' that millions wanted and that the British Prime Minister Neville Chamberlain finally and falsely claimed to have brought back from Munich in September, 1938.

One outcome of Koeppler's discussions was a short book, written with Maxwell Garnett, and published by Allen and Unwin in London in 1940. Its optimistic title was *A Lasting Peace*. The opening sentence of Koeppler's section began: 'There can be no Anglo-German understanding without France.' Already, in other words, he was looking ahead to some form of European understanding on more than just a bilateral basis.

Meanwhile, there were more urgent personal problems. Heinz Koeppler's University lectureship continued into 1940, when he also finally took his Oxford MA degree. But although he was a naturalised Briton, nervousness in the spring of 1940, especially after the fall of France, attracted unwelcome and often unjustified police attention to all 'enemy aliens', briefly including Koeppler himself. This misunderstanding was quickly and firmly dealt with. But as a fit, well-educated, male citizen just thirty years old he wanted to contribute to his adopted country's war effort. On August 4, 1940, he was recommended for a commission in the Army Education Corps. This, which had in peacetime played a minor role, was soon to be greatly expanded to cope with the large numbers of troops based in Britain after the Dunkirk retreat and before the Normandy landings. But to use a speaker of perfect German to teach British soldiers seemed a waste of talent when he could be more directly engaged with the enemy, gathering intelligence and using the truth to undermine Nazi propaganda.

The British Foreign Office had among its ramifications a Political Intelligence Department (PID), and in 1940 Koeppler joined it as an Intelligence Officer. It was in this capacity that he later visited prisoner-of-war camps. In 1941, moreover, Winston Churchill established the Political Warfare Executive (PWE). Koeppler was transferred to it, as Assistant Regional Director, in 1943. PWE's remit was not so much information-gathering as disinformation and propaganda. PWE was headed by the veteran intelligence officer Sir Robert Bruce Lockhart. Also involved in Britain's 'political warfare' were such luminaries as Rex Leeper, Ritchie Calder, and Richard Crossman. With Crossman Koeppler had been friendly at Oxford – so much so that he had been willing for Koeppler's sister to use his flat. Crossman was now involved, among other things, with what was known as 'black propaganda', including broadcasts from fictitious independent radio stations supposedly in Nazi Germany, zestfully run by the former *Daily Express* reporter Sefton Delmer.

Koeppler's role was less cloak-and-dagger. He was concerned chiefly with 'white' – i.e. officially acknowledged – broadcasts to Germany by the BBC, of which nearly 40,000 words went out every twenty-four hours. In addition to his work as liaison officer between the BBC and PID's German Regions (1941 to 1943), and from 1943 onwards as Crossman's deputy and Assistant Director of the German and Austrian Region, he eventually headed PID's Lecture Section, comprising some 60 people. More significantly, he was also Secretary of a joint committee representing the Foreign Office (including the PID), the BBC, and the Ministry of Information. Its task was to prepare plans for the educational and information services to be set up in Germany after the war.

In this context, in 1943 and 1944, Heinz Koeppler twice produced, as has been seen, his plan for 'an institution ... to provide an opportunity for men and women in the public life of Germany to ... look at German problems from outside Germany' – the kernel of what was to be Wilton Park. But, in the urgency of wartime, the plan lay dormant. It was not until 1945 – when, incidentally, PWE was subsumed into PID – that Koeppler received a summons from the Deputy Under-Secretary in the Foreign Office, Sir Ivone Kirkpatrick, the veteran intelligence officer responsible for establishing the British part of the Allied Control Commission in postwar Germany. 'Given the political atmosphere and the very real problems of transport and selection', said Kirkpatrick, Koeppler's ideas were 'premature as regards German civilians'. But they were 'admirable for dealing with German POWs here and now'.

CHAPTER 3

POW Camp 300

'During walks in the Buckinghamshire countryside and over beer and tobacco, confidences – even friendships – were formed which might be as fruitful in ideas to the German side as they were productive of information to the British.'
Donald McLachlan, *Room 39: Naval Intelligence in Action 1939–45*

When World War II ended, Heinz Koeppler had intended to return to his work at Oxford. Now, however, Ivone Kirkpatrick's encouragement offered a chance that his wartime efforts for democracy in Germany could continue and his 1943/44 ideas might eventually bear fruit. 'It appeared to me', he wrote later, 'that trying to set up a centre for prisoners–of–war would provide us with a good testing ground for the practicability of these ideas.' But it was still by no means certain that he himself would be asked to run such a centre; nor was there any notion of where, if anywhere, his proposed 'institution' might be housed.

During the war, when the Prisoners–of–War Section of the Foreign Office's Political Intelligence Department had asked the War Office for a camp in which to locate a special training centre, the War Office had refused, 'on the grounds that it was not able to supply the accommodation or the extra guards that would, in its view, be necessary'. In June 1944, PID was allowed to share with Military Intelligence's interrogators (MI 19) the largely 'white' POW camp at Ascot Park, with a view to forming 'missionary teams' to work elsewhere; but this proved rather unsuccessful, and at the end of 1945 Ascot Park was in any case shut down.

Towards the end of 1945, however, MI 19 privately told the head of PID's Prisoners–of–War Division, Wing Commander F.H. Hitch, that part of its POW Camp 300 at Wilton Park would shortly be freed. The Director General of PID thereupon authorised a new approach to the War Office;

and after negotiations that also involved Military Intelligence, PID obtained part of Camp 300. Later, MI 19 withdrew entirely. In the gratified words of the official record:

> PID thus ultimately acquired for its special camp an ample site little more than an hour's distance from London. In addition there were buildings which had been erected by MI 19 for use as cells and interrogation rooms, and which could serve for holding lectures and classes after conversion. The P/W Division's section of the Wilton Park camp was formally taken over in November, 1945, with a Directorate of Prisoners of War (War Office) establishment to run it.

Wilton Park stood about a mile north-east of Beaconsfield, and some ten miles south-east of Benjamin Disraeli's home of Hughenden Manor. It was not only a park, but a large white-plastered late-eighteenth-century country house of Portland stone, Palladian with later additions including one-storey wings with big arched windows. Inside, it had elegant James Wyatt plasterwork, screens of paired columns, a marble staircase with an ironwork balustrade, and a round glazed dome over the stairwell. Outside, as well as the wooded park, it had a well-kept croquet lawn. Today, the house no longer exists, and the grounds are largely playing-fields. In World War II, the White House, as it was called, housed the British Army officers' mess; the grounds were not only dotted with the 'buildings' put up by MI 19 – mostly Nissen huts – but also surrounded by double barbed wire, with sentry towers. For Wilton Park had been the second of the Combined Services Detailed Interrogation Centres for coaxing information out of prisoners of war.

These were not scenes of threats or brutality. Donald McLachlan, who served in Naval Intelligence during World War II, described in detail British interrogation techniques: 'No third degree, hypnotism, truth drugs, threats of violence, starvation diet or solitary confinement. That kind of treatment was not only forbidden under the Geneva Convention, but was also regarded as useless by good interrogators and hankered after only by lazy and bad ones.'

There were of course tricks, of which the enemy was well aware: placing a 'stool pigeon' in captivity with a prisoner to elicit confidences, and in particular hiding microphones and transcribing unwary chat. At Wilton Park, such 'bugs' were concealed in electric light-fittings, and – astonishingly in retrospect – remained undetected. Later, however, they were to cause embarrassment.

The Commandant of Wilton Park was, of all things, an Australian economist. Born in Melbourne in 1890, Leo St Clare Grondona had begun life as a farmer and then a newspaper reporter. He had served in World War I, and been seriously wounded. In 1923 he had been a delegate to the Imperial Conference, and had settled in Britain. As a civilian, he proposed plans to stabilise commodity prices and exchange rates: he published *Empire Stocktaking* in 1932, followed by *Britons in Partnership*. In World War II he became a senior officer in British intelligence.

As the war progressed and more senior officers fell into Allied hands, Wilton Park was transformed into what one German historian called 'a camp for Generals'. The doyen of wartime scientific intelligence, Professor R.V. Jones, who went there in 1945 to interrogate some of them, described what he called 'an extraordinary sight'.

> Fifty or more German generals were taking their exercise inside a barbed wire compound in the plan of an equilateral triangle of perhaps 80 yards [a] side. Several were already famous names with us, including Field Marshals von Rundstedt and Milch, and I felt rather as one does in a restaurant on going up to a tank of swimming trout and pointing a finger saying, 'I'll have that one!'.

Among the senior Italian officers at Wilton Park was Marshal Giovanni Messe, who with seventeen generals and two admirals had surrendered to General Bernard Montgomery at Tunis on May 13, 1943. 'It was decided', as Matthew Barry Sullivan recorded, 'to give them special treatment.'

> Grondona ... was ordered to make two floors of his officers' mess in the White House at Wilton Park available for them as high security quarters. Having the right connections, he quickly obtained from Windsor Castle the searchlight equipment last used at the coronation of George VI. He was instructed by the War Office not to shake hands with Messe, and to expect a film camera team. But when the small, affable Marshal advanced towards him with hand outstretched, Grondona, an Australian of great courtesy, could not refuse it, nor the warm hand-clasp of each member of his staff. (This was, of course, cut from the newsreel pictures.) Later, while hammering was still going on above, he escorted Messe up the broad marble staircase to the well-appointed bedroom just vacated by himself. The Italian expostulated when he saw three sappers cheerfully fixing stout barbed wire frames to the bay windows overlooking what had been the finest croquet lawn in England. His ADC and interpreter tried to keep up with his voluble protests. 'The Marshal has not the intention of trying to escape – it would be absurd! And is not England an island?' Grondona asked him if he would not give his parole d'honneur. No, his King's Regulations forbade it. An informal *modus vivendi* was amicably found, all the special security measures were dispensed with and Messe, his staff and

the two admirals settled down for the next six months to a rather pleasant existence. They could play croquet or tennis with two ball-boy Italian POWs always provided. Messe had arrived not only with cigars and liqueurs in his baggage, but with 1,000 pounds in 5-pound Bank of England notes, his staff with rather less each. It was allowed back to them in a weekly allowance. Grondona gave his own staff, who still used the ground floor of the White House, special instructions on their behaviour. All conversations on the lawn and the terrace were to be carried out in a low tone. The first reason was security, the second 'courteous considera-tion for people who are at a disadvantage ... undertones evincing obvious caution should be avoided'. When Mussolini was overthrown in July the Italians were all delighted, and sent home by the end of the year in order to co-operate with the Allies.

Grondona's relations with senior German officers were more wary. To deal with a large contingent of them who arrived in May 1945, he stepped up the security precautions. Matthew Barry Sullivan described the reaction:

> When the taciturn sixty-nine-year-old Field Marshal von Rundstedt was shown to the best bedroom, he appeared not to notice the barbed wire at bay windows. The searchlights were turned on at night and an extra acre had been enclosed with double barbed wire and two sentry towers with machine-guns. If the Germans found these precautions absurdly excessive, they made no protest and walked stiffly round their cage for an hour each morning and afternoon.

A year older than von Rundstedt was Field Marshal Ernst von Busch, a veteran of World War I and of Hitler's Russian campaign: he had even been chosen to lead the proposed invasion of Britain at the head of the Sixteenth Army. He had been captured in 1945 while Commander-in-Chief North West, in charge of German forces in Denmark, Schleswig-Holstein and the northern Netherlands. At Wilton Park, on July 17, 1945, he died in bed of a heart attack. The War Office instructed that he could be buried with appropriate military honours. However, von Runstedt was appalled at the simplicity of the service, as he complained afterwards. Matthew Barry Sullivan takes up the tale:

> That evening von Rundstedt asked Grondona to come and see him. He poured him a whisky and, speaking with unaccustomed emotion, asked why he and his colleagues had been subjected to a bitter experience none of them would ever forget. Grondona replied that, as commandant, he had no comment to make, but speaking 'off the record' and man to man, asked von Rundstedt if he had seen the pictures of the concentration camps and

whether he understood the detestation of all things German that had consequently spread over the country. The War Office did not believe that the dead man was personally involved, but had von Rundstedt noticed, when at the cemetery, the solitary figure of a policeman in the distance to keep the public and press-men away? Did he not understand that questions would have been asked in the House of Commons, had there been more than a simple ceremony. Pale and tense, Rundstedt put his head down and his face in his hands. 'We do realise what you say, and have the utmost shame. But I give you my word of honour as a soldier that the revelations concerning the concentration camps have appalled the Wehrmacht even more than the people of Britain.' Grondona had several more private conversations with von Rundstedt, whose dignity never relaxed and who never tried to vindicate himself. His private purgatory was to continue and even increase during the remaining seven years of his life.

Gradually, security at Wilton Park was eased. The generals were introduced to cricket, which they played on the nearby Beaconsfield ground. One group started an allotment to grow vegetables and supplement their rations: some of its produce they sent to the British officers' mess. Finally, as the summer of 1945 turned into autumn, the captains and the kings – or rather, the generals and the marshals – departed. Many of them went to Grizedale Hall in Grizedale Forest between Hawkshead and Coniston in the Lake District, before their final departure in January of the following year. By November 7, 1945, Wilton Park was ready for its new role.

CHAPTER 4

Captive Audience

'He that goeth about to persuade a multitude, that they are not so well governed as they ought to be, shall never want attentive and favourable hearers.'

Richard Hooker, *Of the Laws of Ecclesiastical Polity* (1593)

Wilton Park formally assumed its new role in January 1946. But its administration was still run by Leo St Clare Grondona, who had been asked by the PID to continue as Camp Commandant. Before the changeover, he sent the following circular to those of his former staff who were also staying on:

> The *raison d'être* of the new baby is to re-educate groups of 300 Jerries in the way they should go. Courses will last varying periods, after which the victims will return to their Fatherland – all white or, should one say, all red, white and blue! Instruction will be imparted by a staff under an Oxford don ... We've met only a couple of the long-haired section of the new establishment as yet, but they seem God-fearing folk and bid fair to being good mixers in the time-honoured fashion ... Structurally, the guts will be torn out of the original offices – partitions will be ripped down to make large rooms on the north side of the grille; all barbed wire, compounds and iron bars are going west ... The Jerries will provide their own police.

The 'Oxford don' was of course Heinz Koeppler, who had indeed been scheduled to resume his Oxford career and his lectures on mediaeval history. He had not been the first choice to head the Institution he had himself proposed. One obvious candidate had been Henry Faulk, now a Lieutenant-Colonel and Executive Field Officer in the Ps/W division: but his work in the camps gave him wider responsibilities than 're-education' in just one of them. The next possibility had been Wing Commander Norman Roffey. A former schoolteacher, small and slim, he was fluent in

29

German and had been an RAF interrogator before working under Cyrus Brooks on 're-education'. During the summer of 1945 he began sounding out possible lecturers and drafting a syllabus, balancing cultural and political concerns. In view of his experience as an interrogator, he planned to make sure that hidden microphones were removed. But before he could proceed any further, the Controller of the Ps/W Division, Wing Commander F.H. Hitch, had to send for him and admit that a decision had been taken at a higher level – in fact by Ivone Kirkpatrick: Dr Heinz Koeppler was to be in charge of Wilton Park. Hitch personally, wrote Matthew Barry Sullivan after a later conversation with him, 'had many misgivings – and so did Faulk – but could do nothing about it. Hitch feared that the ambitious Koeppler, with his many good connections, would make Wilton Park into a "show place"; he was also much too German and too domineering in his whole way of doing things.'

Koeppler's character – and the tone of Grondona's circular – suggested that their relationship might be prickly. The division of labour between them was itself potentially abrasive. Grondona had been in full charge of No. 300 Camp; now that it was the 'Training Centre', he remained responsible for its administration (custody, feeding, clothing, and discipline). But Koeppler, as its Principal, was determined to control what it did. *Patti chiari, amicizia lunga* (clear agreements, long friendship)? The future was to validate the warning.

Meanwhile, however, preparations for the new Wilton Park were well in hand. Grondona, wrote Wing Commander Hitch:

> knew all the ropes and was of very real help in the transfer, particularly regarding alterations. It is no exaggeration to say that he saved us a great deal of hard cash by negotiating with the Ministry of Works to use existing material with Ps/W labour. I think I am right in saying that instead of the estimated total of around 2,000 pounds, the bill was only a matter of pounds. I have always found Grondona a most helpful and amiable individual.

Koeppler, on his side, was busy assembling a dozen or so teaching staff. 'The tutors', he wrote later:

> who had to be collected in a hurry and were at first a motley crew with very different backgrounds, soon developed into a most enthusiastic and efficient team whose contribution to the success of our work with prisoners of war cannot be over-estimated.

A number of them were British. One of the first to arrive was George

Roundell Greene, a teacher and Oxford graduate who as an RAF officer had spent five years in a German POW camp. Politically, he was a Liberal. Alongside him was a keen Socialist, Captain Alex Glasfurd, who had already been at Wilton Park as an interrogator. The trio in the political spectrum was completed by a Tory Cambridge graduate, Robert D.J. Gibson, who had been interned in the Netherlands in 1940 while trying to get members of his family back to England, and spent five years as a civilian prisoner of the Germans in Holland, Germany, and Austria: as a result, he said, he had 'a certain sympathy' for anyone in a similar situation. A fourth recruit was Ken Morgan, previously an unaggressive interrogator of POWs at the London District Cage. Most of the remaining British tutors were either officers or academics from Oxford or Cambridge. Their friendliness with each other, despite political differences, was an object lesson in tolerance that astonished some of their pupils.

The other group on Koeppler's team comprised mainly German refugees. Outstanding among them was the remarkable 'Captain Holt'. Like Koeppler's alias of 'Professor King', this was a wartime cover name. The Captain was really a Bavarian aristocrat, Baron Waldemar von und zu Knoeringen, who in the pre-Hitlerian Weimar Republic had been a member of the Socialist Workers' Youth Movement. When Hitler came to power in 1933, Knoeringen had emigrated to Czechoslovakia, and from there in 1939 to Britain. During the war he had worked for Richard Crossman, who in 1943 had sent him to North Africa to talk to POWs in the camps. In Algiers he had collected a group of anti-Nazis, who were brought to Britain in 1944. Together with other like-minded prisoners-of-war, they broadcast to Germany. 'They spoke up passionately and anonymously', wrote Matthew Barry Sullivan, 'for, as they put it, the honour of their country, for Germany against Hitler and for the ten thousand anti-fascists who were their fellow-prisoners.' Knoeringen brought seven of his team, both officers and other ranks, to Wilton Park to work with Koeppler. An especially distinguished recruit was Dr Fritz Borinski, a North German who had been a youthful Social Democrat even before 1933. In Britain he had toured the POW camps in search of talent for the postwar rebuilding of Germany; but he had carefully kept out of politics, and was at first afraid of compromising his independence by working at Wilton Park. Knoeringen reassured him. 'I intend to return home soon,' he said. 'Do you think I will compromise myself at Wilton Park?' So the two of them set up a special section staffed by refugees, under the name *Aufbau* ((re)construction). Borinski's assistant, Fritz Borges, became Wilton Park's Librarian. Another notable

German refugee tutor was Godfrey Scheele, a young historian born in England who had served in the British army and whom Borinski described as 'terribly English in everything but name'. Knoeringen, true to his word, left Wilton Park in April 1946 and returned to Germany, where he built up the Social Democratic Party in his native Bavaria. He was replaced by K. Werner Lauermann, a trade union refugee printer from the Sudetenland who had already worked with Knoeringen in the Socialist Resistance group *Neu Beginnen*. Borinski likewise returned to Germany in April 1947, to be replaced by Richard K. Ullmann, a Jewish emigrant who had taught in the German School in Hong Kong.

The task of Koeppler's team had been laid down by Cyrus Brooks, Director of 'Re-education' in the PID, as early as October 1945:

> It was decided that there should be two different schemes: one a course for the final vetting and preparation of prisoners selected as suitable for work with the Control Commission in Germany, and the other a course for the training of missionary teams for dispatch to other P/W camps in this country.

The Control Commission course was to deal with up to 250 students at a time: it was to include the study of National Socialism, Prussian militarism, current problems in Europe, and democracy 'as exemplified in Britain'. Students were also to learn English. The 'missionary-training' course, to run parallel with the other, was to be for 50 or 60 students, and to cover mainly the practical ways of 'retraining' prisoners-of-war. It came to be known as the 'Action Group', and was largely conceived and run by Knoeringen and his refugees. The courses were to run for six to eight weeks.

The first combined course began on January 12, 1946 with exactly 300 students. Wilton Park selected them from camps near London – 'in the greatest hurry', as the official record admitted, but according to criteria laid down by Koeppler on December 19, 1945. Some were already known to training advisers, some had been proposed by camp commandants, some had been previously nominated by Knoeringen for the Action Group, some were picked in the last weeks of 1945, often by interview on Christmas and Boxing Days, and a very few were chosen from card-index records. All were volunteers. Since the main course was to prepare people for work in Germany with the British Control Commission, those whose homes were in the British Zone had priority. All, however, were firmly told that attending a course would not lead to any special privileges such as early release and repatriation. Of any two similar candidates, the younger was preferred; but although a certain level of education was needed, intelligence and open-mindedness – and what Koeppler called 'brightness and alertness'– mattered more than academic attainment. 'An active and eager trade official who has only been to elementary school may yet be preferable to a dull and pompous professor.' A large majority on the first combined course were politically 'white' or 'Category A', although those under twenty years old were chosen regardless of their ideological colour, and included thirty young 'blacks'. 'They must, of course, be not only intelligent but also ready to listen to other views and to behave as decent human beings and not as SS or Storm Troopers.' Later, in the light of experience, the selectors became politically stricter. But Koeppler happily recalled working

> with German soldiers of all ranks from privates to generals, with convinced anti-Nazis who had paid for their convictions by being put into penal battalions, with people who thought that the only thing wrong with Hitler was that he had lost, and above all with young men whose whole world, the only one they had ever known, had been shattered and who felt lost and bewildered.

Although Wilton Park promised no privileges, students on the first combined course found their surroundings an improvement on most POW camps. They lived in Nissen huts in groups of eight or ten, grouped around a sprawling one-storeyed brick building which looked, according to one visitor, 'very much like what it is – a cross between a prison and a school'. They had to do their own cleaning, wore POW patches on their uniforms, and were paid at the same rate of six shillings a week as POWs doing ordinary work. But they had beds to sleep in rather than military bunks. For special outings to London, they later discovered, they were lent civilian clothes. Normally, they were allowed out within five miles of Wilton Park. Their meals were spartan – as in normal camps, their rations were half those of the British guards: but they were served at table and were spared washing dishes. They received 15 cigarettes a week. The extensive library included the *Oxford English Dictionary* and its 20-volume German counterpart *Brockhaus*; one browser was surprised to find Hitler's *Mein Kampf* alongside a work by Churchill – a deliberate ploy by Koeppler. They had a wide selection of German, as well as British newspapers; and they could listen to the radio.

To face so sudden an influx of so many German prisoners-of-war, a score of them unregenerate Nazis, was daunting. To anyone less robust than Koeppler, it might have been intimidating. Even Koeppler, remembering his hostile reception at Shap Wells, was uneasy. The night before the first course opened, he walked round the camp with his administrative assistant Captain Griffiths. When they came to the newly arrived POWs' reading room, they met the suspicious stares of a roomful as uneasy as themselves. Scanning the walls for a way out, Griffiths said to Koeppler: 'There's only one exit, Sir, but I've got my revolver.' Matthew Barry Sullivan, who tells the story, adds: 'It was not a joke.'

Mutual wariness was indeed a key problem on the first days. Koeppler complained of 'a very serious drawback, which has undoubtedly hampered the work of Wilton Park and created a great deal of suspicion – suspicion which we were at first unable to overcome as we did not understand its origin'.

> When I was first shown Wilton Park I was not told – no doubt for reasons of security – that until the time we were taking the camp over it had been used not as an ordinary prisoner-of-war camp but as a special interrogation camp, complete with all the necessary modern apparatus for obtaining technical information from prisoners.

Muddle, rather than security, was probably the reason for Koeppler's ignorance. The War Office had assumed that the Foreign Office would tell him, and the Foreign Office assumed that he knew already. In fact, he only found out when one of the students said, 'Don't you know, Sir, what this place was once used for?'

> While I did not know this, quite a number of prisoners who came to Wilton Park did, and of course their views of what had been going on there soon spread among all members of the courses. I am quite sure that their accounts were untrue, but of course it was most unfortunate that the work should have been put at such a handicap.

The POWs' fears of still being bugged were indeed misplaced. As Camp Commandant, Grondona had given orders for the 'guts to be ripped out' of Wilton Park's Camp 300 structure, including the secret microphones and recording system. But not everyone believed that it had happened, and the atmosphere remained tense.

Welcoming the students on the first day of the course, Grondona did his best to put them at their ease. He remarked 'what excellent settlers the Germans had made in New South Wales, and that he had served in the First World War under its outstanding Commonwealth Commander General Monash, whose parents came from Germany and *who was a Jew*.' He also stressed: 'We haven't invited you to volunteer to come here for a course with a view to turning you into good little flag-waving Britons. But we think it might be useful to show you how we muddle through in a democracy.'

The assembled students were greeted more formally a few days later, on January 17, in a speech in German by Major-General Kenneth Strong, the Director-General of PID. Work at Wilton Park, he said, was

> an experiment that has no precedent in previous war and post-war periods ... We believe that an attempt must be made to bridge the gap in trends of thought between victor and vanquished ... We hope that this ... will assist to build up, within a well-ordered social and economic framework, a peaceful and co-operative Europe.

Many, he said, wanted to forget the Third Reich and devote all their energy to building anew. But to do so on a solid foundation, and to enable Germany to be received once more as a trusted member of the fellowship of nations, it was essential to understand the background and origins of the catastrophe.

> For this reason, a large part of the course will be devoted to working out with you the main points of German development during the last eighty or hundred years. I say purposely 'with you', for your active co-operation in everything which happens here is an indispensable condition for the success of the experiment ...
>
> We do not intend to deny nor to ignore that the world and Western civilization owe a great deal to Germans, especially in the fields of music, science and technical achievements. Nevertheless, we do not intend that the achievements of these men should be reckoned in any way against the abominations of the recent past. To express myself concretely: Beethoven cannot excuse Belsen, nor Goethe the Gestapo. The good name of Germany lies deeply buried under the millions of corpses and under the shattered structure of Europe ...
>
> We are convinced that it is not National Socialism alone that is responsible for the catastrophe, but also those German circles which helped National Socialism to power: namely, the supporters of that devilish type of policy which, since Bismarck, has borne the name of Realpolitik ... To put it in a nutshell I would remind those of you who know Berlin what struck me during my tour of duty there. It seemed to me to be not without symbolical meaning that the Bismarck-Strasse led, via the Kaiserdamm, to the Adolf Hitler Platz.

After pointing out that 'after every lecture you will have the opportunity of asking questions and of taking part in the subsequent discussion', Strong went on to raise three matters he feared might be 'extremely destructive':

The first is what I would call the distortion of history and the creation of myths. The majority of you, not only those who have grown up since 1933, but also those who were at school before or after the First World War, imbibed an official version of history which has very little to do with reality and truth ... It will be quite easy to show you that there have been many German historians who have come to the same conclusions as their British or French colleagues. Only, it was not these men who were entrusted with the compiling of the official school books ...

The second factor that can hinder discussion is the tendency to avoid facing unpleasant facts by pushing the responsibility for them on to super-natural powers ... 'Fate' and the 'Law of History' are good scapegoats, but they do not help to bring a discussion nearer to the truth.

The third factor in your work about which I should like to warn you is the attempt to blame everything on to other people ... It would be like an emergency exit that does not lead to safety, but back into the burning building.

However, Strong added, there were three other fields of study to be pursued at Wilton Park: international relations and organisations, present-day Britain, and relations between the individual and society. He concluded with some words that Koeppler, in particular, must have been glad to hear spoken:

The fundamental fact can of course not be changed: namely, that you are prisoners-of-war in Britain, but, above this fact, the spirit which will pervade Wilton Park lies in your own attitude. We have set up this Training Centre on the model of the British Residential Colleges, establishments where people pursuing collective intellectual studies live and work together.

Whether Koeppler had any hand in Strong's speech is uncertain. It seems possible, since it was given in German, and had imaginative Koepplerian flourishes. What is certain is that Koeppler imprinted his own stamp on the theory and practice of Wilton Park even in its earliest days.

When the course proper started, the working day began at 8.30 a.m. At 10.30 a.m. there was a parade and roll-call, during which the teaching staff held a daily meeting. The working day ended at 10.30 p.m. Some of it was set aside for private study, and twice a week for sports. Each class had one day a week free, and Sunday mornings were free, for optional worship, until 12 noon. The curriculum included lectures (some of them by visitors from London and elsewhere), discussions, and 'brains trusts' in which lecturers or tutors answered questions on current affairs from a personal point of view. There were also study groups (called 'societies' or 'classes') on music, the press, drama, etc.

A notable feature of the drama group was a cabaret at the end of each course using puppets made by Willi Brundert, an old friend of Borinski's from their youth movement days. He had been discovered at Featherstone Park POW camp, and at Wilton Park became Borinski's assistant. He devised a *Kasperlspiel* – a mild form of Punch-and-Judy show – based on Wilton Park, with Koeppler as the arch-devil and his sergeant interpreters as minor demons. The tradition lasted, but Brundert left in July 1946, being repatriated to the Soviet Zone of Germany, where he became Professor of Economic Law at Magdeburg with an additional post in the Ministry of Economics. In 1949, however, he was arrested on a trumped up charge of espionage: he had been trained, the prosecution alleged, at the 'Spy School Wilton Park'. After eight years in prison he was amnestied and fled to the West, where he became State Secretary in Wiesbaden and Mayor of Frankfurt. He died in 1970 of a liver ailment contracted in prison. But some of his puppets survive in the store rooms of Wilton Park – a memorial both to him and to Koeppler, who enjoyed and encouraged their mocking wit.

There was a wall newspaper, *Die Wilton-schau*, written and printed every other day by the *Aufbau* team of sixty handpicked students, who also produced a magazine at the end of the course. There were also weekly films – including the Nazi propaganda film *Bismarck* which used its subject's expansionary policy as a justification for similar aggression under Hitler – a fact pointed out in a running commentary by one of the Wilton Park staff. No commentaries were needed when prisoners-of-war anywhere in Britain were shown a film of the Nazi concentration camps. As the PID reported on March 27, 1946:

> The effect of this film is exemplified by the fact that after seeing it numbers of Ps/W discarded their Nazi insignia and military awards, while several camps made spontaneous collections amounting in one case to 52 pounds, with the request that the money be credited to the I.R.C.C. for the relief of victims of the concentration camps.

Films, lectures, discussion groups, and so on, were all used in orthodox POW camps. One special feature of Wilton Park, made possible by Koeppler's 'Establishment' connections, was a series of evening lectures by eminent outsiders from every walk of life. Their subjects were a judicious blend of general topics, exposition of British policy, and specifically German concerns. The speakers were equally mixed. A.L. Lloyd wrote in the weekly magazine *Picture Post* on April 6, 1946: 'What Tory Lord

Soulbury [former Minister of Education, who lectured to the second Wilton Park course on March 21, 1946] says one evening may be contradicted by Labourite R.H.S. Crossman the next ... A Brains Trust of Labour MPs may follow one of Conservative MPs.'

As Koeppler told Lloyd, 'The pupils get different answers to their questions, but that's good for them: it's something non-totalitarian; they learn there is no single official answer.'

The first evening speaker, on February 2, 1946, was Koeppler's friend and wartime colleague Richard Crossman, now Labour MP for East Coventry. His subject was 'The Labour Government's task in Europe'. He was followed, on February 6, by the lecturer from the Foreign Office on his 'Impressions of Nuremberg', and on the next night by the African specialist Thomas Hodgkin. He had been a Senior Demy at Magdalen before Koeppler, in 1932–33, and was now at Balliol College. His subject was 'Adult Education for Citizenship'.

On February 12, Harold Nicolson spoke as 'An Englishman on the German Character'. Perhaps he reminded his listeners that in 1939, in his little book on *Diplomacy*, he had quoted Prince Buelow as saying, on a visit to Windsor in 1899, that 'The English politicians do not know the Continent well', and that he himself had declared: 'Underneath all the solid and magnificent virtues of the German race there lies a layer of nervous uncertainty.

If Nicolson provoked his listeners, Koeppler was well content. On the very next day a former RAF interrogator, Geoffrey Forrest, called in on Wilton Park and found him 'very hospitable, tired and triumphant with justification'. Tired he might well be. Even the visiting lecturers' series was barely without a break. On February 14 Norman Mackenzie of *The New Statesman* discussed the 'Home policy of the British Government'. On February 26 another Oxford don, the economist G.D.N. Worswick, surveyed 'Industrial problems of the post-war era'. On February 19 a senior civil servant from the Colonial Office talked about 'Higher Education in the Colonies'; and on February 21 the lecture series for the first Wilton Park course concluded with Amy Buller, former Secretary of the International Students Service and author of *Darkness over Germany*, on 'A challenge to German Youth'.

A challenge to the POW students was that they were encouraged to ask questions. 'A free and open discussion', wrote Koeppler, 'is the basis for our work.' Harold Nicolson, in his 'Marginal Comment' column in *The Spectator* on March 1, 1946, a fortnight after his lecture, described how lively it had been, in contrast to his first impression:

It was dark when I arrived and in the light of the hurricane lamp that guided me along the cinder path I saw the raindrops glistening ... When I entered the large hut I detected that smell of prisoners all over the world from Opocno to Wormwood Scrubs. Three hundred faces stared at me ... that were uniform only in the fact that they wore the grey mask of unhappiness that captivity brings ...

I lectured for some forty minutes, and thereafter there were questions which lasted for almost an hour and a half. It must be realized that the Commandant of the prison camp was present, as well as the Principal of the training course; yet there was no sign whatsoever that the prisoners were deterred from asking leading questions by the presence of their gaolers. In fact, one man asked me why it was, if we disapproved of Prussian discipline and Nazi methods, that we ourselves adopted such methods in our prison camps. I knew that he was referring, not to the British officers in charge of the camp, but to the German NCOs who in the earlier stages of the war were perhaps given too much authority. I ignored this distinction and asked him in his turn whether he would have dared to put such a question to a visitor in the presence of the Commandant of Dachau or Buchenwald. The prisoners laughed heartily at this comparison.

Attendance at the evening lectures was voluntary, and some speakers were a bigger draw than others. To avoid the embarrassment of less popular lecturers having to face a near-empty Nissen hut, Koeppler installed sailcloth curtains at intervals, blocking off unwanted seats – unless they were filled, in which case, after some scuffling, the curtains would be risen to reveal more rows of listeners. Dexter Keezer describes this device as an application of 'Koeppler's law for satisfying speakers': ... 'A full house is far more important ... than the size of the crowd.'

Some speakers needed few curtains, if any. The inaugural speech in the second Wilton Park course of lectures, which ran from March 19 to April 26, 1946, was by Grondona himself, speaking as an economist on 'Price stability as the foundation for World Economic Reconstruction'. The speaker's identity as Commandant no doubt ensured a decent turnout. But it was an arcane subject for most of them, to judge from the results of a general knowledge questionnaire recorded towards the end of the course. The examiner reported that, although

students at Wilton Park are normally considered above the average standard of intelligence and receive here instruction in most of the subjects dealt with in the questionnaire ... , results showed that a considerable percentage of students had only a very vague idea of these events. Subjects revealing the greatest lack of knowledge were:

	Right answer	
	25 years & younger	*over 25*
Kellogg Pact	50%	62%
Kapp Putsch	53%	71%
Country and Epoch associated with:		
Govt. of the People ...	17%	31%

There was practically no question which more than 90% could answer correctly. Notable examples are:

Out of 279 students

    24 students did not know who Karl Marx was
    30 students were ignorant of Shakespeare
     8 students could not explain who Beethoven was
    11 students knew nothing of the League of Nations
    45 students had never heard of the Treaty of Brest-Litowsk
    76 students knew nothing of the Congress of Vienna.

'These results', the report noted, 'may help to indicate which events and ideas will require particular attention'. They certainly did not lead to a watering-down of the evening lecture programme. Its notable speakers, on this second course, included Lord Soulbury on 'The Development of a Responsible Self-Government'; the Oxford historian and *Sunday Times* columnist R.C.K. Ensor on 'Political Parties in Europe'; the editor of *The New Statesman* Kingsley Martin on 'The Truth about the British Press'; the Master of Balliol Lord Lindsay of Birker on 'The Principles of Democracy'; and a 'Brains Trust' team of no fewer than six serving MPs, all – against Koeppler's normal principle – members of the Labour Party.

At the third Wilton Park evening lecture course, from May 20 to June 25, the roster of speakers was still more distinguished. The first, on the opening night, was Dr George Bell, Bishop of Chichester, who had long made himself unpopular by speaking up for the plight of prisoners and the work of the German anti-Nazi Resistance. His subject was 'The Task of the Churches in Europe'. He was followed a week later by the former senior civil servant Sir Arthur (later Lord) Salter, who was now Independent MP for Oxford University. His publications included, in 1933, *The United States of Europe*, and he had worked in two World Wars with the 'Father of Europe', Jean Monnet. At Wilton Park he looked ahead to 'European Reconstruction'. Oxford's Regius Professor of Greek, E.R.

Dodds, discussed 'Academic Freedom'; while the Dean of St Paul's Cathedral, the Very Reverend W.R. Matthews, spoke on 'Christian Civilisation'. From a Quaker viewpoint came E.B. Castle, then Headmaster of Leighton Park School, Reading, the title of his talk was 'William Penn and the principles of political freedom in England'.

If these were broad and general topics, this third course of evening lectures also dealt with matters closer to their listener's personal, practical, even patriotic concerns. Nine days after the lecture course began, into the hut strode a 29-year-old Captain in the Grenadier Guards. It was Harold Nicolson's second son Nigel, a product of Eton and Balliol, and Conservative candidate for North-West Leicester. A veteran of the Tunisian and Italian campaigns, he had won the MBE. In his diary he recorded the reaction to a very personal talk:

My subject is 'A British officer looks at the German Army'. I speak in English, and it is translated into German sentence by sentence. I take a matter-of-fact point of view, a post mortem attitude: this is what puzzled us about you. I give them credit for courage and fortitude, but discredit for tactical folly and poor security and intelligence. They react very well, and there are loud cheers when I sit down after speaking for an hour. Then questions for another hour. These take the form of standing up and saying that they were very wicked, that they abused the Geneva Convention, that they are dirt under my feet. This flagellant attitude is strange and very embarrassing. Many of them tell long stories of how badly the Germans behaved. One parachutist who had been in Cassino (and to whom I had given great credit) said that he had been wounded six times, and was sick of the whole thing. I ask them some questions: about the *Soldbuch* slip which told them what they might and might not say when taken prisoner-of-war; this arouses great discussion; about the rumour in the German army that all prisoners-of-war were shot by the British. They also ask about the treatment of British prisoners-of-war in Germany, for which I give credit, but say that they treated the Russians, 'our allies', like dirt. One man asks what was our attitude towards deserters. I whisper to Heinz [Koeppler], who is sitting beside me, that of course they threw away the lives of their comrades; he is horrified: 'For God's sake don't say that.' I had no intention of saying so, and make probably my most effective answer of the evening, that we admired these people for their courage, and that they came to us as friends from the other side, though we gave them no different treatment to the rest. At the end, I break away from my interpreter, and speak for five minutes on my attitude to war: I describe them as a nucleus of the new Germany: I am glad I fought and won, but what a waste it all was: now both of us, in England and Germany, are about to turn our hands to reconstruction, etc. This goes with a terrific swing, and Heinz is very pleased with the result of the whole meeting.

41

The next evening an RAF officer, Flight Lieutenant John Haire (later Lord Haire of Whiteabbey), Labour MP for High Wycombe, discussed 'British Policy in Central Europe'. Still closer to home, for the assembled POWs, were lectures on 'The German Radio Today', 'The Development and Present Position of the German Press', and 'German Youth Today', all given by speakers from the British Zone of Germany.

The final evening lecture of the course, on June 25, 1946, was by Philip Noel-Baker, Labour MP for Derby, and Minister of State. After a distinguished academic career, in World War I he had been the First Commandant of the Friends' Ambulance Unit and an officer in the First British Ambulance Unit for Italy. He was soon to be Secretary of State for Air and then for Commonwealth Relations, and eventually a winner of the Nobel Peace Prize. Now, he gave his listeners 'My Impressions of Germany'.

For the fourth Wilton Park lecture course (July 12 to August 19, 1946), Koeppler pulled off a series of notable coups. The inaugural evening speaker was his old friend and patron Gilbert Murray, OM, formerly Regius Professor at Oxford, whose subject was for many German prisoners-of-war very near the knuckle: 'The Problem of Hopelessness'. Another old friend, Richard Crossman, made his second appearance at Wilton Park, lecturing on 'The Jewish Question'; and no fewer than five more Oxford dons followed him. They included a Magdalen contemporary of Koeppler's, William James Millar Mackenzie, who had switched from Classics to Politics in 1936 and had served in the Air Ministry during the war, going on later to be a part-time Official War Historian dealing with the Special Operations Executive (SOE). His lecture at Wilton Park was on 'Freedom and Government'. Another Magdalen colleague was Alan (A.J.P.) Taylor, who had become Tutor in Modern History there in 1938, when he had published *Germany's First Bid for Colonies 1884–85*. He spoke on 'Germany and the East'. On July 31, the former Magdalen Senior Demy, Thomas Hodgkin, made a second appearance at Wilton Park, advocating 'A People's University as the means for Democratic Reconstruction'. A Fellow of Brasenose, Michael Holroyd (not the biographer of Lytton Strachey, who was only eleven at the time), further pursued this theme in a talk on 'Reconstruction of the European and German Universities'.

The last of the Oxford dons to speak at Wilton Park's fourth course of lectures was from Queen's College; but he had another connection with Koeppler. This was Lindley Frazer, formerly Professor at Aberdeen, but during the war a leading figure in BBC broadcasts to Germany. Not surprisingly, he lectured on 'The Development and Future of the BBC'. A second wartime colleague whom Koeppler roped in to speak at Wilton Park was Dr Werner Burmeister, a refugee broadcaster, journalist, and author who was a Lecturer at London University and who specialised, then and later, in European affairs. He described 'A Journey through Germany', which many of his audience were longing to make.

As on the previous course, in fact, several of the summer lectures were devoted to what was happening in the POWs' homeland. On successive evenings, officials from the Control Commission reported on 'The Situation in Berlin' and 'Lower Level Administration in the British Zone'. Still more important, to some, was 'The Present Spiritual Situation'. That was the subject of an impassioned address by Pastor Birger Forell, the heroic Swedish Protestant minister who had long worked in Germany. In wartime Berlin until 1942, when he was recalled to Sweden, he had used his diplomatic passport and status to help the German resistance. Since 1944, invited by Bishop Bell of Chichester, he had been working in Britain for the War Prisoners Aid of the World Alliance of YMCAs.

True to Koeppler's principle of balancing speakers from both Left and Right, two unmistakeable Conservatives addressed the fourth lecture course. One was Lady Apsley, National Chairman of the Women's Section of the British Legion, previously MP for Bristol Central. The other was Viscount Hinchingbrooke, the MP for South Dorset who was later, in 1962, to become President of the Anti-Common Market League and in 1964 to disclaim his peerage for life.

The fifth course of evening lectures at Wilton Park ran from September 11 to October 14, 1946. By now, virtually all the speakers were household names. The one exception was the 22-year-old who opened the series. This was Robin Marris, billed as ex-President of the Cambridge Union Society, since he was speaking on 'The Politics of English University Students', but very soon to serve in the Treasury and at the UN in Geneva before returning to King's College, Cambridge and to a brilliant career, as both an academic and, like his younger brother Peter, a practical economist. It was typical of Koeppler to choose so young and so promising a newcomer to start the series. Marris was followed by the MP for Cambridge University (and Harold Nicolson's editor at *The Spectator*), Wilson Harris: his subject was 'The British Press'. The next evening, the Conservative MP for Hertford, Derek Walker-Smith, discussed 'The Role of an Opposition in a Parliamentary Democracy'.

Prisoners-of-war eager to hear more about Germany had to wait until September 20, when Koeppler himself took the rostrum to talk about 'Adult Education and the Universities in Germany today'. On September 25, the topic was 'The Economic Problems of Europe', and the speaker was C.W. Guillebaud, Fellow and Tutor at St John's College, Cambridge. He was not only an eminent economist with particular practical experience on wages and prices, but also the author of two pioneering works on Germany – *The Works Council: A German Experiment in Industrial Democracy* (1928) and *The Economic Recovery of Germany 1933–38*. Later in the course, Barbara Ward, Assistant Editor of *The Economist* and recently appointed a Governor of the BBC, spoke on 'Present Conditions in Germany'.

The remainder of that course's evening lectures were more general, or oriented more towards Britain. On the evening after Guillebaud's talk on Europe, Kenneth Adam, Director BBC Publicity since 1941 (and later to become Director of BBC Television), discussed the BBC as 'A National Institution', stressing to an audience accustomed to Dr Goebbels's state-run propaganda broadcasting that the Corporation was that wonderful anomaly, a non-commercial, public-service institution speaking for the nation – yet independent of government control. The next evening – making three lectures in a row – Robert Birley, then Headmaster of Charterhouse, spoke on 'The Teaching of History'. It was his first public appearance at Wilton Park, with which he was to be long associated; in 1947 he was to become Educational Adviser to the Military Government on the Control Commission, Germany, before returning in 1949 to be Head Master at Eton, where he had been an assistant master before the war.

The political balance shifted leftwards on October 2, 1946, when another Oxford Professor, the veteran Socialist G.D.H. Cole, spoke about 'The Fabian Society', on which he was the greatest living expert. Two days later, T.D. Weldon, a Fellow of Magdalen and frequent broadcaster, lectured on 'The Free Citizen in a Free Society'; and soon afterwards Ernest Green, JP for Surrey and the General Secretary of the Workers' Educational Association, talked about 'Adult Education in Britain'.

The last two lectures of this course covered foreign affairs: 'Recent Developments in India', by Sir Stanley Reed, MP for Aylesbury, who had had long experience in the sub-continent as a correspondent and later editor of *The Times of India*; and 'Anglo-Soviet Relations', by another Magdalen contemporary of Koeppler's, also once a Senior Demy, Max (later Lord) Beloff. Having seen war service in the Royal Corps of Signals, Beloff had returned to Oxford as Nuffield Reader in the Comparative Study of Institutions and was soon to publish, in 1947, the first of his two volumes on *The Foreign Policy of Soviet Russia*.

But the greatest 'catch' among the speakers on Wilton Park's fifth lecture course was yet another Oxonian, the newly ennobled Lord

Beveridge. Born at Rangpur in India in 1879, the son of a British civil servant, he had begun his lifelong concern for unemployment, its causes and cures, when at the age of 25 he had become Subwarden of Toynbee Hall in London. After work as Director of Labour Exchanges and Permanent Secretary of the Ministry of Food, he had been Director of the London School of Economics and Political Science from 1919 to 1937, when he had been elected Master of University College, London. His crowning achievement, in 1942, had been his report on *Social Insurance and Allied Services*, best known as *The Beveridge Report*, which helped to work out the policies and institutions for Britain's postwar social security system or welfare state. Now, at Wilton Park on the evening of October 10, 1946, he addressed the POW students in German on 'The Essentials of British Democracy'.

The sixth and last evening lecture course of 1946 began on November 5 and ended on December 6. Once again, education had a prominent place, and prominent speakers were placed upon the programme. On the first night, Thomas Hodgkin returned again to speak on 'Adult Education'. 'Postwar Education' was addressed by the civic-minded Kenneth Lindsay, Independent MP for the Combined English Universities. And the internationally celebrated poet, philosopher and art critic Herbert Read spoke on 'Contemporary Painting and Sculpture in England'.

Democracy, as always, featured largely in the sixth lecture series. Duncan Wilson, a Foreign Office official later to be knighted but now on the Control Commission, Germany, examined 'Some Problems of Democratic Administration', while Sir Alfred Brown, Legal Adviser to the Control Office, concluded the course with a talk on 'Democracy and the Rule of Law'. As civil servants, these two speakers were naturally non-partisan; but two others were members of Clement Attlee's Labour government. The first was Arthur Skeffington, MP for Lewisham and Parliamentary Private Secretary (PPS) to John Hynd, who was not only Chancellor of the Duchy of Lancaster, but also Minister for Germany and Austria. Skeffington spoke on 'Freedom in a Planned Society'. The second Government speaker was another PPS, this time to the Minister of Transport, Alfred Barnes. This PPS was Alfred (or Alf) Robens, later to be Minister of Labour and National Service, then Chairman of the National Coal Board and finally a life peer. His subject was 'The British Trade Union Movement and the Co-operative Societies'. At a less official level, the Chairman of the Oxford Branch of the Workers' Educational Association, gave a talk on 'The Reaction of the Man in the Street to the First Year of Peace'. And from a point much further Left on the political spectrum came Jennie Lee, Labour MP for Cannock, Stafford, the daughter of a Fifeshire miner and the wife of the Health Minister, Aneurin Bevan. Her subject was 'Relations between Press and Parliament in a Democratic Community'. Long afterwards she wrote:

> In all the bitterness and fear left by the war, Wilton Park will always remain for me a happy memory in a barbarous world. By doing a civilized job with delicacy and intelligence, it will, I am sure, recall the better side of English life to many who came here as prisoners and, I hope, have left as friends.

Koeppler was careful to balance these Left-wing lecturers with spokesmen from the Right. Clifford Glossop, Conservative MP for Howdenshire in the East Riding of Yorkshire, who had worked in the Ministry of Food during the war, had travelled extensively, and was later to settle in South Africa, described 'The British Method of Colonial Administration'. But the most effective counterweight to this lecture series' Left-leaning speakers was the Hon. William Waldorf Astor, Conservative MP for East Fulham until the 1945 Labour landslide. He came to Wilton Park, just eight days after Jennie Lee, to expound 'The Principles of Tory Policy'. In *The Daily Graphic* for December 31, 1946, he described his experience with good-humoured zest:

> As several previous lecturers had been supporters of Mr Attlee, I was encouraged to state the Conservative case vigorously. I pointed out that every plane designed by the Air Ministry before the war had proved a flop, while the planes that defeated the Luftwaffe ... all owed their existence to private aircraft firms going against the Air Ministry's views. I then suggested that if our aircraft industry had been nationalized before the war I would probably now be in the audience and they would be lecturing me, a point they took uproariously.

Closer to home, for Astor's audience, were three talks about the present state of Germany. The first was on 'The American Zone Today', by its Chief of Adult Education, Professor Willem van de Wall. The second, by an official from the Research Department of the Foreign Office, offered 'Sidelights on the Social and Political Situation in Germany Today'. And the third, on 'The SDP in Germany Today', was by none other than the German Social Democratic Party's leader, Kurt Schumacher. He himself had long been Hitler's political prisoner, in Dachau, Buchenwald and Neuengamme, since 1933. In World War I he had lost his right arm; two years after his visit to Wilton Park, his left leg would have to be amputated. Now, at 52, he was in painfully poor health and looked ten years older – tall, bowed, and gaunt. 'I felt humble,' said George Roundell Greene, 'towards a man who had been through so much.' One of the anti-Nazi prisoners, the artillery lieutenant Horst Woetzel, long remembered that October evening:

> Just to see this man from the past was an extraordinary experience. With bad sight and bad teeth, which made it hard to articulate, he came in on someone's arm, which naturally aroused sympathy among us. But the harsh provocative tone of his voice shocked me – it was almost like Hitler's. Not a single passage did he put over soberly.

Back in his room afterwards, Schumacher slumped into a chair, sweat pouring from his face. Among other things, he had insisted that, for German Socialists, Marxism, humanism, and Christianity were all legitimate and had to be recognised – a novelty for many of his audience. It was provocative even in Britain, prompting questions in the House of Commons; while Schumacher's very presence in the UK caused a protest from France. But for most of his audience, here was an authentic voice from pre-Nazi, anti-Nazi Germany, speaking realistically about life amid the postwar ruins, and prophetically about the hopes of rebirth and reunification.

This, far more than just the 're-education' of prisoners-of-war, was what Heinz Koeppler had always believed should be Wilton Park's overriding aim. Not everyone in the War Office and the Foreign Office agreed.

CHAPTER 5

Nissen–Hut University

'Seine Magnifizenz Herr Rektor Dr Koeppler.'
Engelbert Brandt, addressing a letter, September 25, 1946

To attract to Wilton Park lecturers so distinguished and disparate as Lord Beveridge and Kurt Schumacher was a remarkable achievement. But in London it confirmed something that Wing Commander Hitch had feared when appointing Koeppler – that he would turn Wilton Park into a 'show place'. He had certainly done that. One further result had been publicity in the press. By the end of 1946, as well as the articles in *Picture Post*, *The Spectator*, and *The Daily Graphic* already mentioned, Wilton Park had featured in the Quaker periodical *The Friend*, in the London *Evening Standard*, in *The New Statesman*, in the Catholic *The Tablet*, in the BBC's *The Listener*, in *The Times*, and in *The New York Herald-Tribune*.

What was more, to many people Heinz Koeppler was a very dominant figure. As Alec Frank, his later family doctor, recalled in conversation:

> Heinz used to come into the surgery – he was a big man and he had a big presence: I think he was six foot three and weighed about sixteen stone. He wore a smart pin-stripe suit and had a fresh rose in his buttonhole every time you saw him. He was really a larger-than-life man, a very strong personality ... He smoked heavily, drank a lot of black coffee, but he was very healthy ... He was a man of fairly boundless energy: he didn't complain of exhaustion, or tiredness, or not coping; I don't think he complained of tension ...
>
> He was obsessional, he was knowledgeable, he was immensely able ... a very able politician: he knew the politicians and the academics, and he picked his way through them ... [At conferences and suppers] he would hold court, and he had a sort of verbal shorthand, so you would start a

sentence saying 'But of course – ' and he said 'Yes, I absolutely understand your point': he would anticipate the point almost before you had a chance to articulate it. And I think he was usually right …

He was astonishingly adept with words, and ideas. That was one of the things that made him very formidable … I don't think he was in awe of anyone.

He had this enthusiasm – infectious enthusiasm … and he was prepared to fight his corner: he believed in the future of Wilton Park, and he had this absolute certainty that it was doing good.

As Principal of Wilton Park, Koeppler had to fight his corner from the start. Looking back at the end of Wilton Park's POW phase, he wrote:

> Concerning our relationship with the Military, it must be admitted that we presented a great problem since, quite clearly, the situation of prisoner students had not lain within the previous experience either of the Camp Commandant, or of the General Commanding Eastern Command, or of the War Office authorities responsible for prisoners-of-war … Considering that the bodies of the prisoners belonged to the War Office and their minds to the Foreign Office while they were at Wilton Park, the possibility of conflicts and misunderstandings was enormous.

Initially, Koeppler and Grondona, in Matthew Barry Sullivan's words, 'did not hit it off': 'When at the outset Koeppler began to assert himself with his usual force the Commandant dug his heels in. There was an awkward official confrontation, after which their areas of authority were precisely defined.'

Even so, friction remained. Wing Commander Hitch, who headed the Ps/W Division in the PID and later when it was attached to the Control Office for Germany and Austria, explained that:

> In our work of re-education great difficulties had been experienced as the then Secretary of State for War [J.J. Lawson, succeeded in 1946 by Captain F.J. Bellenger] was against it … I had a talk with Koeppler about the necessity to go carefully and to help Grondona, particularly with the War Office, so that our methods were evolutionary rather than revolutionary. After a time there were rumblings and differences but they were smoothed over as the last thing we wanted was a break with the War Office. They led up eventually, unfortunately … to a real rumpus over Koeppler's methods, and wanting special privileges etc.

Hitch further reported that Grondona, 'while admitting that Koeppler was "clever" and able, just did not like some attitudes and was a bit het up about certain "sincerities"'. To avoid any suspicion that he was going direct to Hitch behind Koeppler's back, he agreed to deal with his War Office colleagues first: they in turn agreed to contact Hitch before taking any action if further difficulties arose. 'But the net result', Hitch added, 'is of course that even in small matters Grondona just digs his heels in and rules his side of the roost good and hard.'

In November 1946, Camp Commandant Grondona felt obliged to issue orders reminding everyone of the need to economise with fuel and light. Radiators had been left full on with windows open, lights had been burning in corridors, empty classrooms, and staff common rooms, coke had been thrown away. Breaches of economy orders were punished by temporary suspension of fuel supplies and of free cigarettes. Part of the problem was due to hut leaders being changed each week on a rota system 'in compliance with Koeppler's wishes (quite understandable)', Grondona admitted, 'that as many prisoners as possible should be vested with authority in turn, but the objection is that almost before a prisoner has learned to exercise the necessary control of his fellows he is replaced'.

'It is not easy', complained Grondona in a letter to the War Office on January 16, 1947, 'to maintain ordinary discipline in this place'.

> Today I pulled up a prisoner who passed me with a mere nod, quite out of keeping with the usual brace up and smart eyes left or right which is the German way of paying compliments when hatless. I asked him why he had not conformed to the usual procedure and he told me that he had been instructed that the ordinary method of saluting, even of British officers, was not to be carried out in this camp. I asked him the source of this information and he told me his hut leader, whom I paraded at once. This man would not say that he had been so instructed, but he said that he had gathered that impression since he had been here.
>
> I left him in no doubt as to what would be expected in future and promulgated an order on the subject. I spoke to Koeppler on the matter and he said that the difficulty was that he was trying to make the men forget that they were soldiers, whereas I, in the exercise of my duties, seemed to remind them very much that they were still soldiers. I replied that so long as there were British Military personnel in this camp I certainly would not tolerate any departure from the strict letter of the law in the matter of compliments from German prisoners.

In the long run, however, Koeppler and Grondona solved their mutual problems. 'Of course,' wrote Koeppler, 'there arose some difficulty and now and again even unpleasant situations,' but looking back I should like to pay tribute to the co-operation which, after a somewhat shaky start, we got from the Military authorities, and in particular from Lt-Col. Leo St Clare Grondona ... The co-operation which was achieved proved that goodwill and common sense can deal satisfactorily with the oddest of administrative arrangements.

It was indeed an anomalous arrangement. Officially, Wilton Park was still a prisoner-of-war camp. Yet even the perimeter wiring was not impassable. On one occasion, Horst Woetzl helped a veteran Communist fellow-prisoner, Wolfgang Abendroth, through a broken section to get out on to the London road, where a car took him to a meeting with Left-wing British comrades. As Kingsley Martin wrote in *The New Statesman* after his own visit, 'any prisoner could escape if he wished, but none do, or wish to do so'. Nor was it necessary to find holes in the wire. Church parties were allowed to walk to St Theresa's in Beaconsfield without supervision; once, they were joined by an ex-SS officer who claimed to be Catholic and wandered off on his own, returning unpunished later in the day. Although 'fraternisation' was still officially outlawed, prisoners encountered local people at nearby Jordans, with its Friends' Meeting House, or at socials arranged in Beaconsfield by the Christian Council and the Fellowship of Reconciliation. One POW artist, cadet-officer Werner Düttmann (later the leading architect in postwar Berlin), held an exhibition of his paintings in the house of a Jordans resident, Betty Jenkin: it was visited by Walter de la Mare, Herbert Read, and Henry Moore, who invited him to London to see his work. Later, in Berlin, Düttmann obtained a Moore Reclining Figure for display outside his Academy of Arts. From Wilton Park, trips to London or Oxford were a regular item – three at a time in three civilian suits, small, medium, and large, that Koeppler had obtained from his staff.

For reasons of tact, he arranged such outings without officially consulting the Camp Commandant – although (as Matthew Barry Sullivan surmised) 'he would probably have approved'. Sullivan went on:

Grondona's very human side inspired the affection of one of his personal clerks, Hans Freibusch, who glued together a matchbox-holder out of dock-stems and inscribed it 'made in Sing-Sing'. But nothing gave Grondona (who was no mean staff officer) so much satisfaction as what he could do for Corporal Herbert Krause, a young man arrived at Wilton Park from a hostel in Cumberland and found to have leukaemia. He was put in Amersham Hospital and was not expected to live long. His mother who lived in Hamburg had lost both her husband and other son in the war. 'Why can't she be flown over?' asked Mrs Grondona ... This was a tall order, but the War Office gave permission for the Commandant to go ahead on his own. It happened he was about to inspect the fifty British personnel in the camp; he told them about Herbert Krause and immediately – it was pay day – half the air fare from Hamburg was produced, 27 pounds. He then assembled the 400 German students and staff, told them what the Tommies had done and immediately they collected 40 pounds from their meagre pay of 6 shillings a week. Meanwhile the Salvation Army in Hamburg was locating Frau Krause and getting her a civilian travel permit, Jean Grubb, a hospital almoner, arranging for a Methodist family to put her up and the Soldiers', Sailors' and Air Force Families Association tracing the boy's girl friend in Carlisle. The mother was met next afternoon by the Grondonas and taken at once to the hospital. Screens were put round the bed. In the tense silence of the ward the amazed boy's frail voice was heard, '*Ach, Mutti, träume ich?*' (Am I dreaming?) Next day the girl friend arrived. A dramatic improvement in his condition continued and he was sent home by hospital ship. In Hamburg he recovered sufficiently to take up civilian employment. Grondona wrote up the story for the *Empire News* which syndicated it round the world in a series entitled 'Did This Really Happen?' Sadly Herbert Krause's remission from leukaemia did not last and he died within a year.

So Grondona was as compassionate as Koeppler. But one was an Army officer, the other a civilian. And one of Koeppler's innovations was especially striking to the military mind, British and German alike. He had decided, as he put it, that

> membership of Wilton Park should be open to all German prisoners, irrespective of rank in the German Army. The precondition of this arrangement was clearly that while students at Wilton Park there could not be any distinction either in class or in living conditions between officers and other ranks. This was, after some hesitation, accepted by the British Military authorities and gladly accepted by the German officers who volunteered to join Wilton Park.

German other ranks took more convincing, because many resented the way their officers had behaved. Nevertheless, as Koeppler wished, officers and men at Wilton Park lived in the same conditions, were addressed alike as '*Herr*' or 'Mr' So-and-so, and were to address each other in the same way.

What was more, those of their instructors who had university degrees were to wear academic gowns, even over military uniforms. In other words Wilton Park was to resemble a university college rather than a POW camp. Koeppler – who was still referred to as an Oxford lecturer in September 1946 – made the point explicitly when he objected to the English lessons prescribed for early morning sessions on the first course:

I was not quite happy about this, because I did not feel that this was part of the purpose of our work; in so far as prisoners could or should learn English there were much better opportunities in their ordinary camps. We therefore took a leaf from the educational system of Oxford, and from the second term [sic] on have devoted our first session every morning to informal discussion in small groups, which we call 'tutorials'. If I had to single out one factor which was the most efficient in overcoming the suspicion of the prisoners it was the institution of the tutorials and the way in which the tutors handled them.

This meant, as in the long question-and-answer periods after the evening lectures, a two-way relationship between students and tutors:

It was ... from the beginning our principle to ... give in every session, to each member, complete freedom to ask questions, to state his own views or to voice his disagreement of the views of the lecturers. This seemed to us a most vital precondition of our work, as it seemed the only way to create the confidence without which such delicate but essential problems as formed our curriculum could not profitably be discussed. I am convinced that no other step in our work so impressed our members or contributed so much to the success of the work. It was a great joy to see how the clouds of suspicion, mistrust and cynicism towards our work lifted during the six weeks of the session. This does not mean that everything which was said by our lecturers was accepted as gospel truth – far from it.

Koeppler himself experienced this on July 20, 1946, when he remarked in a lecture that July 20 had three times been unlucky for Germany: 'in 1932 through Franz von Papen's coup against the Socialist Government, in 1933 through Hitler's Concordat with the Vatican, and in 1944 through the attempt to assassinate Hitler, whose failure had been a blessing for the world, since otherwise German militarism would have seized power in another guise.' This caused uproar. Some of the officers present had friends or acquaintances among the July 20 plotters against Hitler. Many understandably resented the charge of militarism. And the selection process for Wilton Park meant that most of them were anti-Nazi. What Koeppler had meant was that not all Hitler's opponents had been determined to overthrow the regime itself and that, even if Hitler had been killed in 1944, the Third Reich might have survived him. What he might have said, less controversially, was that the plot's *failure* had been 'unlucky for Germany'. But it was typical of Koeppler that he gave his own opinion bluntly, and was glad of heated debate that ensued. Frankness was vital. The whole point of Wilton Park was to allow conflicting opinions to be expressed openly, without violence or fear. This often meant disagreement but, as Koeppler continued in his assessment; 'it does mean that the very great majority of members at each course left convinced of our goodwill, our sincerity and the honesty of our purpose.'

Proof of this came very early from pupils who had moved back to their previous camps. On March 29, 1946, Alfred Klug wrote from Goathurst Camp near Bridgwater to friends in Germany:

> We finished our 6 weeks course at Wilton Park on February 28, and can say without exaggeration that it was the high spot of my time as a POW. From my earliest youth it has been my principle to develop my mind in such a way that I would be able to act and think for myself. This idea has been strengthened here and I find it very gratifying. Former officers of the 'Wehrmacht' and others came at the end of the course and they had to admit that a fundamental re-adjustment of their history was necessary. I see in this a very important step towards the successful recovery of Germany. The German nation and German life have everywhere been discredited though Nazi ideologies and barbarous conduct. However, it has been my experience that people are already at work holding out the hand of reconciliation ... These are certainly the spearhead, who are ahead of public opinion. It is to be hoped that the German people realise this, and that they do not push aside these helping hands either through stupidity or through a desire to be left alone, or even through thoughtlessness. We must first of all give proof of our sincerity, and only then can the German nation be admitted into the community of peace-loving nations.

This letter was intercepted (and translated) by the British censors. But the same picture emerged in letters that former students now back in their camps sent to their lecturers at Wilton Park. On May 12, 1946, Eric Rüssinger wrote to George Roundell Greene from Lodge Moor POW camp:

> I have much enjoyed this amiable kind of 'propaganda' which had been connected to your former captivity. You are particularly qualified for your occupation, not only on account of your knowledge of German language but also because of the very fact that you had been a POW ... Let us hope that the growing sentiment of understanding and indulgence will give ground in the public opinion of your country before the wave of misery and despair will drive the continent to new excesses of radicalism and wickedness.

Rüssinger apologised for his 'bad English'. So, on May 22, did another of Greene's correspondents, Kurt Otten from Hempton Greene POW Camp:

At first I beg your pardon for the mistakes I commit in using your language, but I prefer to write in English as one can talk in it more frankly than in the German tongue.

Now being back at my old camp I often remember Wilton Park and I feel, Mr Greene, that you have been the lecturer by whom I was most impressed. And that is, as you are the only man who could have a real understanding of a POW. Therefore I resolved to influence my fellow prisoners on the same lines you taught at Wilton Park. But I never thought this to be so difficult as I find it now to fight against misunderstanding, ressentiment and even hate. Just now we had a new intake of prisoners, who came from America hoping to be repatriated as promised to them. Now they are mostly bitter and hopeless and often stubborn ...

Once more I thank you very much for all the kindness you showed at Wilton Park and so I remain with best wishes and kindest regards to you and your wife ...

Greene wrote across the top of this letter: 'Fulsome! Perhaps better check if possible if he has written to others like this – if so, down-grade him!' But the comment seems unduly sceptical. Otten's letter was typical of many. On May 26, from Carburton Camp, Worksop, Dr Hans Kranz wrote 'remembering the nice and fruitful time spent at Wilton Park ... and the sincere and friendly atmosphere of understanding in which we met each other'. On May 28, from Camp 57, Alfred Fuhrmann sent 'my very first letter I ever wrote in English, and I know it cannot be a well-styled one':

First and foremost I may repeat my sincere thanks I already expressed to you orally. By your kind guidance all members of Class I have learned a new and successful method of teaching and learning ... It is my definite purpose to become a teacher of the English language: I think that your language has a great future and if many Germans would strive to obtain its knowledge we could broaden the narrow path of understanding among the nations to a grand road of friendly intercourse. The help in providing for such a desirable road will be the main task of my life, and I am convinced that all my fellow-students will strive to the same end.

I beg to say that your personal charm has contributed very much to my encouragement, and I will never forget the many signs of undeserved benevolence I met at Wilton Park.

On June 2, Georg Langer wrote in German from Hampton Green Camp, Fakenham, to 'Dear honourable Mr de Mopurgo'. This was no doubt the late Lieutenant-Colonel Jack Morpurgo, soon to be better known as General Editor of the Pelican Histories and Director-General of the National Book League: he was one of the many daytime lecturers who came from London to Wilton Park, quite apart from the evening VIPs. Langer confessed to Morpurgo:

> It was not so easy to get used to camp life again after the Wilton Park atmosphere ... I should almost compare the return to Camp with a hot and cold sauna, with the Camp as the cold water. Wilton Park impressed me enormously: without exaggeration I can say that it gave me basic training for camp life as well as for future work in Germany. I rediscovered that one has a brain with which to think and work. It is only now that I realise how comprehensive and valuable the lectures were, when I am designing my own lectures with the aid of my own notes and the help of my comrades.
>
> I see now that one cannot stand idly by any longer, but has to take in everything that is needed for understanding other people and reconstructing a new democratic Germany. The basis for this was in Wilton Park. I shall continue to work on it.
>
> You know from our conversations how very grateful I am to you personally for your great understanding and untiring care, bringing light into the darkness of our thoughts and deeds.

On July 18, Dr Hans Kranz of Carburton Camp followed his letter of May 26 with thanks for Greene's response and the enclosure of a class snapshot, which would always remind him 'of the fine time at Wilton Park':

> You see, for me this time was not so much a six weeks' school of democratic thinking and feeling from a purely political point of view: it was much more a strongly welcomed opportunity of getting in close and personal touch with British gentlemen like you and your fellow-teachers, whose attitude towards us was one of sincere understanding and readiness to help each other on the basis of humanity, free from this propaganda-incited hatred which has done so much wrong on both sides.

Greene and his colleagues always replied to these letters of appreciation, in at least one case – with Walther Eckhardt, from North Hinksey Camp near Oxford – involving an exchange of books and of thoughts about literature that lasted several months. One of Eckhardt's remarks, in a letter of September 11, 1946, was prophetic:

> I am convinced that the main problem of European peace is not the relation of England and Germany (there never was a deeply rooted aversion of German people to English) but of France and Germany. Without considering reasons and guilt (both have a share in it), there is to state that in the

course of three centuries France first invaded Germany eleven times and then Germany invaded France five times. I personally see the only constructive solution in an economical and customs union preparing the political federation of Europe ...

I am glad to learn from my friend Stauffenberg (a cousin to Count Stauffenberg who tried to kill Hitler) that he has become a secretary to the newly founded Swabian society in Tuebingen where German and French philosophers meet to talk on important questions of their countries.

On October 15, sending back to Greene a borrowed copy of *Le Silence de la mer* by 'Vercors', he delved into the issue raised by that Resistance novel – and denounced not only Nazism but also ex-Nazis now currying favour with the Allies by parading as 'superdemocrats':

I must confess that in spite of having been quite distressed about the German war against the very roots of our common civilisation, I myself had a faint hope that there would rise a renewed belief and a new German unity: I tried to work to this end in several countries. But subconsciously I was dominated by a lasting melancholy and sadness in consequence of the bitter feeling that German rulers were Neronic figures rather than human beings – that they had not any human values. You cannot estimate how much I have been oppressed by this fact. But I think that you will comprehend that I do not like to confess in the servile manner of those superdemocrats now appearing in Germany and, I suppose, occasionally in Wilton Park. These newborn confessors of guilt and fault are despicable in my opinion, and weighing down the credit of democracy in the very beginning.

'It is a curious thing', wrote Eckhardt in a later letter, on November 21, 1946, 'to write as a prisoner to a free man living in a free and happy country ... Please do not trouble on account of answering my letters. You have too little and I too much time. I am pleased to be allowed to write you and, by doing so, to remember the days of Spring and Easter that you made so agreeable for me.' As another prisoner-of-war, Ferdinand Acon, wrote earlier from a camp near Norwich about his time at Wilton Park: 'I shall always remember it as it was the only good time I had during the 5 years of captivity.'

Lothar Hegewisch, who attended the third Wilton Park course in May and June 1946, had first heard of the place from a POW newspaper in Camp 306 in the Suez Canal Zone of Egypt. In a note of his impressions written in German on September 17, 1946, he expressed his amazement at how mixed were the students' ranks and professions; 'These people ... for six weeks turned from POWs to full citizens of a democracy such as many of them had not experienced even in the Weimar period.'

Another former Wilton Park student, Engelbert Brandt, wrote in German to Koeppler from the British Zone of Germany on September 25, 1946:

> For me, the weeks at Wilton Park are still a major experience in my life. One thing I shall always have to thank Britain for – that through Wilton Park it gave me, on an open and honourable basis, new perspectives on political thought and behaviour. Today I see politics in quite a different light, and above all far more clearly.

A fine if abstract tribute. But Brandt's letter was addressed to 'Seine Magnifizenz Herr Rektor Dr Koeppler'. George Greene might have called the expression 'fulsome'. Walther Eckhardt might even have thought it 'servile'. Yet if Koeppler himself may have smiled at it as over-obsequious, the term nonetheless fitted his view of his own role as 'Principal' or 'Warden', and of Wilton Park's role as very much more than a 'retraining centre'. These were not views then widely shared in London.

> *5. The official title of the senior member of the G.1(d) resident staff [Koeppler] is 'Head of the Training Centre, G.1(d) C.O.G.A' [Control Office for Germany and Austria]. For official purposes including correspondence this title will always be used. For convenience within the camp and within G.1(d) the courtesy title of 'Principal' may be used. This courtesy title will be kept within the prescribed limits ...*

> *15. The use ... of any such terms as 'university', 'college', 'Wilton Park graduates', 'old Wiltonians', etc. ... will on no account be encouraged or used.*

This testy 'Administrative Instruction' from Wing Commander F.H. Hitch early in 1947 dealt not only with titles it reaffirmed that Koeppler was '*responsible to the Head of G.1(d) [Hitch] for carrying out the work in connection with the re-educational scheme under the agreed policy and instructions issued by C.O.G.A. through the Head of G.1(d)*'. And it reiterated that '*the Training Centre is not a separate entity. It is a section formed as an integral part of the establishment of G.1(d) C.O.G.A. for work in connection with the scheme for the re-education of German Ps/W in Great Britain and the Middle East.*'

Wing Commander Hitch's issue of such orders was a culminating point in growing friction between Koeppler and his official superiors in London. Writing early in 1947, Hitch recalled that relations had been potentially uneasy even before Koeppler had been appointed to run Wilton Park:

> There were grave doubts about giving Koeppler the job as head: though his academic qualifications were good, his personality record was not. However, it was finally agreed because at that time we were so short of personnel, but General Strong (then head of P.I.D.) made it quite clear that he wanted no side tracking on Koeppler's part. I had a talk with Koeppler on this and for a time all went reasonably well.

Hitch went on to claim that the task of preparing selected POWs for work in their base camps had been 'swamped out – we felt deliberately' by Koeppler's concern to prepare them for use in Germany.

> Around this period we were changing over to C.O.G.A., P.I.D. were packing up and 270,000 more Ps/W were arriving. This meant a great deal of additional work for the Ps/W Division's headquarters staff. I cannot help saying that Koeppler took full advantage of this to be just as difficult as possible and to foster a 'separatist' movement for Wilton Park.

Earlier, the friction between Koeppler and Hitch had been lubricated by the skill and diplomacy of Cyrus Brooks, Director of Re-education in the Ps/W Division, whom Hitch described as 'very able'. In August 1946, however, Brooks left. As Koeppler afterwards reported,

> Since this account is confidential I consider it my duty, although not a pleasant one, to refer in one sentence to one of the greatest psychological handicaps of the work. The relationship between Wilton Park and the heads of the Prisoner-of-War Department after the departure of Mr Cyrus Brooks deteriorated rapidly and reached such a level in both official and human relations as I never wish to meet with again.

Hitch, for his part, admitted that 'Koeppler ... took the strongest exception to this issue of the [above-quoted] Standing Instruction and the ensuing rumpus was dealt with by Wilberforce' – Richard Wilberforce, an Oxford-educated lawyer later to be a knight and a life peer, a Fellow of All Souls since 1932, and since 1946 Under-Secretary, Control Office for Germany and Austria. Hitch continued: 'Richard opened the door, Koeppler was defiant and jubilant, and as far as the Ps/W Division is concerned there has been no holding him since. Any form of co-operation at all ceased.' The phrase 'Richard opened the door' was an allusion to a so-called novelty song, 'Open the door, Richard' that was popular in 1946 and 1947. The 'Richard' alluded to was Wilberforce himself, who clearly seems to have sided with his fellow-Oxonian Koeppler.

In retrospect, each side in the dispute had an understandable case. What divided them were not only bureaucratic disputes but contrasting conceptions of Wilton Park's main purpose. Both sides shared similar overall aims. The Ps/W Division sought: 'to project the democratic way of life; to provide an impartial view of German social and political developments during the last 80 years; and to bring into a proper perspective the relation between individual and State.' Koeppler largely echoed this. 'Very briefly', he wrote later: 'the curriculum dealt with four main groups: the historical background, present problems, the projection of Britain, and our common future.'

But there was one crucial difference. Wing Commander Hitch was concerned with prisoners-of-war in all the camps. As he wrote:

> Long before Koeppler was appointed Head of the Training Centre the plan for its activities was drawn up. There were to be two functions: (a) preparing selected Ps/W for greater use in Germany ... and (b) preparing selected Ps/W as leaders for re-educational activities in their base camps ... Gradually the (b) side was swamped out – we felt deliberately.

This may have been so, although several letters from Wilton Park students back in their base camps make clear that they had tried to spread the word – often against great hostility. What was certain was that in the long run – some eighteen months later, as it turned out – all German prisoners-of-war would be leaving Britain, and that government policy would be concentrated more and more on the British Zone of Germany. In this respect, what Wing Commander Hitch called 'the (b) side' of Wilton Park was bound to be of limited duration.

Koeppler, by contrast, had always looked beyond the POW camps towards Germany itself. Lured away from his prospective return to Oxford, he had (as he wrote afterwards) made stipulations from the beginning:

> I assume that I was chosen partly because of my previous work within the prisoner of war section and partly because of the proposals I had made during 1943 and 1944 to the joint F.O./P.W.E./B.B.C./M. of I Committee on Post-War Planning in Germany. These proposals amounted to the setting up of an institution very much on the lines on which Wilton Park exists today, i.e. to provide an opportunity for men and women in the public life of Germany to overcome their isolation and to look at German problems from outside Germany, to gain a better understanding of British policy and by exchanging views on the basis of the running of a free society,

to be stimulated into making efforts, or increasing their efforts, for the building up of German society in such a way that Germany could live in peace and friendship with her former enemies. This programme I have always considered as an instrument of British Foreign Policy which would also be an instrument of German Foreign Policy, provided that Germany choose what I cannot but consider the right path.

Given the political atmosphere at the end of 1945 and given the very real obstacles of transport and selection, it was obvious that this programme could not be carried out at that time in the way I had envisaged it. It appeared to me that trying to set up a centre for prisoners-of-war would provide us with a good testing ground for the practicability of these ideas. Accordingly, when accepting the offer to start Wilton Park, I made it clear that I should be permitted to try and find out if it were possible to convert the Wilton Park for prisoners-of-war to the original scheme ...

It is necessary to give this background to make it quite clear that from the beginning there were inevitable differences between Wilton Park Centre and the Prisoner-of-War Division, the latter quite naturally considering Wilton Park as one of the many aspects of the prisoner-of-war scheme while we at Wilton Park considered our prisoner-of-war population as a forerunner of future developments.

'Future developments' came sooner than even Koeppler had expected.

CHAPTER 6

From the Waste Land

Long is the way
And hard, that out of hell, leads up to light.
John Milton, *Paradise Lost* (1667)

The idea of sending civilians from Germany to Wilton Park was first offi-
cially mooted in the British Control Commission for Germany (CCG/BE)
in May 1946, and first seriously discussed on September 9 at a meeting in
Berlin attended by representatives of the Control Commission and by
emissaries from the London Control Office for Germany and Austria
(COGA). COGA's Under-Secretary Richard Wilberforce, Koeppler's
Oxonian ally, was particularly keen on the idea. Recalling the event,
Koeppler thanked 'the support of the Foreign Office and the interest of
Control Commission officers', which made it possible to 'convert' Wilton
Park from POWs to civilians from Germany 'sooner than I had dared
hope'.

Koeppler naturally saw such conversion as beginning to implement his
'original scheme' for Wilton Park as 'a centre for free people only'. So it
turned out to be. But that was not how it looked at the time to COGA or
the Control Commission. Their concern was not with the future of Wilton
Park but with the urgent plight of postwar Germany.

When the war ended, Germany was a wasteland of destruction, privation, hunger, and despair. Ten million homes had been destroyed. Berlin,
wrote General Lucius Clay, 'was like a city of the dead'. Ninety-five per
cent of its urban area lay in ruins: there were four hundred million cubic
metres of rubble. Everywhere, people scrabbled for a living. There were
two million cripples in West Germany alone. Famine was a constant threat.
One young British army officer described a railway trip:

Crowds of people throng round all the troop trains at every station. Wherever there is any sort of habitation, the railway track is lined by children. The sight of them, perfectly spaced out along our route, many crippled, many barefoot, and all of them mechanically waving at our train, with their cries of '*Schokolade*', remains the most vivid memory of the journey. Outside Karlsruhe, this amazing formation persisted for miles into the country. Nobody with any humane feelings can possibly resist the natural impulse to throw out all the food one can. To see the children fighting for the food was like watching animals being fed at the zoo.

And penury persisted. In the spring of 1946, the meagre rations had to be cut – to 1,275 calories a day in the US occupation zone and 1,040 in the British. This was about one-fifth of the amount needed by a physically active man. The British Prime Minister, Clement Attlee, although under pressure to ease 'austerity' at home, felt obliged to divert to Germany 400,000 tons of food, including 50,000 tons of grain – partly at the cost of imposing bread rationing on Britain in July 1946 – something that had never happened during the war.

To physical hardship was added demoralisation. As the Political Intelligence Department observed on February 21, 1947, 'empty stomachs are a bad basis for the tolerance and patience that democracy demands'. In the midst of rationing, the black market was flourishing. Cigarettes had become a virtual currency. In public administration, the old, Nazi order had been destroyed. The Occupying Powers, perforce holding the fort, were anxious to replace it with a civic building – democratic government by the Germans themselves. But former leaders were discredited: so, understandably, was the word *leader* – *Führer* – itself. From the Control Commission's point of view, what Germany needed was a cadre of reliable Germans to take responsibility, at first under Allied supervision but eventually in new, independent, democratic institutions of their own. To prepare the ground, the Control Commission staff suggested forming discussion groups similar to those set up by 'ABCA' (the Army Bureau of Current Affairs) for the civic education of British troops. The Control Commission endorsed the project.

It also approved the idea of sending selected German civilians to be trained as leaders of such groups at somewhere like Wilton Park. It was stipulated that the participants were to be shown other centres of 're-education' and other British institutions, that they were to dispel rumours that Wilton Park 'indoctrinated' prisoners, and that they were to narrow the gap between former Wilton Park students and the rest of the population. Some of this emphasis was no doubt due to misgivings on the part of Wing Commander Hitch and his colleagues. Nevertheless, operational necessity had helped to relaunch Koeppler's long-cherished plan for the future. It offered one answer to an immediate need.

The first group of 25 German civilians came to Wilton Park on January 1, 1947 – coincidentally the day the UK and US zones of Germany were combined in the 'Bizone' – a stage in the impending division of the country between East and West. There were to have been 35 visitors, but ten were delayed by administrative complications. The first selection process, in October 1946, had produced journalists and educationists; a second, in November 1946, had added administrators, trade unionists, and members of co-operatives such as the *Konsumengenossenschaften* and the *Grosseinkaufsgesellschaft Hamburg*.

At Wilton Park, they lived in the school building rather than the POWs' Nissen huts, with two or three sharing a room. There were no sheets on the beds, to avoid favouritism *vis-à-vis* the POWs. It was a bitterly cold winter, and the visitors' rooms were centrally heated only when there was coal. However, those coming from Germany were used to privation. As one of them – Max Dahlhaus, the communist editor of *Die Freiheit* – reported there at the end of the month: 'The food, accommodation and clothing are good in Wilton Park. There can be no talk of hunger and the German civilians are repeatedly urged to eat enough: they collect their second helpings from the kitchen with pleasure.' Dahlhaus added his more general impressions:

> The British are not anti-German. I did not see any queues in front of shops. Food is rationed. Large families can manage with the rations, but persons who live alone find things more difficult.
>
> In the restaurants and cafes one receives everything without coupons and there is plenty, just as during peacetime, and at almost prewar prices. The worker cannot, however, afford to eat several times a week in a restaurant. The shops are full of goods; cocoa, coffee, etc., one receives unrationed. In the cafes one can eat all kinds of cakes without coupons, in restaurants everything one can wish, without coupons. For us Germans it was a wonderful feeling to order just what we wanted to eat without having to worry if we had enough coupons. But in Germany one cannot get with coupons that which is unrationed in England.
>
> In comparison, textile goods are fully rationed. The prices are enormously high and the result is that many Englishmen are unable to use the full amount of their clothing coupons. Everywhere when one talks with the English one hears the remark, 'the taxes are too high, we shall not be able continually to pay such high taxes'.

Even though reported in German and translated back into English, the remark sounds familiar. Equally familiar were the worries of the POW students at Wilton Park. Dahlhaus and the other German civilians, plus a few POW students, had special seminars there on Britain and British foreign policy, conducted by Koeppler's old friend Richard Crossman and by another Oxonian, Duncan (later Sir Duncan) Wilson, at that time on the Control Commission for Germany. Other such seminars covered 'England and the German Problem', 'Democracy Here and Abroad', and 'German Internal Problems as Seen by an Officer of Milgov [Military Government] and the Control Commission'. Otherwise, the civilians largely shared the routine of their POW colleagues. Nor, as Koeppler later reported, was there any 'psychological clash'. Max Dahlhaus wrote:

> The POWs could come to us when they wished and we could go to them. We ate with them and received the same rations as our German comrades. We hardly managed to eat, because we were always being asked new questions.

After years of captivity, the POW students were desperate for news of home, and they virtually mobbed the German civilians right from the start:

> Upon our arrival we were immediately overwhelmed with all sorts of questions, the chief ones being – 'How are our women behaving towards the occupation troops?' – 'What does it look like in the town?' – 'Are the statements about the food situation correct?' – 'What will happen to us, why can't we go home, and why doesn't the German population do still more to have us set free?' We had great difficulty in answering all these questions. Every night we sat with them together in one room.

Dahlhaus was impressed by the quality and vivacity of Wilton Park's work:

> The tutors, who are composed of Englishmen and German emigrants, understand admirably how to render the lessons interesting and lively. We German civilians were allotted to the various classes so that we could take part in the discussions. The classes are conducted on very democratic lines. The POWs express their opinions quite frankly, and it is rare that one of them becomes aggressive. All political and religious tendencies are represented here and the discussions are made livelier still by the introduction of German civilians. There are also lecturers from London who lecture here regularly on Bismarck, England, Germany and the Third Reich during study time ...

The English do not talk much, but they have a good understanding of how to handle a subject in half an hour's debate. It needs, however, over an hour to answer all the questions put to the lecturer by our German comrades ...

During the evening sessions prominent politicians and economists speak, even a Lady Astor can have her say here! Such a person would be unthinkable in Germany.

Viscountess [Nancy] Astor, the widow of the first Viscount Astor, whose son had lectured at Wilton Park on November 21, 1946, was a 67-year-old American of enormous energy, wit, and persistence. The first woman to take her seat in the House of Commons, she had succeeded her husband as Conservative MP for Plymouth after his death in 1919. As well as acting as a political hostess at Cliveden, the Astors' country house near Taplow in Buckinghamshire, she campaigned tirelessly to raise the school-leaving age, improve conditions in catering and distributive trade, and – most famously – to curb the consumption of alcohol. In 1923, she had successfully carried through the Intoxicating Liquor (Sale to Persons under 18) Bill. She was also passionately outspoken; and early in the first POW-plus-civilian course at Wilton Park, on January 13, she gave an evening lecture on 'Women in Public Life'. Her off-the-cuff (and off-the-subject) talk raised eyebrows among the Germans – and hackles among the British. Camp Commandant Grondona wrote to a colleague in the Control Office for Germany and Austria:

She was extremely entertaining and not much exception could ordinarily be taken to her remarks had they been addressed to a British audience, but her castigation of Catholics and of Russia was most injudicious when delivered at a Ps/W Training Centre.

She condemned the Russians from Stalin down, detailing her conversations with Stalin (whom she described as a 'cunning old fox'). She said she asked him 'When are you going to stop shooting your own people and putting them in jail?', that the interpreter blanched and said 'Surely you don't want that question translated?', to which she answered 'Indeed I do.' What she reported Stalin to have said in reply I was unable to gather owing to the laughter of the audience.

She went on 'I hate dictators ... I hated Hitler, Mussolini, and Mustapha Kemal; – and I hate Stalin' ... a pause to the accompaniment of more laughter ... 'No, I should not say I hate anyone ... I should merely say I dislike him' ... pause, then (sotto voce – which everyone heard) 'But I do hate him all the same' ... loud laughter. She said she hoped that the Germans would provide a bulwark against Bolshevism.

She said she expected a great deal from German women whom she liked. She had found that women of the Nordic countries, Scandinavians, Dutch, and Germans 'were very easy to deal with and very sensible' – but that 'the Wops and other Latins were quite hopeless'.

Alluding to Martin Luther she said that we had primarily to thank him for the Reformation and for the liberty of thought which followed, which was in striking contrast to the ignorance which appeared to be fostered in Catholic countries.

One would not dispute many of her statements and contentions (in private), but there were many Catholics and several Communists (including, I believe, a civilian Editor of a German Communist paper) in the audience and I fear that like Queen Victoria they were 'not amused'.

It would be quite easy for the Communist Editor on his return to Germany to take out selected juicy extracts from Lady Astor's speech (of which several present took notes) and to publish these, allowing it to be inferred that they were typical of addresses given at the British Government Re-education Centre for selected German personnel. And if anything of the sort were done, the Moscow press might easily take up the issue and use it in an attack upon the British Government.

I have no doubt Koeppler was alive to this when, in his speech of thanks to Lady Astor, he dissociated himself from her remarks about the present Government's policy and about Russia.

My own view for what it is worth is that the requisite re-education work can be carried out here without calling in entirely irresponsible speakers, and that criticism of foreign states, especially of Russia by visiting lecturers should be rigidly banned. I may add that I am quite capable of criticising the present Government and of voicing strong opinions on Russia – but I would see no point in doing either for the edification of the Germans. It is quite a different matter for the Germans in the course of their discussions to criticise Russia. But I think we should steer clear of doing anything under official auspices which could have a boomerang effect, and I shall be greatly surprised if nothing about Lady Astor's comments on Russia appears later in the German Communist press.

But I must say that in any other surroundings I should have unreservedly enjoyed her address. No one who was present is ever likely to forget it.

Koeppler himself, in a later report on the first course, had the last word:

It is interesting that although Lady Astor's lecture provoked an official complaint from a British source, the Germans were not in the least perturbed by it. A conservative wrote that it was rather unfair to Conservatism not to have led off with someone you could take seriously; a Socialist wrote: 'Lady Astor has a great deal of charm but is certainly not taken very seriously by her hearers'; the communist editor of *Die Freiheit* wrote in his newspaper on his return to Germany that the appearance of Lady Astor on the platform was a proof of the astonishing tolerance of the British in political life.

Other evening lecturers on the first joint POW/civilian course were less controversial, but no less eminent. The first, on January 7, was Karl Barth, the Swiss theologian who had been a professor at Bonn before being dismissed in 1935 for refusing to take an unconditional oath to Hitler, and had become Professor of Theology at Basel. His subject was 'The Protestant Church in Germany today'. Professor Arnold Toynbee, the well-known author of *A Study of History*, spoke on that subject on January 22, while further famous names on that first joint course included General Sir Ronald Adam, Chairman of the British Council, and Ritchie Calder, British delegate to the UNESCO conference. The subjects ranged from 'The Commonwealth of Australia' (by the Camp Commandant) and 'Universities in Present-day Germany' through various aspects of British life – imperialism, education, law, trade unions and co-operatives – to 'Public Schools – especially Eton' by the college's Senior History Master, A.K. Wickham. There were two brains-trust discussions, and the usual multi-party turnout of MPs, including such colourful opposites as Derek Walker-Smith and George Brown.

As well as outside lecturers, the civilians at Wilton Park enjoyed a choice of organised outside visits. In London, they could visit the House of Commons, the Law Courts, the London County Council, the trades union headquarters at Transport House, the Royal Institute of International Affairs, the BBC's German Service and its POW educational section at Bush House, and representative journalists in Fleet Street. In Oxford, they could meet and debate with dons and attend the Union Society. Elsewhere, they could see slums and slum clearance schemes, factories, local councils and local governments offices, and every kind of school including Eton. 'We have tried to organise the visits', Koeppler reported 'to ensure that in the short time available the students can see really representative institutions and have an opportunity to talk to the experts who can really explain them.'

Altogether, Koeppler adjudged the first joint POW/civilian course at Wilton Park to have been a success:

It was never intended that these visits by civilians should serve solely to increase the value of Wilton Park for the prisoners-of-war. [But] the amount gained by the prisoners from contact with the civilians was a most gratifying by-product of the course ... The main point was the atmosphere which made the course possible ...

The present mental and psychological situation in Germany coupled with intense party rivalries are not conducive to an undertaking which aims by impartial discussion to clear the ground and to tackle problems which are controversial and at the same time vital for the reconstruction of a Germany fit for her neighbours to live with. There is in Germany such a bitter division, such general distrust that it will be next to impossible to start discussions amongst people of different social views ...

Occasionally the fear has been expressed – though not by our staff or by our students – that our work is much too 'academic'. We are academic if by this term is meant integrity in the approach to controversial topics. We are not academic in the choice of our curriculum; rather could we be accused of being too severely practical in our desire to counter the German tendency to develop a *Weltanschauung* about everything.

The secret of creating the right atmosphere, Koeppler was convinced, was the tutorial system he had borrowed from Oxford:

Tutorials consist of a period during which the topic discussed and the manner in discussing it varies continuously. The main function is the active participation of the students while the tutor's job consists in keeping the ball rolling and preventing it from going off-side. A tutorial may consist in a discussion of a debate in the House of Commons; in a discussion of a topical or controversial article in the Press; in the delivery of two short papers taking opposite views followed by a general debate; in the formation of a Brains Trust from among the members of the class, and last but not least the tutorial may be turned into a 'definition' society in which an attempt is made to define some of the political or social terms constantly used by everybody. The value of such exercise in definition is not to arrive at final conclusions, but rather in teaching the participants the need for clear thinking and the need to avoid slogans and phrases which sound well but may easily be misunderstood. By taking part in all these activities the civilian students are learning the practical principles and methods of political adult education better than by any theoretical lectures on education and citizenship.

Such activities, Koeppler believed, were uniquely possible in such a milieu as Wilton Park:

The civilians of the first course were unanimous in agreement that what they had gained from the course could not have been accomplished in Germany. The sharp divisions in political views and social status have certainly been in evidence at Wilton Park (the mutual feeling of contempt in some discussions, for instance, between worker and University student). But the most conservative of the civilians has said that for him the most valuable part of the course was that in England, as distinct from Germany, he can talk to German Socialists and have it out with them. The Leader of the Socialist Youth in the British Zone perhaps can be said to have summed up the general feeling when he wrote: 'During the seminars and discussions many things have become clear to me which I would never have learned in Germany. It seems incredible, but I am coming slowly to the realisation that I am likely to learn more in these six weeks than I would have done in two years in Germany; quite apart from the fact that in Germany one could not make such an experiment.'

Koeppler's impressions were confirmed by at least one outside observer. Shortly before the end of the first joint POW/civilian course, an official from the German Political Branch of the Control Commission, Mr Pitt Hardacre, came to the UK to prepare the second. At Wilton Park, with none of the staff present, he spent two hours with all but one of the German civilians, 'to discuss with them, very frankly, their impressions of the whole scheme'. He asked them to be 'equally frank, critical and constructive if possible, in any suggestions they might wish to make for improvements in the course'. He reported on March 3, 1947, while their remarks were still fresh in his mind:

> They were very emphatic as to the value and positive necessity of the courses and, if possible, expanding them to cover more people ...
>
> They further stated that there were no irksome restrictions and everything had been done for them to stimulate interest in all that they had seen and heard, both by explanation and example. They had no idea that the workers in Britain were so well organised and had such democratic workers' institutions. They were particularly impressed by our system of Adult Education and the atmosphere surrounding it ... When they saw the British democratic institutions and so forth actually functioning, they were so taken aback that they were quite flabbergasted ...
>
> We were under the impression that there was too much emphasis on celebrities; maybe there was, but I think without doubt there must be a leavening of celebrities to talk to the Germans. German civilians consider that mixing with the German prisoners-of-war at Wilton Park, and visiting PW camps, is a good thing and should continue. They say that the prisoners-of-war had not realised the actual state of affairs in Germany; in fact, prisoners-of-war were expecting to go back to their homes and find things just somewhat less than what they envisaged to be normal. German civilians had been able gently to disillusion them. They were able to tell them the facts. The civilians admitted that telling them the facts had very

probably lowered the morale of prisoners-of-war but it had brought them up against realities, and it was better that such facts should come from Germans, prior to the repatriation of the prisoners-of-war, rather than that they should come upon them suddenly on their return to Germany ...

The German civilians mentioned the coal crisis, then existing in England. They had themselves no idea that we were so short of commodities like coal ...

I was very impressed indeed with the Wilton Park scheme and, if the money can be spared, (it would be a very small drop in the ocean), I suggest that we move heaven and earth to get the scheme expanded, as I believe these enlightened Germans could have a tremendous influence for good in Germany. It is merely a question of 'seeing is believing'.

Not everything, of course, had been plain sailing. In the first place, most of the German civilians had been inadequately briefed on what was expected of them. Two had been sent a written Military Government order saying '*You will proceed to England for six weeks to give lectures.*' Several had been told that the course lasted for ten days; one or two had been offered a visit to England with no further information. Several had simply received letters from the Control Commission inviting them 'to spend six weeks in England contacting professional colleagues', and not mentioning the course. Most visitors had adapted well to the reality of Wilton Park; but one Berlin newspaper editor, whom it would be invidious to name, had followed to the letter the misleading terms of his invitation. As Koeppler reported, witheringly:

He was determined to use his six weeks entirely for the purpose of making professional and social contacts in England. He spent three or four days every week in London, disappeared near the end of the course for about a week on end, took part in hardly any of the tutorials, classes or seminars, and responded to none of the requests for written work or reports. It is somewhat peculiar that [he] should have made an unfavourable report on some aspects of the course to higher authority, considering that he alone among the students took so little part in the course that he can have very little idea of what actually went on.

Even those who appreciated Wilton Park had suggestions to make. Some found the living conditions spartan, and wanted laundry facilities: no laundry within miles could take their clothes, which they had to wash themselves. Others felt that the course crowded too much into six weeks: they found it strenuous. In their conversation with Pitt Hardacre, the civilians suggested that future visitors be given 'some sort of pamphlet' before leaving Germany – 'a brief description of the workings of [the] democratic functions and institutions with which they would come in contact ... By this method their minds would be prepared in some measure for what they would see.' They also hoped that more of them could make private contact with ordinary people in Britain. This might require more than their five shillings a week pocket money – which went in fares on one weekly visit to London. 'They did not make this statement in any critical sense as they said, quite frankly, that they quite appreciated they could not look to the British Treasury to finance them any more than was being done.' But they hoped that some way might be found to change Marks in Germany against 'reasonable amounts of sterling in London, so that they could bear out of pocket expenses themselves'.

Some of the civilians, too, like some of the first POW students, had initially been 'full of suspicion and quite ready to find fault with every-thing'. One at least of these, a Communist youth organiser from Cologne, Koeppler later described as 'joining in more and more each week' and 'a good deal less suspicious of our intentions than he was at the beginning'. But Koeppler was dismayed, in a different way, by another of the first German civilians at Wilton Park, who had become a teacher in 1937 and was 'destined for the headmastership of a large and important secondary school':

> He firmly maintained in seminars the point of view that in about 1740 something went 'click' in the tortured and sensitive German soul, and that therefore it is no good discussing <u>facts</u> with Germans; they must be given psycho-therapeutic treatment until with some sudden stroke of magic their souls click back again to where they were in 1740 and all is well. It must be said for the other students that they protested almost as a man ... But it would surely be a pity if his charm and polish should lead him to a respon-sible position where he could instil into German Youth theories that would make them more convinced than ever that whatever happened or might happen in the future, they or their poor little Fatherland could in no possible circumstances bear any of the blame.

Blame and war guilt, Koeppler insisted, were subjects 'never proposed' by the tutors; but they arose inescapably in discussion of the past. He admitted that

> The most frequent criticism of the curriculum is its alleged concentration on the past and its alleged lack of constructive thought for the future ...
> We must help them to acquire a clear impression of the picture which the rest of the world has of Germany and they must honestly try to compare it with their own views ... We attempt to make it clear that it is

not true to say that 'all nations are equally responsible, the Allies as much as the Germans'. This attempt is vital not simply as a statement of historical truth but for its practical consequences. How else can we avoid German resentment and a craving for revenge in years to come ... ?

The analysis of the past is also necessary for ... the older of our students. Quite a few of them believe that because they were never members of the Nazi Party their views and actions are bound to be those of good Europeans. They have always objected to the methods Hitler employed and also to some of his aims and they feel that they are making a wonderful concession if they say as much. This group is not very large but its influence in Germany is certainly very strong. They may be defined as the 'Bismarck instead of Hitler' group. It comes as a shock to them that we do not bother, in our curriculum, with Nazism as such ... We ... prefer to concentrate on the discussion of those forces and thoughts which have helped the Third Reich to come into existence, which have kept it alive and which are by no means dead today ...

It is clear ... that we are bound to meet with the greatest psychological resistance from quite a few of our students ... We are therefore conscious of the need for tact ...

Those to whom any criticism of Germany appears as 'anti-German' and who are ever ready to take offence, often overflow with criticism of other nations and with vicious attacks on people of differing opinions. '*Der Geist, der stets verneint*' [the spirit of constant denial], so prevalent in Germany today, does not leave Wilton Park untouched.

Some of the German civilians on the first joint POW/civilian course were unhappy not only about the curriculum, but about the selection of prisoners to attend Wilton Park. As Max Dahlhaus reported: 'The present course, the seventh [since the beginning], consists mainly of students, academical POWs, engineers, etc. Only a very small percentage of workers is included.'

The prisoners, for their part, were unhappy about the delays and anomalies in their repatriation. But some were also critical of their civilian fellow-students – who, after all, could go home at the end of the course, and some of whom, as George Roundell Greene recalled, were 'rather bores and self-important, and not nearly so nice as the POWs'. Matthew Barry Sullivan records that one former Wilton Park POW, writing afterwards in Camp 18's *Zeit am Tyne* about his civilian colleagues,

was amazed at how starved and shut-in their minds were and asked himself who had been the free men, who the prisoners. For most of them the world began in 1945; therefore everything wrong in Germany was due to the occupation. Some too had come expecting to be able to fill their pockets with chocolate, or believing that butter had vanished from Germany because it was on the London market; they had no idea that coal and cigarettes were short. Some (such was the legacy of the Nazi era) wanted to know if the *Manchester Guardian* they had been reading was not a propaganda edition for Germany.

To dispel mistakes and illusions, Koeppler later spelled out very crisply for potential civilian students what their coming to Wilton Park implied:

> In view of earlier misunderstandings it might be useful to explain what is not intended to be the purpose of their visits.
>
> It is not a sight seeing tour of London or Great Britain.
>
> It is not a reward for services rendered to the British occupation authorities.
>
> It is not a lecture tour of prisoner-of-war camps although we expect all civilians to go and visit at least one of them.
>
> It is not a course intended to improve their knowledge in their various professions and occupations, although it is hoped that by meeting representative British people and visiting British institutions they may indirectly profit in this respect.
>
> It is not an opportunity for renewing or making personal or professional contacts, although here again this might be a by-product in a few cases.
>
> Finally, it is decidedly not a *Schulungskurs* or training either in DEMOKRATIE or in journalism, education, trade unionism, local government, etc.

The second joint POW/civilian course at Wilton Park took place in March and April 1947. There were 29 German civilians. Six were newspaper editors, six trade unionists, and six politicians, one from each party. Four were local government officials, one from each *Land* in the British Zone and one from Hamburg. Three were educationists. Two were representatives from co-operatives; and two were journalists – one of them from North-West German Radio.

In several ways, this second joint course proved more difficult than the first. Once again, the civilians had not been adequately briefed. As Koeppler complained:

> One of the criticisms of Wilton Park by Higher Authority has been that we do not pay enough attention to the individual wishes of civilian students; it is therefore rather a pity that with the second course the students do not appear to have had any proper briefing until they met students from the first course or until they were brought together at Hanover, that no

complete information was available at any time beforehand as to who the students would be, and that the 'background information' on each student which it had been promised to provide was not forthcoming.

But inadequate briefing was only one reason why the second joint POW/civilian course at Wilton Park had a slightly rocky start. A further handicap, paradoxically, was what Koeppler called 'the very generous hospitality given to the visitors on the various stages of their journey'.

> They were made welcome in Officers' Clubs and not having been briefed about the spartan simplicity of Wilton Park some of them found their quarters something of a shock … It is always only a few who feel aggrieved and fewer still who voice their complaints. Even allowing for the fact that they had been expecting greater comfort we cannot feel very great sympathy with the particular complaint of a minority in view of the general conditions both in this country and Germany.

As one of the civilian visitors said of his colleagues, rather bitterly, 'these people are taking an unfair advantage over millions of their countrymen and over many of their colleagues and competitors'. However, as Koeppler continued:

> We must avoid comparing the attitude of the second group of civilians after a fortnight in this country with that of the first group at the end of their course. The atmosphere during the first course was much less satisfactory at the beginning than at the end. Even so we feel that the second group are both mentally and physically in a worse state than the first. This may well be due to the catastrophic situation in Germany's big cities which has assumed particularly acute proportions during the month of January which the first lot spent in this country.

As a result, some of the German civilians had come to Wilton Park in the hope of sending food parcels home from Britain; and others planned to look for jobs (or even books). What was more, 'The present visitors are physically in a worse shape; almost half of them have been in bed for a day with minor ailments.' One reason, it seems, was that many of the visitors, half-starved in Germany, found food relatively plentiful at Wilton Park, and at first ate more than they could easily stomach.

> Until the situation in Germany improves [Koeppler continued] we may, in future courses, have to allow for a period of two to three days for the civilians to get acclimatized to the living conditions here.
> But much more important is the mental attitude not indeed of all of

them but at least of a strong minority. They have arrived believing in a dangerous myth, viz. that Germany was the only country suffering today and that such suffering was mainly due to the incompetence and corruption if not to the intentions of the Allies ... While tutors and lecturers here are fully conscious of the chaos in Germany they are also fully conscious that the cause of this chaos is to be found essentially in German policy. To many members of our second course this fact has been obscured, if they have ever been aware of it, by their experience of the British Zone in January 1947. They have arrived here full of burning indignation, ready and eager to improve on Zola's 'J'accuse'. This attitude became evident during the various Regional Brains Trusts in which civilians from, say, Rhineland Westphalia answered questions asked by the prisoners from the same district. A good number of the civilians in answering the questions did not make any effort to link the present calamity with the policy of the Third Reich ... On the other hand we feel justified in thinking that most of those on the course have not yet sufficiently hardened in their views, are ready to discuss the causes of the present chaos and are even prepared to change their views ...

Finally we would like to emphasise that these observations are based on a very short acquaintance; but for what it is worth we feel that the work with German civilians here is both more difficult and more necessary than we had expected.

Routine on the second joint POW/civilian course followed much the same pattern as before. The seminars for the civilians included two discussions of Germany, one led by Koeppler on 'England and the German Problem', the other by the Hon. T.M. Lindsay on the very pertinent subject of 'Germany through British Eyes'. The evening lecturers included familiar faces at Wilton Park: Ernest Green from the WEA; Kingsley Martin of *The New Statesman*; R.C.K. Ensor of Corpus Christi College, Oxford and *The Sunday Times*; Professor E.R. Dodds from Oxford; Harold Nicolson; and T.D. Weldon from Koeppler's old College, Magdalen. As well as assorted MPs, literary men, and journalists, there was an Oxford Union Society Brains Trust – an innovation typical of Koeppler's concern to involve young people in Wilton Park's work.

Even with more troubled participants than before, the second joint course had its effect. One student on it, the theatre critic and *feuilleton* editor of a Kiel newspaper, said shortly afterwards: 'I have a new outlook. I can understand things better since Wilton Park and see most things in another light ... In many ways it will be difficult for the teachers who attend, especially the older men. One told me that in his mind there is now indecision. All his old ideas have been disturbed.'

1. Heinz Koeppler in 1919 age 7.

2. Heinz Koeppler as a young man.

3. Heinz Koeppler's birthplace in Wollstein (Wolsztyn), Poland (born 1912).

4. Heinz Koeppler talking to students at the Wilton Park in Beaconsfield in 1947. The cottage in the background is where Heinz lived.

5. Cartoon from the newspaper *Die Wilton-Schau*.

6. The White House at Wilton Park, Beaconsfield.

Punch and Judy Show

**The last day of Judgement
alias
Punch and Judy at Wilton Park**

by
Friedrich Broeger

Represented in the Puppet Show are:

Punch:
"You" PoW ('familiar' form)
"You" PoW ('polite' form)
Student
Big Devil
Little Devil
Caretaker
A Girl
An Index Finger

Place and Time: not disclosed

Music:	Heinrich Heun
Stage Management	Gerhard Güntzel; Aly Franke
Technical Equipment:	Max Bergmann
Heads of Puppets:	Gerhard Güntzel
Costumes:	Franz Nass

Enacted by the 8th Course – March–April 1947

Actors:
Rudolf Lautherbach
Hans Meyer
Clemens Stoll

Voices:
Friedrich Hellwig
Hans-Joachim Hoerder
Helmut Reuter
Wilfried Schneider
Harry Ziems
Gerd Zitzewitz

Musicians:
Harry Ziems

Technical Management:
Herrmann Graefe
Hans-Günther Huch

Play Management:
Siegfried Schley

A CULTURAL-POLITICAL COOPERATIVE

– Let it Grow –

When at the 4th Course FRIEDRICH BROEGER wrote the Punch and Judy show following ideas from the Cultural-Political Cooperative, he made the point that the show should develop and grow in accordance with the characteristics of each course re-enacting it.

Therefore, at the 6th and 7th Courses some timely additional feature covering camp life and current political concerns e.g. "repatriation", "imprisonment in the Middle East", "Fake Election in the PoW Camp", reaction to the "Nürnberger Trials", etc.

At the 7th Course the 'civilian' participant is a new feature in the play. Also, the stage layout was re-designed and implemented.

At the 8th Course the scene "Beaconsfield" was recreated and conversations with 'civilian' participants were expanded. The additional texts were written by Friedrich Hellwig und Gerd Zitzewitz.
We hope that the current shows, which have now become a tradition, will not only entertain you but also give you cause for reflection. We would like to pass on to the next Course the Punch and Judy show tradition, in accordance with the words of the Index Finger:

– Let it Grow –

7. Original Programme from the 'Kaperlspiel' – a Punch and Judy Show performed by the students, circa 1948.

8. Willi Brundert's surviving puppets.

9. Wiston House, West Sussex, circa 1950s.

1	Richard Marmein	13	Walter Kargl	25	Herbert Jux	37	Anton Setzwein
2	Hans Binder	14	Dr. Otto Raesch	26	Werner Hagen	38	Jobst Suhr
3	R.D.J. Gibson	15	Heinr. Borg	27	K.W. Laudermann	39	Herr Gawronski, Switz
4	Konrad Friedrich	16	Dr. E. Ingenday	28	Thomas Wolf	40	Theo. Gantefähr
5	Heinr. Rücker	17	Dr. G.V. Unruh	29	Rudolf Ebel	41	Dr. Hermann Junge
6	Hans Gengnagel	18	Dr. Herm. V. Lindheim	30	Dr. Rud Schlinker	42	Frau Grete Brass
7	Peter Godde	19	A.L. Glasfurd	31	Hans Helm. Klimm	43	Fr. F. Elsinghorst
8	Dr. H. Koeppler	20	Nicholaus Jenniches	32	Josef Lanzhammer	44	Miss M.D. Black
9	Bruno Eisenburger	21	Hans Bock	33	Hans Darwig	45	Freir v. Ketelhodt
10	Georg hollenkamp	22	Arno Kosmale	34		46	Fr. G. Knobel
11		23	Manfred Fichtner	35		47	
12		24		36			

10. 'The First Session in a new home' January-February 1951.

11. Lord Pakenham (on right), who later became Lord Longford, at a conference reception, 1950s.

12. Werner Lauermann (left) giving a tutorial to participants in his study at Wiston House (now the Common Room), 1950s.

When the second joint course had begun, the British authorities in Control Office (COGA) and Control Commission still regarded it as an experiment. But on March 13, 1947, those responsible held a meeting at which they proposed it should continue. This required, and received, widespread agreement – from the Home Office, the War Office, and the Foreign Office. It was proposed that the number of German civilians should be raised to sixty, with more from Berlin; that they should include more trade-unionists; that they should all have more extramural visits; and that even more emphasis should be placed on the practical side of adult education in working and social life. Rather to Koeppler's annoyance, it was also suggested that the historical part of Wilton Park's curriculum – 'The Development of Germany in the Past 100 Years' – be slightly reduced.

Soon afterwards, however, a number of bureaucratic changes took place that greatly strengthened Koeppler's hand. They reflected, at some distance, the growing rift with the West's former Soviet ally, and the growing desire to deal with the Western Zones of Germany less as occupied territory and more as an emerging part-nation. In political terms, they looked modest: but in bureaucratic terms they meant greater autonomy for Wilton Park. COGA, the Control Office for Germany and Austria, was reorganised as the German Section of the Foreign Office, under Lord Pakenham, who succeeded John B. Hynd as Chancellor of the Duchy of Lancaster, with Sir William Strang as his Permanent Under-Secretary. Within it, the German Political Department and the German Education Department were placed under Assistant Under-Secretary Sir Ivone Kirkpatrick, who had responded to Koeppler's wartime proposals for an institution like Wilton Park. More significantly still, Robert Birley (who had spoken at Wilton Park and became one of its major champions) gave up the headmastership of Charterhouse to become Head of Education Branch in the Control Commission in Germany and Educational Adviser to the Commander-in-Chief and Military Governor, General Sir Brian Robertson – a key post Birley was to retain when it was later split from – and placed above – the Education Branch. On July 1, 1947, responsibility for Wilton Park passed from Political Division to the Educational Adviser. This meant that Birley was responsible for all questions of principle and guidelines and that Education Branch was responsible for the administrative arrangements in Germany. Political questions concerning Wilton Park, and the selection of politicians to attend its courses, were still to be discussed with Political Division, but letters and inquiries were to be addressed to Education Branch in Berlin.

Meanwhile, towards the end of April 1947, the third joint

POW/civilian course had got under way, and continued into the month of June. Again, the overall pattern was the same, with the usual muster of VIP lecturers. As well as such veterans of the series as Lord Lindsay, G.D.N. Worswick, Alfred Robens, Thomas Hodgkin, and Camp Commandant Grondona (on Australia again), they included Patrick Gordon Walker, MP for Smethwick, and Major J.A. Boyd-Carpenter, MP for Kingston-upon-Thames. There was again an Oxford Union Brains Trust, led by the Union's President, the Hon. Anthony Wedgwood Benn; there was a two-way Brains Trust between the POWs and Beaconsfield Workers Educational Association; and a third Brains Trust assembled representatives of youth organisations and further education bodies, together with another schoolmaster from Eton. A novelty this time was the presence of three lecturers from Switzerland. Professor Besseler, of the Adult Education Centre in St Gallen, spoke on 'Problems of German Reconstruction'; a journalist, Dr von Schenk, examined 'The Meaning of Federalism'; and a Swiss High Court Judge, Dr Hans Schultz, considered 'Applied Science and its Effect on Culture'. This link with Switzerland was the first of many contacts to come.

The third mixed POW/civilian course was still in progress at Wilton Park when a cloud the size of a man's hand appeared in the blue June sky. It was pointed out on June 3, 1947 in a letter to Robert Birley from Robert Crawford, who had been Assistant Secretary of COGA, the Control Office for Germany and Austria, and was now the Head of the Foreign Office's German Education Department. He wrote:

> There are already rumblings in the War Office which indicate that as soon as Wilton Park is no longer needed for prisoners-of-war it will probably be needed by them for some other purpose. So far as I can see we shall wish to go on sending Pws there for at least another year, but if there is to be any question of our keeping it for civilian re-education after that time it is not too early to start thinking about this now. I feel sure that we should have the very greatest difficulty in getting the War Office to agree to our taking over Wilton Park from them for a civilian use if they do in fact want it for themselves, and apart from this we should have to face the problem of the Foreign Office looking after the administrative services which have so far been a War Office responsibility. If, therefore, we are to try to keep it for civilian purposes we ought to weigh in soon.

Crawford was clear that questions would be raised about creating a smaller, cheaper operation in Germany, or spending the funds on other forms of contacts. He went on:

A question which we will almost certainly be asked is whether we could not conduct a similar establishment in Germany where, even though the facilities were smaller and the atmosphere more clouded, at any rate most of the cost would fall on the German economy. It would also be said that by that time the opportunities for travel between the two countries will be greater and the need for a special establishment in this country reduced. I do not know whether this will in fact be true, but it will undoubtedly be said. It will also probably be maintained that by that time we shall get more value from spending our money on facilitating professional contacts between educationalists, journalists and trade unionists in Germany and this country and that there will not be the same need for an establishment of a general nature.

Koeppler duly travelled to Germany to discuss these problems, and more immediately the selection of civilian students. One difficulty was that they had to be chosen not only by profession, age, and aptitude, but also as fairly as possible from the various regions. This meant that large numbers of British officials, geographically scattered and usually overworked, had to be involved in the selection process. There was no guarantee that they all knew much about Wilton Park, or that they could use consistent criteria in choosing people to go there. Too often, choices were hasty or ill-judged, while those invited at the last minute could make no plans for their absence. Over time, Koeppler was able to suggest solutions – notably a supervisory committee, the compilation of waiting lists, and above all the preparation of a leaflet to explain Wilton Park both to future students and to the officials selecting them.

In its final version, the leaflet was welcoming but firm. Its aim, in the official English translation, was:

> to tell you about the opportunities which Wilton Park offers, opportunities which can only be used to the full if you are prepared to devote your time in England to the work at Wilton Park; it is also intended to save you from disappointments ...
>
> It is not necessary for you to be able to speak English nor to have a university degree or a secondary school education. Of course, we have no examinations nor certificates at the end. Wilton Park is not an institution for absorbing undigested information ... It is hardly necessary to mention that there is no 'official Wilton Park view', neither do we consider our students from Germany as delegates whose function it is to force one particular point of view on the other participants ... Whenever the subject permits the introductory talk may be prepared by one of the students and this might well be you ...
>
> Work at Wilton Park deals with four main subjects:

(a) <u>The Individual and the Community</u> ...
(b) <u>International Relations</u> ...
(c) <u>Projection of Britain</u> ...
(d) <u>The Development of Germany during the last century</u>. This is the most difficult and certainly not the least important of the subjects. Germans have been cut off for too long from the outside world and are often in danger of considering their own problems without relation to those of other countries. The most burning questions today in Germany are food, coal and housing; but even when these problems are nearer solution than they are today, a long-term task will remain, the reintegration of Germany into Europe. This reintegration cannot wait until the emergency is over; it must begin now. The first step is for Germans to understand how responsible people look at Germany, her past and her future. Wilton Park enables Germans to consider their country's problems in a saner atmosphere provided by a certain distance from those problems, an atmosphere which cannot, in the nature of things, prevail in Germany.

It was clear that Koeppler had successfully resisted – perhaps with Birley's help any attempt to limit consideration of Germany's past. The leaflet concluded:

Before you come to Wilton Park we would ask you to realise that your acceptance of our invitation presupposes your readiness to play an active part and thus to contribute to the success of the course. This demands a certain amount of self-discipline, the only form of discipline that exists at Wilton Park. We would like to stress that it is not an invitation to a sightseeing tour of England. The object of your visit cannot be to earn some money or to organise relief for yourself or your family, however necessary such relief might be. By far the largest part of your time in England will be claimed by your work inside and outside Wilton Park, for your honest co-operation will provide you with few opportunities to satisfy special interests of a professional or personal nature. If you think this too great a restriction of your personal liberty, please do not come. But, however sceptical you may be, you should come if you believe, as we do, that this course with its balance of work inside and outside Wilton Park may help you to participate more actively in the reconstruction of Germany and Europe. If you are prepared to work under these conditions we shall be glad to see you.

The leaflet helpfully added some 'Useful Details' about Travel, Luggage, Money, etc. Its note on Accommodation introduced a novelty. As before, 'in order not to distinguish their position from that of prisoner students', the German civilians were to have only blankets on their beds. But now there was an exception. 'Women students will be provided with sheets.' Wilton Park had taken another step forward.

CHAPTER 7

Sheets and Dances and Tough Talk

'When men and women meet as we met at Wilton Park, truth is amongst them, and to dispense with truth means ruin and death.'

Dr Hilda von Klenze, lecture on 'Wilton Park –
A Bridge Between the Nations', 1947

One of the results of World War II had been to accelerate the long overdue recognition of women's right to equality with men. Some had served in the forces; many had worked in the factories or on the land. Replacing absent men, they had undertaken new responsibilities. Few were prepared, after the war, to put up with traditional, subordinate roles.

This was perhaps most marked in Germany. The stereotype of the blonde, pig-tailed *Hausfrau* was now confined to old comic books. The slogan encouraged by Hitler, purporting to define women's realm as limited to '*Kinder, Kirche, Küche*' (children, church, and kitchen), had become an object of scorn. In practical terms, the casualties of war had left huge imbalance between the sexes. What after World War I in Britain had been called 'a surplus of women' was in Germany now an appalling death-roll of men.

Already in April 1946, the Women's Affairs Section of the Foreign Office had pointed out how much had changed. Economically, socially, and politically, there was enormous scope for German women: but – partly owing to previous indoctrination – many lacked self-confidence. The Occupying Powers, desperately needing democratically minded Germans to take over more and more of public life, should see women as an under-valued resource, and help them. Civic education as at Wilton Park might be an answer.

The Women's Affairs Section was right. Women's organisations in

Germany, well aware of the problem, had approached the Control Commission for help in civic education for their members; and the German Political Branch itself agreed that this could perhaps be done at Wilton Park. In May 1947, on the initiative of General Sir Brian Robertson, the Control Commission in Berlin formally recommended to the Foreign Office that German women be admitted to the Wilton Park courses. This caused top-level concern in London at both the Foreign Office and the War Office: as Koeppler put it, senior officials feared 'that the first German female civilians who came to Wilton Park would be set upon by sex-starved POWs'. Nevertheless, on June 18, 1947, it was agreed that ten German women would take part in the fourth mixed POW/civilian course, from July 5 to August 15, 1947. They included two *Landtag* members, two housewives, a trade union secretary, a radio journalist, a pastor, a Communist Party official, and a university lecturer.

> Our first overwhelming experience was when we saw German prisoners-of-war lining the camp road in Wilton Park waiting for us. I may say that some of us ten women could scarcely control our voices when we alighted from the coach and greeted them.

So said Dr Hilda von Klenze, quoted above. The men were no less moved. Before the women's arrival, Commandant Grondona had issued instructions about how the POWs were to behave, and actually arranged segregated dining and sitting rooms. As another of the visitors, Ursula Gravenhorst, remarked, they were surprised by the 'chivalry and politeness' of the POWs, one of whom echoed Winston Churchill in praising the women's influence: 'Never in the history of Wilton Park have so few done so much for so many.' Within a week, the segregation arrangements were ignored and officially abandoned. So relaxed did relations become that before the end of that summer the POWs were allowed to organise a dance. As one of them later explained:

> Two barriers had to be taken by storm: the Commandant and the Rector of Wilton Park.
>
> To everyone's surprise, however, the Commandant accepted the plan with joy, shared even more by the Commandant's wife. Herr Dr Koeppler, although a confirmed bachelor and temporary guardian of the morals of his protegées, could no longer withhold his consent ...
>
> Two hundred girls were invited and the Commandant's wife earned unforgettable gratitude by her efforts to welcome so many guests ...
>
> Heaps of cake ... were served with coffee or tea by our German civilian lady students ... While the last tune was fading away, an English girl

exclaimed with enthusiasm: 'How nice it has been, just like a big family', and the parting and goodbyes at the gates ... took a long time. Many POWs returned to the barracks with joy in their eyes, some unable to sleep, some finding their dreams more beautiful and wonderful than ever. Many a sweet secret could be revealed by Wilton Park ... if only they weren't secrets.

The picture – and the description – of 'our German civilian lady students' serving the refreshments sound anachronistic today; and the coyness cloys. But for the prisoners-of-war this, like the arrival of women students, was a momentous change. Earlier, one POW student, Commander Grandjean, whose U-boat had been sunk in the first year of the War, had broken down on a visit to a British household, when he spoke to a woman for the first time in seven years. A few close friendships and attachments, some of them lasting, were formed between men and women at Wilton Park: one POW, Horst Devers, met his future wife there when she was a journalist on *Die Welt* and came as a student early in 1948.

Appropriately, the first evening speaker to the first course with women students was Jennie Lee again, this time on 'Women in England under the Labour Government'. Having left her humble Fifeshire background for Edinburgh University, where she had taken an MA and LLB before becoming an MP and the wife of Aneurin Bevan, she was a lifelong social-ist. She believed that everyone – and that included all women – should have the opportunities she had enjoyed, educational and cultural: she fiercely opposed what was later called 'dumbing down'. True to Koeppler's policy, the next evening lecturer from outside (after Grondona had spoken on Australia) was the Conservative Lord Soulbury, followed by a multi-Party House of Commons Brains Trust. As well as Jennie Lee and Lord Soulbury, several other familiar figures reappeared, including Thomas Hodgkin and David Worswick; there was also another speaker from Switzerland, the journalist Dr Zbinden, whose subject was 'The Future of Germany'. Lord Lindsay was one of several distinguished people who made a return visit to the evening seminars for civilians; while the main evening lecture series included two experts on the Left: Christopher Hill, formerly in the Foreign Office Research Department's Russian Section (on 'Russian Foreign Policy') and the publisher Victor Gollancz (on 'The German Problem'). One woman student said after-wards: 'The visit of Victor Gollancz ... was for us, from the humanitarian point of view, a great event.'

What Koeppler called 'the extra-mural activities' for the civilian men and women included nearly fifty organised visits to schools and colleges,

the three main political party headquarters, the TUC, Co-operative societies, local government meetings, youth clubs, welfare institutions, clinics,
factories, physical education centres, police courts, young offenders' institutions, Fleet Street, the BBC, a labour exchange, and the city of Oxford.
These trips and activities were funded by Wilton Park. For private
expenses, the civilians were given twenty shillings a week plus a lump sum
of thirty shillings to buy books of their own choice. Some brought cameras
with them, but were warned that 'it is at present almost impossible to
purchase films in England'. Those who were invited by British groups or
individuals to stay on after the course could do so if they told the authorities and if 'satisfactory arrangements' could be made for their return. They
were reminded that 'visitors who spend less than six months in Great
Britain are not permitted to export any goods or foodstuffs'. The war was
ended, but austerity lingered on.

When the course ended on August 15, 1947, Koeppler looked back on
it with mixed but mainly positive feelings: 'This was the first course in
which women participated and there is general agreement amongst the
staff that they were a great success.' One of the women – Fräulein
Rudnitzki of the Münster Institute of Social Economy – agreed. Her
tutors' report described her as 'a splendid choice. Very regular attender,
most active in debates, thinks about what she is going to say, stands up
bravely to the men.' She sent them in return her own report on the course:

> We were the first women for whom the gates of Wilton Park had opened,
> and I think that people in and out of the camp had regarded this 'Ten-
> headed experiment', as it was described in the camp wall newspaper, a little
> sceptically. A POW ... said in his closing report: 'The women have brought
> those tones into the concert which could not have been sounded in an all-
> male atmosphere and they have given expression to many an idea which
> men among themselves all too easily forget.' I can only confirm that we
> were not only given many opportunities to air our opinions on current
> questions in tutorials and discussions but that we also very often and with
> great pleasure made use of the opportunities. We also assured that, through
> conversation in small circles, particularly among the prisoners-of-war, full
> importance was attributed to the 'women's question', and I think that we
> have made it quite clear and shown it in its right light. With the inclusion
> of women students one has certainly performed a good service for Wilton
> Park and I would like to request that in future the percentage of women
> should be increased as much as possible.

Koeppler attributed the course's general success to 'careful selection'.
Even so, there had been awkward customers – especially among the men:

There can be no doubt that some students have proved difficult and that they have given the staff much food for thought. Reports which have reached us of educational meetings and conferences in Germany seem to indicate that what we have observed here is by no means an isolated instance peculiar to Wilton Park.

It would appear that the atmosphere of anarchy and of destructive criticism for its own sake has taken a powerful hold of some Germans; if they are representative of responsible German opinion there might be reason to despair of Germany ever being re-integrated into a free and peaceful Europe. There were amongst our students some men of all parties who had lost all sense of self-discipline and civic responsibility if they ever possessed it. They considered the most elementary forms of organisation as a violation of what they chose to call academic freedom. They refused to approach our discussions with an open mind, being so filled with a sense of grievance and with their own importance that it appeared well nigh impossible to achieve anything constructive with them.

One of them stated that we ought to realise how difficult it was for them to be constructive when they had always before their eyes the sight of an undestroyed London but in their minds they saw the destroyed German cities.

It was a familiar and saddening situation. But, Koeppler went on:

What proved disappointing was a tendency of a few participants to consider opinions differing from their own as evidence of a low standard of morality and if proffered by the staff or by visiting lecturers as proof of an anti-German attitude, if proffered by their fellow-students as undemocratic, unpatriotic and bordering on high treason. The same people who accused the British of deliberately starving them intellectually would not condescend to make use of our library, and those who protested against being treated as schoolboys would not honour a study group with their presence even when they were due to read a paper. The outstanding example was provided by two elderly civil servants who felt they had nothing to learn yet refused to contribute to the discussions while doing their best in private conversations with their fellow-students to make their minds as impervious to new ideas as were their own. We feel that this is a further proof of the need for the utmost care in selecting people above the age-groups of 20–40, to which it was agreed our students should normally belong …

In fairness to the majority we would like to stress that those who behaved badly got told off in no uncertain manner by their countrymen and it was rarely necessary for the staff to deal with the obstructionists in discussions; as one tutor writes: 'I don't remember hearing any really monstrous remark which was not squashed by one of the Germans before I could get a word in.'

If some of the men had been aggressive, some of the women had been wary. 'We Germans,' wrote Dr Hilda von Klenze, 'have become highly sceptical and as sensitive as seismographs':

> Whenever we hear someone in the distance mentioning Fascism, War, or even Concentration Camps we begin to tremble with indignation and loudly to protest our innocence. I think most of us went to England with the intention of looking for the catch in Wilton Park. Several of us believed that the catch would be found in the mask of hospitality and goodwill with which we were being lured to England, where we would be put into the dock or indoctrinated. On looking at my diary I find entries concerning this visit to England on the very first page. In Düsseldorf, for instance, I wrote: 'Everyone seems to think that the British are trying to bluff us or to "show us how". Of course they want to show us amongst other things how they manage their affairs, but they are not nearly so self-satisfied about it as we are apt to think.' That was the catch for which some of us were looking.

Fräulein Rudnitzki, too, was aware of 'the distrust ... which many students ... feel at first': it 'should be removed as quickly and completely as possible'. Like Koeppler himself, she was critical of 're-education':

> Here it should be taken into consideration that a large number of the civilian students were already in opposition to National Socialism before the collapse and were persecuted during that regime. Today many of them hold high positions and are themselves responsible for re-educating such circles as may need it.

As tension mounted between the Soviet Union and the West, debates everywhere tended to polarise, not least at Wilton Park. 'In many discussions', said Koeppler, 'the widening rift between the Occupying Powers was making itself felt.' One young woman Communist student, Dr Lotte Schellewaldt, praised Wilton Park for having given her 'a feeling of tolerance and patience for my fellow-men'. She stressed that 'the tutors and the Rector ... have taken great care to fulfil their tasks in an exemplary fashion'. But she had her reservations:

> I personally considered that there was something lacking in that not sufficient stress was laid upon Russia as a victorious power side by side with the other allied powers ...
>
> In discussion with the POWs and also the civilians we often had an impression of mistrust as if in Wilton Park one only wanted to play off Germans of separate '*Weltanschauungen*' one against the other. Generally

most said that Wilton Park was an SDP [Social Democrat Party] officials' school …

I personally often noticed, which interested me a great deal, that among the POWs (in other camps as well) an anti-Russian feeling existed. I observed that among the rich number and assortment of newspapers, there was neither a German nor an English paper with a 'Left' tendency. I hope this report will not seem too presumptuous, but honestly it is written in pursuit of democratic ideals and this I learnt at Wilton Park.

The confidential report on Dr Schellewaldt called her 'definitely one of the better sort of Communist. Had made a lot of dominantly sensible contributions to discussions.' Dr von Klenze, in her own remarks about Wilton Park, said:

Those of us who went there looking for the anti-Communist catch found we were barking up the wrong tree. Whilst I was there I heard English speakers lecturing publicly on the necessity for co-operation with Russia and pleading for understanding to be shown for the Russian attitude. That these views were not shared by every lecturer in Wilton Park does not affect the issue. The vital point is that every opinion could be heard there …

It also helped us Germans to see our own internal political problems more clearly. We had among us excellent representatives of the KPD [German Communist Party] and the SED [(Communist) Socialist Unity Party], who succeeded in gaining the respect and confidence of civilians and prisoners from the Right to the Left. I think there were many who learned in Wilton Park that it is actually possible to sit with a Communist at one table and to discuss such delicate topics as, for example, the Marshall Plan, without the direst consequences.

Summing up his impressions of the first course with civilian women, Koeppler quoted diaries kept by two students to illustrate the attitude of what he called 'the constructive members of the course':

It was right to applaud vigorously the lecture by Mr Gollancz, almost everything he said deserved to be taken to heart. And yet I felt a little humiliated to hear so many people applaud him whom I had heard frequently express views which did not fit within the framework of Gollancz's ideas. These people see that he is conscious of Germany's desperate position and demands redress, but they overlook that he also imposes obligations on the Germans which it will be much more difficult for us to fulfil than it will be to overcome the present emergency.

It cannot be assumed that anyone who comes to Wilton Park will change his moral or political attitude fundamentally. The Nazis were sufficiently naïve to assume such change could be brought about by a course of a few weeks. I believe Wilton Park has a different object. It seems to me important that men of goodwill and only such should come to Wilton Park. They will experience ... a strengthening of their moral forces through the repeated and impartial discussions of burning topics of the day and through a clear exposition of the problems. Even if at the end we recognise that the individual can do little to influence developments we also recognise that we must properly use even the tiny opportunities which every individual has to influence public affairs.

When Koeppler quoted these words, the fifth mixed POW/civilian course was well under way. 'We are very encouraged', he declared, 'to find that its atmosphere is much better and that the students are more willing to play their part.' This, he thought, was 'most likely due to their having a clearer picture of what is expected of them'.

Soon, in fact, the mixed POW/civilian courses settled into a regular routine. Leaving aside the civilians' extra-mural activities, which took up two days a week, the internal timetable was intensive. Each period of work filled 90 minutes, at least half of which was devoted to questions and discussion. As Koeppler reported on November 4, 1947:

Every student from Germany takes part in

> 7 formal seminars (without Ps/W)
> 1 formal class (with Ps/W)
> 5 formal discussion groups (3 with Ps/W, 2 without them)
> 3 reading periods, during two of which he may instead join a class with
>   Ps/W

The students from Germany are divided into 4 syndicates, and during the present course their seminars, the mainstay of the curriculum, deal with these subjects:

> International affairs (political): 1
> International affairs (social and economic): 1
> Civics: 2 (for two syndicates: 2)
> Projection of Britain: 1 (for two syndicates: 2)
> German Problems: 2

For the three classes with Ps/W (one of which only is compulsory) they have a choice of nine lecturers who cover various aspects of international affairs and citizenship, and two periods of German history, from Bismarck to Versailles and the Weimar Republic.

It is in the nature of the tutorials that it is impossible to give an exact account of the topics covered but the following is a list of constantly recurring themes:

Allied intentions for the future of Germany and the world; comparison of British and German institutions; the East–West problem; Pan–Europe; Germany's frontiers; Church and State; the crisis of the young generation; youth movements; youth amnesty; the place of the universities in society; race; freedom of the individual, and of the Press; pacificism; political parties; socialism versus free enterprise; agrarian reform; denazification; war guilt and responsibility (a subject never proposed by the tutors) ...

It should perhaps be stressed that the educational value of the tutorials lies as much in the practice of tolerant discussion of controversial issues as in the subjects discussed.

Koeppler once again confronted what he called 'the most frequent criticism of the curriculum' – 'its alleged concentration on the past and its alleged lack of constructive thought for the future'. After rehearsing the familiar argument that understanding the past was a necessary basis for building a solid future, he memorably added: 'What all Germans of goodwill will need in the years to come, and what recent history has shown they do not possess, is patience.'

Koeppler had some detailed suggestions about the future selection of German civilians. He proposed, for instance, that no more members of the co-operative movement be brought over since 'almost every co-operator sent to Wilton Park has been interested only in the machinery of co-operation and not in the problems of a free society'. He hoped for more young university dons and undergraduates, and fewer elderly educational administrators. He envisaged students preparing papers in Germany before coming to Britain.

Problems, however, subsisted. Some were typical of Europe's postwar plight. After a year's experience of receiving civilians at Wilton Park in 1947, Koeppler complained: 'The difficulties in the way of proper selection are formidable. Since selection is both on a regional basis and a functional basis the number of officers involved has been considerable and it has taken some time for the purpose of course to become known.' He proposed several ways to improve matters without adding to the selecting officers' workload. But he added:

It would appear that the circulation of the leaflet for British selectors also leaves much to be desired. It seems that it has hardly penetrated beyond Regional headquarters ... We wonder whether it is not possible to circulate the leaflet to all the *Kreis* (District) officers ...

While the leaflet will probably have to be the main instrument of information we feel that the following practice adopted in one or two Regions might become universal. A meeting is arranged between candidates for Wilton Park and people who have been on earlier courses. This personal contact may be a valuable source of additional information ...

We should not forget that the first impressions our students will get of the Wilton Park scheme are the arrangements for their journey to England. These have, unfortunately, not always been successful.

Koeppler appended the report written by the tutor, T.J. Durkin, who brought the last 1947 party of German civilians to England. 'We should be grateful', he added, 'if remedial action could be taken'. Durkin's report was cogent:

I should like to place on record my surprise that the travel authorities should find it so difficult to move a party of 60 Germans from various points in the British zone [of Germany] and in the British sector [of Berlin] to the UK. One gets the impression that the whole thing is regarded as something of a nuisance: one attends to it reluctantly, at the last moment, and hopes that everything will turn out well.

From many points of view it seems convenient that most of the parties should meet at Hanover, but in that case surely it would be possible to arrange for the Berlin party to spend the early morning hours somewhere while waiting for the train. At the last moment in Berlin I was informed that they should go to Klages Markt but in fact the hotel was closed and they were not able to get in. The RTO [Rail Travel Officer] at Hanover expressed surprise that we were travelling on that day, but we were allowed to occupy a coach which eventually proved too small for the whole party so one had to take turns at sitting although of course there was a certain amount of accommodation in the rest of the train. The feeding arrangements in this CCG [Control Commission Germany] were good and everyone was satisfied.

A hot meal was provided in the NAAFI [Navy, Army, and Air Force Institute canteen] at the Hook, but it was rather unpleasant having to wait from 8.30 p.m. until just after 1 a.m. as it was rather chilly. We went aboard then. Accommodation was poor; we were not expected, there was no food for us, which meant that apart from a sandwich at Harwich no one had anything to eat from 10 p.m. on Monday until 7.30 p.m. on Tuesday. Moreover it was cold below decks and most of us were not even able to lie down as there was no room. We were not expected at Harwich: the boat authorities and the immigration people at Harwich were most insistent that they had not been informed of our coming. Surely it might be required of the lower military ranks to treat visitors to the UK with the ordinary courtesies that one expects in a civilized country.

I should like to suggest that some single scheme be worked out by which one would know in advance what to expect. It may be necessary or desirable that the party should travel with the European Volunteer Workers, but in that case surely the purser of the boat should be informed in advance. It would be an advantage if the various groups were issued with similar travel documents. Some had separate tickets, some travelled as a party, some were issued with vouchers entitling them to draw £1 at Hook, others were not. It seems better to choose a leader of a group and give him the travel documents for his party. This makes it more simple for the leader of the whole group who cannot know each individual.

There were, of course, no such transport problems for the prisoners-of-war at Wilton Park. But their presence was soon to come to an end. The last POW course took place in June 1948. By that time, more than 4,000 POW students had passed through – a tiny fraction of all those in the UK, but an impressionable and influential group. George Roundell Greene, one of the tutors who had himself been a prisoner-of-war, later wrote feelingly about 'the detachment from practical reality which is in any case natural and almost inevitable for men living in prison camps':

German politics and economics, in any ordinary sense, were not even to be read about in newspapers. On the other hand this detachment may have enabled the intelligent POW to think more clearly than his brother at home (or visiting Wilton Park), simply because his main attention was not occupied by such transitory conditions as those of the black market and of an occupation which was still in essence largely hostile. He could only think in general categories; but it was <u>something</u>, to be able to think in general categories.

Consequently, I myself nearly always found it refreshing to get back ('get <u>back</u>', because I had more to do with the POWs than the 'civilians') from some miserable recital of the wrongs inflicted on or the calamities suffered by Germans since the war, to a lively discussion on free trade, or trade unions, or federalism: a discussion confessedly based largely on inexperience, but usually sustained by interest, and intelligence, and sometimes wide reading, and observation of non-German politics, and now and then, of course, memories of Weimar. Such discussions were thus not entirely in the void; and I should say that the emphasis which was necessarily given to <u>principle</u> (not, or not only, in a moral sense) made the Wilton Park course particularly valuable to <u>young</u> Germans as their first real introduction to political thinking.

At the risk of being obvious, it is perhaps worth remembering that the most accessible political examples then were British ones, and that British politics were particularly lively at that time. In every group of German POWs were at least one or two who had read Hayek and Roepke; and what with rationing, permits, prolongation of the Control of Engagement Order, delegated legislation, the guillotine, the Parliament Bill on the one side, and all the new social legislation on the other, the POW could see, though he could not share in, the dispute on <u>the most essential</u> problems of democratic domestic politics in modern times, and could further see that the dispute was not, by and large, being badly handled.

The serious young POW at Wilton Park had at least one further advantage if he wished (as, indeed, he required, and as his 'free' contemporary in Germany requires) a solid grounding in political principles: a regular timetable. He knew that next Tuesday morning Adams was going to deal with another aspect of 'The Welfare State', and that Demuth, on Tuesday afternoon, was coming on to Bismarck's dismissal, and that on Wednesday Burmeister was to deal with the Weimar electoral system: and <u>he could read it up</u> – after the first lecture of each series (and there were five lectures to come) he could to a great extent plan his course and allocate his own time so as to get the best out of it.

In brief, I should say that Wilton Park enormously widened the perspective of the average POW student, but did not, because it could not, do much to enable him to see <u>himself</u> as an essential part of the picture. On the other hand, he gave the impression of being very much more a social being, essentially, than the average participant from Germany did or does. 'Team spirit' among the POWs is one of my own personal most lasting and most heartening memories – the extraordinary good humour with which they used to differ from each other, sometimes passionately, in discussion.

Koeppler, too, felt that he and his colleagues had done an honourable job. 'Many former students have told us when we met them in Germany', he recalled, 'that this part of our work is in the nature of a delayed action bomb and that they find the new approach gained at Wilton Park a great help long after they have left.' One of them, who attended the very first course for prisoners–of–war, wrote years afterwards:

When I came to Wilton Park in January 1946 it was half a year after the end of an awful world war, brought about by Hitler, with millions of dead people and chaos in many countries. We all had just heard the truth about the unbelievable atrocities committed by Germans in concentration camps. In occupied Germany the British troops had strict orders of 'No Fraternization' with the Germans. It is against this background that we German prisoners–of–war experienced Wilton Park. What Heinz Koeppler did was most surprising. He gave us Germans the possibility to become partners. He did not 're-educate' us ... , he did not tell us how things ought to be handled in Germany, but he made us think for ourselves; he believed it to be 'vital' in the real sense of the world, that Britons and Germans should get to know and to understand the other fellow's point of view. I

SHEETS AND DANCES AND TOUGH TALK

cannot describe the encouragement and confidence Heinz Koeppler and his colleagues gave to us, German prisoners-of-war, by having ministers of the British Crown, leading Opposition speakers, economic leaders like Lord Beveridge, professors like Lord Lindsay of Birker and so on come and talk to and discuss with us.

Behind barbed wire one could sometimes, of course, feel discouraged and pessimistic. What was the use of Wilton Park? Our possibilities were limited and wasn't the task too big? Heinz Koeppler's conviction and humanity coped with such situations. He told us that small numbers are not necessarily a bad thing, for we have, after all, good *biblical* authority for the belief that from small seeds great results may follow.

The witness was Willi Brundert, the Wilton Park puppeteer who eventually became Mayor of Frankfurt. Many no less distinguished figures could have said the same. Gerhard Richter, a leading socialist politician from Berlin who had been librarian while a prisoner-of-war at Wilton Park, said: 'Berlin is my homeland, but Wilton Park is my spiritual home.' Several admitted that nowhere else had they been taught about German history from Bismarck to Weimar. One affirmed: 'This … laid the personal basis for my future.'

Koeppler cherished such tributes, and – like Roundell Greene – had warm memories of work with prisoners-of-war. But in November 1947, as the time approached for the last POW courses at Wilton Park, he looked ahead with barely concealed eagerness to all-civilian courses and the implementation of his original plan, when Wilton Park would become, as he put it, 'a centre for free people only':

> Inasmuch as the complaint about a 'militaristic' atmosphere is anything more than an excuse for lack of elementary self-discipline, it will disappear with the military element at present required because of the presence of prisoners …
>
> If our arguments [about the need for history teaching] are accepted, it follows that the main structure of the curriculum should be maintained after the last prisoners-of-war have gone.

Already, in fact, Robert Crawford and his Foreign Office colleagues had been making the case for continuing Wilton Park after the last German POWs had left, by the summer of 1948. They had been backed by the Control Commission in Germany, by Birley and by others, including James Marjoribanks, who had moved from the Cabinet Office to be HM Minister (Economic) in Bonn. The only mildly dissentient voice was that of the Foreign Office's Deputy Under-Secretary of State (Political), Sir

Oliver Harvey. The consensus was that the Office should draft its esti-mates for 1948 to include some £34,000 for taking over the costs of Wilton Park from its original War Office paymaster.

Accordingly, plans were made to adapt Wilton Park for purely civilian use. In particular, the Nissen huts were to be replaced by buildings more suitable, more comfortable, and more permanent.

But then, only a few weeks after Koeppler's November 1947 report, the 'rumblings' that Robert Crawford had detected in the War Office became a thunderclap. On December 19, 1947, the Director of Quartering at the War Office wrote to the Foreign Office:

> Due to the number of Army Units returning to the United Kingdom as the result of the evacuation of India and Palestine, it is regretted that the War Department must request the return of Camp 300 at Wilton Park, Beaconsfield, which is at present on loan to you … We will require posses-sion of this camp by the 20 January 1948.

This sparked off frenzied Christmas Eve activity – to postpone the next Wilton Park conference, due to begin on January 8, 1948, and above all to reverse the War Office ultimatum. It was time to wheel in the big guns.

CHAPTER 8

The Captains and the Kings Depart

The tumult and the shouting dies –
The captains and the kings depart.
Rudyard Kipling, 'Recessional', 1897

Fortunately, not only Heinz Koeppler had been giving thought to the future of Wilton Park as a purely civilian institution. Two separate strands of policy were soon, in fact, to converge. In Germany, the Occupation authorities were still anxious to help prepare leading Germans to serve what would eventually become the Federal Republic. And in London, as East-West problems became more pressing, the Government was wondering whether to establish some sort of centre where British and foreign visitors could increase international understanding.

The former was the more urgent; and Robert Birley viewed with regret the possible demise of Wilton Park. On November 5, 1947 – the day after Koeppler's latest report – he had sent a handwritten letter from the Travellers' Club to Robert Crawford, Head of German Education in the Foreign Office:

If Wilton Park were to be closed, we should have to do our best to arrange all visits through the normal channels. The result would be to reduce the number very considerably, for two reasons. First, the number of Germans who can be looked after by their 'opposite numbers', for instance school teachers at an English school is inevitably strictly limited, and we already do pretty well all that is possible in this way. Secondly, Wilton Park enables us to bring to England and so under direct English influence Germans who could otherwise not be brought over at all, as there would be no suitable 'opposite numbers' in England to look after them as guests …

Wilton Park is a place where we can do some definite teaching of Germans, explaining to them the essential characteristics of the democratic way of life. They cannot expect to get this from ordinary visits. Wilton Park, in fact, is one of the ways in which we are able to bring a positive influence to bear on the Germans, especially those likely to be the leaders of Germany in the future. I am sure that if it were abandoned our positive influence would be greatly diminished.

Lord Pakenham, who was in political charge of the German Section of the Foreign Office, shared Birley's and Crawford's views. Born in December 1905, the second son of the Earl of Longford, Frank Pakenham had been educated at Eton and New College, Oxford, where he had been a Student and then Lecturer in Politics in the 1930s. When Wilton Park was set up he had been Parliamentary Under-Secretary of State at the War Office, moving on to become Chancellor of the Duchy of Lancaster in 1947. A devout Catholic, he saw Britain's mission in Germany as a 'Christian Crusade'. 'Every German', he pointed out, 'is as much a human being with an immortal soul of infinite worth as we ourselves'. In a speech to the Foreign Press Association in London at the end of September 1947, Pakenham had reaffirmed what he regarded as the reasons for the continued occupation of Germany: 'First, the security reason, secondly the educational reason, thirdly the economic reason.' All, he thought, were very closely intertwined:

> Wars were made in the minds of men. What matters far more than anything else, therefore, in doing this job in Germany – the real standard by which history will judge us – is what effect we have had or have not had, at the end of it, on the mind of the German people. In that sense security – the task of averting another war – is merged inseparably into German re-education and everything done under one head must be studied in reference to the other.

'Re-education', admittedly, was an expression that Koeppler detested, and had always avoided at Wilton Park – just as he had objected to its being called a 'Training Centre'. On this subject, he was soon to express his views at great and eloquent length.

On terminology, Birley agreed with Koeppler, and even instructed his colleagues in Education Branch to avoid the 'horrible word "re-education"'. Semantics apart, however, Birley, Koeppler and Pakenham saw eye-to-eye. Birley in particular recognised the need for what he called the 'stimulus of mind on mind'; and, like Pakenham, he believed that Christians above all had a particular duty to help the Germans themselves overcome the crisis afflicting them. Nor was this, he thought, just a German phenomenon. A clear symptom 'of the spiritual disease of our civilisation', he argued, 'is the widespread feeling among men that they have lost all control of their own destinies'.

Encouraged by Birley and Crawford, as well as by Koeppler, Pakenham took up the cause of Wilton Park. Perhaps from conviction, perhaps for tactical reasons, he continued to use the language they disliked. 'To close the centre down', he declared, ' ... would constitute a serious blow to our plans for the re-education of Germany'.

The first task was to put on hold the War Office's request to reclaim Wilton Park by January 20, 1948. As a substitute, the War Office had offered Ontario Camp at Liphook, between Haslemere and Petersfield. 'Quite out of the question', said Crawford: it was too far from London and Oxford; it would need slow, costly renovation; and the Wilton Park staff could hardly move house so fast. Eventually, the War Office postponed its return until August 1st, 1948, when the last German prisoners were due to leave. Meanwhile, broader questions were on the agenda, prompted by dramatic events in Germany and in Europe generally.

The zoning of Germany among the victorious Allies had been agreed in principle in 1944; and although the Potsdam Conference in July 1945 had stipulated that 'during the occupation period, Germany shall be treated as a single economic entity', the Soviet Union had followed its own separate agenda, stripping the Eastern zone of resources that should have helped Germany as a whole.

Divergence and disagreement with the Soviets had eventually led the British and Americans to merge their own zones with each other on January 1, 1947. Despite Soviet protests and obstructionism in the four-power conferences on Germany, the British and Americans had set up the 'Bizonal' Economic Council of delegates from the *Land* Assemblies, with an Executive Committee representing the *Land* governments.

That had been in May 1947. In June, the Soviet Union retaliated by establishing an East German Permanent Economic Commission. In July, the Soviet delegation walked out of a Paris meeting on the Marshall Plan, and the Western Powers had extended Marshall Aid to their own zones of Germany. In the autumn, the USSR set up the Cominform; and in December 1947, while a further four-power conference was deadlocked in London, the Soviet authorities held the first of a series of German People's Congresses, supposedly pan-German but boycotted by the Western parties and dominated by the communists in the East. The *de facto* division of Germany was proceeding apace: soon, it would become *de jure*.

In February 1948, the Western Allies enlarged the Economic Council and added an upper house or *Länderrat* composed of two governmental delegates from each *Land*, and remodelled the Executive Committee to group the heads of the various administrative agencies. General Lucius Clay, the US Deputy Military Governor, described this as: 'a realistic political structure of the federal type even though it had no sovereign powers, was limited in its authority to fiscal and economic measures, and its acts were subject to Military Government approval ... We had the machinery for government, if not a government.'

It was completed by a High Court and by a central bank, the *Bank Deutscher Länder*, serving all three Western zones. Soon afterwards, with the Benelux countries, the Western Allies agreed to establish international control of the Ruhr. They added that they favoured 'a federal form of Government' as 'the most appropriate to make possible the ultimate re-establishment of German unity'.

At once, the Soviet Union formally protested. It increased the powers of the East German Economic Commission, and staged a second People's Congress which elected 400-member People's Council, which in turn appointed a committee to draft an 'All-German Constitution'. Soon afterwards, the Soviet member of the four-power Control Council in Berlin, Marshal Vassily Sokolovsky, read a long, aggrieved statement and walked out. In practical terms, as General Clay put it, 'the Allied Control Council was dead'.

The Western powers continued semi-official consultations among themselves, and in June 1948 they recommended the establishment of a German Constituent Assembly to draw up a federal Constitution. They also issued a new West German currency, the *Deutsche Mark* (DM), exchanged at the rate of one DM for ten old *Reichsmark* (RM) – later reduced to 6.5 DM for 100 RM. The result was a brief spending spree, and renewed faith in paper money after years of quasi-barter. Shortly afterwards, to the Western powers' surprise, their German Director for Economic Administration, the bulky, cigar-smoking Bavarian, Ludwig Erhard, removed price controls. 'It was strictly laid down by the British and American control authorities', he confessed later, 'that permission had to be obtained before any definite price changes could be made. The Allies never seemed to have thought it possible that someone could have the idea, not to alter price controls, but simply to remove them.'

When currency reform had first been suggested, the Soviet Union had thought of using the *Deutsche Mark*, and had asked for a set of printing plates. But on a previous occasion, when they had had duplicate plates for Allied 'military Marks', they had failed to account for them; so Clay refused. He proposed instead that the banknote printing works, which was in the American sector of Berlin, be placed under four-power control. The Russians refused, and conducted their own currency reform in the East.

They also walked out of the four-power *Kommandatura*, and imposed a land blockade on the city of Berlin.

The West responded with the Berlin Airlift of supplies to the beleaguered city. It lasted nearly a year. By the time it ended, in May 1949, the Western powers had signed the North Atlantic Treaty, and East and West Germany were on the brink of establishing their rival Constitutions. The West Germans held their first postwar election on August 14, 1949. On October 7, without any pretence of election, the East German People's Council set itself up as a 'Provisional People's Chamber' or *Volkskammer*; three days later, the Eastern *Land* Assemblies chose delegates to the *Länderkammer*; and on October 11 these two houses elected as President of the East German Republic the Communist leader Wilhelm Pieck.

The division of Germany into two rival states – the Federal Republic and the German Democratic Republic, the DDR – embodied and symbolised the East-West division of Europe. In Eastern Europe since the war, one country after another had fallen under Soviet domination: Poland, Bulgaria, Romania, Hungary, with Finland, Albania, and Yugoslavia following only partly divergent courses of their own. The most dramatic coup, in Czechoslovakia, culminated in March 1948, when the non-Communist Foreign Minister Jan Masaryk was murdered.

Meanwhile, Western Europe was groping towards closer co-operation – not entirely in reaction to events in the East. In September 1946, Winston Churchill spoke in Zurich of the need to build 'a kind of United States of Europe', and two years later was one of many European statesmen who attended the unofficial 'Congress of Europe' in The Hague. On the official level, American Marshall Aid led to the establishment in 1947 of the Organization for European Economic Co-operation; in 1948, Britain, France and the Benelux countries signed the Brussels Pact; and in 1949 they formed – with Ireland, Italy and the three Scandinavian countries – the Council of Europe.

Such was the evolving international background against which the British Government – independently of the Control Commission in Germany – began considering how to spread Britain's democratic influence in Western Europe. At first, the main aim was to counter Communist encroachment. On January 3, 1947, the Prime Minister Clement Attlee – it was his sixty-fifth birthday – delivered a New Year's broadcast predicting a sombre year ahead. Three weeks before, the Foreign Ministers' conference in London had broken down over Soviet intransigence; and Attlee now drew a gloomy contrast between 1848 and 1948. A hundred years ago, he said, 'Europe revolted against absolute governments which suppressed all opposition, but today the absolutists who suppress opposition masquerade under the name of upholders of liberty.' Perhaps as a sop to Left-wing critics like Richard Crossman, he conceded that Britain might be a potential 'third force' between 'outright capitalism and tyrannical communism'. But Britain and the United States – despite their differences over Palestine – were being drawn closer and closer together by the growing aggressiveness of Soviet policy, especially over Germany.

Two weeks later, the Foreign Secretary, Ernest Bevin, spoke in a parliamentary debate on foreign affairs. The Soviet Union, he declared, seemed bent on dominating Europe. To prevent this, the Western democracies must draw together: 'I believe the time is ripe for a consolidation of Western Europe.'

For Bevin and the British Government, 'consolidation' did not mean integration or union, but co-operation between sovereign states: OEEC, the Brussels Pact, the North Atlantic Treaty, and the Council of Europe. For Britain's continental partners, it implied a great deal more. But even in Britain there was concern, as Jean Monnet later put it, not just to make coalitions of states, but to unite people. Bevin's Parliamentary Under-Secretary of State for Foreign Affairs was the 31-year-old former President of the Oxford Union, Dunkirk veteran and ex-Major, Christopher Mayhew. With three senior Foreign Office officials, including C.F.A. Warner, he proposed a way to promote democracy abroad. On January 27, 1948, he minuted Bevin that, with them:

> I have been giving some thought to the following paragraph of our recent Cabinet Paper on anti-Communist propaganda, which your speech in the House has made very pertinent:
>> 'In order to influence important trade unionists from abroad and other influential non-communist foreigners in favour of our way of life and thought we should organise visits by them to Britain in a systematic fashion. We should set up, under the British Council, a "Wilton Park" at which we could offer them attractive courses on British life and institutions, and "brief" them on the ideas contained in this paper.'

Evidently, 'Wilton Park' required no comment. But 'our way of life' did. It was a phrase whose 'frequent use on the F.O.' Bevin had noticed, and 'would like ... dropped'. Accordingly, Mayhew crossed it out in favour of 'democratic systems'. He went on:

> From our discussions the following questions emerge on which I would welcome guidance:-

<u>Who should be invited to attend these courses?</u>
 (i) Should we invite only young, influential trade unionists; or
 (ii) any young working-class people, whether actual trade unionists or not;
      or
 (iii) should we allow any students or other young people likely to be influ-
       ential in their own country, irrespective of their background, to be
       invited? I think, on the whole, we should approve some such qualify-
       ing formula as:
          'Influential young people, especially trade unionists from
          Western Europe, who have shown themselves friendly to the
          British way of life and wish to know more about it.'

The next question was who should set up and run such a college? One
option was the British Council, but it might not fit into their current terms
of reference which barred them from any political work. 'The Cabinet
should allow the British Council to run the "college" as a special exception
to the Council's terms of reference (the Council might even then object to
taking on the job, as damaging to their non-political reputation).' The
alternative was:

> That the 'college' should be run by the Foreign Office (Information
> Departments). Mr Warner points out that the Information Departments
> have no experience in the practical details involved in setting up and
> running such a 'college' and would probably have to find and take on at
> least one suitable extra man to do the job. This difficulty is not, of course,
> insuperable but it would no doubt be better if the 'college' and courses
> could be run by some body who already knows how to tackle it.

On the geographical spread, he suggested that, 'I think that most of the
visitors should come from Western Europe, but that we should leave
ourselves free to invite suitable people from elsewhere, e.g. the colonies,
Middle East, etc.' Two days later, Bevin minuted back: 'This document is
very important, and I should like to discuss it when I come back. I do not
like the method outlined.'

Less than two weeks later, on Tuesday February 10, 1948, Bevin held a
meeting in his room to discuss what the minutes called 'the establishment
of a "Wilton Park" at which we could offer to foreigners courses on British
life and institutions as part of the campaign against Communism'. Among
the half-dozen present were C.F.A. Warner, the Minister of State, Hector
McNeil, (whom Harold Nicolson once described as 'Scotch and dour'),
and the diminutive, brilliant and birdlike Frank Roberts, Bevin's Principal
Private Secretary, later (as Sir Frank) to be Ambassador to Moscow and
then to Bonn.

Bevin felt, he said, 'that we ought to aim at something on a considerably larger scale and with bolder conceptions'. He did not want the courses to be mainly or directly anti-communist. Nor did he want those attending these courses to be mainly trades unionists. What he wanted was that 'rising men from Western Europe, from various walks of life, should be given a real insight into the way we did things here, in every branch of our national life'. In his view, the proposed College – in the official record it had now dropped its quotation marks and acquired a capital letter – should not be run as a government organisation. Instead, it should be a national institution with an independent governing board. It should, however, have a Government grant. Bevin hoped, he added, 'that it would be possible to collect money to establish it from such organisations as the Nuffield Trust and from public-spirited private individuals'.

C.F.A. Warner chipped in to remark that the British Council was already bringing to Britain, or helping to look after, people who wished to study various aspects of British life; but the consensus of the meeting was that the courses envisaged would be 'definitely of a political character', and that it would therefore 'not be suitable for the British Council to undertake the running of the proposed house'.

Where the 'house' should be caused considerable discussion. Bevin mentioned, among others, the possibility of getting Bewdley; McNeil was anxious to find out whether Newbattle Abbey could be used. Frank Roberts suggested that it would be well to find a place within easy reach of the universities, so as to get a ready supply of lecturers; but Bevin wanted to avoid too academic an approach and in any case not to favour Oxford or Cambridge over the newer universities. McNeil wondered whether people from Britain's 'overseas territories' might not attend the courses. Others feared the effect of this on foreign visitors. Bevin thought that the Workers' Travel Association might deal with travel, physical organisation and catering, but obviously not with the curriculum.

At the end of the meeting, it was agreed that the Foreign Office should look for 'a suitable person of wide experience to make the preliminary plans for the establishment of the College, since no one in the Office was sufficiently aware of the problems involved, and the same person or another should later explore the possibility of raising funds'. At this time, it seems, none of those present proposed Heinz Koeppler, despite his 'wide experience' and his running of Wilton Park. Instead, Bevin suggested the 57-year-old Air Vice-Marshal, Sir John Cordingley, who had just retired from the RAF after spending most of the war at the Air Ministry dealing with educational questions. He, however, went on to concern himself chiefly with the welfare of ex-servicemen.

Another name suggested at the meeting in Bevin's room was that of Sir Harold Butler. Formerly Director of the International Labour Office, Butler was Chairman of the British Section of ELEC, the European League for Economic Co-operation, whose other members included Harold Macmillan, Edward Beddington-Behrens, Lord Layton, and General Sir Colin Gubbins, ex-head of the wartime Special Operations Executive. Soon afterwards, Butler was put in charge of a Working Party to carry the discussion further. The Working Party took just over two months to prepare a 3¼-page 'Preliminary Memorandum', completed by April 13, 1948. Despite marked patriotic *hubris*, understandable at the time, it was a wise and thoughtful document. With one startling exception, it also read uncannily like a prospectus for a revivified Wilton Park:

> Britain has taken the lead in drawing Western Europe together in order to promote its recovery from the effects of two disastrous wars and to organize its spiritual defence against the Communist assault. To achieve these ends it is essential that the ideological ties between Britain and the Continent should be reinforced. As a step in this direction it is essential that the other Western countries should realize more vividly than in the past how much the Western way of life owes to Britain and how closely it knits them together with her, not merely in their common fight against the totalitarian doctrine of the East but in their common effort to restore the dynamic power and the prestige of European civilization in the world.
>
> The main purpose of the institution will therefore be to afford a certain number of fellow Europeans from the Continent the opportunity for studying the British contribution to Western civilization at first hand. An understanding of the British conception of representative government, the freedom of the citizen, social security and social justice should create a bond of sympathy between them and this country and a sense of sharing a great common heritage. It is on such psychological foundations that the new Europe must be built.

In retrospect, the notion of benighted 'foreigners' from, say, France, the Netherlands, or any other democratic European country being invited to study 'the British conception of representative government', etc. seems overweening. It reflected, however, a general pride in Britain's having 'stood alone' in 1940, and a genuine concern that France and Italy, in particular, seemed under threat from Communist unrest. There may also have been an anxiety to recruit support domestically – not only from other Departments including the Treasury, but also from the public and from potential large-scale donors. Even so, the Working Party was not beating a crude anti-Communist drum:

It is suggested that emphasis should be laid on this positive and constructive aim of the enterprise rather than on the negative aim of strengthening
the common front against Communism. The former necessarily includes
the latter ... The credit of the institution will stand much higher if looked
upon as a contribution to the spiritual unity of Western Europe rather than
as instrument of anti-Communist propaganda.

Butler's Working Party proposed that students chosen – initially fifty,
later up to a hundred – should be drawn mainly from France, Switzerland,
Benelux, and Scandinavia. It gave careful consideration to their selection,
proposing a national committee of prominent people in each country
concerned, liaising with the local British mission. The students should
preferably be potential high-flyers aged between 25 and 30, not necessarily graduates but with at least a minimum standard of English. Either
significantly or inadvertently, the paper referred only to 'men'. Students
should perhaps pay their own fares to Britain, unless the distance was too
great, but the cost of board and lodging and travel within the country
should be met by 'the institution'. They should live together in one
building 'so as to obtain the benefits of debate and discussion among themselves and with the permanent staff'.

The course should last six months: 'it would be impossible to cover the
ground at all adequately in a shorter time'. It should give 'a practical
insight into the working of democratic institutions in Britain by a combination of theoretical and field work'. This would cover: parliament and
government; the civil service, judiciary and police system '(particularly
from the standpoint of the rights of the ordinary citizen and their protection against arbitrary state action)'; trade unionism, social services and
protection of labour; local government; education and religious life; press
and the BBC. Lectures should be given by active practitioners and illustrated by organised visits.

The 'institution', it was proposed, should not be a Government body:
'any purely official establishment would at once acquire a propagandist
character in the eyes of enemies and even of many friends'. Instead, it
should be 'a national institution', funded not only by government (which
should supply the initial capital and an annual grant for running costs), but
also by the universities, the Trade Union Congress, 'munificent bodies and
individuals', and educational trusts such as the Nuffield Foundation, The
Pilgrims' Trust and the Rockefeller Foundation. It would be controlled by
a Board of Governors of up to nine people; initially, they should be
appointed by the Prime Minister, but with three seats reserved for representatives of the universities, the TUC, and the Foreign Office. After that,

the Chairman would continue to be appointed by the Prime Minister of the day, but the other vacancies would be filled by the Board itself, perhaps subject to prime ministerial approval.

The Board in turn would appoint a Warden, who would recruit a small staff with the Board's approval: the staff could include three or four lecturers or tutors, a Secretary, a Librarian, and a Bursar in charge of establishment and the house staff. Outside specialists would be enlisted to give specific talks. Although of high standard, the course should not be too academic; and the Warden and staff should not be 'too elderly'. Recreation would be provided for, and debates and informal discussions would be encouraged.

To accommodate the 'institution', the Working Party proposed a large house within 1½ hours' distance from London, and accessible to one or two universities and to some large industrial centre such as Birmingham. The house should be able to contain small bed-sitting rooms for 50–100 students and at least two resident members of staff, plus a large hall for meals and debates, four lecture rooms for 30–40 people, a library and reading room, and a recreation room.

Finally, the paper raised the question of naming the 'institution'. It concluded, rather lamely: 'A title is needed which suggests the general aim of the institution, which implies that it is distinctively British and which will make an appeal to foreign ears. These three requirements are not easy to reconcile.' In retrospect, reading the paper's specifications, it seems surprising that no one at once suggested 'Wilton Park'.

A further six weeks elapsed before these ideas were again discussed with Ernest Bevin. Then, on the afternoon of June 1, 1948, he called a meeting with Hector McNeil, Christopher Mayhew, Frank Roberts, C.F.A. Warner, and James C. Wardrop. Their purpose, Wardrop minuted that day, was 'to discuss the recommendations put forward by Sir Harold Butler's Working Party in regard to the financing of their modified version of the "Wilton Park" scheme'. Clearly, the analogy with what some called 'Koeppler's College' had not been lost to view. Bevin, indeed, was 'very anxious for the scheme to be realised as soon as possible: he had in mind more particularly the urgent need to educate German opinion'. But if this might have seemed to imply that Wilton Park itself should take over the whole enterprise, McNeil and Mayhew argued that 'Sir Harold Butler's plans might be upset if the Germans were included … It would probably prove very difficult in practice to get Western Europeans, at any rate for the present, to take part in courses side by side with their former enemies.'

In the meeting with Bevin, this view finally prevailed. 'It was agreed that a separate scheme should be worked out for the Germans and that no publicity should be given to this; it was also agreed that the German scheme must be wholly government-financed.' As to the 'non-German scheme', Bevin said he would have preferred to have it financed entirely out of voluntary contributions, but he undertook to ask the Chancellor of the Exchequer (Sir Stafford Cripps) to put up half the money. Wardrop's minute concluded with the agreement 'that we had better go to the Chancellor of the Exchequer on both schemes simultaneously in spite of the delay to the non-German scheme'.

With Wilton Park so long up and running, there might have seemed little need for 'a separate scheme' to 'be worked out for the Germans'. The proposed new 'institution' had already been nicknamed (by Christopher Mayhew) 'a "Wilton Park"' and (by James Wardrop) a 'modified version of the "Wilton Park" scheme'. Was there a general assumption that Wilton Park would cease operations now that the War Office wanted the grounds and buildings back, or as soon as the last German prisoners-of-war had gone? Was there an unspoken prejudice against it, or against Koeppler? Whatever the explanation, once the competing plans reached the Chancellor of the Exchequer and the Treasury, financial good sense, like Occam's Razor, condemned duplication – or triplication – of effort. The eventual outcome was predictable: a gradual compromise between what Wilton Park was already doing vis-à-vis Germany and the longer-term hope of doing something similar vis-à-vis other countries in Western Europe.

Meanwhile, although Wilton Park's future remained uncertain, it at least had temporary respite. On January 2, 1948, the Director of Quartering at the War Office wrote to tell the Foreign Office:

> In view of your difficulties in moving from Camp 300, Wilton Park, by 20th January, it has been decided that we must make other temporary arrangements to accommodate the Intelligence Corps Depot until Wilton Park can be made available.
>
> I am, therefore, further directed to inform you that we will definitely require Camp 300 to be returned to the War Department by the 1st August, 1948, at the latest.

A possible alternative was Bletchley Park, wartime home of the code-breaking 'Station X'; but Koeppler considered it too far from London. And despite the War Office's draconian letter, some in the Foreign Office believed that they might be able to negotiate using part or even all of Wilton Park. This was confirmed when Koeppler had an informal chat with Colonel Walford, the Head of the School of Military Intelligence, who told him that they were moving down to Sussex and that, so far as he knew, the War Office did not have in mind an alternative tenant for Wilton Park. As Koeppler wrote to Robert Crawford on February 16, 1948:

> The removal of the military both from our present abode and from the School of Military Intelligence would considerably increase the attraction of Wilton Park for our purpose. I think there can be no doubt that next to the title 'Training Centre' the close proximity of a school for what to most Germans has a sinister implication has helped to keep suspicions of our intention alive.

At a pinch, Koeppler believed that Wilton Park could be concentrated in only part of the property, since it would have to cater only for 60–70 students. It transpired that the War Office might well be needing the White House at Wilton Park for the School of Military Administration; in which case Koeppler would have to be content with another camp within the Park. 'It is, however, essential', Robert Crawford pointed out, 'that if there is any question of staying on at Wilton Park itself, then we must have full title to the accommodation, since we cannot be exposed to the sort of alarm which was raised last Christmas.'

The War Office ultimatum, in fact, had helped to generate debate in the Foreign Office about Wilton Park's future as an entity and not just about its premises. On February 17, 1948, Maurice Dean, Deputy Under-Secretary of State in the German Section, asked his boss Sir William Strang, the Permanent Under-Secretary, for his formal approval 'for Wilton Park to continue as at present, at any rate until the end of the financial year 1948–49'. He added: 'The matter can, of course, always be reviewed later.' Strang agreed; so did Sir Ivone Kirkpatrick, with the proviso that 'before we decide to keep on Wilton Park as a permanence we should consider whether we could not spend the money more effectively' – perhaps by bringing over more Germans to mix more in English life. Lord Pakenham endorsed Dean's proposal, but wondered whether the Wilton Park staff might not now need 'higher academic or similar qualifications'. While agreeing with this recommendation, Robert Crawford pointed out on February 25, 1948, that it would be difficult to find good staff if their expected tenure was only some nine months. He hoped, therefore, that the Foreign Office would approach the Treasury in 'an expectation of a minimum life for the Centre of two years'.

Meanwhile, on January 17, 1948, the 13th Wilton Park Course had begun in an atmosphere of moderate hope for the future. Not that the work was problem-free. That Spring, one woman student at Wilton Park was described as 'very unpromising material':

> She is quick-witted, tough, cynical, utterly contemptuous of anyone else's point of view. She 'writes off' Poland, Russia and other 'inferior peoples' with a sneering laugh. She has just that sort of spiritual intolerance that makes gas-ovens possible ... In matters of attendance she is the worst of the group, and she is particularly shameless about being 'ill' on a day when she wants to dine and wine in Town and reappearing in blooming health immediately afterwards.

This was from her Wilton Park tutor's report. Despite its strictures, she was allowed to extend her stay in Britain. A woman official of the German Education Department in the Foreign Office wrote to a colleague in Hamburg on March 4, 1948:

> It would be interesting to learn why she thinks that she was finally given permission to stay. If by any chance she thinks that it was because of her vociferous admiration for England and liberty, she might be told that this almost decided us not to let her stay because it was so obviously phoney. We also feel that an eye should be kept on her in future.

Only two days later, another minor storm blew up. The German Communist trade union newspaper *Tribüne* published an article claiming that German trade unionists had no help from Wilton Park in seeking either contact with their British counterparts or information about British workers' standard of living. It recommended making contact with the chairman of the London Trade Council who, it alleged, had been the only person willing to co-operate.

When these claims were investigated, several facts emerged. One was that German trade unionists had been welcomed at Wilton Park as soon as it was open to civilians, and that organised contacts had been made with their counterparts in Britain. A second was that the German Communist Party and the Communist Trade Union Federation had both imposed conditions on sending people to Wilton Park. They would do so only if representatives were sent from all the Occupation Zones, including that controlled by the USSR. Thirdly, the London Trade Council chairman was himself a Communist.

The whole dispute, in other words, was a skirmish in the emerging 'Cold War'. It corresponded, in particular, to Clement Attlee's move in March 1948 to purge Communists in the Civil Service and to insist that the Trade Union Council should reveal any Communists among its members. On May 5, 1948, in fact, Industrial Relations Branch (Manpower Division) actually warned Education Division that participants on Wilton Park courses should be protected against 'undesirable

influences of doubtful loyalty'. Robert Crawford agreed that when selecting candidates one should avoid those who would exert only a 'subversive
and destructive influence'. But he remained philosophical. 'That *Tribüne*,
the Communist paper, should pick up a story of this kind is, I suppose,
unavoidable.'

A far more promising student, who actually attended the January 1948
Course, was the young Ralf Dahrendorf, later to be variously a university
professor, a government minister, a member of the Commission of the
European Communities, the Director of the London School of Economics,
the Warden of St Anthony's College, Oxford, a knight, and a life peer. In
1948 he was still a Hamburg student of philosophy and classical philology.
Looking back in 1982, he wrote:

> For the young German, armed with a 'Temporary Travel Document'
> issued by the Military Government, an 'Exit Permit', a 'Re-entry Permit',
> and above all the entry visa to the United Kingdom, the train trip to the
> Hook of Holland was a source of great excitement. I was eighteen; it was
> January, 1948, and the War was still very much on most English people's
> minds, especially when they met a German. However, neither this nor the
> stormy Channel night in the bowels of a military transporter could dampen
> the excitement: England, at last! ... England began with one of those
> legendary breakfasts on the Boat Train from Harwich to Liverpool Street.
> Then we were taken across London and out again from Marylebone
> Station to Beaconsfield, or more precisely to Wilton Park, where German
> PoWs and groups of Germans like ours spent six weeks being 're-
> educated'.
>
> This was not my first contact with the country with which I had fallen
> in love even before I first saw it. There were, for example, the officers of
> the occupation army who looked after young Germans, invited them to
> their homes, arranged discussion evenings, and gave them cigarettes and
> even an occasional gin and tonic. Some of them were, and are, famous, such
> as the great Sir Robert Birley, who has done more for liberty in a practical
> and personal way than anyone else I ever met.

This was Birley's last full year as Educational Adviser to the Military
Governor in Germany: in 1949 he was to become Head Master of Eton,
where he had been an assistant master before the war. But throughout his
life he remained deeply involved with Wilton Park, as both a critic and a
candid friend. On March 4, 1948, he heard from Robert Crawford that Sir
Ivone Kirkpatrick had been asking whether the cost of Wilton Park could
be justified, in view of the small numbers attending the courses. The
annual bill was said to be £35,000, of which £10,000 came from the Import
Budget. This seemed to Kirkpatrick a large slice of the total expenditure

on 'education and information services'. He wondered whether it might not be better spent on 'British Cultural and Information Activities' in Germany itself, including the other occupation zones. The British had in fact been sounding out the Americans about sending to Britain Germans from the US zone – partly in the hope of American largesse. Kirkpatrick, via Crawford, put to Birley a tempting question. Should £34,000 or so go on being earmarked for Wilton Park, or would Birley prefer to have £24,000 for new projects in the other zones, with the remaining £10,000 used on further visits to Britain? Crawford added, 'If you felt that we definitely ought to press for Wilton Park, ... then I should be glad to know very quickly, as the sands are running out.'

Birley understood Crawford's argument, but he was also inclined to agree with Kirkpatrick. He was keen for more British people to visit Germany, preferably for a year or even longer; but he wanted to increase the number of young Germans visiting Britain. On March 19, 1948, he wrote a long manuscript letter to Crawford from 8 Cavendish Road, Bournemouth. In view of his later support for Wilton Park, it was startling.

I thought it would be as well if I sent you a letter on the subject of the future of WILTON PARK.

I have come to the conclusion that in all the circumstances we should not be justified in applying for the considerable sum of money that would be necessary to keep it going, (at some other place) after it ceases to be under the control of the War Office.

In the course of the last year or so it has been possible greatly to increase the number of Germans who visit the United Kingdom, other than to Wilton Park, and it seems very probable that that number may be further increased. This bears on the question of the future of Wilton Park in two ways. First, Wilton Park is no longer as strictly necessary as it was when such visits could rarely be organized in any other way. Secondly, as these visits increase, so does the amount of money needed for them, and Wilton Park is inevitably an expensive way of arranging them. We have now to face the position that visits, which we believe would be of great value, and other projects, will have to be given up if Wilton Park is kept going under the Foreign Office.

I have no doubt whatever of the value of Wilton Park in the past. I gave long consideration to the question whether it should not be retained for the future. If there had been no question of alternatives, that is expenditure either on Wilton Park or on other projects and visits, I should have recommended that it should continue. But it was a matter of weighing up the value of alternatives. Even then, I should have been in favour of retaining it, on one condition. I came to the conclusion that it was essential that Wilton Park in the future should be directed by someone with first-hand

110

experience of the problems of post-war Germany. The qualities demanded of a Director are various, and I have been unable to find anyone with the requisite experience who possesses them, and who is prepared to accept the post.

Regarding Koeppler he concluded:

In my view he has done a great piece of work, which has proved to be of real value. It has, however, seemed to me clear that any instructional course now given to Germans should be organized by someone with personal experience of the problems that Germans have to face in their own country. I have been so impressed by the value of Wilton Park in the past, that I have made an earnest search to find someone with that experience, who could carry on the work. As I said, I have failed in this. I have failed because I have deliberately set myself a high standard, bearing in mind the fact that Wilton Park would inevitably be an alternative to other projects.

Was there a hidden agenda here? There had been minor disputes with Koeppler about expenses, and most recently about mock elections now that the presence of German civilians at Wilton Park brought present-day party politics into what had previously been a harmless academic exercise in civics for the prisoners-of-war. But Birley's letter was transparently honest – even confusingly so. Would he have recommended continuing Wilton Park if he could have found his ideal candidate to run it? His quest was real: he had considered at least two possibilities – Harold Nicolson and Harry Wilfred House, the Master of Wellington College, who had lectured at Oxford and served with distinction as an officer in both world wars. But neither met his high criteria, and especially the need for 'a close knowledge of the present position in the Zone now and ... of the tasks on which the Control Commission are engaged'. Could Koeppler have been brought to Germany to familiarise himself with conditions on the spot? Or was Birley inclined to believe, as were some in the Foreign Office and the Treasury, that Wilton Park had outlived its period of greatest usefulness?

Robert Crawford, who had earlier recommended asking the Treasury for a stay of execution lasting two or three years, had perforce to take account of what he called 'Mr Birley's new recommendation'. On March 23, 1948, he discussed it with Lord Pakenham and Sir Ivone Kirkpatrick. 'The decision was taken', in his carefully neutral words, to recommend to the Treasury that Wilton Park should go on until the end of the 1948–49 financial year, and that it should then close 'unless changed circumstances made it desirable to extend its life'. Accordingly, the German Section of the Foreign Office wrote to the Treasury on April 20, 1948 asking for its agreement to continuing Wilton Park until March 31, 1949. Even this was at first queried, partly because Wilton Park sought to raise the level of its courses to university standard, which the Treasury thought 'altogether too ambitious, too costly'. However, after further negotiation over staff and financial economies, the Treasury agreed.

Pakenham meanwhile asked Emanuel Shinwell, the Secretary of State for War, to allow Wilton Park to use 'No. 20 Camp' within the grounds: this was agreed within a few weeks, and before long measures were in hand to adapt the camp. Pakenham also wrote to Koeppler and his staff 'so that they would know where they stood and could make plans for the future'.

'I am afraid that the enclosed will be a big disappointment to you.' So began Pakenham's personal covering note to Heinz Koeppler on March 25, 1948. 'Believe me, (as I know you will), when I say that I admire very much indeed all that you personally have done and shall always be pleased to help you in any way within my power.' The 'enclosed' was an apologetic statement of the conclusions reached two days before:

> The delay has not at all been due to doubt about whether Wilton Park has been doing good work: of that I am quite sure, and all the evidence shows that it has had a salutary effect on the people who have been able to attend it. The decision on whether to go on with it after June is not, however, an easy one, since the total cost of the institution and of bringing German civilians over is high and has to be considered in relation to our other expenditure on German educational activities. Moreover, we are very short of money and there is keen competition for what there is.

With a probable future life of only nine more months, Pakenham went on, it would be unrealistic either to move from Beaconsfield or to recruit new outside staff. He added:

> I repeat that this decision has been taken very reluctantly and I should not like you in any way to think that the value of your own good work and that of your colleagues is impugned by it. You have done magnificently and I am sure that the effect of a stay at Wilton Park on POWs and civilians in Germany will continue to influence them for long after they have returned. It is only our financial position which compels me to say that it is very unlikely that we shall be able to continue it after March 1949.

Perhaps mindful of the adage *'C'est le provisoire qui dure'*, Koeppler wrote back to 'My dear Frank' on April 9, 1948:

> I can assure you that we shall endeavour to do our best during the coming nine months so that if there is 'some unforeseen development which alters

the picture' you may feel satisfied that the work done at Wilton Park justifies its continuation.

Unknown to Koeppler, this raised a highly personal and even agonising
problem. Birley, as his letter of March 19, 1948, made clear, wanted to
replace Koeppler even if Wilton Park continued after the end of the
1948–49 financial year. He had asked Robert Crawford to discuss with
Lord Pakenham 'how Koeppler should be told that he would not be
expected to stay on at Wilton Park after next Spring even if the Centre
continued'. Crawford did consult Lord Pakenham, the Chancellor of the
Duchy of Lancaster, and as he wrote confidentially to Birley on April 14,
1948, 'he has asked for your advice'.

> His view is that he is the proper person to tell Koeppler, but that it would
> be rather embarrassing for him to do so, since he had himself in conversa-
> tion assured Koeppler that if the Centre continued he would undoubtedly
> wish him, Koeppler, to remain in charge. He therefore feels that to tell him
> something different now would both look rather odd and also make it clear
> to Koeppler that it was not really the Chancellor [of the Duchy of
> Lancaster (Pakenham's post)] who had made this decision. He does not
> want to shirk his responsibility, but feels that the alternative of your noti-
> fying Koeppler in the first place should be considered. He would like your
> advice on whether you think it would be right for you, rather than he, to
> write to Koeppler.

Birley answered promptly on April 19, 1948:

> I feel it would really be better if I told him in the first place. There have
> been many criticisms of Koeppler, which were, to my mind, quite unjusti-
> fied. I think Koeppler knows my view on these. I ought to be able to
> persuade him that the decision rests on other grounds and does not reflect
> on his past work. As a supporter of Koeppler's in the past I feel that it is
> right for me to tell him and I strongly recommend that I should do so.

How Koeppler took this can readily be imagined. Whatever his
personal feelings, however, he went on fighting for Wilton Park. He
certainly inspired – and very probably wrote – an account of its work
which appeared in *The Times Educational Supplement* on May 1, 1948. It
concluded:

> The achievement of Wilton Park cannot be measured in a short period. But
> it has now existed long enough to have produced encouraging reactions
> from those who have passed through. The divergence in educational

qualifications, social status, and political and religious views among its students makes it inevitable that such a topical and difficult curriculum should lay itself open to the charge of bias. Most of the students agree on the fairness of the Wilton Park course – a fairness achieved by the encouragement of the expression of all opinions honestly held. The minority who complain of bias are nicely balanced between those who find Wilton Park too 'reactionary' and those who think it too 'radical'. Perhaps the comment most frequently made by those who have passed through is that Wilton Park has helped them to face the national and international problems of to-day with a clearer and more open mind, and to learn that merely being good at one's particular job will not suffice to build a better world.

Koeppler assiduously collected such comments. They included one dated May 19, 1948, from Hanns Manfred Stumpf of Munich, a translated copy of which he made sure reached the Foreign Office:

> The very excellent idea to assemble Germans of all political concepts and from various social backgrounds, has made me more conscious than before, that we live in a community of which we have no adequate knowledge. It may sound absurd: but I had to travel 1,000 km to Wilton Park in order to become acquainted with e.g. representatives of communism, and I am to fill out certain gaps of my knowledge and views which I have not been aware before their attacks. I also had opportunity to become familiar with officials, trade union leaders and politicians through discussions and personal conversations. I emphasize this since within Germany we seem to live in a painful isolation.

Herr Stumpf clearly felt Koeppler in no way handicapped by his lack of what Birley had called 'personal experience of the problems that Germans have to face in their own country'. On May 21, 1948, at Koeppler's request, George Greene wrote a 12-page note epitomising the gist of letters from former students. In one, dated March 10, 1948, Mr and Mrs Klaass Vogt wrote:

> Just as some secret societies are to be recognized by a pin-head in the coat collar, so do old Wiltonians recognize each other by the spirit of tolerance and fair discussion which is imparted to them in six weeks, even though on arrival they behave like hedgehogs, bristling with quills on all sides.

On June 15, Regierungsrat Buening wrote from Stade a report on his attendance at Wilton Park's Course No. 14. This too, in translation, reached the Foreign Office. Buening was wholly positive, especially about the way in which 'Wilton Park transfers German problems into a neutral atmosphere beyond the every-day politics which in Germany always forms the basis for all negotiation between the English and the Germans'. He was especially observant of his fellow-students:

> I noticed that about one week after the commencement of the Course the student body split into three equal groups:- first, those who regarded Wilton Park without any reservations as absolutely positive and who were actively co-operating; secondly, those who regarded Wilton Park without prejudice but who did not actively contribute to its success; and thirdly, those who obviously did not like the Wilton Park atmosphere and for that reason were strongly critical ...
>
> What were the objects of criticism?
> 1. Compulsory attendance at lectures,
> 2. Imperfect objectivity,
> 3. Lack of 'depth' in some of the lectures and papers read.
>
> It is obvious that the first point is unjustified ...
>
> The second point very ingenuously overlooks that objective truth is only to be found with God; that – while in England – one is mainly exposed to English people and English opinions; that Wilton Park follows an educational purpose; and that an institution run by the British Foreign Office is not just a propaganda centre for the KPD, the Soviet Union, the CDU, SPD, or the former German Nationalists ... Wilton Park preserves the greatest possible objectivity in its aims.
>
> The third point is the 'depth' missed in lectures by many Germans; hence the reproach of shallowness.
>
> This criticism is a result of the difference between English and German mentality, of the German inclination for abstractions and absolutely complete logical systematizations which contrast with the British sense for facts ... The person making such a criticism is in fact merely expressing his surprise at not being in Germany when in Wilton Park. In addition, he feels he is not being taken seriously, and he is annoyed when the English Tutor seasons even the most serious problems with funny anecdotes and ironic remarks. He feels hurt in his dignity when wisdom is offered in an easily understandable manner ...
>
> This criticism ... is actually only an expression of the discomfort created by the Wilton Park atmosphere ...
>
> At Wilton Park discussions are continuous and animated. In discussions only mental weapons are of any use ... At Wilton Park a lot is tolerated, except stupidity.

It was a motto of which Koeppler and his colleagues had reason to be proud.

CHAPTER 9

Teach the Free Man

> In the deserts of the heart
> Let the healing fountain start,
> In the prison of his days
> Teach the free man how to praise.
> **W.H. Auden**, 'In Memory of W.B. Yeats' (1940), pt 3.

June 21, 1948 saw a transformation of Wilton Park. It no longer held prisoners-of-war; it was no longer called a 'Training Centre'; it was no longer a War Office responsibility, but 'a detached unit of the Foreign Office, German Section'. During the period July 21, 1948 to March 31, 1949, five courses were to be held, each lasting six weeks, with an average of 60 students per course. The total expenditure for the nine months was to be £19,576. The Ministry of Works was to be responsible for accommodation, and its cost; the Ministry of Supply would provide vehicles, although these would be paid for by German Section. Koeppler was given 'local responsibility', but he and the academic staff were to be under German Section, and an Administration Officer was to be appointed to deal among other things with travel arrangements.

The Administrative Instruction setting out these details was strikingly elaborate for what was still technically a temporary, nine-month expedient – suggesting that German Section had hopes of persuading the Treasury to support Wilton Park for longer. But uncertainty remained. Later that summer, on September 25, 1948, an official from German Section reported to Birley, who was still Educational Adviser in Berlin, that Koeppler had been asking whether Wilton Park was to continue after next March:

He said that he had been offered an appointment at Jamaica University about which he would have to make up his mind within three or four weeks. He also mentioned that one or two of his permanent staff had also received tentative offers of alternative employment ...

I assured him that the question of Wilton Park's future was being very carefully considered at the moment, and that I hoped that a decision would be taken within the next month or two ...

He added that he had heard suggestions (emanating he believed from the Secretary of State) that the college should be thrown open to nationals of other Western European countries and should become a kind of Western Union cultural institution. [This was an echo of Sir Harold Butler's Memorandum.] He expressed the view that this might be a desirable development later on, but not for the next two or three years. He felt that the Germans were at present the least 'house trained' of the European family, and that it would be unthinkable to expect Frenchmen and Belgians etc. to mix and study with them at present on terms of absolute equality at an institution like Wilton Park.

Meanwhile, uncertainty or not, Koeppler had plunged zestfully into running Course No. 16 – the first for 'free people only', as he put it – in July and August 1948. As he wrote in his report:

This has been the first course in our new home and without prisoner students ... We have noticed an increased readiness to co-operate combined with a great decline in the suspicious attitude of the students. No doubt the change in the international situation has helped here; currency reform, improved rations, the air lift to Berlin, have helped to make the students feel that it is worthwhile to think about and work for the reconstruction of Germany in Europe ...

Our new home is still situated within Wilton Park but on a better site free from any lingering suggestion of a prison camp. The students live and work in two modern one-storey buildings, centrally heated, in friendly and airy rooms. Instead of the windowless Nissen huts which used to serve as dining and common rooms we now have pleasant quarters and thanks are due to the Ministry of Works for what they have done for us. This has ensured a happy atmosphere, and a great improvement on our former standards without making Wilton Park in any way luxurious; as a result students have made much more use of our common room, reading room and information room facilities; in short, they have felt at home. While in previous courses most people wandered off to their bedrooms after the evening lecture or other activities, they now are to be found in the common room for reading or discussions, serious and otherwise.

Only now have we realised the tremendous psychological strain produced by having as students free people and prisoners side by side. It is much easier to establish friendly contact with 65 rather than 300 students, and the many personal problems of the prisoners are no longer acting as a brake on the studies of the students ... On this, as on all earlier courses, students were more sceptical of our intentions in their first week than in their last but the change came much quicker than in previous courses and was easier to accomplish ... We gained the impression that there is now a greater diffusion of knowledge about Wilton Park and its aims amongst the social and political groups from whom our students are drawn.

Koeppler and his staff had also made changes, reducing the number of compulsory lectures, giving students more chance to read papers and introduce seminars, and setting up working parties to prepare reports on special subjects, as well as mixing in a weekly Dutch visitor, and encouraging contacts with English people. Greater flexibility had reduced absenteeism: 'There was hardly any inclination to interpret "democracy" and "academic freedom" to mean licence to do as one pleases.' However, Koeppler had reservations about two groups of students:

The first group who with a few exceptions have been persistently unsatisfactory are the very young journalists. This is not really surprising in view of the type of person who before currency reform decided to go into journalism. Most of them are bright and sharp witted enough but they are sadly under-educated and exhibit an almost complete lack of social responsibility ... The second group who appear unsuitable for very different reasons are the elderly trade union and party representatives. They are as a rule too set in their ways to be able to profit by the work here.

Koeppler also noted that 'concerning the composition of this course the tendency of the last few courses towards the Right in politics has continued. While it is difficult to be certain it seems safe to say that the majority of the students inclined towards the C.D.U. and the F.D.P.' Willy-nilly, in fact, the polarisation of opinion in Germany affected life at Wilton Park. Partly because of Communist reluctance, partly because of the professions from which participants were selected, the political Left had begun to be under-represented.

More particularly, Koeppler noted on the 17th Course, in September and October 1948, Right-wingers had changed. 'Their greater self-confidence and their greater sense of security has stiffened their attitude.' The Left, by contrast, 'feels rather less sure of the part it has to play in the reconstruction of Germany'. At the beginning of the September–October course, many of the participants were aggressive and almost hostile – partly because one of them had received a document stating that he had been sent on a 'course for political rehabilitation'. No wonder this caused suspicion. Only gradually were sceptics disarmed:

> I had some misgivings as I learnt that for this Course about sixty Germans would travel together to England and would live together in one camp. I had painful memories of the student camps of bygone days with P.T. before breakfast, hoisting of flags and propaganda sessions; and these memories somewhat spoilt my hitherto pleasant expectations.

So said a participant on the 17th Course, Dr Gertrud Harms, a member of the Senate of Bremen and a lecturer on the history of art. Broadcasting on Radio Bremen on November 28, 1948, she confessed that when she was first invited, she had little idea of what Wilton Park involved:

> During the journey from Hamburg to the Hook of Holland it began to look as if the worst might really come to pass. We were shunted about from one track to another, and we had eight hours wait in the Hook of Holland in none too comfortable circumstances. I began to feel less and less like my previous idea of a guest of the British Foreign Office. The 'democratisation' (as some of my colleagues, assembled together on the train from all parts of Bizonia, were calling it) was beginning with a vengeance.
>
> These first impressions, however, altered rapidly as we reached England and landed at Harwich. My confidence and the pleasant expectations for my six weeks stay in England began to return as we were welcomed, given tea and shown to comfortable motor coaches for our drive along the tidy English roads to Wilton Park ...
>
> The old English estate has a notice at the entrance to the drive reading: 'German Section, Foreign Office'. This made me think that it must be an indoctrination camp after all. But when I saw the well constructed buildings, with pleasant rooms, wonderful bathrooms and showers, a big hall, common rooms for reading, writing, and listening to the wireless and a library with all the books we can't get in Germany, the barometer began to rise again.

Gertrud Harms went on to describe the contents of the course, including six lectures and discussions on each of the five main subjects: European history from 1648 to the present day, the Great Powers, European Economic Problems, Individual and State, Problems of Modern Politics – plus working parties on trade union questions and education. Of the extra-mural visits – including appointments with the political parties and trade unions – she added:

It is worthwhile noting that these visits never took place in the old manner of 'sightseeing parties for foreigners', but nearly always began with a reception which gave one the opportunity to talk to men and women of importance in every sphere (and it was astonishing how many found time to talk to us) and to ask all sorts of questions. There were mostly talks before and after our visits to complete the picture.

Of Wilton Park she said:

In spite of the tradition that the guest should preserve politeness towards his host, we met every Monday ... for a so-called 'grumbling hour' in which every participant could voice perfectly freely any criticisms he had to make of Wilton Park or of the way in which the Course was carried out. Many of the participants seized upon this opportunity and with typical German thoroughness exploited it, often in the most uninhibited manner ...

There was opportunity enough for plain speaking. Take, for instance, the series of historical lectures. One could have prefaced these by the motto: 'What you call the spirit of the times is mostly your own point of view of politics.' When we think of the stuff which was served up to us in bygone times as an interpretation of history! But for all the objectivity even here in Wilton Park history was always tinged with the imperialistic English point of view, especially when the lecturers were English historians. This was most instructive for us, and gave us all the more opportunities for attack; though we were often robbed of these opportunities by the praiseworthy tolerance of the lecturers and their astounding faculty for self-criticism.

Gertrud Harms's more general impressions of Britain in that still postwar period were perhaps surprising to her radio listeners. With only £1 a week pocket money, she took to hitch-hiking, and enjoyed talking with her travelling hosts:

I found again and again that English friendliness towards Germany was very much greater than I had expected. The most negative reception I ever encountered on these journeys was one of reserved politeness. I found out also that the difficult economic conditions of England, about which so much has been said, had not been in the least exaggerated. Even in 'Merry Old England' there is a great deal of rationing of food and clothing, only with the difference that in England there is hardly any black market. I must admit that the self-discipline of the English is, for us, quite astounding. However, one should not forget that conditions in England during and after the war were not so chaotic as in Germany and that therefore the general moral level has not sunk so low in England as it has in our country.

Altogether, she was well pleased with what she called 'the most inter-esting and exciting experience I have had for years'. Not the least valuable aspect of it had been the chance to meet and freely talk with, 'on neutral ground, fellow Germans from the most varied social, political and confes-sional groups'. These included: 'University teachers, trade unionists, school teachers, party functionaries, government officials, journalists, radio reporters, welfare officers, and so on.' She had a proviso:

> German and English alike regretted that two groups were missing, not only in this Course but in most others: communists and employers. What was the reason for this? It appears that the communists have, in general, been very reluctant to take part – and the reason for this you can think out for yourself. The employers seem to have been prevented from coming by the difficulty of leaving their business behind for six whole weeks. With the exception of these two groups practically every type of homo sapiens was represented among the 42 men and 18 women who were gathered together with the firm intention (for such was the impression – particularly in the first weeks) of giving the English a good big piece of their mind …
>
> Every free minute was taken up by discussions between the various groups of Germans. It was remarkable and gratifying that as the Course went on these debates between right and left became steadily more objective and more tolerant, and this applied to all except a few extremists who saw in Wilton Park a battle ground for their own political aggression.

Concern about 'extremists' was very pervasive in the later months of 1948. On September 1, the West German Parliamentary Council met in Bonn to draw up the Basic Law that became the Federal Republic's Constitution. The East–West division of the country was becoming a definite split. Communists in West Germany now seemed *ipso facto* suspect; and the German Christian Democrats in particular were reluctant to see them invited to Wilton Park. Education Branch remained liberal: its policy was that anyone who might benefit from Wilton Park should go there, irrespective of party membership. But the German Political Branch of the Foreign Office rather agreed with the Christian Democrats. On December 20, 1948, it announced: 'It has been decided that there is little point in allowing such people to occupy places which might be more prof-itably filled.'

'Such people' of course meant primarily Communists. But restiveness among Germans was stirring elsewhere in the political spectrum. The notion of a West German contribution to defence was to be debated hotly from 1950 onwards in the context of the proposal for EDC, the European Defence Community or European Army. But already, two years before, what was then and later called 'German re-armament' came under discussion at Wilton Park. In Heinz Koeppler's report on Course No. 18 (November–December, 1948), he noted that a clear majority of the participants were against the idea. But a small group had shown stubborn and almost arrogant nationalism. Nor were all its members from the Right: some Berlin Socialists were more nationalistic than the representatives of the CDU. They seemed to believe that the Western Allies knew 'that they had made a mess, had no arguments against the German case', and would now be coming 'cap in hand' to seek German help against the Soviets. However, when the Wilton Park tutors argued against them, they were taken by surprise. Towards the end of the course, 'most of them were seeing things in a more proper perspective'.

Satisfactory as this may have seemed, in the later months of 1948 the longer-term fate of Wilton Park still hung in the balance. The Treasury's agreement for it to continue was still valid only until March 31, 1949; and even within the Foreign Office certain elements seemed to be sceptical. On October 5, 1948, to try to resolve the issue, the Deputy Director of Education Branch, Herbert Walker, circulated all the British offices in Germany concerned with the selection of candidates. Should Wilton Park continue? And, if so, what changes to its curriculum should be made in view of the forthcoming Occupation Statute, which would alter German relations with the Occupying Powers?

On October 14, 1948, Miss R. Ostermann of Political Branch wrote a critical Minute: 'It is clear', she claimed, 'that the need for Wilton Park in its present form is becoming less each month ... By March 1949 Wilton Park will have completely outlived its purpose.' The £34,000 or so per year that it cost would be better used on private hospitality and on 'an Information Centre or Anglo-German Centre, conveniently situated in London'. Duncan Wilson, the Head of Political Branch, did not entirely agree. 'I am sure', he wrote, 'that the Wilton Park organisation in any case needs a change ... I am not sure, however, that for the next year it may not have, in revised form, a useful function.' The Military Governor's Political Adviser also thought in terms of an eventual Anglo-German centre, with no stigma of 're-education'. But, in the meantime, Wilton Park was running well, and he doubted whether it could be replaced by March 1949. Amid this debate, Birley and the Head of Education Branch, Brigadier R.V. Hume, set their sights on at least preserving Wilton Park for one more financial year – i.e. until the Spring of 1950. On October 19, 1948, Hume sent his Deputy Herbert Walker to Wilton Park to see for himself.

A three-day visit was enough to convince Walker that Koeppler and his team were doing a valuable job. 'I think I should state at once', he reported on October 25, 'my general conclusion that ... we should be lacking in common sense if we abandoned this valuable experiment and permitted Wilton Park to come to an end in March, 1949.' The suggestion had been made, he noted, that it should 'assume an international character and even become a sort of Western Union College' – again a reference to Sir Harold Butler's work for Ernest Bevin. 'The best advice seems here to make haste slowly.' Walker proposed instead that Wilton Park 'might assume gradually a more international character', with more Dutch lecturers and some German-speaking English students (as Koeppler had mooted). Courses, he thought, should be more flexible, with shorter stints for VIPs and occasional courses for people in their twenties. The selection of candidates, he stressed, required 'particular care'. 'In the present course a freelance journalist of Nazi sympathies with an able and persuasive manner is a centre of disturbance. It was gratifying to note that his following now appeared to be small, and that his contributions to discussion were received by the majority with impatience.' Most students, in fact, were positive. 'A senior Local Government official said to me: "I came to Wilton Park full of prejudices, particularly the prejudice that I should be subject to indoctrination. How could it be otherwise in an institution run by a Government department? I have been on the look-out the whole time for propaganda, and now, in the fifth week, I know it will not come. It is most extraordinary."' The basic truth about Wilton Park was that it involved 'six weeks of citizenship and politics with the emphasis on realism and impartiality and with an encouragement to students to think independently and to examine statements before accepting them'.

> It brings together ordinary German men and women, who in the usual run of exchange visits are overlooked. In a real sense these are the people who should matter in a future democratic Germany, for it is axiomatic in a truly democratic community that the impulse should come from below and not be imposed from above. The numbers affected by Wilton Park are, of course, extremely small (which underlines the necessity for the most careful selection), but there is something to be said for the claim that the course is making a contribution, important, if modest, to what is referred to at Wilton Park as 'priming the pump' of German democracy.

With Walker's clean bill of health, Duncan Wilson was able to assure Koeppler privately that he was recommending the continuation of Wilton Park. Koeppler wrote to him on October 27, 1948, restating his impassioned case for the task; and two days later he wrote a personal note to Walker too. British policy, he recalled, aimed at creating a stable, prosperous, and peaceful Europe. This would require a powerful contribution from the Germans. The policy of Wilton Park – whose cost per student per course was £56.19s.2d – was not to try to turn them into 'good little Englishmen': 'we rather look down on French attempts to inculcate "*l'esprit français*".' Even so, many Germans seemed to feel like 'benighted niggers who must be educated to learn from the higher civilisation of this country'. Such a 'colonial approach' was unjustified and unsound. The purely technical, vocational aspects of German education were not the problem. Where the Germans lagged behind was in citizenship, in their duties as '*Staatsbürger*':

> If one lesson has emerged from my work at Wilton Park it is just this, that there is no hope of a better Germany unless the people in responsible positions grasp that being good at one's particular job is not sufficient for the establishment and maintenance of a free society. That Germany should become such a society is not only a German but also a British interest.

In London, too, Foreign Office opinion had swung in favour of maintaining Wilton Park. On December 15, 1948, W.R. Iley of the German Education Department visited Koeppler. Among other things, they discussed security of tenure for the staff. They agreed that action would have to await a formal decision on Wilton Park's future. But, as Koeppler wrote to Iley the next day:

> I need hardly stress that from every point of view the longer the period to which the Foreign Office are going to commit themselves the easier it will be to plan ahead. I am not only thinking of the effect on the staff but very much also on the attitude of the selecting bodies in Germany. I am sure that one reason why not sufficient attention has been given to the selection has been the feeling in CCG [Control Commission, Germany] that Wilton Park was coming to an end anyway and that it was not worth taking very much trouble over it. The decision to establish it, at any rate in the first instance, for a period of, say, five years would change this attitude and would also raise the status of Wilton Park in the eyes of the Germans.

This, no doubt, was typical Koeppler optimism. Equally characteristic was his raising again a subject that he had first broached two years before, in a letter to COGA, on November 17, 1946. Then, he had written:

> Ever since Wilton Park began I have been wondering whether it would not be helpful to have an advisory body for Wilton Park composed of men who are prominent in education and in politics. The expected arrival of civilians and the possibility of this side of our work assuming increasing importance would appear to make it even more desirable to have such a body at our

disposal. I am not afraid of [for?] the liberty which I have been fortunate enough to enjoy concerning policy and curriculum ... I hope, and I feel confident, that the creation of such a body would not interfere with it and from the point of view of parliamentary and public interest it might be advantageous to have their support.

The names he had then suggested had included Lord Beveridge, Lord Lindsay of Birker, R.A. Butler, R.C.K. Ensor, Patrick Gordon Walker, Harold Nicolson, Sir Arthur Salter, and Major-General Strong.

Returning to the charge now, Koeppler wrote: 'As I told you, I feel very strongly that we should obtain such a council. It clearly must not interfere with Foreign Office control of Wilton Park but it may be a help if there were ever questions in Parliament or in the Press on the level and the objectivity of our work. I do not think there will be, but one never knows.'

That same day, December 16, 1948, the Foreign Office sent an urgent telegram to the Control Commission in Berlin:

We are still anxiously awaiting to receive your recommendations for the continuation of Wilton Park after 31st March 1948 [*sic*: clearly a misprint for 1949], as we have officially received no such recommendation to date. We have been unable to include any provision for Wilton Park in the draft of the 1949/50 estimate which has already been forwarded to the Treasury. It is imperative that we should receive your recommendations without further delay, otherwise we may be out of time to obtain financial authority.

The answer came by telegram four days later: a despatch was on its way by bag:

The main recommendations affecting the financial aspect are:-
    (a) that Wilton Park should continue at least for financial year 1949–50;
    (b) that plans should be made for its retention on a longer than a year to year basis.

The despatch, signed by Sir Brian Robertson, Military Governor and Commander-in-Chief, endorsed Walker's Report (though adding that 'it might be a pity' to submerge Britain's particular contribution 'by endeavouring to create a pronouncedly international atmosphere'.) 'I strongly recommend', Robertson went on, 'that an early decision should be taken to continue Wilton Park after the end of the financial year 1948/49. In the interests of continuity and of security for the staff it would be greatly preferable that plans should be made for a continuation of the institution on some thing longer than a year to year basis.'

Nor was that all. 'I further suggest', concluded Robertson, 'that an Advisory Council of men and women of high academic standing in the United Kingdom should be set up to advise on Wilton Park and to assist it in making the right contacts with British education.'

Birley's, Walker's, and Robertson's pleas were successful: Walker's had been forwarded to Ernest Bevin himself. On January 3, 1949, W.R. Iley of the German Education Department minuted Robert Crawford, now of the German Finance Department, with a long brief for approaching the Treasury. It cited:

> It is the general belief that the greater independence which Germany is to enjoy in the political and economic sphere under the Occupation Statute is a reason for increasing rather than diminishing our efforts to influence the trend of German events by educational means. This view is held not only in the Foreign Office and the Control Commission (B.E.) but is shared by representative organisations of our Allies, who have interested themselves in German Education. It was endorsed in a resolution at an international conference convened in November by the Educational Adviser [Birley], and attended by representatives from Norway, Sweden, Denmark, Holland, Belgium and Switzerland, as well as observers from the French and U.S. Military Governments. This same conference emphasised the value of the work done by Wilton Park and strongly urged that it should be enabled to continue after the end of the present financial year.
>
> In recommending the continuance of Wilton Park, I have discussed with the German Political Department its possible relationship with the Scheme for a Western Union College which is under consideration. I find that the two schemes are so dissimilar that there can be no question of the one superseding the other, at any rate in the at all immediate future ...
>
> If possible we would like to obtain agreement for the continuation of Wilton Park for a longer period than one year.

On January 7, 1949, Crawford wrote along these lines to the Treasury. It replied tartly – and within twenty-four hours – over the signature of D. O'Donovan:

> Your letter of the 7th January about Wilton Park *has been very carefully considered here* [my italics], and we have felt very much doubtful about continuing the expenditure of money and manpower which would be involved ...
>
> We are also inclined to think that the benefit conferred by the course will wear very thin in a short time. Such a course cannot be anything but an obvious piece of 're-education', and it seems pretty clear, even apart from recent trends in German opinion, that a country of the standing of

Germany is bound sooner or later to react pretty vigorously against the idea of re-education.

Having delivered its verdict on German psychology and politics from the vantage-point of Great George Street, London, the Treasury response continued:

> In view, however, of the weight of opinion which you bring to bear on your side, we are willing to sanction the continuance of Wilton Park, on the understanding that you will agree to bring it to an end not later than 31st March 1950. We hope that you will be able to confirm that you agree to accept this condition. I do not think that it has at any time been argued that Wilton Park should be a continuing institution, and there would seem to be a risk that unless some time limit is set, there may be pressure to continue it for further periods. I imagine that you will agree that it is better to finish with an experiment of this kind before and not after it has become apparent that it has outlived its purpose.

Koeppler's reaction to this grudging reprieve was immediate and impassioned. He was vexed, at the same time, by similar sentiments from elsewhere. On February 15, 1949, *The Times* published an editorial suggesting that in Germany there was 'the feeling that those who co-operate with the Western Allies are in some ways Quislings'. Writing that day to W.R. Iley in the German Section of the Foreign Office, Koeppler commented:

> Our experience shows clearly that this view is being spread by people who belong, again in the words of *The Times*, 'to the very class which welcomed Hitler and made possible two world wars' ... In the specific case of Wilton Park I would go so far as to maintain that closing down in 1950 would be interpreted by the positive elements in Germany either as a lack of faith or of interest in German reconstruction ... Perhaps the best proof of this is the question of finance. When there were rumours in the British Zone that Wilton Park may have to close for financial reasons, we got letters from former students in influential positions offering to start a subscription amongst interested German organisations to help and pay for Wilton Park. Members of the Landtag of Rhineland Westphalia and of other Diets belonging to the three main non-communist parties, SPD, CDU, FDP, have told me that they felt sure that once German currency is convertible their parties would be in favour of Germany making a contribution to Wilton Park, a view supported by some senior officials of both Hanover and Schleswig Holstein, who have been on the course.

On February 19, 1949, commenting on the Treasury's scornful (and long outdated) remarks about 're-education', Koeppler wrote a virulent denial that this had ever been Wilton Park's aim:

> The enthusiasm so prevalent at the end of the war for 're-educating the enemy' is rightly and rapidly disappearing as people realise how futile the assumptions were on which much of this process was based. It is, therefore, perhaps inevitable that observers who have no first hand knowledge nor a very detailed picture of the aims, methods and syllabus of Wilton Park, should include Wilton Park in their scepticism concerning re-education as an instrument of British foreign policy. Wilton Park, like other pioneering experiments, suffers from the inclination of most people to fit something new into familiar categories.
>
> A definition of re-education in the pejorative sense in which it is generally used now would appear necessary. I would say that people who are against re-education think of it, not without justification, as the work of enthusiasts who with little understanding of their own history and institutions and none of Germany's tried to preach to the pagan barbarians who were expected to listen because they were beaten. While I do not think that this definition is a caricature of much that has been undertaken I would claim emphatically that it is not and never has been a description of the work at Wilton Park. Right from the beginning we banned at Wilton Park the very word 're-education'; we also objected to the term 'Training Centre' which was, happily, abolished officially a year ago and we have always pointed out that the word 'democracy' should only be used in our discussions after its various meanings had been understood.

But the problem, for Koeppler, was not just one of vocabulary. Whatever expression was used, there was a need to be met:

> Unless we accept the dogma of historical materialism and explain all politics by the automatic working of economic forces we cannot deny that political ideas in the widest sense of this term have an influence on the political activities of both individuals and nations. When such activities lead to wars they become a perfectly legitimate object of concern for those affected. It is the painful and direct experience of German politics from which this country is still suffering that provides to my mind the justification for a British effort to stimulate a healthy change in Germany's political outlook. This change is not likely to come automatically as a result of a lost war, nor will it be helped by the present economic difficulties and by the quarrel between the occupying powers.

So, despite the Treasury's argument that 're-education' was now inappropriate (as for Koeppler it always had been), this was no reason for abolishing Wilton Park. He took the opportunity to repeat a horse-racing metaphor he had used many times before:

> Granted that the pedigree of 're-education' proves it to be by ignorance out of arrogance and that it is therefore right to scratch, the fact remains that something must take its place. For the present prevalent German attitude to politics is dangerous to Germany and to Europe alike. It is therefore a British interest to help Germany to face the national and international problems of today with a clearer and more open mind ...
>
> This was the basic reason for inviting to Wilton Park people from Germany whose positions enable them to play a part in the shaping of German public opinion. The argument in favour of the continuation of Wilton Park is not only based on the reason mentioned above, valid as this reason remains, but also on another which follows logically from it. I refer, of course, to the argument generally accepted now, that Germany must form part of Western Union.

'Western Union' was not, of course, Western European Union (WEU), set up in 1954 after the rejection of the European Defence Community (EDC). At the time, however, the term 'Western Union' was loosely used to refer to the growing cohesion of the West – in Europe and, eventually, with North America – as the Cold War divided it from the East. The emerging German Federal Republic was not to contribute to Western defence until it joined WEU in 1954 and NATO in 1955. But there was a growing desire not only to anchor Germany to the rest of Western Europe but also to harness its potential for greater prosperity and security. How to achieve this remained uncertain: there were doubts and fears as well as potential benefits. But Koeppler was convinced a solution must be found. Although the form and degree of 'Western Union' remained to be determined, Koeppler's reasoning closely resembled that of Jean Monnet when in 1950 he proposed the European Coal and Steel Community and EDC: 'Germany's contribution is needed for the well being of Western Union, and the legitimate fears of new German aggression can only be overcome by making Germany a part of the greater unit.' This in turn, as Monnet himself knew, required psychological change. Koeppler saw the need for it in Germany as well as in her neighbours:

> Western Union really demands Western Union mindedness on the part of the participating nations. This is a difficult problem in all countries but particularly so, for historical and sociological reasons, in Germany. The interests of British foreign policy and of Western Union will not be served if Germany's enthusiasm for such union is based solely on the belief that

thereby she can escape all the awkward consequences of the late war or on the hope that once she enters Western Union it will be only a question of time before she dominates it.

Six months earlier – perhaps in response to those advising Ernest Bevin – the Head of Education Branch, Brigadier R.V. Hume, had written a memorandum suggesting that the courses at Wilton Park should gradually become more international. The same idea had been taken up by his Deputy Herbert Walker after his visit there in October 1948: Walker had suggested taking on more Dutch lecturers. From the Foreign Office in London, the Head of German Education, Robert Crawford, agreed. 'If anything of the Wilton Park character were required after March 1950 it would be something of a wider international basis.'

Koeppler, in fact, had been thinking along these lines. His broader horizons were clear from his concern for 'European Union'. But he had long backed his ideas with practical action to extend the scope of Wilton Park from purely bilateral, Anglo–German relations. As early as July 1947, he had increased the contacts with Switzerland initiated on previous courses. At that time, under a project known as *Schweizer Bücherhilfe* (Swiss Book Aid), 42 Swiss had come to Britain to give talks in POW camps. Some of them had visited Wilton Park: they had included the Federal Judge Hans Schultz. And Koeppler's thoughts about Europe beyond Germany had emerged in the 50 or so pages of the privately printed review that was issued at the end of each course. Initially known as *Der Anruf* (*The Call*), this had been retitled *Die Brücke* (*The Bridge*), then *Wilton Park*, until the fourth joint POW/civilian course (July 9 – August 7, 1947, the first with women members), when it began to appear with the *Wilton Park Review*, intended as an alumni magazine. The issue following the fifth joint POW/civilian course (August 30 – October 11, 1947, the second with women members) had had as its theme 'The Uniting of Europe'. In the preface, Koeppler had written that Europe could no longer afford 'the luxury of thirty absolutely sovereign nation/states', and that 'the uniting of Europe does not deepen the gulf between East and West, but bridges it'.

By 1949, the hope of directly bridging East and West had faded; but unity in Western Europe was nevertheless to prove, forty years later, the catalyst for freedom in the East. Meanwhile, the national frontiers to be transcended lay in Western Europe; and Wilton Park, as Koeppler noted, was already responding to these new needs:

There has been much development at Wilton Park in the three years of its existence. Changes in the subjects, changes in the working methods, particularly the participation of Dutch and now of Swiss people, the planned inclusion of some English people as students, all these developments are designed to stimulate the Germans more effectively to become good citizens and good Europeans. This is clearly a very different thing from turning them into tools of the occupational authorities, a view which can only be taken by Germans who are either ignorant or malevolent or both.

Although other nationalities were now included, Koeppler had not wholly embraced the idea of an 'international college' as mooted by Sir Harold Butler's working party. The Germans remained his primary concern. This was natural enough in view of his origins, upbringing, and wartime efforts, as well as his experience over the past three years:

Our methods of work are not those which have made 're-education' a term of abuse. We do not lecture our students; in fact there are no lectures as such, only introductions to discussion. The students carry much of the work, by reading papers, forming working parties and by their active participation in the discussions both at Wilton Park and at the many conferences which form the most important part of our extra-mural activities. Such discussions lead to the conclusion that the individual German must assume responsibility for the future of his country within the greater European unit. For Germany's intellectual reconstruction must be done by the Germans themselves; all that can be done from this country is to prime the pump.

But Heinz Koeppler could not help reverting to wider issues:

Western Union will be effective only if it is based on member states with free parliamentary institutions. Even well meaning Germans have two profound doubts: one is whether such institutions can provide efficient government and the other whether even if the first be the case in this country it can ever be so in Germany. Our curriculum in both its internal and extra-mural parts endeavours to show by the example of this country that a free democracy can work efficiently. In doing this we never hide the great difficulties. This is the only way to gain their confidence. It also answers the fatal German demand for absolute perfection which has played such havoc with practical politics in Germany. We demonstrate that it is more realistic, and in the long run even more moral, to practice that form of government which on balance is the least bad form rather than to look for a non-existing 'best' form of government and to end up in a destructive dictatorship. This realistic approach has the advantage of helping to answer the second German doubt, viz. that democracy works in Britain because

131

she is supposed to have had it since 1215 but that it could not be started in Germany now. This doubt is perhaps not always allayed by schemes to show the high lights and the smooth running of British institutions.

This last remark was perhaps a dig at the British Council. There was undoubtedly pressure at this time to devolve some of the Foreign Office's educational role in Germany on to the Council, whose task was promoting Britain's image abroad generally, and to the newly established British Relations Boards (BRB), also responsible for projecting British policy and points of view. The BRB's President was the Military Governor with the Political Adviser as chairman, and the Educational Adviser as one of the members. At the same time, the German Education Department was under Treasury pressure to reduce its budget; and on February 10, 1949, Policy Instruction No. 40 reduced the British role in German education to 'observing, assisting and advising' rather than control.

It was in this shifting situation that W.R. Iley of German Education Department told Birley that even in that Department there were some people who sympathised with the Treasury's argument for wanting to close Wilton Park. It was, he thought, highly dangerous: 'the same argument is being used for disbandment of Education Branch in favour of the British Council and other similar bodies, and we could scarcely accept the argument against Wilton Park without weakening our case all along the line'. In these circumstances, the defence of Wilton Park was highly relevant, and Koeppler's words were apt:

> The purpose of Wilton Park is to stimulate civic responsibility and now more than ever to encourage German public opinion to help make Germany a good European. The evidence coming out of Germany shows that they cannot do it all by themselves. It is a British interest to help in the process; the problem is how. I would claim that the work of Wilton Park is aimed at the very core of this problem. I do not claim that our methods are the most effective under ideal conditions; for specific cases others are certainly better. But Wilton Park is particularly well adapted to reach all influential sections of German society including those who for reasons of language and social background are not often invited abroad although their political importance is very real ...
>
> In fact, Wilton Park by providing a link for Germany with the efforts to which the Brussels Powers have committed themselves under Article III of the Treaty of Brussels, is making a contribution towards the ultimate acceptance of Germany into Western Union.

What Koeppler called 'the evidence coming out of Germany' and the testimony of 'those who have come to Wilton Park' had been accumulating for some time. Many Wilton alumni were, or were to become, well-known. As well as Ralf Dahrendorf, the January 1948 course had included Willi Weyer, then President of the Young Liberals and later an FDP politician and President of the German Sports League. A few months earlier, the future CDU leader Rainer Barzel, then a journalist on the *Rhein-Ruhr-Zeitung*, had attended the eleventh course; 'Ideology or Politics' was the title of an article he had contributed to the wall newspaper, attacking 'any totalitarianism from Right or Left'. A number of other Wilton alumni also made their names in German politics, including Karl-Wilhelm Berkhan, Ilse Elsner, Wilhelm Kaisen, Heinrich Köppler, Lauritz Lauritzen, Ernst Majonica, and Hans-Jochen Vogel. The same was true of many of the POW students: Fritz Borges, Erhard Dornberg, Horst Grabert, Johann Baptist Gradl, Karl Hemfler, Hermann Höcherl, Heinrich Kröller, Gerhard Richter, Oskar Rummel. As Frank Roberts later remarked (after serving as British Ambassador to the Federal Republic): 'I was continually finding those who had been at Wilton Park in key government posts, particularly at the regional and local level. There is no doubt that Wilton Park has had an impact on the post-war development of Germany.'

On March 1 and 2, 1949, Herbert Walker convened and chaired a special meeting in Bad Rothenfelde of all the British offices, plus some Germans on the second day, to discuss Wilton Park's future. Walker was now Director of Education Branch, since Brigadier Hume had moved to become Birley's Deputy; and he was determined to look at the problem root and branch. Formally, the Treasury had yet to give its financial approval for continuance beyond the end of the month, but it was 'probable' that it would agree to one more year, until March 31, 1950.

Koeppler, who came from Britain for the occasion, summarised the essence of his February 19 paper on – or against – 're-education'. He put forward, as a point for discussion, the benefit of including other nationals. The Dutch were coming regularly; so had some French, Belgians, and Americans; and the next course would include some Swiss. As soon as the continuance of Wilton Park was assured, he hoped to introduce British students as full-time members of each course.

On the second day, Walker raised three main questions. First, were there enough people in Germany to go on benefiting from Wilton Park? Secondly, how could those who knew it influence the choice of candidates? Thirdly, how could Ministries, firms, and so on be persuaded to send colleagues to Wilton Park while continuing to pay their salaries?

To the first question, the Germans present gave a resounding Yes – and added that the range of participants should be broadened to include doctors and lawyers as well as businessmen. In response to the second question, the meeting recommended that a committee of interested individuals and organisations be formed to help the regional British Relations Boards select candidates. Thirdly, to tempt more key Germans to attend, the meeting proposed – as Walker had in his October 1948 report on Wilton Park – special shorter, ten-day sessions alongside the full six-week courses.

This last suggestion helped to defuse a recurrent complaint – not only from the Germans – that Koeppler's courses were 'too academic' and that the programmes were overloaded. As always, Koeppler denied the charge; and in the end the majority agreed with him. The other suggestion that Walker had made in his October report – of special courses for people between 20 and 30 – was rejected, because it was felt that mixing age-groups was beneficial; but it was agreed that most participants should be under 35.

To help British officials in Germany to select candidates, the meeting decided to issue more elaborate documentation for those recruiting candidates. As well as the programme of the previous course, this was to contain the text of Gertrud Harms's Radio Bremen broadcast of November 28, 1948, and an Introduction by Heinz Koeppler. Never one to waste a well-argued text, Koeppler incorporated in it the whole of what he had written about 're-education' two weeks before. He prefaced it with an invitation:

> I would like to say first of all that the best way of getting to know Wilton Park is to come and see it. We are only one hour's journey from London and we are always very glad to welcome members of CCG [Control Commission, Germany] who are interested in our work.

The meeting also agreed that exhibitions about Wilton Park should be laid on at Britain's information offices in Germany. Beyond emphasising that its courses would now, naturally, concentrate on preparing for the future, no great changes were proposed – except in the selection process. Hitherto, candidates had been chosen at *Land* level by a committee normally chaired by the Regional Governmental Officer: now, it was to be done jointly by regional and local British Relations Boards, supported at *Land* level by a Wilton Park committee of prominent citizens in contact with employers. These would be advised by a local committee composed of former students. Regional officials were to invite Mayors or Ministers-President to put forward candidates; but, so long as Wilton Park was financed from public funds, the British Relations Boards were to have the final decision.

All this looked like a substantial moral victory over Treasury and other critics. On March 12, 1949, the British Relations Boards held their second meeting. Robert Birley was present. He was soon to retire as Educational Adviser to the Military Governor and return to Eton as Head Master; but he still strongly backed Wilton Park. Britain must primarily aim, he said, at influential Germans so as to spread democratic ideas and strengthen Anglo-German understanding. Pleased, no doubt, with the new selection procedure which gave them the last word, the British Relations Boards adopted the proposals made at Herbert Walker's meeting. They were encouraged by an offer from the German Trades Union Federation, the DGB, to pay DM3000 per course for its members, and by plans for a special conference to bring influential Germans to Wilton Park in October 1949.

But a moral victory was not necessarily practical. Although the Treasury had agreed to maintain Wilton Park until March 1950, it was still pressing for it to be closed after that date. It was time for the Foreign Office to fight back. Heinz Koeppler promptly supplied it with eloquent ammunition:

> As a general argument it should be emphasised that there is a great weight of opinion in favour of the prolonged continuance of Wilton Park, in addition to that of the Military Governor, the Educational Adviser and the Director of the Education Branch C.C.G. Lord Lindsay of Birker is but one of many prominent protagonists for the future of Wilton Park. Lord Lindsay had a discussion on the matter with Lord Henderson [Parliamentary Under-Secretary of State at the Foreign Office] on 18th March and it is understood that Lord Henderson expressed himself as warmly supporting a prolonged continuance ... Most significant is the fact that German opinion has recently come out clearly in favour of Wilton Park, both among former Wilton Park students and also among other Germans holding influential positions ...
>
> The main arguments for the continuance of Wilton Park for one year appear to have been accepted by the Treasury; yet they apply no less to a prolonged continuance after 31st March 1950 ...
>
> The Treasury view is based both on an ignorance of the purpose of Wilton Park and of the way in which its work is actually carried out, and on an incomplete perception of current reactions in German opinion ...
>
> The purpose of Wilton Park is a direct expression of the foreign policy of H.M.G. Under Article III of the Brussels Treaty, H.M.G. with the other Brussels Powers committed themselves to creating conditions which would make possible the ultimate acceptance of Germany into Western Union. It follows that a continuous effort must be made to encourage German public opinion to help make Germany a good European ...
>
> The present prevalent German attitude to politics is dangerous to

Germany and to Europe alike. It is therefore a British interest to help Germany to face the national and international problems of today with a clearer and more open mind.

Koeppler went on to point out that offers of funds from Germany would alleviate the cost, and that savings could also be made by hiring out Wilton Park and its staff to other organisations. He concluded:

The precise duration of any prolonged extension after 31st March 1950 can perhaps be argued further, but a period of 2–3 years seems to be the minimum desirable to enable the courses and general work to be planned effectively in advance and to give reasonable security to the staff.

At the beginning of April, 1949, representatives of the three Western powers (Britain, France, and the United States) met in Washington to settle the final details of the Occupation Statute, adopted on April 10, and the establishment of the Allied High Commission in the future German Federal Republic. The Occupation Statute was due to come into force on September 21, 1949. Its purpose was to define the frontiers of power between the Allied Control authorities and the future Federal Republic. In this respect, as the future German Chancellor Konrad Adenauer insisted, it was a step on the way to full West German autonomy. To his critics, however, it was a humiliating reminder that Germans were still not fully free and equal members of the European family of nations – especially as the Allies retained the right to take over full or partial authority in Germany if need arose. The Lower Saxony *Land* British Relations Board, for example, pointed out that publication of the Statute 'has had the effect of making the Germans ultra-sensitive to anything that smacks of inter-ference or patronage on our part'. The Boards accordingly recommended that all officials concerned with education, information, and youth should have offices separate from those of the Allied Control authorities, and that exchanges, visits, and contacts should be intensified, deepened, and stepped up.

Such was the political context in which John Churchill (of the Foreign Office's German Education Department) discussed with Robert Birley and Sir Ivone Kirkpatrick the response they should make to the Treasury's ultimatum about Wilton Park. As Churchill minuted to the Head of the Finance Department, Robert Crawford, on April 13, 1949:

It is agreed that we cannot give an undertaking that Wilton Park shall close at 31st March 1950. Until the latest situation created by the Occupation

Statute has been clarified we cannot say how education in Germany will develop. On the face of it, however, it appears that the Occupation Statute will make it more difficult for us to influence German education and German opinion by action within Germany: it is therefore all the more important that we should try to retain an establishment such as Wilton Park which enables us to carry on our task from this country ...

At the moment Mr Birley agrees, however, that we cannot ... specific-ally ask the Treasury to approve now an extension of Wilton Park for, say, two or three years. For this we must wait for a clarification of the general situation.

On April 21, 1949, therefore, Crawford warned the Treasury that the decisions reached in Washington would probably have the effect of reducing Britain's own education programmes in Germany. If, as also seemed likely, there were financial constraints, these too might hamper the work of the Information Centres. The overall result could be to make Wilton Park more necessary rather than less. Crawford therefore proposed postponing any review of Wilton Park until the autumn of 1949.

W.R. Iley, now Head of the German Education Department, felt that this response to the Treasury left the Foreign Office on the defensive. In a Minute on April 26, 1949, he argued:

We have strong support in Germany and in this country for Wilton Park, and the balance of argument in favour of its continuation seems to me quite overwhelming. It would, I think, have been better to have told the Treasury that we strongly disagreed with their opinion, and felt we had a more than adequate case for retention, but that the financial and political considera-tions which would be uppermost in March 1950 were as yet so insecure that we preferred to await developments before we pressed our arguments.

On August 16, 1949, Iley wrote to Herbert Walker asking for his help in preparing the case. Both the Foreign Office's Finance Department and the Treasury, he said, were stressing the 'internationalization' of Wilton Park, about which he had doubts; and among other things he wanted to know the attitude of the Germans on this score. As regards possible German contributions to the cost: 'My view is that we should do all we can to encourage German participation in finance by informal contacts, but that it would be unwise at present to make any formal approach.' As a realist, however, he believed that 'we can justifiably express to the Treasury a hope that German contributions may expand'. He added that the Wilton Park Advisory Council – 'a most distinguished body' – was likely to meet in September.

In inviting its members to serve on the Council, Lord Henderson, Parliamentary Under-Secretary of State at the Foreign Office, had spelled out its aims:

(a) to link Wilton Park with the best British educational thought and practice;
(b) to assure that the high standard necessary for such important work is maintained;
(c) to be ready to advise the Foreign Office on academic and educational questions arising from the work of Wilton Park; and
(d) to assure the standing of Wilton Park with British and German public opinion.

This last was particularly important: especially in the Russian Zone – the future East Germany – Wilton Park was regarded as at best a Foreign Office propaganda outfit and at worst a Western 'spy school'.

The Academic Council's Chairman was Lord Lindsay of Birker, and its members included a number of other familiar speakers at Wilton Park: Birley, Lord Beveridge, R.C.K. Ensor, Ernest Green, and Harold Nicolson. Their colleagues were Miss H.C. Deneke (who had often lectured in Germany on women's problems), Dorothy Elliot (Chair of the National Institute of Houseworkers), the Lord Bishop of Sheffield, the Social Economist Gertrude Williams of Bedford College (wife of W.E. Williams, Director of the Bureau of Current Affairs), S.H. Wood (who had been Chairman of the voluntary German Educational Reconstruction founded in 1943 by Eleanor Rathbone), J.C.V. Wray, Education Officer of the Trade Union Council, and Professor Thomas Marshall of the London School of Economics, who was shortly to succeed Birley as Educational Adviser in the British Zone of Germany.

Altogether, things seemed to be progressing in good order. On September 9 and 13, 1949, Wilton Park had a staffing inspection, at which Koeppler was able to explain his need for better German-speaking secretarial assistance. Meanwhile, the British Relations Boards in Germany met on September 10, 1949, to finalise the case they would put to the Treasury. They agreed to concentrate on five main points:

(i) the Germans were very keen on Wilton Park; places were over-subscribed;
(ii) although the Occupying Powers had been criticised during the elections for the first Bundestag, this was just electoral rough-and- tumble;
(iii) Wilton Park should remain chiefly Anglo-German rather than being rapidly internationalised; the German trades unions agreed;
(iv) the German Land Governments were showing signs of willingness to help finance it;

(v) the new selection procedure would greatly improve the quality of candidates.

In the Foreign Office ten days later, on Wednesday September 21, 1949, the Academic Advisory Council met for the first time. The quorum consisted of Lords Lindsay and Aberdare, Dorothy Elliot, Ensor, Nicolson, the Bishop of Sheffield, Gertrude Williams, and S. H. Wood. Also present was Heinz Koeppler, with – from the Foreign Office – Lord Henderson, John Churchill, and the Canadian-born Rolland Chaput de Saintonge, late of COGA and the CCG, and now Head of the German Information Department. The atmosphere was sanguine. True, the Treasury's pressure was still heavy: in July, it had told the Foreign Office to expect cuts in the budget for the German Education Department. But now that the Germans were willing to share the cost of Wilton Park, Treasury doubts must surely be on the wane.

On October 13, 1949, commenting on the Wilton Park inspection, Chaput de Saintonge remarked that 'The centre would appear to be cheaply run. I think you can take it for granted that Wilton Park will continue beyond the present financial year.'

To this end, Koeppler was already busy with what some might have considered a high-level week-long public relations exercise. He called it a 'VIP conference' – and its official subject was 'The Basis of British Policy with which is combined a Study of the Work of Wilton Park'. Its 29 German participants included MPs, mayors, industrialists, trade union leaders, Land Prime Ministers, Ministers, and Deputies, newspaper editors, bankers, lawyers, senior civil servants and university professors. Also present were delegates from Denmark, Holland, Switzerland and UNESCO. It began on Friday October 7, 1949, with a welcome from Lord Henderson. The list of speakers sounded like a roll-call from the very early days of Wilton Park: it included Jennie Lee, Kingsley Martin, Wilson Harris, Douglas Woodruff, Richard Crossman, Lord and Lady Pakenham, R.C.K. Ensor, Alfred Robens, Denis Healey, Peter Calvocoressi, Bertrand Russell, Robert Birley, and Dame Evelyn Sharp.

The VIP Conference seemed to me to go very well and I understand that both [Heinrich] Weitz [Minister of Finance, *Land* North Rhine Westphalia (CDU)] and [Wilhelm] Kaisen from Bremen [where he was Head of the *Land* Government and Lord Mayor (SPD)] had said that they mean to get some more financial support from Germany. They have said that they are now deciding whether it is better to raise this from the various Laender or from the Bund. It seems to me quite significant and I feel it would be a pity for us to snuff out something which the Germans seem ready to support.

This was from Robert Birley, writing to Christopher Steel, Deputy High Commissioner in Germany on November 1, 1949. Yet the future of Wilton Park, he said, still seemed to be uncertain. 'As far as I can make out there is some sort of division of opinion at the Foreign Office about it. I have been asked to ask you whether you could support it from your end, if you think it is a good thing.'

There was indeed 'some sort of division of opinion at the Foreign Office'. Another visitor to the VIP Conference that October had been Miss R. Ostermann of Political Division. 'The aim of the Conference', she reported on November 8, 1949, 'was to gain the interest and support of prominent Germans for the work of Wilton Park, and in this it undoubtedly succeeded'. That sounded unequivocal: but a year earlier Miss Ostermann had declared that 'by March 1949 Wilton Park will have completely outlived its purpose'. Her views, she now wrote, had not materially altered. 'I believe even more firmly that some kind of Anglo-German centre, with a counterpart to balance it somewhere in Germany, would be more in keeping with present circumstances.' Yet even she had to admit that much of the criticism once levelled at Koeppler no longer applied. 'His handling of the VIP Conference, during which he took the chair for most lectures, was quite masterly, for he combines a scholar's gifts with a sense of showmanship quite indispensable to the job.' Among her conclusions was a recommendation 'to continue the grant to Wilton Park for one further year, i.e., up to April, 1951, as a provisional measure during which time the possible advantages of some form of Anglo-German Centre could be explored'.

Miss Ostermann was one of a number of people who offered Steel, Walker and others their opinions. On November 14, 1949, Major-General W.H.A. Bishop wrote from the Private Office of the *Land* Commissioner in Düsseldorf, North Rhine Westphalia, to Professor Thomas Marshall, following a visit to Wilton Park on November 9, 1949:

> I have reached the conclusion that it is most desirable to retain this establishment and, despite the financial stringency, to try to ensure that the necessary funds for this purpose are provided ...
>
> I have been impressed by the enthusiastic manner in which those Germans who have visited Wilton Park have spoken about it on their return to Germany.

They emphasised, said Bishop, 'the complete absence of patronage or of anything which savoured of dictation or propaganda and the fact that all the speakers were highly qualified'. He recommended, among other things, that 'we in Germany should do all we can to ensure that at least the equivalent of £10,000 per annum is provided from German sources ... , that we should strongly recommend to the Foreign Office that everything possible should be done to keep the Centre open'.

Christopher Steel, in his eventual reply to Birley, was less definite: his views, as expressed on November 22, were clearly influenced by Miss Ostermann's:

> I cannot speak with any authority on Wilton Park but Political Division's experience leads us to believe that it has done, and will still be able to do, useful work, in spite of the changed conditions in Western Germany.
>
> I imagine, however, that any uncertainty as to its future must result largely from the high cost of running it. I am certainly prepared to support its continued existence on its merits if and when I am asked for my views but I have a feeling that the system may not be entirely appropriate to present conditions and that some kind of new deal might be a good thing besides impressing the Treasury with the vitality of the organization. I am thinking here really of a more direct tie up with some permanent German body which would select the students and work things more on an exchange basis.
>
> As you say, Kaisen was certainly most favourably impressed, but Deutsche Marks will not pay for a British institution nor would the Americans allow them to be converted. They might however well be used to finance the German end of a joint project.
>
> I am afraid this is a very vague idea but you will I think see the point. Empires cannot stand still, however beneficent, and Koeppler's is no exception.

With this partial proviso, however, virtually all those consulted in Germany pleaded that Wilton Park should be continued beyond the 1950 deadline. One of their key arguments was that, as German autonomy grew, so would the importance of Allied influence. The political situation, moreover, made Anglo-German understanding still more vital. On April 4, 1949, NATO had been founded; in August, the Soviet Union had broken the US monopoly of nuclear weapons; and now the German Occupation Statute had come into force.

Nevertheless, the Treasury remained a stumbling-block. At last, on November 28, 1949, Robert Crawford wrote to O'Donovan there confronting the subject head-on. After describing a number of measures to streamline educational and information activities as regards Germany, including staff cuts, he added:

We have looked again at the question of the continuance of Wilton Park beyond next March, on which you agreed ... that we could make recommendations this Autumn. The question has been most carefully considered at a high level both in Germany and here. As a result we have come to the definite conclusion that Wilton Park should continue throughout next financial year, and I am accordingly writing to ask for your agreement to this. We shall be including provision for Wilton Park in the Estimates figures which we shall be sending to the Treasury in the next few days ...

[He added]: Indeed, the evidence of support for Wilton Park in responsible German quarters has been growing, not only among Trade Unions which have, for some time, been providing funds to enable their members who could not otherwise afford to attend Wilton Park to do so, but also among the Land Governments themselves. The Finance Ministers of both North Rhine and Schleswig-Holstein have stated their readiness to make available Deutsche-mark funds if these can be usefully employed in enabling students to attend the Centre.

Contrary to what Koeppler and others had hoped, Crawford asked only for the Treasury's agreement to continuing the Wilton Park Centre for a further twelve months from the end of the current financial year – i.e. until March 31, 1951. He concluded:

We should propose to review the question again in the Autumn of 1950. Although the character of the courses will probably change as time goes on, the administrative framework will remain the same, and consequently the level of expenditure. The cost works out at about £26,000 a year on our Vote and about £8,000 a year on the Vote of the Ministry of Works.

Two days after this submission to the Treasury, the High Commissioner Sir Brian Robertson made a statement on Wilton Park at his staff meeting, which Con O'Neill, then serving the Foreign Office in Germany, thought 'should solve the problem of the attitude we are to adopt towards it'.

He said he thought its work was very important and of very great value. A number of Germans who had attended Wilton Park had expressed views to him, and his opinion was based in part on this. He knew there were divided feelings about Wilton Park in the Foreign Office, and that pressure might be exerted to put an end to Wilton Park because of its costs. He intended to resist such pressure, since to abolish Wilton Park would be a false economy.

142

Christopher Steel, the Deputy High Commissioner, to whom Con O'Neill sent this Minute, wrote on it: 'W.P. has so many powerful advocates I think it can do without me.'

Perhaps the most powerful advocate was the *Deutschemark*. On December 2, 1949, the Treasury official, Mr O'Donovan, who had originally been so sceptical, wrote a note to the Treasury Under-Secretary Lionel Thompson:

> You will remember that 12 months ago we discussed Wilton Park, the re-educational [*sic*] centre for Germans. You were extremely doubtful about the value of the scheme, but agreed to allow Wilton Park to continue for one more year. They now want to continue it for yet another year and probably longer ...
> F.O.G.S [Foreign Office German Section] now tell me that German trade unions and governments have been willing to make contributions ... It seems to me that if this principle could be carried a bit further, it might alter the whole character of the thing. If (though it is unlikely) we could get the Germans to pay half the cost, whether in sterling or in deutschemarks, and the Germans thus felt that it was partly their own show, I think that my main objection would be answered.

So, just before Christmas, on December 22, 1949, the Treasury grudgingly agreed that Wilton Park could survive for a further year, until March 1951 – provided that the Germans paid travelling expenses and pocket money, and contributed to the cost of board and lodging. It felt obliged to add, however, that current staff cuts in the British Civil Service might effect Wilton Park, and that as new financial year began in April 1950 it might have to contemplate reducing its academic staff or even shutting up shop altogether.

Robert Crawford, Head of the German Finance Department, responded over the Christmas and New Year holiday with commendable speed. On January 4, 1950, he wrote to O'Donovan at the Treasury saying that the Finance Ministers in four *Länder* Governments – Bremen, Hamburg, North-Rhine-Westphalia, and Schleswig-Holstein – had stated their willingness to make some contribution. '*As soon as we have your confirmation that Wilton Park can continue* [my italics] we shall follow these offers up and also seek to get something, if possible, from the Federal Government once it gets its financial affairs into some sort of order.' Did this sound a little like a simultaneous exchange of hostages at Checkpoint Charlie in divided Berlin? There was certainly new firmness in the tone.

Crawford's strategy worked. On February 7, 1950, the Treasury accepted the bargain. Wilton Park could continue until March 31, 1951, on condition that every effort was made to get German financial support. Koeppler's college had weathered another Christmas crisis. Was the barometer at last set fair?

CHAPTER 10

Goodbye to All That?

> Wandering between two worlds, one dead,
> The other powerless to be born,
> With nowhere yet to rest my head.
> Like these, on earth I wait forlorn.
> **Matthew Arnold**, 'Stanzas from the Grande Chartreuse' (1855), l.85.

The year 1950 began well – deceptively well – for Wilton Park. It had a new lease of life. It was promised German funds. The Academic Advisory Council was in being. A second VIP Conference was in the offing. The struggle for survival seemed over. Now, at last, it was possible to deal with matters that had too long been neglected. To begin with, Koeppler wanted to refresh contacts with Germany. He had not forgotten Birley's past concern about the need for local knowledge. Now, between courses, seemed a good opportunity. As he wrote to Rolland Chaput de Saintonge on January 16, 1950:

The reasons are:
1. The need for keeping in regular touch with the German scene.
2. Contact with the new selecting bodies for Wilton Park.
3. Discussion concerning the proportional representation of Germans from the American and French Zones amongst the members of the Wilton Park courses. This will necessitate entry into the American and French Zones.

He left eventually on February 19. After two days in Berlin, he went to Hanover for a day, then for three days to Düsseldorf. He spent most of the first week of March in the American and French Zones, then came back from Bielefeld to London. He returned with, among other things,

145

confirmation of the desire gradually to bring other nationals to Wilton Park. As he wrote to Rolland Chaput de Saintonge on March 15, 1950:

> Both the opinion of the German members of our Sessions and of the British, Allied and German officials I met in Germany ... is unanimously and strongly in favour of this international admixture. I say 'admixture' advisedly as I am quite sure that we should not try and get large numbers of other nationalities, even if this were technically and financially possible; but the contribution which even a handful of Dutch, Swiss, French, and Belgians can make, and are making, to the success of our Sessions cannot be over-estimated.

The upshot was a series of letters to British embassies in Brussels, Copenhagen, Oslo, Paris, and Stockholm, seeking to recruit likely candidates.

Before his German trip, however, Koeppler had had to air a serious grievance that was causing unhappiness and unrest at Wilton Park. This was the insecure situation of the academic staff: R.D.J. Gibson, A.L. Glasfurd, G.R. Greene, K.W. Lauermann, and the Hon. T.M. Lindsay. As Koeppler wrote – 'with great urgency' – to the Foreign Office German Section's Establishment and Organizations Department on January 17, 1950:

> When the present status and salaries of the Warden and tutors at Wilton Park were fixed in the summer of 1948 this, like the whole budget of Wilton Park, had to be in the nature of a cockshy. It had to be done in a hurry and everybody concerned was aware of the fact that there was no certainty whatever concerning the life of Wilton Park. We have now had 18 months working experience of this system which is a sufficiently long period to enable us to reconsider this position.

For this reason, Koeppler argued, salaries should no longer be fixed, but be subject to increments. When the tutors were first engaged, their £800 income corresponded to the starting salary of a university reader. The latter was now £1,000 or £1,100 a year. Koeppler himself had had his salary fixed at its present rate in September, 1943, when he was serving in what he now called 'a secret department of the Foreign Office [PID] where the nomenclature of the position was different from that of the civil service proper'. At the time, he wrote he had been told that 'in fixing his salary the salary of an Assistant Secretary was taken into consideration'. Today, his salary was well below that, and his responsibilities had increased. At the same time, Koeppler pleaded for Wilton Park's academic staff to be given greater security, in particular by being made members of the Federated Superannuation System of Universities (FSSU). This in turn would require their contracts to cover not less than two years.

Innocuous as these suggestions seemed, they caused a minor storm. Quite properly, Koeppler sent a copy of them to Rolland Chaput de Saintonge; but he also sent one, for information, to Lord Lindsay as Chairman of the Academic Advisory Council. Lindsay had already raised the matter of Wilton Park staff's status and salaries at the Council's first meeting in September 1949; and at the second he had declared his intention to raise it again at the third – due for January 1950 but postponed until March 9. The agenda for that meeting – with no reference to staff matters – Koeppler sent to Chaput de Saintonge before departing for Germany. While he was away, Lindsay wrote to Koeppler asking him to send his note of January 17 round to members of the Academic Council. Koeppler's secretary opened the letter; and, after consulting the next senior member of staff, she obeyed Lindsay's request. The subject of staff salaries accordingly figured on the revised agenda for the March 9 meeting. It incensed Rolland Chaput de Saintonge:

> I do not consider that the Academic Council has any jurisdiction over this matter and I shall be forced to object to the discussion of this question under the agenda, as not being within the competence of the Academic Council.
>
> I am sorry that this situation should have arisen. It would have been much better for you to have sent us a draft of your agenda, or at any rate mentioned the item to us. You will realise that the Academic Council are not like the Board of Governors of a school but are advisers to the Foreign Office who retain the sole responsibility for Wilton Park. Under these conditions, administrative details are certainly not within their competence.

This letter, sent to Koeppler in some haste on March 8, 1950, was too late to prevent the Academic Council's discussing the staff question when it met in the Foreign Office on the following afternoon. Lord Lindsay had begun by suggesting that a member of the Wilton Park staff should be invited to attend meetings of the Council and put forward any views they might consider appropriate. Chaput de Saintonge had objected, fearing that the staff might raise 'questions which should properly be discussed by the Establishment Department and were therefore, in the first instance, matters of domestic concern within the Foreign Office (German Section) with which the Academic Council *would not like* [sic] to be troubled'. Chaput's report of the meeting, written that day, continued:

The discussion which followed was difficult but Mr Birley and Mr Nicolson understood the position and emphasised the delicacy of the situation. Lord Lindsay, however, was very strongly of the opinion that staff questions were a matter for the Advisory Council, as the whole standard of the work of Wilton Park could be adversely affected by the position of the staff ...

The matter is certain to be raised again at the next meeting when we may be faced with strong recommendations by the Academic Council on the whole of this question. The general feeling was that the Council should make a very strong recommendation on staff matters if they consider the conditions of service are not satisfactory, and I fear we may be in considerable difficulties unless the Council is satisfied on the official case concerning the academic staff.

Chaput detected in this imbroglio a familiar, ever-present hand:

It is evident that Koeppler has strongly enlisted Lord Lindsay's support and is using him as a lever on the whole question of Wilton Park.

The Academic Council evidently considers itself in a position to take decisions or at any rate to make recommendations in such a form that they are tantamount to decisions. This came out on Item 2 of the agenda, namely the official designation of Wilton Park. Koeppler raised this on his own initiative and said that he wished Wilton Park to be known as a college, advancing as an argument that German officials whom he visited in Germany had suggested such a designation. Several members, including Marshall and Birley, supported the proposal and before I could say anything Lord Lindsay said it was decided that it should be called a college. I shall instruct Koeppler to make certain that the minutes of the meeting put the decision as a recommendation ... I feel that this is another instance of Koeppler trying to enhance the importance of the institution and to give it a place in English academic life which it has no right to hold but which might later make it more difficult to bring Wilton Park to an end.

Within a few days, on March 14, 1950, Koeppler was able to explain how the staff question, and his note on the subject, had reached the Advisory Council and its agenda. Geoffrey Kirwan of the Foreign Office duly acknowledged that Koeppler 'personally was blameless'.

But in a way the harm has been done, and the Council appears to have got its teeth into pay questions. It looks to me as though firm action may have to be taken to steer the Council off matters which really do not concern it (e.g. title of the place).

This took some time. On March 27, 1950, Lord Lindsay wrote to Lord

Henderson, the Parliamentary Under-Secretary of State at the Foreign Office, transmitting the Advisory Council's recommendations; but not until May 1 did Henderson reply. Politely but firmly, he assured Lord Lindsay that if 'questions of establishment' – i.e. staff pay and conditions – impinged so closely on the working of Wilton Park that the Advisory Council must take notice of them, 'I shall always be pleased to consider your recommendations'. But

> much as we would value your advice on these matters, I do not consider that they are questions which could usefully be discussed at your meetings.
>
> You have, I understand, already discussed on the Council the Warden's minute to the Foreign Office (German Section) Establishment and Organisation Department on the position of the Academic Staff at Wilton Park. It is unfortunately not possible to adopt either of the proposals put forward by the Warden and he has been so informed.

On salaries, the basic problem was the government's wage freeze; on superannuation, 'experts' believed that the Wilton Park tutors were not comparable to university teachers. Several officials in the Foreign Office, including Chaput de Saintonge, C.F.A. Warner, and George Anderson of the Establishment and Organisation Department, were sympathetic to the problem, and were later to discuss matters seriously with Koeppler. But for the time being, that was that.

Even on the minor point of Wilton Park's name, the Foreign Office seemed hesitant. Henderson had 'no strong objection' in principle to the expression 'Wilton Park College'; but he suggested that it was not the moment to change the name. Why? Because of two uncertainties. One was familiar: 'for financial and other reasons we can never hope to get more than annual authority to carry Wilton Park on'. The other was far more ominous. 'There is, as you no doubt know, doubt about our being able to retain the present accommodation. I suggest that it would be premature to change the name to Wilton Park College until we know whether it is going to remain at Wilton Park.'

This cloud the size of a man's hand had already made its appearance at the meeting of the Academic Council on March 9, 1950. In the words of the official minutes,

> Mr CHAPUT de SAINTONGE reported a War Office request that Wilton Park should be vacated by September 1st. After it had been pointed out that the War Office had agreed in June 1948 to the use of the premises by the Foreign Office for as long as they were required, Mr Chaput de Saintonge told the Council that the matter was under discussion and,

failing a withdrawal of the request, would have to go to Ministerial level.

There was, and remained, some uncertainty about why the War Office so suddenly wanted Wilton Park back. It first told the Foreign Office that it needed to house the Army Education Corps. This hardly seemed vital or urgent. In the wider world, however, tensions were growing – not only between the two Germanies but also in the Far East. Eventually, at dawn on Sunday, June 25, 1950, North Korean troops crossed the 38th parallel dividing the north from the south of the country; and some feared that this might be a prelude to war in Europe. In July, partly under US pressure, the five members of the Brussels Treaty agreed to increase their armaments and prolong military service. It was against this background that on August 4, 1950, the Secretary of State for War, John Strachey, wrote to Kenneth Younger at the Foreign Office that Wilton Park had been 'designated as the site of General Headquarters, Home Forces, in the event of mobilization'. He explained that this decision, like others, had had to be taken 'as a result of the recent review of our position in the light of the worsened international situation'. A week after Strachey's letter, on August 11, 1950, Major-General Nevil Brownjohn, Vice-Chief of the Imperial General Staff, told Chaput de Saintonge that Wilton Park was to be used for a special Signals and Telecommunications Section.

Whatever the real reason for the War Office's volte-face, matters had come to a head on Friday, April 14, at a meeting hosted by the War Office in the White House at Wilton Park. Koeppler was not there, but Chaput de Saintonge was, with George Anderson. In the afternoon they went to have tea with Koeppler and told him that Wilton Park would almost certainly have to move that September. 'Frankly', wrote Koeppler afterwards, 'I was somewhat staggered at the sudden collapse of our case.' As Chaput ruefully explained to Lord Lindsay on the following Monday:

> The arguments advanced by the War Office are I am afraid compelling; the Treasury have agreed that they should purchase the estate on condition that it is fully occupied by the War Office, and there are certain other security requirements which will make it undesirable for Wilton Park to remain there ...
>
> It may still be that we can find a weak point in the case put forward by the War Office and press for the retention of our existing premises, but I am not hopeful.

Koeppler, on the contrary, hoped that 'we are not going to commit ourselves to the War Office to vacate Wilton Park by September'. But, as he wrote to Chaput on April 17, 1950: 'It would now appear that we must concentrate on finding another suitable abode ... It may well be that a suitable property might not be available till the end of the year.'

'Suitable' was the key word. The Ministry of Works had a number of places in mind, including several Emergency Teacher Training Colleges, soon due to be closed. One of them was at Ashridge Park, near Hemel Hempstead in Hertfordshire, a former wartime hospital. Its main building, Ashridge House, was a vast Gothic revival mansion begun in 1808 by James Wyatt; but its main practical accommodation was as a semi-permanent hutted camp. Wasting no time, Chaput, Anderson, Koeppler and other officials inspected Ashridge on the afternoon of Wednesday, April 19. There was plenty of room, some of it rather dingy, and the surroundings were delightful; but it was four miles from the station, and there were not enough single or double bedrooms. Worse, Wilton Park could probably not move in until the Spring of 1951 – and the Ministry of Works wanted to end the lease before June 1951 to avoid paying 'dilapidations' or reinstatement costs. 'I think it might do', was Anderson's non-committal verdict.

'I realise', Koeppler had told Chaput two days earlier, 'that the finding of a place will have to be undertaken by the Ministry of Works, but as a very much interested party I think there could be no harm if we kept our eyes open and mentioned to them informally any suitable place.' Koeppler was as good as his word – and his promptness, characteristically, got him into hot water.

On April 20, 1950, Sir William Strang, Permanent Under-Secretary of State at the Foreign Office, was surprised to receive a letter from the J. Arthur Rank Organisation. It was testy. Its signatory was one Sydney Wynne – who, an alert official pointed out, was the son-in-law of Ernest Bevin, the Secretary of State. Wynne's letter read:

> This is a matter with which I would not normally bother you except that we appear to be the victims of an exasperating action which I am sure you will agree should not go unchallenged. For some time past we have occupied premises at Moor Hall, Cookham. There we built up a cartoon film production organisation which unfortunately we have now had to abandon as a consequence of the difficulties through which this industry is passing – difficulties largely the result, in our view, of excessive Entertainments Tax.
>
> The premises and contents of Moor Hall have been offered for sale and among the visitors yesterday [in fact on Sunday April 16], was a Mr Koppler [sic] who announced that he was from the Foreign Office at Beaconsfield. He spoke with a heavy German accent and is alleged to have

said before witnesses 'We need new premises – Rank owes the British Government money – we will take these over'!

If the Foreign Office is indeed a potential purchaser we should be delighted to enter into negotiations; but we are not in the habit of dealing with gentlemen such as Mr Koppler [sic] whose manners and apparently slanderous comments on our economic relations with the Government alike appear to require correction! I am sure this is a matter that you would wish to have investigated and I shall look forward to hearing from you.

When this letter reached Chaput de Saintonge, he at once telephoned Koeppler. Much distressed, Koeppler apologised for the additional work the incident would cause; but declared that he was 'surprised and somewhat irritated'. What had happened, he explained, was that on the Saturday morning after the War Office meeting at Wilton Park on Friday April 14, a member of staff had told him about Moor Hall. It was only a few miles away from Wilton Park; so next day, Sunday, he had gone to have a look at it, and asked for the prospectus to be sent to him. 'I made it quite clear', he wrote to Chaput on April 25, 'that I was not acting in anybody's name and I was taking good care not to talk of the Foreign Office or any Government Department. In the letter asking for the particulars which I wrote I used my own stamp and not an O.H.M.S. label … Nothing I did could lead anybody to assume that I was acting in an official capacity.' Even the notepaper on which he had written had been his own, although it included the Wilton Park address. Koeppler replied that he only wished to be helpful, as past experience had led him to believe that 'the devil helps those who help themselves'. As to the offensive remarks about taking over Moor Hall against Rank's alleged debts, Koeppler 'denied having made them'. On this point Chaput remained unconvinced. As he noted on April 25:

> During a discussion at Ashridge with representatives of the Ministry of Works, Koeppler mentioned Moor Hall and suggested that the Ministry of Works should take over the property as part payment of the debt of the Rank Organization to H.M. Government. This suggestion was quickly disposed of but it shows that the statement attributed to Koeppler in Mr Wynne's letter was probably rightly so attributed.
>
> Koeppler is an able man but his judgment is sometimes at fault. His zeal often runs away with his discretion.

In the end, Sir William Strang wrote a conciliatory answer to Sydney Wynne, explaining that Koeppler's had been a private initiative and that he denied the words ascribed to him. Koeppler was admonished, and reminded by the Permanent Under-Secretary of State for the German

Section, Sir Ivone Kirkpatrick (who was shortly to become High Commissioner in Germany) that he was 'part of a Government Department'. He was only slightly chastened; but Moor Hall slipped quietly from the picture.

The next alternative, produced by the Ministry of Works, was another Emergency Teachers' Training College, due to close in November, 1950. This was Morley Hall, Wymondham, Norfolk – a moderate-sized Georgian house with some 15 rooms, in 18 acres of parkland, adjoining a further 48 acres with huts. Altogether, it could take about 500 people. It was held on lease; but the owners were prepared to sell it. The main disadvantage was its remoteness, over 100 miles from London. This was important because many of the speakers at Wilton Park were Members of Parliament, and because visits to London by students were a major feature of the curriculum.

Distance from London (55 miles) was a slighter problem in the case of another property: Newton Hall, six miles from Cambridge. This, owned by Harry (later Lord) Walston, whose wife became a close friend of Graham Greene, had been used during the war as a Civil Defence Reserve Headquarters. Koeppler, Chaput, and George Anderson went to see it on Wednesday May 17, 1950. Next day, Anderson summed up his impressions:

> Newton Hall is a dignified, well-built house, in remarkably good condition (considering that it has been requisitioned for a number of years) and the surroundings are extremely pleasant. It should also be fairly economical to run; and daily domestic help can be had in the village.
>
> Because it has sufficient big rooms on the ground floor, and a large number of fairly small bedrooms on the first and second floors, it could be adapted for our purposes without much trouble or expense. And, being a fairly new house (it was built in 1910), it is reasonably well supplied with bathrooms and lavatories. Also, there are some quite good huts. The accommodation of the married members of the staff may present a certain amount of difficulty, but I am told that there are flats to be had in the neighbouring village of Harston.

It sounded promising; and a detailed inspection was scheduled for June 29. But there were problems. One was the length of lease. On June 8, 1950, Harry Walston telephoned the Foreign Office to say that if there was a firm prospect of Wilton Park's taking only one year's lease, or two at the most, 'this was an awkward proposal from his point of view'. Unless the Ministry of Works could find somebody who was prepared to take the place on a 7- or 14-years lease, he told Chaput on June 24, 'I would much rather have it back as soon as possible'. The reason, he explained when they met for lunch at his home at Thriplow Farms on June 29, was that he needed to find accommodation for one of his managers, and had to decide quickly whether to build him a house. From Wilton Park's point of view, Newton Hall was rather small, especially for housing married staff; and Walston's mother, who was the Hall's legal owner, was unlikely to agree to Wilton Park's occupying all of it. Finally, the cost of adaptation, 'roughly between £1,500 and £2,000', was likely to be more than originally thought. Altogether, as Koeppler wrote to Chaput on July 1, 1950, it was 'unlikely that Newton Hall will fill the bill'.

While Newton Hall was under consideration, the Ministry of Works had come up with another site. This was an ex-War Department Camp at St Paul's Cray just off the Sidcup bypass. At present occupied by the Ministry's Mobile Labour Force, it was due to be free near the end of August. 'It comprises,' the Ministry wrote on May 25, 1950:

> Some 25 huts, mostly timber, in a good state of preservation, complete with ablution facilities. Some of the hutments are already partitioned to form single bedrooms. The Camp has been extended to accommodate about 400 people and kitchen and dining facilities are sufficient to deal with this number at one sitting.

Not surprisingly, the Foreign Office officials concerned were dutiful but doubtful. 'I am getting rather tired of these excursions', wrote George Anderson, 'but I suppose we had better look at the place at St Paul's Cray, if only because it is so much closer to London than Newton Hall'.

On the afternoon of Wednesday, June 2, Anderson and Chaput went down with three officials from the Ministry of Works. As Anderson reported next day,

> It is an ex-Army camp of exceptionally unprepossessing appearance. On two sides it is surrounded by waste land containing a disused and flooded claypit and a large rubbish dump ... The whole camp, though occupied, is overgrown with weeds and looks unkempt and forlorn. And in order to reach it, whether by road or rail, one has to pass through some of the most dismal and uninviting parts of London.

The Ministry of Works agreed with Anderson; but it had another site to offer – Fernhurst Militia Camp, between Haslemere and Midhurst in West Sussex, near the Surrey border. 'Do you want to look at this place?' Anderson asked Chaput on June 13. 'I think it would be impolitic not to', Chaput replied, 'as it has been offered us by W.O. [the War Office]. If it is like St Paul's Cray, we shall have wasted another day.'

In fact, it was an improvement – so much so that Chaput asked Koeppler to inspect it on Friday July 7. A provisional estimate of what it would cost to bring Fernhurst up to Wilton Park standard was £7,500. 'I imagine', wrote Anderson next day, 'that the cost of adapting Fernhurst Camp will rule it out, and I am not sorry for this.' 'In general', he had said earlier, 'we regard hutted camps with abhorrence.' Chaput agreed. 'They are not the best places', he had written on June 30, 'from which to show people the value of English life and the meaning of England'.

Somewhat to his colleagues' surprise, however, Koeppler preferred the Fernhurst camp to Newton Hall. He said so at the meeting of the Advisory Council on the following Monday July 10. Newton Hall, he thought, would be less suitable because it would afford little or no accommodation for married tutors. Wilson, Harris and others agreed with Koeppler; but Chaput said that the official Foreign Office line was 'that a camp was not the ideal solution and it was felt that an old country house would be preferable'.

So househunting went on, taking most of that golden summer. It was complicated by further uncertainty. Just how soon was the War Office going to take over the whole of the Wilton Park grounds? But even this was a minor worry compared with another threat that now loomed. The Treasury was renewing its effort to close Wilton Park altogether.

This too was linked with the need to move house. As Chaput de Saintonge told the Wilton Park Advisory Council on July 10, 1950: 'The Ministry of Works would not undertake any expenditure without a guarantee from the Treasury that the premises would be required for at least three years. The Treasury was being approached on the subject.'

The approach was made just two days later, on July 12, 1950, when Brigadier P.R. Antrobus wrote from the Foreign Office to Arthur Clough in the Treasury. After explaining the need for Wilton Park to move, and the alternatives suggested by the Ministry of Works, he revealed the dilemma:

> In all cases … alterations will be necessary to make them suitable for our purpose and the Ministry of Works are loath to undertake any expenditure for alterations in view of the fact that we have agreement from you to continue Wilton Park only until the end of the present financial year.

Antrobus went on to describe the successful efforts made to secure funds from the Germans:

> They have donated the sum of DM 45,000 (£3,823) as a token of their appreciation of the work done by Wilton Park, and this sum has already been placed to the credit of the Foreign Office (German Section) in sterling at the Bank of England. This contribution is for the past. [It had

originally been hoped that it would be annual.] As regards the future, we have reached agreement with the German Ministry of Finance that foreign exchange will be made available for pocket-money of Germans coming here under our educational scheme. In addition, the Educational Adviser hopes that foreign exchange will be available as a contribution towards the maintenance of some of the Germans. This depends upon the outcome of the present trade talks. We also hope to save on the fares of German visitors under our education schemes ...

You should also know that the Dutch and the Swiss Governments have shown interest in the work of Wilton Park by sending lecturers to the Courses and paying their travelling expenses and some pocket-money, and further the Governments of France, Belgium and the Scandinavian countries, who have been approached, have also shown their willingness to participate in the work of Wilton Park in the same manner. The Nobel Committee of the Norwegian Parliament has made available 800 kroner to cover the expenses of one of their visitors ...

I would therefore ask you to agree in principle to the continuation of Wilton Park for a period of at least three years after the end of the present financial year. This would facilitate our negotiations with the Ministry of Works in finding alternative accommodation and would justify the expenditure necessary to make available premises suitable for Wilton Park.

Two days later, on July 14, 1950, the old boy network swung into action. E.J.R. Edwards of the Ministry of Works, who had known Clough of the Treasury when they had served together in the War Office, wrote direct to him to seek an early answer. 'All I am writing to ask you is for an early decision.'

The sound of plain speaking was refreshing. Was it also dangerous? The Treasury's response to Brigadier Antrobus's plea for Wilton Park was decidedly and stubbornly negative. It came on July 26, 1950, from A.J. Platt, who pointed out that 'my division is responsible for overseas information expenditure'. Later, he explained to Clough that he was 'following precedent'. He was – even in his phraseology:

We have given *careful consideration* [my italics] to the arguments which you put forward for continuing Wilton Park after the end of the current financial year, but I am afraid that we cannot agree to your doing so ...

In these circumstances I am afraid that we have no alternative but to ask you to close Wilton Park as soon as possible.

As soon as the Foreign Office received this letter, George Anderson held an urgent meeting on the morning of Thursday, July 27, 1950, at the Ministry of Works in Lambeth Bridge House, with colleagues from the

Ministry and the Office: they included Chaput, Koeppler, and E.J.R. Edwards. Hoping that the Treasury letter was 'not to be taken as their last word', they determined, as Anderson put it, to return to the charge: 'we should do this with the least possible delay and at a sufficiently high level'.

By this time, indeed, 'the highest level' was involved in several respects. On August 4, 1950, the Secretary of State for War, John Strachey, wrote to Kenneth Younger, Minister of State at the Foreign Office, repeating that Wilton Park had to go: 'I am afraid I must press you to arrange for the school to be moved by 30th September or at least very shortly afterwards.' The Foreign Office interpreted 'very shortly' in very liberal terms. A.J. Platt of the Treasury wrote to Clough on August 9 that the War Office 'now appear to have agreed to the Foreign Office staying till the end of the financial year', but repeated his opinion that 'the centre should close down when it has to vacate its present quarters'. Two days later, he received a terse reply that Brigadier Antrobus has sent on August 5:

> Our information is that the War Office are prepared to allow us to remain at Wilton Park up to the end of this financial year and we propose to do so ... I cannot accept a proposition that the education work for Germans which has been carried out at Wilton Park must cease. The policy is one on which our Ministers have strong views, and we are now obtaining their instructions.

That same day, August 11, Platt changed his tune. As he wrote to Clough:

> Since I wrote my minute of 9th August I have seen General Robertson's report, with which the Chancellor agrees, recommending that we should exercise influence over Germany by educational means and provide funds to facilitate the exchange of visits between Germany and the U.K.

After explaining his previous opinion that 'the Wilton Park centre should close down', he went on:

> I do not think we can now maintain this view, though we can still ask for reasonable economy ...
> Brigadier Antrobus' letter of 5th August gives us an opportunity of withdrawing on these lines, and I propose, if you agree, to write to him as in the attached draft.

The draft conceded:

> If, as you say, the War Office have agreed to your remaining at Wilton Park until the end of the financial year this clearly alters the situation, and as you

already have financial sanction up to the end of the year, we do not press the suggestion that the centre should be closed forthwith.

So far so good; but there was still no mention of what the Brigadier Antrobus had asked for – 'the continuance of Wilton Park for a period of at least three years'.

Within less than a week, by August 17, 1950, a strongly-worded minute was ready to send to Ernest Bevin, recommending that he 'should approach the Chancellor of the Exchequer with a view to his affecting a change in the present policy of the Treasury'. It pointed out that:

> The Treasury have not only refused to consider our case favourably but have sent three letters, the arguments in which threaten the continuance of the educational work already planned for this financial year and raise points which not only are in direct opposition to the educational policy we are pursuing in Germany but, if accepted, will render such a policy impossible.

It dismissed as 'nonsense' the Treasury contention that 'special arrangements for Germany are no longer justified':

> Germany is to-day one of the most vital areas in the world where the cold war is being raged with great fury and determination, and with real danger of being converted into a shooting war. Being nearer the United Kingdom, conflict in Germany would be more immediately dangerous to us than conflict in some other parts of the world. We are now engaged in an attempt to prevent war by increasing our strength and that of the Western democracies.

The Permanent Under-Secretary at the Foreign Office, Sir Donald Gainer, speedily endorsed and signed the paper; and on August 29 Ernest Bevin wrote a more moderate letter to the Chancellor, Sir Stafford Cripps, himself to retire owing to ill-health. Instead of calling the Treasury's case 'nonsense', Bevin simply said 'I do not agree with this argument'. But he repeated almost word for word his officials' arguments, adding references to the Berlin blockade, to the state of German morale, and to the recent Soviet encouragement of civil disobedience to the Occupying Powers. He drew the conclusion:

> We cannot hope to achieve lasting results if we operate on a year to year basis. I am not now asking for more money … , but only the admission of the principle that since Germany remains a special case deserving special treatment, these activities, including the Wilton Park school, should continue for a period of at least three years at the level foreseen at 1st January, 1951.

While the Treasury and the Chancellor were considering this letter, officials continued bickering about Wilton Park. As E.J.R. Edwards of the Ministry of Works had written to Mrs Johnstone, his regular interlocutor at the Treasury on August 23:

> The Earl of Chatham, with his sword drawn
> Stood waiting for Sir Richard Strachan:
> Sir Richard, longing to be at 'em,
> Stood waiting for the Earl of Chatham.

The wait was to continue for a further three weeks. In the absence of the Chancellor Sir Stafford Cripps, the Minister of State at the Treasury, Hugh Gaitskell, answered Ernest Bevin's letter on September 21, 1950. The Treasury was still reluctant, but was yielding a little:

> I am not sure that the Chancellor would go the whole way with you in your assessment of the value of the Wilton Park Centre. In particular it seems rather doubtful whether a Centre which must be conducted in German need necessarily be in this country, with resultant higher costs. However, in view of your very emphatic request, I am prepared to agree in principle to the continuance of the Centre after 31st March 1951 at approximately the present cost of £26,000 a year on Foreign Office Votes, provided that the cost of alternative accommodation, which will fall on Ministry of Works Votes, is reasonable.
>
> I do not think that we should commit ourselves to continue the course for three years ahead. In the light of the ever-changing picture of our relations with Western Germany, it should, I think, be subject to annual review.

The Treasury decision was a great relief. As Chaput de Saintonge pointed out to Koeppler, the stipulation about 'subject to annual review' was an improvement: it put Wilton Park on the same footing as other parts of the service, implying that 'we continue with the Centre and the burden of proof for non-continuance would lie with the Treasury'. Chaput also believed, as he minuted on September 16, 1950, that the way was now 'open for us to raise again the question of the salaries of the academic staff'. In particular, 'We are, I think, all agreed that it is not fair to the members of the staff at Wilton Park to treat them as Civil Servants and not pay them on an annual incremental scale.' The Foreign Office accordingly proposed a scale of £800–£900 for the Tutors and the equivalent of a Senior Principal's salary for the Warden.

The focus of anxiety now shifted to the question of Wilton Park's move into a new home. Two questions were still in suspense: the date and the destination. As the weeks had worn on, the date had slipped. By September 30, 1950, Wilton Park was still in its old quarters, but Koeppler believed that it would have to move by November 15. This would just give it time for the further VIP Conference that he was now planning. As to the destination, the first choice had narrowed down to Rushbrooke Hall, Suffolk, recently turned down by the National Trust. 'My first reaction', wrote the Foreign Office's Deputy Under-Secretary of State (German Section), Eric Seal, 'had been very adverse, mainly on the ground of inaccessibility.' However, as he continued in a letter to Robert Birley on October 9, 1950, 'The Ministry of Works and Koeppler between them managed to persuade me that it was the best chance open to us. It is at any rate that rare bird – a country house with efficient plumbing, heating and electric wiring!'

Seal's letter to Birley was in reply to unexpected – and, as it turned out, vital – news. Birley had just succeeded Lord Lindsay, who had retired owing to ill-health, as Chairman of the Wilton Park Academic Council; and on October 5, 1950, after 'a good deal of hesitation', he intervened with a fresh proposal for Wilton Park's future home:

> I was first told of the alternative accommodation of which I shall speak, by one of the staff there. I asked Koeppler about it, and found that although he knew about it, he was not doing anything. Partly, I think, because he had burnt his fingers once before in making his own enquiries, and partly because he felt that it would be too much of a nuisance to suggest somewhere else after so much trouble had been taken about Rushbrooke Hall.
>
> However, I feel that I ought at least to tell you about this other place, which I can do now that I am Chairman of the Wilton Park Advisory Committee. There seem to me to be two disadvantages in the choice of Rushbrooke Hall. First, it is going to be very difficult to get accommodation for the staff, and I know from my own experience how much that matters to an educational establishment. Secondly, it is a long way from London, and what is more, the address of the place gives the impression of being a long way off. I think this is bound to make it more difficult to get visiting lecturers. Against this, it is near Cambridge, which should be a good source of supply on a good many subjects.
>
> The place of which I was told as being now in the market, is Wiston Park, near Steyning. This is said to have two advantages over Rushbrooke Hall. First, it would be easier to find accommodation for the staff. Secondly, it is nearer London ... It is 13 miles from Brighton, to which, of course, there is an excellent train service.
>
> Wiston Park is said to be available, and to be in a good state of repair, and to have satisfactory accommodation. It will be possible to move there at once. The small alterations necessary could be carried out while they are

there. There is one obvious disadvantage. I understand that Rushbrooke Hall would be offered free, and it would be necessary to pay a rent for Wiston Park, but the people at Wilton Park believe that the saving in running costs, repairs and transport charges, would make up for the added cost and expense of the rent.

Seal was away when Birley's letter reached the Foreign Office; but when he returned on Monday October 9, 1950, he found that colleagues had already set enquiries in train. They took just over a week to convince George Anderson that, as he minuted on October 17, 'We should take Wiston Hall, which, from every point of view, seems the more attractive proposition.' Wiston would be rather more expensive than Rushbrooke Hall for the Ministry of Works, but cheaper for the Foreign Office. What was more, the Ministry of Works believed that 'the necessary alterations (which are not substantial) could be carried out by the end of the year'. Rushbrooke Hall, after all, had been unoccupied for some time, whereas Wiston, until six months ago, had been 'a finishing school for girls'.

Koeppler, for his part, was delighted. 'I entirely agree with your conclusion', he wrote to George Anderson on October 18, 1950:

> I have no doubt that Mr Morrison of the Tunbridge Wells region of the Ministry of Works was very pleased indeed with the small amount of work which would be required ... He mentioned £5,000, but made it quite clear that he did not for one moment believe that this sum would be reached ... I feel, therefore, that we may reasonably expect the Ministry of Works to think again about helping us with accommodation for the staff outside the main buildings. You will have been told that we feel satisfied that we can house the administrative, secretarial, clerical and domestic staff in the three cottages which we were shown by the owner's agent ... But, in this case, we shall not be able to offer accommodation to the Tutors. As I told you, they would be prepared to face it but, on the principle that a contented cow has the best milk yield, I venture to suggest that it would be a very great help if we could house one or two tutorial families in Wiston Park accommodation.

The staff situation had long preoccupied Koeppler. When the Academic Council held its next meeting, on November 8 in the Foreign Office, he had to report that one of the tutors, Martin Lindsay, had resigned to take a job at the Trinity College of Music, and that others too had been feeling the strain of uncertainty. George Anderson said that the Foreign Office's proposals for salary improvements had not yet been accepted by the Treasury; but it was prepared to come and look at matters on the spot. As to accommodation, the hope was that cottages and outhouses at Wiston could be adapted without much expense. The Council agreed, moreover, that the new name and address of Wilton Park should be Wilton Park at Wiston, Steyning, Sussex: the previous idea of calling it a 'College' was quietly dropped.

All that now remained was the removal itself. The January course was well in hand; and on November 14, 1950, Koeppler proposed to Chaput that he use the interim period of late November for another visit to Germany. He planned to go to the French and American Zones, the Rhineland, Berlin and, if time permitted Schleswig-Holstein, 'as the political situation has changed completely up there'.

So, of course, had the political situation generally. The years 1949–50 had marked several turning-points. The immediate postwar period, all urgency and improvisation, was now over. The major international institutions – the United Nations, the World Bank, the IMF, NATO – were in place. In the Far East, Mao Tse-tung headed the People's Republic of China; Indonesia had declared itself independent from the Dutch; Laos, Cambodia, and Vietnam had become independent while still linked with France; while in Korea the North had invaded the South and war had broken out. In Europe, the 'Iron Curtain' had divided East from West. Western Europe had set up OEEC and the Council of Europe, and in May 1950 had witnessed the Schuman Declaration that was to herald the eventual European Union. The West Germans had held their first postwar election, and acquired a Chancellor, Konrad Adenauer, as well as a Federal President, Theodor Heuss – the former director of the Berlin Hochschule für Politik where Heinz Koeppler had debated, and the organiser of the public speaking contest for schoolboys that he had nearly won.

The old Wilton Park had lived through these changes, and survived several attempts to close it down. Now, as Christmas 1950 approached and Koeppler returned from his German trip to supervise the removal to new headquarters, the prospects were challenging and the surroundings apt. In his letter of October 18 to George Anderson, welcoming the decision in favour of Wiston, Koeppler had added a postscript: 'As a fellow historian you may be interested in the result of very rapid research I have undertaken into the back history of Wiston Park.' He was quite clearly delighted with what he had found.

CHAPTER 11

Aspiring Dreams

'Il y a dans tout changement quelque chose d'infâme et d'agréable à la fois,
quelque chose qui tient de l'infidélité et du déménagement.'
Charles Baudelaire, *Journaux intimes*, 1887.

Wiston House, near Steyning in Sussex, was barely further from London than Beaconsfield was. In that respect it met everyone's stipulations. In another, it surpassed them. Standing at the top of a long drive curving up from near the village, on a noble site under the Downs near the Iron Age hill-fort of Chanctonbury Ring, Wiston House was several centuries older than Wilton Park: it was originally built in about 1575. Although much altered since then, it retained its main front, and at the back, alongside an originally 14th-century church, it had rows of stately chimneys and a range of mullioned windows overlooking the sloping lawns of the park. For a man as nostalgic for Oxford as Heinz Koeppler, it was instantly appealing. It might lack Matthew Arnold's dreaming spires, but it was a perfect setting for aspiring dreams.

Its chequered ancestry matched its changing architecture. Some of Wiston's successive owners lived switchback lives, lurching from prominence and prosperity to disgrace and ruin. Three were briefly imprisoned, two of them in the Tower of London. One sought temporary exile in Belgium. Twice, their vicissitudes made national constitutional history. The estate was ravaged, like many, by the English Civil War. But it long predated the 17th century. Before the Norman Conquest, an Anglo–Saxon thane named Azor held Wiston from Earl Godwin. Twenty years after the Conquest, the manor appeared in the Domesday Book as 'Wistanestun', in the possession of William de Braose, one of William the Conqueror's most powerful retainers, who had received large parts of Sussex as a reward for his services to the king.

In 1357, a mediaeval manor-house was recorded at Wiston. No trace of that survives; but the property remained in the hands of the de Braose family until the early 15th century, when John de Braose – buried in the Wiston church under a fine brass plate – died without a male heir. Thereafter, only five further families owned and lived on the Wiston estate.

Its next owner was John de Braose's great-nephew, Ralph Sherley – a local member of a very widespread family, usually spelt 'Shirley' else-where, although 'Shurley' at Isfield near Lewes. It was one of Ralph Sherley's descendants, Thomas Sherley, born in about 1542, who in about 1559 married Anne Kemp from Kent and had twelve children. Although three of them died in infancy, leaving six daughters and three sons, it may have been this numerous family that prompted Thomas Sherley to replace the old mediaeval stone and timber manor house. He had the means to do so, holding the post of Deputy Lieutenant of Sussex until 1601, becoming Member of Parliament for Sussex in 1572, and being knighted by Queen Elizabeth in 1573. Work began, in fact, shortly after his knighthood, some of the interiors being completed by 1576.

Sir Thomas Sherley's new house was conceived on a grandiose scale, built round a paved court. It had a south wing stretching further westward than the surviving building (which has a conservatory there), a now vanished three-storeyed wing running parallel to the existing west terrace at the back of the house, and a range of buildings (also now demolished) enclosing an east courtyard outside the present front door. Inside this opulent mansion was a hall with a double hammer-beam roof, a great chamber, a panelled parlour, a chapel, and a gallery 90 feet long.

It was a house fit for a Queen's servant; and Sir Thomas Sherley was determined to fit the part. In November 1577 he was appointed Sheriff of Surrey and Sussex for a year; later, he was to be a JP for over two decades, while his eldest son was to be Member of Parliament for Steyning. In 1585, in his early forties, he set off with two of his three sons, Thomas the younger and Anthony, for the Netherlands with the Earl of Leicester, accompanied by 1,000 mounted troops and 6,000 foot-soldiers, to help the Protestant Dutch in their rebellion against Spain. Two years later, in 1587, he was appointed to succeed Richard Huddilston as Treasurer-at-War in the Netherlands.

This, though a non-combatant post, usually made its holder an influ-ential member of the Council of War. It was also reckoned the most lucrative in the army – not because the basic salary was high, but because the perquisites were great. Huddilston had been paid some £500 a year, but he had been allowed a commission of 1 per cent on the money passing through his hands. Sir Thomas Sherley's yearly legal perquisites were said to total £2,000. The heart of the job was dealing with pay and supplies. These depended on accurate musters, which were hard for muster-masters to obtain from the captains, and for the Treasurer-at-War to obtain from the muster-masters: at both levels, bribes could inflate the numbers, creating artificial surpluses and ill-gotten gains. The Treasurer-at-War had also to deal with suppliers – merchants who often vied unscrupulously for military custom. He was therefore subject to both personal temptation and the offer of inducements. It was hardly surprising that, at many levels, fraud and corruption were rife. Even if scrupulously honest, any official could well be accused of fraud or corruption.

Two who fought for honest accounting were Thomas Digges, the first muster-master in the Netherlands, and his brother James. Both aroused great hostility by their zeal. James Digges in particular clashed with Sir Thomas Sherley. During Sherley's first four years in office, his books were three times subjected to a special audit. Three times, he was exonerated.

Pride went before a fall. Back in England, the rents from Sherley's farms and iron interests in Sussex were relatively modest; and he was finding it hard to make ends meet. In 1588, when the English and Dutch had stationed a fleet off the Netherlands to resist the Spanish Armada, Sherley's unpaid debts were so great that the Sheriff seized some of his possessions at Wiston. They included 71 feather beds, 70 pairs of blankets, 60 pairs of sheets, 32 Turkish carpets, 30 embroidered stools, seven great chairs of velvet, scarlet, and cloth of gold, two cushions of embroidered satin, and a valance of yellow taffeta embroidered with black velvet. It was no doubt humiliating; but Sherley must have been spending at a great rate, for in the following year – 1589 – he was accused of making an annual £16,000 on top of his salary. His alleged methods included advancing money to officers before their full pay was due, but taking a cut by way of interest, selling concessions to victuallers, taking over soldiers' debts when their full pay seemed in doubt, and generally using public money to act as a private moneylender. Sherley complained that Queen Elizabeth and Lord Burghley were listening to slanders by officials whom he had prevented from milking the Treasury; and he requested a third audit. As before, nothing was proved against him, and he continued in office. In 1591 he also become Treasurer of the army in France.

Sherley's luck ran out in 1596. In nearly ten years, almost £1.5 million had passed through his hands. Asked by Burghley for an estimate of his annual income, he replied that it was about £1,700. In reality, he was thought to have been making some £20,000 a year – nearly a fifth of what it cost to keep British forces in the Netherlands. The government reduced his stipend; and it was now rumoured that 'he owes the Queen more than he is worth'. Shortly afterwards he was dismissed, and in March 1597 was made bankrupt, spending some months in the Fleet prison, charged with owing the Queen £35,175.

Of this sum, improbably small by comparison with what was suspected, £12,702 was excused and £10,000 recovered by seizure of property and putting an 'extent' – a writ for seizure – on his land. Still owing £12,473, Sherley was released in January 1598.

He remained Deputy Lieutenant of Sussex for another three years, but made no attempt to pay the rest of his debt. Eventually, Elizabeth and her Ministers lost patience. On August 20, 1602, they put into effect the sequestration of his estate at Wiston, conveying it to the Attorney and Solicitor General 'to the use of the Queen' so that its rents went to the Crown.

The Queen's death on March 24, 1603, may have been fortunate for Sherley. In February 1604, he was elected 'burgess' – Member of Parliament – for Steyning. The result was a case that made constitutional history. On March 15, 1604, four days before the opening of Parliament, Sherley was riding through London when he was arrested for a debt of £3,000 by a Serjeant-at-Mace, William Watkyns, and his assistant Thomas Aram. The creditor was a City goldsmith, Gyles Sympson. Sherley was first taken to the Compter prison in Poultry, and then to the Fleet. The House of Commons considered that this was 'contrary to the liberties, privilege and freedom accustomed and due to the Commons … who have ever used to enjoy the freedom in coming to and returning from the parliament and sitting there without restraint or molestation.'

On March 22, the House ordered that a warrant be directed, under the hand of the Speaker, to the Clerk of the Crown, for the granting of a writ of Habeas Corpus. Five days later Sherley was brought to the bar of the House, and those involved in arresting him, Watkyns and Sympson were brought in 'as delinquents'. There was much debate in the House and by a committee of 18; then, on April 11, after the Easter recess, the House resolved that Watkyns and Sympson be committed to the Tower. On May 8, the House even summoned the Warden of the Fleet, John Trench, for having failed to free Sherley, and committed him too to the Tower. Three days later, Trench was still recalcitrant, and the House 'thought fit to increase his punishment' by committing him to 'the prison called Little Ease, in the Tower'. Four days of 'Little Ease' changed Trench's mind. On May 15 Sherley was released and took his parliamentary seat, and on May 19 Trench knelt at the bar of the House, 'confessed his error and presumption and professed that he was unfeignedly sorry'. He and the other 'offenders' were duly pardoned – and parliament had finally secured freedom of MPs from arrest except for treason, felony, or breach of the peace.

In June 1604, no doubt mindful of this spectacular case, which had coincided with a second issue of parliamentary privilege concerning a disputed election in Buckinghamshire, King James I showed clemency and generosity to Sir Thomas Sherley. He restored Sherley's property and lands, while securing some income from them, and ordered that the rest of his debts to the Crown be paid off at £400 per annum for 33 years, with three relatives standing as guarantors.

Since Sherley was now in his early sixties, it was an optimistic arrangement. Within a year, he was complaining that he could not afford either the arrears instalments or the income from his restored property. The most dramatic news came on April 9, 1610: at the suit of creditors in Somerset, he was formally outlawed from England. Perhaps on account of parliamentary privilege, this never took effect. Two and a half years later, on October 16, 1612, Sir Thomas Sherley died. He left no will, and nothing but debts to his son and heir. Yet he had played a role in constitutional history; and at the end of his life he played another. One of his friends was Sir Robert Bruce Cotton, the antiquary, manuscript collector and grand-father of Sir John Cotton, who left the Cottonian Library to the nation. Together, they evolved the idea of baronetcies to be sold as a source of revenue for the Crown. The first of these, in 1611, brought in £1,096. A few years later, Thomas Sherley the younger reminded the King that

> My father (being a man of most excellent and working wit) did find out the device for making of baronets which brought to Your Majesty's coffers well nigh a hundred thousand pounds for which he was promised … good recompense which he never had.

The burden on the young Thomas Sherley was heavy. Six months before his father died, he had tried to commit suicide while in prison. As MP, first for Hastings, and then – in 1614, 1615, and 1620 – for Steyning, he was soon able to claim parliamentary immunity, and try to salvage something of the family estate. But the debts were crippling. On May 23, 1614, the Wiston estate was again 'extended' to the Crown, and a year later given to King James's favourite Robert Carr, Earl of Somerset. He, however, was soon disgraced by a murder scandal, and supplanted in the king's affections by George Villiers, later Duke of Buckingham; and he seems never to have visited Wiston. Sir Thomas Sherley's widow, Dame Anne, was still living in Wiston House, which had been her home for half a century. But her role had long been akin to that of a sitting tenant. Her son Thomas Sherley the younger, retained only a precarious financial interest in the estate; and this – like his finances – became more and more tenuous as time went on. He already had seven children by his first wife when in 1617 he married again, to father eleven more. And if the Sherley family had debts, others were both willing and able to purchase the claims upon them in order to acquire the property.

One such was the London merchant Sir Lionel Cranfield, who had become Surveyor General of Customs in 1613, rising to be Lord Treasurer in 1621. Known as a prudent and diligent money-maker, he began buying up claims and titles to the Sherley manors so as to obtain the Wiston estate. By 1622 he had succeeded, making his family the third to own Wiston since the Norman Conquest. He gave the 80-year-old Dame Anne Sherley a £400 annuity, persuading her to move to a neighbouring estate; and in August 1622 he held a 'very merry' housewarming party at Wiston House, with the king's new favourite, George Villiers, among the guests. In September, Cranfield became first Earl of Middlesex. In 1623 he installed at Wiston House a non-paying tenant and housekeeper, his friend Lady Frances, the recently widowed Countess of Exeter, whose husband Thomas had been the son of Lord Burghley.

A political career in Stuart England was no less hazardous than under the Tudors. The new Earl of Middlesex had made influential enemies, including the Chief Justice of the Common Pleas, Sir Edward Coke. In 1624, Coke engineered his impeachment on corruption charges: he lost all his offices, was fined £5,000, and – like Coke before him – was temporarily imprisoned in the Tower. After a few days, he was released and his fine was reduced to £2,000; but he gave George Villiers, now Duke of Buckingham, his house in Chelsea and other favours, including a cash payment of £5,000.

Meanwhile, Lady Exeter was holding the fort at Wiston. In the following century, Daniel Defoe shrewdly remarked: 'An Estate is but a Pond, but Trade is a Spring.' Sometimes, Wiston could be productive: shortly after Middlesex's troubles, his *châtelaine* sent him six figs from the gardens to the north of the house, apologising for the small number, but explaining that in a bad summer 'common fruits' had not flourished. In 1628, £1.16s was spent 'felling and cutting the woods in the Pk' – an operation that raised £1,500 from the sale of timber to ease Middlesex's financial problems. In the same year, however, his secretary wrote to him:

There are some things about Wiston House which I would not meddle wthatall, wthout your honours direction, the howse is much decayed, and much monye may be layd out about yt, but I strive to avoyd extraordenarye expenses, and to do onlye that wch of necessity must be donne.

One task that Middlesex clearly deemed a necessity was to install a new water system. Early in 1630, Sir John Lawrence – a family friend and amateur engineer – set about it. In September he reported that the new supply ran: 'delicately into every office [lavatory] ... The wast passes through yo garden ... there falling into oval cisterns wch I have made wth bricks ... At yo stable door ... the horses may drink fro yo pure fountain and be washt in a new pond.' So successful was the new system that Lady Exeter was able to brew two batches of beer and yet have plenty of water left over. The feat was commemorated in a poem by Middlesex's nephew Sir John Suckling:

> And is the water come? sure't cannot be;
> It runs too much against philosophy ...
> twas the water's love that made it flow;
> For love will creep where well it cannot go.

The liquid triumph was short-lived. Charles I had succeeded James I in 1625; and he had never much liked the Earl of Middlesex. Buckingham, with whom Middlesex had negotiated his earlier liberation, had become unpopular because of his incompetent administration: Parliament tried to impeach him in 1626, and in 1628 he was stabbed to death. King Charles was appalled by the resultant public rejoicing; but he himself had other worries – a quarrel with Parliament, and huge debts. These no doubt contributed to the Crown's decision, in 1632, to re-open the inquiry into Middlesex's alleged financial misdeeds while a public servant. He was fined £25,958; distraints were set against him in nine counties, including Sussex, and the Wiston land was 'extended' to the Crown for £1,100 on account of 'certain several bonds which Sir Thomas Sherley entered into about forty years since'. This sum was more than a year's normal income from the Wiston estate. Further, the bonds in question had been discharged under the Great Seal when Middlesex had acquired Wiston in the early 1620s. Angry and disgusted, he decided to get rid of the estate. In 1634 he sold it for £16,500 to Sir John Tufton, Earl of Thanet, the grandson of his friend and sitting tenant, Lady Exeter. So Wiston House passed to the fourth family to own it since the Conquest.

A rich man and a devoted Royalist, the Earl of Thanet too had a tumultuous career. In August 1642, at the start of the Civil War, he joined Charles I at Nottingham with 100 horse. He fought at Edgehill on October

23, and later at the siege of Chichester; but at Bramber Bridge, a couple of miles east of Wiston, he had to surrender to the parliamentarians. He requested 'an accommodation', and in the spring of 1643 he managed to escape to Belgium, leaving his pregnant wife and his children at Wiston House. Parliament then sequestered all his estates.

In December 1643, as the fortunes of civil war ebbed and flowed, royalist troops seized Wiston House and held it for three weeks. In January 1644, after the royalist defeat in the rain and mud at Arundel, they had to flee for their lives. They left behind three cartloads of booty. The parliamentarians promptly seized this, and occupied the house for the next eighteen months. Many of them were sick, and all were short of fuel for heating and cooking. Like cold and hungry soldiers everywhere, they seized whatever they could burn, dismantling wooden buildings and removing some three thousand fencing posts round Wiston's deer park. No doubt they killed and ate many of the deer. They drained seven fish-ponds, eating 'Carpes and other fish'. They stole fodder, cattle, sheep, pigs, and horses. They eventually rented out the park as a bivouac for itinerant cavalry, charging six pence per horse for a 24-hour stay.

Thanet saw these depredations for himself when he returned in March 1644, paying Parliament a fine of £9,000. He reckoned that he had lost £17,000 on his Kent and Sussex estates. At Wiston, £1,600 worth of silver plate had been stolen, plus £1,400 worth of other goods, as well as furniture, weapons, books, and a trunk of documents. The house, he complained, had been 'totally defaced'. Perhaps, by comparison with some royalists, whose lands were confiscated, he felt himself lucky. At all events, in May 1649, three months after the execution of Charles I, he sold Wiston House and a great part of the estate to a 22-year-old parliamentary commander, John Fagge. The price, in that buyers' market, was £6,870.

The young John Fagge was one of many. As one historian put it, 'In all parts of England army officers suddenly appeared as the proud possessors of great estates, and seemed on the way to found a new landed aristocracy.' Even at the time, they were known as 'the new gentry'. And in 1660, when good King Charles's golden days dawned, it was perfectly legitimate (*pace* the Vicar of Bray) for former parliamentarians to side with the monarchy. As John Evelyn observed, Charles II had been invited to return 'by that very army which rebelled against him'. So – again one of many – John Fagge acquiesced in the Restoration and served the King as a valued local administrator. He became Member of Parliament for Rye, Steyning, and Sussex, and acquired a baronetcy.

Sir John Fagge's was the fifth family to own Wiston House since the Norman Conquest. But it had not quite shaken off the second. A quarter of a century after Fagge had bought the property, he found himself embroiled in a bitter dispute with His Majesty's Physician in Ordinary Dr Thomas Sherley, the great-grandson and last male heir of the original Sir Thomas Sherley. The complex 'extensions', conveyances, sequestrations, purchase of liabilities and clearance of titles to do with Wiston had evidently left loose ends. In 1664, Dr Sherley was actually taxed for lands valued at £5 and described as 'the miserable residuum of the once great estates of the elder line of the Sherleys of Sussex'. This 'residuum' eventually led Sherley to make a claim which in 1675 produced an important constitutional landmark in relations between Lords and Commons.

Sherley's claim against Fagge was heard in the Court of Chancery. It ruled in favour of Fagge. Sherley, by a petition, brought the case on appeal to the House of Lords. The Lords ordered Fagge to appear and answer at their bar. But Fagge was a Member of Parliament; and on May 5, 1675, the House of Commons promptly espoused his cause. It argued that because of parliamentary privilege its members were exempt from legal process while parliament was sitting, and that the Lords could not hear appeals in Equity cases. The Lords contradicted both assertions on the following day. A week later, on May 14, the Speaker of the House of Commons issued a warrant for Sherley's arrest 'for prosecuting his appeal before the Lords'. There followed a rapid, stately, and barbed exchange between the two Houses, sometimes in notes, sometimes at joint meetings. During the course of it, on June 1, Fagge himself was imprisoned in the Tower – in effect for breaching his own parliamentary privilege. The House of Commons declared that 'without leave' he had 'appeared in the Lords' House, and put in his answer to the appeal of Dr Shirley' when the matter of his privilege was, at his instance, in question 'in this House of Commons'. He immediately petitioned, 'submitting himself to this House, and craving their pardon for his offence, and praying, he might be released of his imprisonment'. The Order for his release was agreed on June 3. The quarrel between Lords and Commons rumbled on until November 22, 1675, when the King prorogued Parliament until February 1677. It was a virtual stalemate. Dr Shirley did not pursue his petition; members of the Commons retained their freedom from arrest save for treason, felony, or breach of the peace; and the Lords continued to hear appeals from Equity courts.

The Fagge family continued to live at Wiston House until the 1740s. Sir John Fagge's great-grandson died in 1740, leaving his sister Elizabeth to inherit the estate, which included other land a property in Kent and Sussex. Three years later, she became the second wife of Sir Charles Goring, of nearby Highden House, Washington. The Gorings, a family distinguished in Sussex since the 13th century, were the sixth to occupy Wiston House since the Conquest. They still own Wiston to this day.

Such was the turbulent history of the mansion to which Wilton Park moved at the turn of the year 1950–51. By that time, the house had shed some older, grandiose features. In the 1740s, Sir Charles Goring had demolished the outer buildings of the eastern courtyard in front of the house, including the original gatehouse. He refaced the ends of the wings on each side of the courtyard: a stone near the ground on the eastern façade of the north wing is inscribed 'April 15th 1747'. He retained the Elizabethan hammer-beam roof and the windows of the Great Hall, embellishing its walls, niches and chimney-piece with plasterwork, perhaps from James Gibbs (whose *Book of Architecture* had appeared in 1728), perhaps from Batty Langley's 1741–42 *Gothic Architecture Improved*. Above the south end of the hall, he placed two heraldic crests with the Goring lion and Fagge ostrich, to symbolise the uniting of the two families.

Charles and Elizabeth had only one child, Charles, born in 1744. In 1760, at the age of 16, he organised the planting of beech trees within the Iron Age earthwork on Chanctonbury Hill. So strongly did he feel about the plantation that shortly before his death in 1829 he wrote a poem about Chanctonbury Ring:

> *How oft around thy Ring, sweet Hill,*
> *A Boy, I used to play,*
> *And form my plans to plant thy top*
> *On some auspicious day.*
> *How oft among thy broken turf*
> *With what delight I trod,*
> *With what delight I placed those twigs*
> *Beneath thy maiden sod.*
> *And then an almost hopeless wish*
> *Would creep within my breast,*
> *Oh! could I live to see thy top*
> *In all its beauty dress'd.*
> *That time's arrived; I've had my wish*
> *And lived to eighty five;*
> *I'll thank my God who gave such grace*
> *As long as e'er I live.*
> *Still when the morning sun in Spring*
> *Whilst I enjoy my sight,*
> *Shall gild thy new-clothed Beech and sides,*
> *I'll view thee with delight.*

Soon after Charles's death, the Gorings decided on further alterations at Wiston House. For these they engaged a champion of the then popular

'Tudor Gothic', Edward Blore (1787–1879). Blore had made his name with Walter Scott's romantic Abbotsford; and as a fashionable if not very individual architect he enjoyed a highly successful career. He worked on Lambeth Palace and Westminster Abbey, and he succeeded John Nash at Buckingham Palace. At Wiston, according to family legend, he first proposed demolishing the house and starting afresh, leaving the Elizabethan hall as 'a romantic ruin' in the park. Cost or taste forbade this scheme; and Blore had to content himself with lesser changes. In the northern part of the house, he replaced the parlour with a ballroom. To the south he added a library, a study and a drawing-room, whose walls are partly lined with panelling from the former parlour, and partly decorated with a copy of the plaster-work from the hall. To the west side of this southern range, Blore added a cast-iron conservatory. The gardens to the south were very probably laid out at the same time.

By the time that Wilton Park moved to Wiston, the Goring family had owned the house and estate for more than 200 years. Time had mellowed its mixture of styles and erased the memory of earlier vicissitudes. The 20th century had nevertheless seen innovations: electricity in 1911, motor transport in the 1920s. The most drastic were death duties. In 1924, when another Charles Goring died, the estate faced a heavy tax burden. Land and properties were sold, and in 1926 Wiston House itself was leased to tenants. During World War II it was occupied by Canadian and British troops: the former, unlike the latter, did no damage. After the war, Wiston House was again leased out, this time to the girls' finishing school known as 'The Monkey Club'. In 1950, it found its new tenant – and not a moment too soon. If it had not, the Goring family believes, John Goring might well have been forced to demolish Wiston House. In the event, Wilton Park and Wiston turned out to be an ideal match.

CHAPTER 12

Stately Home

> The stately homes of England,
> How beautiful they stand!
> Amidst their tall ancestral trees,
> O'er all the pleasant land.
> **Felicia Hemans**, 'The Homes of England' (1849)

Wiston House tallied better with Koeppler's and Mrs Hemans' vision than with Noël Coward's – although the member of staff who had to help cope with its heating and plumbing problems no doubt recalled Coward's lines:

> The pipes that supply the bathroom burst
> And the lavatory makes you fear the worst ...

Koeppler felt obliged to remind visitors that 'This is a very old building which makes for increased danger of fire.' Dexter M. Keezer, an American participant who in 1973 produced the first book about Wilton Park, wrote:

> Into this Elizabethan mansion have been fitted living and sleeping quarters which preserve much of its old English dignity and also provide a substantial measure of modern comfort and convenience, extending even to the provision for the guests of an electric washing machine and dryer. Of these amenities an Italian conference participant remarked that 'the old house, like so many in Britain, is full of 'comforts' which for many Europeans are very uncomfortable indeed'. There is little doubt, however, that a broadly based international poll of Wilton Park conference participants would show this judgement to be much too harsh.

Be that as it may, the daily routine at Wiston House, as at Beaconsfield, was by no means sybaritic. 'Please take your bath in the morning before

7.30 a.m.' said the 'Hints for Participants'. They continued:

> Please help save electricity, and switch off lights when leaving the common rooms ... Wiston House is not particularly sound-proof. Self-interest suggests complying with the following restrictions and seeing in a friendly but firm manner to their adoption by all other participants:
> a) Do not slam doors
> b) Absolute silence in corridors and bedrooms between 11.30 p.m. and 7.30 a.m.
> c) No music in the lecture hall after 11.30 p.m.

The day began with breakfast at 8.00 to 8.30 (half an hour later on Sundays). There was then what Dexter Keezer called 'the only conference exercise which seems to have an almost ritualistic character. This is the filing into the library after breakfast to shuffle through the newspapers to make sure that no major international development has taken them unawares.' Next would come a two-hour plenary session, with the chairman presiding in front of the fireplace from a quasi-throne inherited from an English judge, and conference members ranged round the room in deep upholstered armchairs. Koeppler regularly introduced the first plenary, equipped with a rose in his button-hole and a pungent cigar. His customary opening remarks as chairman were paraphrased by another American participant, William C. Rogers:

> We are here not to discuss the matters that bind us together. We all appreciate that we share common tastes in music and the arts, and in other ways share a common civilization. Here we are more concerned about the matters that divide us. Talking about peace with friends will get us nowhere. (If the Russians were here it might.) Therefore in the brief time we have together let us concentrate on the awkward and vital issues that divide us. Ladies and gentlemen, in your questions please be brief, trenchant and, if possible, witty.

'This straightforward, almost abrupt, greeting', said Rogers, 'sets the tone of the conference'. At each session the discussion leader had half an hour to introduce his subject; then it was open to general discussion, with all interventions addressed 'through the chair'.

Between the plenary sessions, participants met in smaller groups of about a dozen each, which allowed the less self-confident to shine. All discussions were punctuated by tea – at 10.30 in the morning and 3.30 in the afternoon. Dinner was from 7.00 to 7.30 p.m.; and for a purely nominal fee participants could join 'the Chanctonbury Ring Club', a small bar in the basement. Every course included at least one excursion, often to Parliament in London; and all participants had the opportunity of a drink or a meal in Koeppler's Wiston House lodgings, usually to meet a visiting VIP.

For the first course at Wiston, in January 1951, Koeppler redefined Wilton Park as:

> A course in citizenship, in politics, and in common European problems with the emphasis on realism and impartiality. The purpose of these courses is, in brief, to make a positive contribution to the development of a European public opinion. People talk too much about Europe today without really being conscious of the practical problems.

This was part of the general, very gradual process of opening up Wilton Park to more nationalities and new types of course. The six-week courses were reduced to four weeks, with about fifty people on each; and the VIP conferences of one week each were now to be twice a year, with 20–30 prominent Germans plus about ten from other European countries. Non-Germans were now usually funded by their governments or by other sources. Staff from the Allied High Commission were also invited to spend a few days at Wiston to get a better idea of how it worked and what sort of candidates it needed.

On March 7, 1951 in the Foreign Office, the Wilton Park Academic Advisory Council held its first meeting since the move to Wiston House. Reporting on the first two sessions in the new premises, Koeppler said that the public rooms were very much better than at the old Wilton Park but the bedrooms were, if anything, worse. The Germans, however, were settling down very much more quickly and that there was less political antagonism than had been the case hitherto. He could not, he said, attribute this entirely to the new surroundings: selection had improved considerably of late, which undoubtedly helped. This led to the question of selecting participants from the German trade unions, who were now given a block quota that they filled themselves instead of submitting names to the general Selection Committees. Professor Thomas Marshall wondered whether this system was resented by other participants. Koeppler admitted that it caused comment; but though selection varied enormously it was generally improving.

Koeppler reported that the Federal German government had asked for four or five extra places at the one-week VIP conference. Chaput de Saintonge felt that this was a tribute to Wilton Park. Koeppler said that his December visit to Germany had shown him how much it was appreciated by both the Germans and the Occupying Authorities in the French and American Zones. Professor Marshall said he was sure the Americans would gladly pay for people sent to Wilton Park from their Zone.

The next major event at Wilton Park was a citizenship course for 'Youth Specialists', who spent twelve days, from March 8 to March 20, 1951, staying with private families and studying British institutions, then had ten days at Wilton Park, ending on March 30. Over the Easter weekend they were joined by youth leaders from other countries. Of the 26 German participants, only one had mentioned 'politics' as a special interest. At the other end of the age-scale, Koeppler had circularised the Selection Boards in Germany about a proposed 'Old Boy' or 'Old Wiltonian' course, and he was glad to note that the Dutch and the Swiss were also very interested.

The 'Youth' course was drawing to a close when George Anderson had good news about staff salaries. It came in a letter from Jack Rampton of the Treasury dated March 29, 1951. He had come to Wiston on March 6 with an Assistant Secretary colleague, Antony Peck, who coincidentally had known Koeppler at Oxford. The visit had been 'a useful exercise' which they had found 'very interesting and instructive'. Privately, Rampton was not much impressed by the intellectual level of the Wilton Park discussions or the academic calibre of the tutors:

> At the time of appointment in July 1948 these people were certainly not underpaid [at a flat £800 a year]. Apart from general 'nursemaid' duties their official functions are largely confined to promoting discussion groups at a not very high intellectual level. Though the tutorial system which they run has basic similarities with university tutorial systems, the intellectual ability and degree of knowledge required is very much lower. Indeed the job could really be undertaken by anyone with a reasonable knowledge of current political and social affairs, with an interest in people and with a degree of conviction that the work was worthwhile. (I do not mean that such people are easy to find: the job has no prospects and in any event would be unattractive to the first-class man.)

In this minute of March 27, 1951, Rampton seems to have ignored the fact that the tutors had to work in German and (increasingly) other languages. A colleague pointed this out. But he conceded that:

> There are ... two grounds for altering their present salaries. First the general cost-of-living which has been extensively recognised as grounds for improvement. Second the absence of an incremental scale. (If there were a third reason it would be that the Tutors are dissatisfied and threaten to walk out.)

It was clear, in fact, that all the academic staff deserved better treatment. As Dexter Keezer wrote much later from his own experience:

> There are ... certain common characteristics of successful members of the academic staff at Wilton Park, beyond their linguistic skills. One is intellectual alertness. Another is a liking for people, of all the remarkable varieties reaching Wilton Park. Another is an insatiable curiosity about the unfolding British and international scene, and a driving ambition to increase understanding of its significance. To do this effectively a combination of modesty and quiet authority is essential. So is a strong constitution to provide a physical backup for the hard work at hand.
>
> In imparting such enthusiasm Warden Koeppler takes a contagious lead.

So Rampton agreed to the proposed salary scale for the tutors and to a rise in the flat-rate salary for Koeppler, to go up from £1,229 a year to £1,375. Soon afterwards, in April 1951, Cecil de Sausmarez joined the staff to replace Martin Lindsay. Politically he was a Liberal, offsetting two Conservatives (George Greene and Robert Gibson) and two Labour Party supporters (Alec Glasfurd and Werner Lauermann).

In his letter of March 29, 1951, Rampton had told Anderson that he awaited proposals for improving the pay of the Librarian 'I think', he added, 'that you will find us not entirely unsympathetic.' There was good reason. As a later inspector pointed out:

> The Library is in constant use by the members when they are not at tutorials, which means most afternoons and evenings. They are directed by the tutors to certain books, articles and periodicals, etc. and it is the Librarian's function to enable enquiring students to be supplied with matter on any particular subject mentioned. For this reason he must not only be German speaking but have sufficient academic qualifications and abilities to advise members in this respect. The tutors especially attach great importance to the qualifications of a Librarian.

This notwithstanding, work in the Library – including cleaning it – was being done by a German, Mr F.F. Mehlberg, classified in the establishment as one of six ... kitchen-hands. If anything, it was an index of how Wilton Park had had to improvise from the beginning, relying on goodwill where administrative rules seemed inflexible. In the end, he was regraded Librarian; but it took time.

A further instance of how hard it was to reconcile operational efficiency with bureaucratic punctilio arose in the late summer of 1951. The Lord

Mayor of Salzgitter in Lower Saxony, wishing to show gratitude for the work of Wilton Park, offered Koeppler the gift of a Volkswagen minibus, seating eight people. It would be particularly useful for transporting visitors between Wiston House and Steyning, the railway station for London – a job hitherto done under contract by a Steyning private hire firm. 'There is no doubt,' wrote Brigadier P.R. Antrobus on September 8, 1951, in a letter to Jack Rampton in the Treasury, 'the car would be a very useful asset': used for official purposes only, it would save at least part of the cost of hiring. Antrobus went on:

> The Board of Trade have been approached and offer no objection to the granting of an import licence for a car presented to a Government Department who will be the owner and sole user. The Customs Authorities, however, are somewhat difficult and inform me that they would be obliged to charge $33\frac{1}{3}\%$ duty and $66\frac{2}{3}\%$ purchase tax on the price of the car. These charges would make acceptance of the gift quite impossible.

It took nearly three weeks to get an answer from the Treasury. When it came, on September 27, 1951, it was not from Rampton but from another official, Mr M. Lynch. 'We appreciate that it would be desirable to accept the vehicle as a mark of gratitude, but I am afraid that it is impossible in this case to waive the Customs duty and Purchase Tax chargeable on import.' When Roy Portman replied for the Foreign Office, on November 30, 1951, he asked the Treasury to reconsider its earlier decision and agree to purchase tax and customs duty being waived, or to allow the Foreign Office to pay them itself.

All December went by with no further Treasury reaction. It was understandable. On October 25, 1951, the country had gone to the polls and evicted Clement Attlee's Labour Government, replacing it – by a majority of 16 – with a Conservative administration headed by Winston Churchill, now 77. Within Government generally there was 'the pressure for economies'. Writing to the Foreign Office, the Treasury spelled it out: 'The need for economy is paramount and every penny of expenditure which cannot be classified as absolutely essential must be ruthlessly eradicated.' Churchill wrote, in a minute to the Lord Privy Seal: 'Special attention should be paid to the heavy expenditure on education in Germany.' Minuting colleagues in January 1952, Rampton saw this as an opportunity to abolish Wilton Park:

It occurs to me that as part of the economy drive we ought to have another shot at getting rid of this institution …

On our side I do not think that there is much to add to what has been said ad nauseam in the past, except that to my mind it becomes increasingly difficult to fit a thing like this into the general picture of increasing German independence. (Since September 1950 I have seen the place in action and came away as unimpressed as possible!)

He noted (with obvious satisfaction) that Wilton Park's budget 'specifically demands annual review'.

On January 3, 1952, Lynch of the Treasury wrote that 'There is some doubt whether Wilton Park will continue to function after 1/4/52.' Five days later the doubt had hardened into what the Treasury hoped was certainty. On January 8 it wrote to the Foreign Office demanding a cut in the Estimate of its German Section for 1952–53, and directly targeting Wilton Park: 'We for our part conclude that the reasons which have hitherto been advanced to justify its continued existence can no longer be regarded as valid in the present crisis. We must, therefore, ask for the winding up of this centre.'

This obviously dwarfed any question of a minibus. As Lynch put it in a letter to Portman in the Foreign Office on January 17, 1952:

We have reached the conclusion … that the offer should be gratefully declined, because, while it may not be a matter of extreme difficulty to maintain the vehicle in this country, our enquiries lead us to believe that it would certainly be difficult to re-allocate it within the government service when Wilton Park closes down.

As it turned out, however, Lynch's words were premature. With the approval of the new Secretary of State for Foreign Affairs, Anthony Eden, the Foreign Office had already asked the High Commissioner in Germany to make 'appreciable economies' in the Information and Education field. This met Churchill's immediate concern. But the economies proposed deliberately excluded tampering with Wilton Park, which the Foreign Office regarded 'as a vital element in our re-educational programme'. Eden being away in the United States, a final decision had to be postponed; but at official level the Estimate had to be agreed with the Treasury by January 19, 1952. The Wilton Park budget of £27,464 was included, to be endorsed later by Eden himself.

Shortly afterwards, Lynch had to admit that 'Our attacks on Wilton Park have so far been fruitless.' He promised himself 'a new assault in the next Estimate season'; but for the new fiscal year 1952–53 Wilton Park was safe. Among other things, the Foreign Office had successfully pointed out that, although its budget – like that of any government department – still had to be renewed from year to year, the assumption now was that it should continue.

As a result, Portman wrote to Lynch on February 20, 1952, a letter quietly exuding satisfaction at having won both the minor and the major battles:

> I refer to your letter of 17th January and to our subsequent telephone conversation about the offer of a Volkswagen omnibus to Wilton Park.
>
> It has now been decided that provision for Wilton Park can be made in our estimates for 1952–53 and in view of this we feel that we can reasonably and safely assume that there is a very good prospect of Wilton Park continuing for another twelve months.
>
> In these circumstances I am writing to ask you to reconsider the decision notified in your letter of 17th January and to agree to our bearing both purchase tax and customs duty charges, and so enable us to accept the gift.
>
> With every prospect of Wilton Park continuing awhile, we can no longer see any valid reason for refusing this gracious offer by the Mayor of Salzgitter.
>
> We are certain that when Wilton Park closed down there would be no difficulty in selling the omnibus and that, in the meantime there should be no difficulty about spare parts as we think that the gift would include a number of them. Could I ask you to reply at an early date.

Parturient montes, nascetur ridiculus minibus. But the more important result of the mountains' labour had been a further lease of life for Wilton Park.

It was not a life free of care. Staff problems continued to concern Koeppler – including his own. He was still – so far unsuccessfully – seeking FSSU (Federated Superannuation Scheme of Universities) superannuation such as was available to university teachers. Late in 1952, Koeppler recruited the first woman tutor, Miss A.M. Cameron; and on August 2, he raised with the Establishment and Organisation Department of the Foreign Office's German Section the question of a 'Responsibility Allowance' for George Greene, the Dean at Wilton Park.

The Establishment and Organisation Department took quite a while to act on Koeppler's request, 'because', it said, 'of estimates and other extremely urgent work'. But at last, on October 31, 1952, it made a convincing case to Jack Rampton at the Treasury. In doing so, it emphasised that:

One side of the Wilton Park activities of ever increasing importance is the participation of people from countries other than Germany. This participation requires an increasing amount of letter writing which, to a large extent, has become the responsibility of the Dean. Furthermore, the distinguished foreign members of the Sessions do expect, and possibly are entitled to, special consideration while they are at Wilton Park. Whereas the Germans come for 4 weeks and there are generally around fifty of them, those students from France, Belgium, Holland, Switzerland and Norway appear as lone wolves and stay only for a week, knowing no one on arrival and obviously requiring special care and assistance.

A still more crucial point stressed by the Foreign Office was the recurrent problem of selecting the right candidates for Wilton Park. It had caused headaches from the beginning, and certainly from the moment that civilians had begun to be recruited:

> However good the programme is and its execution, Wilton Park cannot fulfil its task unless the people who attend the courses are the right people. In order to get these people there has now developed in Germany a network of Selection Committees. Experience has shown that constant contact and advice from Wilton Park is necessary in order to guide the Committees, tactfully to tell them where they have chosen wrongly and to offer encouragement when it is felt that their choice has been particularly good. The Dean is responsible for sending a letter at the end of each Session to each of the main Committees summing up the Centre's impression of the candidates from the particular area.

Such written contact was supplemented by Koeppler's and the tutors' annual visits to Germany. Especially significant in this respect was the official trip that Koeppler himself made in the summer of 1953. In just over a week, in early July, he covered an immense amount of ground, in both geography and subject-matter. On the key problem of selecting suitable candidates for Wilton Park, he had some fruitful discussions at the Wahnerheide Headquarters of the British High Commission.

Another purpose of such visits to Germany, as Cecil de Sausmarez told a British reporter, was to see 'Whether the flame of Wiston House is still burning brightly.' In Koeppler's report on his July 1953 trip, written ten days afterwards, he devoted two and a half pages to just this:

> When discussing the possible effect of the work of Wilton Park on those who participate in it, the question is often raised how far former members show in later years any effect of their participation in Wilton Park discussions. The nature of our work does not allow an accurate estimate. Even if

182

men and women who have been to Wilton Park later on take a leading part in the public life of their communities, it would be foolish to maintain that this was the result of their visit here, although amongst the many letters we receive from former members not a few make it clear that the writers have either been encouraged to continue with their public work or have started it as a result of their visit.

Koeppler actually kept a collection of appreciative letters in what he called the 'Trumpet File'. Dexter Keezer quoted some, including the following from continental Europe:

From a member of the German Federal Parliament: 'I am particularly grateful that we were able to discuss any problem – even the really hot potatoes.'
From a Swiss Parliamentarian: 'Wilton Park is not a playground for "cold warriors" but a genuine forum and true meeting place of free peoples from free countries: it is a place where one not only thinks but also learns to think and go on thinking.'
From a French lawyer: 'Wilton Park is a melting pot where prejudices and preconceived ideas dissolve and give way to a pragmatic view of the world, more realistic because it is more multinational.'
From a member of the French Military Commission: 'At Wilton Park the clash of ideas cannot fail to produce something positive for every man of good faith, and without any undue self-consciousness let me freely admit that my point of view on certain problems underwent a change.'
From a Chief of Protocol in the Danish Ministry of Foreign Affairs: 'The Warden and his staff have developed political discussions to the sublime. Here is not the next best but the best: the most crystal clear clarity.'

Koeppler also alluded to – but on this occasion avoided quoting – the roll-call of distinguished German statesmen and others whom Wilton Park had received: 'There are indirect ways of estimating the effect of Wilton Park, such as conversations with former members and the reaction of that rather sensitive gauge of German public opinion, the Federal Parliament and federal officials in Bonn.'

The roll-call was long and distinguished. From Wilton Park's days with prisoners-of-war it included such figures as Wolfgang Abendroth, political scientist; Rüdiger Borchmann, journalist; Fritz Borges, activist with the Europa Union; Erhard Dornberg, Minister of Education in North Rhine Westphalia; Horst Grabert, SPD Senator from Berlin; Johann Baptist Gradl, CDU politician; Kurt Halbritter, the caricaturist; Karl Hemfler, Minister of Justice in Hessen; Bernd C. Hesslein, journalist; Hermann Höcherl, Federal Minister of Agriculture; Botho Kirch, producer with the official broadcasting station *Deutsche Welle*; Heinrich Kröller of the

Bavarian SPD; Hans-Ulrich Pusch, broadcast producer; Gerhard Richter, Berlin politician; Oskar Rummel, SPD deputy in the Bavarian *Landtag*; and Chrysostomus Zodel, journalist.

Wilton Park's 'civilian' alumni, in addition to Rainer Barzel and Ralf Dahrendorf, included: Karl-Wilhelm Berkhan, State Secretary in the Federal Defence Ministry; Herbert Blankenhorn, later Secretary General of the CDU; Fritz Borinski, SPD luminary and professor of Adult Education; Leo Brawand, editor on *Der Spiegel*; Willi Brundert, Mayor of Frankfurt after his brush with the Soviet authorities in East Germany; Ilse Elsner of the SPD, political scientist and Hamburg Senator; Ulrich Erfurt, actor, director, and theatre manager; Hildegard Hann-Brücher of the CDU; Winfried Hedergott, FDP representative from Lower Saxony; Theodor Heuss, the Federal President; Alois Hundhammer of the CSU; Wilhelm Kaisen, Lord Mayor and Minister President of Bremen; Heinrich Köppler, a CDU deputy and State Secretary; Lauritz Lauritzen of the SPD, Federal Housing Minister; Ernst Majonica of the CDU; Emil Maltzkuhn of the SPD; Werner Marx of the CDU; Bernd Nelleson, journalist; Helmut Rohde, journalist and SPD activist; Helmut Schmidt, later to be Federal Chancellor; G. Ernst Schnabel, senior producer with the Nordwestdeutscher Rundfunk; Hans-Jochen Vogel, SPD deputy and Lord Mayor of Munich; Friedrich W. von Sell, lawyer and broadcaster; Curt Weckel, SPD President of the *Landtag* of Saxony; and Willi Weyer, Interior Minister of North Rhine Westphalia.

Apart from listing selected alumni, how was one to gauge influence? Koeppler had a suggestion:

> One further method is to see how far people who have been here keep contact with one another, how far they participate in the work for Anglo-German understanding undertaken by the High Commission, how far they join German organisations devoted to the study and improvement of international relations. One form of these activities is the formation of clubs of former Wilton Park members and the organisation of regular meetings.
>
> Throughout Germany there are such Old Wiltonian clubs whose fortunes vary. Some, like Hamburg, would appear to have almost lapsed; others, like Hannover [*sic*], Berlin, Munich, Nürnberg, Stuttgart and Cologne, have now been active for a considerable number of years ...
>
> So far about half a dozen weekend meetings have taken place. Apart from one in Schleswig-Holstein in 1949 they were arranged at the Adult Education College Göhrde, with the active support of its Director, Dr Fritz Borinski, who had himself been a tutor at Wilton Park in 1946. These meetings were considered a great success both by the Germans participating and the several tutors who went to attend and to open discussions.

Koeppler noted that Göhrde was very near the Elbe in the easternmost corner of the Federal Republic, and easily accessible mainly for people from southern Schleswig-Holstein, Hamburg, and eastern Lower Saxony. Yet a sprinkling of Old Wiltonians came to these meetings from as far away as Munich and Trier and other parts of the south and west.

For several years, Old Wiltonians in these areas had planned a more local Old Wiltonian get-together. It was finally held at Hennef (Sieg) in North Rhine Westphalia on July 4–5, 1953. The three organisers – the former head of the *Land* Ministry of Culture, the *Oberkreisdirektor* in Wesel, and a senior Trade Union Official – had all been at Wilton Park for one-week VIP conferences. All that Wilton Park did was to supply a list of local Old Wiltonians, send good wishes, and promise that some tutors – in the event, de Sausmarez and Glasfurd – might attend.

The response, as Koeppler said, was 'astonishing'. More than a third of those canvassed wanted to come, paying their own travel, board, and lodging; and about a fifth of those who did attend had been at Wilton Park as prisoners-of-war – three of them from the very first course. This gave Koeppler especial satisfaction. 'The myth that Wilton Park, at least in its beginning, indulged in "re-education" could hardly be more effectively refuted than by the presence of these "very old" Wiltonians.' And he had another reason to be gratified:

> It was for us a great pleasure to see that, while strongly opposing views were expressed and no punches were pulled, the whole atmosphere was less strident and more constructive than is usual on these occasions in Germany. In the farewell speeches this point in particular was stressed and the speakers found in it a lasting effect of their stay at Wilton Park.

Three similar meetings in different parts of Germany were tentatively planned for the following year.

The discussions at Hennef, Koeppler reported, had shown something else:

> The Wiltonians agreed that in international meetings it was better to tackle political problems, however awkward and difficult, than to avoid these difficulties by activities which might be described as 'cultural' in the narrower sense of that term ...
>
> I also felt confirmed in the belief that we were right at Wilton Park not to avoid the discussion of German internal affairs.

It was a good universalist principle. But then, as if suddenly mindful that he was addressing British officialdom in the Foreign Office, Koeppler added:

Of course, British concern is only with German external policy, but internal issues will exercise a powerful influence on the composition of the next government, and this government will decide Germany's foreign relations. Thus, in order to try and influence German foreign policy, it would appear justified not to resist the discussion of German internal affairs if our members are anxious to discuss them with us.

Koeppler contrasted the candid, free spirit of Wilton Park with what he diagnosed in Germany at that time as 'two-tier politics':

> Leaders of all political parties would give their views in private, but would assure you that in public they would never be able to express the same opinion, either because the public would not stand it, or because their party might object. This affects all vital issues, such as the European Defence Community, Germany's eastern frontiers, reunification, etc. An amusing instance of how far these 'two-tier' politics will go has been reported by my colleague, Alec Glasfurd. He visited a small but distinguished group of Old Wiltonians in a south German town, amongst them the Lord Mayor who is a Socialist and the local member of the Land Parliament who is a Liberal Democrat (FDP). The Lord Mayor arranged a dinner with Glasfurd as guest of honour to which he invited leading citizens of the different parties, in order to show Glasfurd that 'in Germany, too, party political differences did not prevent people from sitting and talking together'. The dinner was a great success and, clearly, these men of different convictions were on good personal terms. Glasfurd stayed the night at the house of the Liberal M.P. and was present the next morning when the M.P. tried hard to persuade the local paper not to report the dinner for fear that his party chiefs would not approve of his having dined in public with the Socialist Lord Mayor.

If anything, this confirmed Koeppler in his belief that Wilton Park succeeded just because it transplanted Germans of all professions, creeds, and political persuasions to a neutral, confidential, British environment where discussion could be free. He concluded his very detailed, nine-page report:

> This visit has strengthened my conviction of the profound differences between British and German society. The façade of daily life, the technical civilisation, the interests and pastimes of the general population are much alike ... It is surely also right to believe that both civilisations share in the legacy of Athens, Jerusalem and Rome. And yet in the assumptions of what makes the good life for the citizen, what are his rights and what are his duties, Britain and Germany are still very far apart.

186

Koeppler wrote this ten days after the end of his German visit, in the very British surroundings of the Warden's lodgings at Wiston House. It was good to be back; but there were tensions – and temptations – to be faced. Academic life still distantly beckoned. This year, 1953, he had been given to understand that, if he cared to apply for a university professorship, he had a good chance of getting it. He declined. He did so, Whitehall officials thought, 'in the light of our assurances that the Foreign Office set great store by his work'. But it was also clear that Wilton Park still had first place in his affections.

On July 27, 1953, just after Koeppler had completed his report on the trip to Germany, a more weighty Report was published by the Drogheda Committee, set up under the Earl of Drogheda to review the value of Britain's overseas information effort – the Foreign Office's Overseas Information Services, the Commonwealth Relations Office, the Colonial Office, the Board of Trade, the Central Office of Information, the British Council, and the External Services of the BBC. Drogheda concluded that the Overseas Information Services played a vital role in support of overseas policy, and that they deserved more funds. He recommended that special efforts be concentrated on Asia, the Near East, Latin America, and the United States, but that Germany should be seen as a case on its own. It was the country where the Cold War was being most fiercely waged; and its future was uncertain. It might later be united: but it might remain divided, with the Federal Republic further integrated into the West. One of the main aims of occupying Germany had always been to introduce and consolidate democratic practices in the media, education, and administration. The work of information and education must continue, with an organisation of its own. So the Foreign Office's Information Division (responsible mainly for the media) and Cultural Relations Division must both be kept, although the Office had planned gradually to hand over Cultural Relations to the British Council.

Contrary, therefore, to what some had feared and others had perhaps hoped, Drogheda largely endorsed existing policy on Germany. Indirectly, this gave a boost to Wilton Park. For some time, it had been changing, with more visitors from outside Germany and, in general, higher-level participants. As Koeppler said in a letter to the Foreign Office on November 13, 1953, there had been a 'considerable increase in the "weight" of personalities active in government and public affairs who attend Wilton Park Sessions'. This naturally affected the budget. Most obviously, it required what Koeppler called 'a comparative raising of the standard of hospitality which we are authorised to offer'. The Foreign Office broadly agreed. It felt that the proposed 1954/55 estimates for food were 'on the high side';

but it was glad to see the Ministry of Works improving the accommodation and furnishings.

Higher-level participants were not only more demanding: they were also busy. And an increasing problem, for Wilton Park, was their reluctance – or inability – to spend too long away from their normal jobs. For VIPs, Koeppler's special one-week sessions were about the limit. Although in 1949 the original six-week courses had been cut down to four weeks, many prospective participants had asked the Foreign Office whether they could not come for a shorter time. But various ideas – of shorter sessions, of more than two one-week VIP courses, and even of long-weekend meetings for Germans already in Britain – were debated between the Foreign Office and the Bonn Embassy. The Counsellor there, Peter Wilkinson, suggested on March 26, 1956, that 'it might be much better if the regular courses could be made nearer a fortnight in length'. He also thought that shorter courses would attract more people from the business world, which was at present under-represented. Koeppler and his Wilton Park colleagues, however, continued to argue for four-week courses. It was a disagreement that was to rumble on for years.

Nor was it the only difficulty with Whitehall. Perhaps the most delicate was the perennial problem of the staff. 'I realise full well', wrote Koeppler, 'how square a peg Wilton Park is in the round pigeon-holes of the Civil Service'. No easy comparison could be made between the academic staff there and the normal grades within the Foreign Office. But for once the Office was sympathetic. On March 1, 1954, Roy Portman wrote to F.R. Barratt in the Treasury submitting a salary claim based on the increases granted to Executive grades, and also seeking approval for a salary scale (rather than a flat rate) for Koeppler. The proposals were for £860 × 40 – £1,100 for the tutors and £1,500 × 75 – £1,800 × 50 – £1,850 for Koeppler, both scales to be consolidated. 'In proposing a scale for the Warden,' wrote Portman, 'we would mention that the recommendation of the Drogheda Report is for long term cultural relations with Germany and we think it would be very inequitable to keep the Warden on a fixed term salary point for a further protracted period.' He asked for his proposals to be approved with effect from January 1, 1953, and that Koeppler be started 'one increment up his scale, i.e. at £1,575 p.a.'.

True to form, the Treasury demurred. 'Even at their current rates', wrote Barratt to a colleague, 'these people are probably over-paid'. He and others sought to compare them to British Council Lecturers. The debate sputtered on until July 2, 1954, when Roderick Barclay, Deputy Under-Secretary of State at the Foreign Office, announced that 'We have finally reached agreement about the Tutors.' But, he continued: 'The Treasury's last offer for Dr Koeppler still seems to us inadequate and, after discussion with Mr [John] Nicholls [Assistant Under-Secretary of State] and Sir F[rank] Roberts [Deputy Under-Secretary of State], I have reached the conclusion that we ought to take the matter up at Ministerial level.'

So on July 8, 1954, Anthony Nutting, Conservative MP for the Melton division of Leicestershire and Minister of State for Foreign Affairs, wrote directly to John Boyd-Carpenter, fellow Conservative M.P. for Kingston-upon-Thames and Financial Secretary to the Treasury: 'We are ... not at all happy about the offer of a salary of £1,570 for the Warden, Dr Koeppler, which with the addition of £50 E.D.A. would leave him £70 per annum better off than at present.' Nutting went on with what amounted to an eloquent tribute to Koeppler:

> A number of our colleagues of all Parties visit Wilton Park and all speak most highly of it and of Dr Koeppler. It would be extremely difficult to get anyone with anything like his personality and qualifications to take on the job if he were to throw his hand in and we should, I fear, have to offer a substantially higher salary than he is now receiving. I know that the Foreign Secretary would be greatly distressed if dissatisfaction with the financial terms offered him caused Dr Koeppler to resign. I fear that there is a serious risk that he may do so, if we fail to offer him what he, and we, think is a reasonable rate for the job. In the circumstances I trust that you will agree to our last proposal that he should receive a salary of £1,700 consolidated.

This letter caused much barbed minuting inside the Treasury. One official, W.W. Clague, wrote on July 21, 1954:

> It seems to me that the Foreign Office are only too well aware that the 'success', if any, of Wilton Park hangs entirely on the personality of Dr Koeppler. One is left in little doubt as to why they are so anxious to retain his services. If he goes the place will lose whatever momentum it may have at present. Incidentally this should help the Treasury in its campaign against the extravagance of Wilton Park. It might conceivably fold up without being pushed!

'I am afraid', commented Boyd-Carpenter, 'this is going to give us a lot of trouble.' It was 'just the sort of issue which, in my experience, Mr Nutting is inclined to take to the Foreign Secretary and raise at the highest level – and ... Wilton Park is their cherished infant'. In the end, it was Henry Brooke, the new Financial Secretary to the Treasury, who replied to Nutting on August 7, 1954: Boyd-Carpenter had meanwhile become

Minister of Transport and Civil Aviation. Brooke's letter made a concession, if in time-honoured words:

> I have considered very carefully ... whether the circumstances of the
> present case are such as would justify some exceptional arrangement.
> Knowing as I do something of Dr Koeppler's abilities and of his outstand-
> ing personal contribution to the work of Wilton Park, I am inclined to
> accept the view that, so long as Wilton Park continues as at present, it is in
> our interests to do what we reasonably can to retain his services there. I
> should therefore be willing to agree that his salary should be increased,
> from 1st August, 1954, from £1,570 to £1,700 a year.

When George Aynsley, of the Foreign Office (German Section)
Personnel Department, announced this decision to Koeppler, he surmised
that he might probably feel disappointed. 'You are quite right', wrote
Koeppler on September 21, 1954, 'and I know you agree I have every
reason to be.'

Robert Birley and Harold Nicolson, who had raised the subject at the
November 1954 Wilton Park Academic Council, went by appointment to
the Foreign Office on February 1, 1955. They had hoped to see Anthony
Nutting, but he was ill: in his place they talked with Lord John Hope, the
Joint Parliamentary Under-Secretary of State for Foreign Affairs. Birley
pointed out that since last October the position had changed: the salaries
of all university professors and lecturers had been raised. Koeppler's salary
was now less than that of any man holding an equivalent position in
university life. Hope was sympathetic to Birley's plea that Koeppler's
salary should be put on an academic rather than a civil service basis, and
he agreed that Birley should see Henry Brooke at the Treasury.

On February 14, 1955, Birley wrote to Brooke in preparation for a brief
meeting or a lunch:

> Every time I go to Germany I hear about Wilton Park, and almost everyone
> I know who has been over there has also heard of it in the course of his or
> her talks and discussions in that country. It has a remarkable prestige ...
>
> The trouble is that the whole thing depends on Koeppler. He invented
> it, and I think he is the only person who could run it. He combines the
> greatest enthusiasm for it with an understanding of the German problem
> and a quite astonishing flair for choosing and securing speakers. He has
> hung on for years at a salary considerably less than he could hope to get in
> an ordinary academic post. I doubt whether we can really hope that he will
> go on doing this much longer. He was a Don at Magdalen before the war,
> and was already making a name for himself as a mediaeval historian. By

now I think he would almost certainly have been a professor at a provincial university if he had not started Wilton Park.

The argument cut little ice with the Treasury official asked for advice, Francis Barratt. Under the new university scales, he minuted, non-medical professors got the standard minimum rate of £1,900 a year – an increase of £300 over 1949 – whereas Koeppler was getting nearly £400 more than he was in 1950. The basic Civil Service doctrine was 'the rate for the job', although this could be interpreted 'fairly liberally' for temporary civil servants with special qualifications. 'We have already done as much', wrote Barratt, 'for Dr Koeppler'. The Treasury also reckoned that Koeppler's accommodation and food were subsidised to the tune of 'at least £300 a year'.

Concern about Wilton Park salaries continued for many months. On December 22, 1955, Roy Portman of the Foreign Office wrote to the Treasury suggesting – unsuccessfully – that Koeppler might be eligible for a pay supplement of £100 a year. On April 11, 1956, Koeppler made further pleas for his staff to George Aynsley, adding one for himself. Because his last year's pay rise had been personal, 'I fall between two stools and receive neither the rise given to Assistant Secretaries nor the one to those below. This appears to me quite iniquitous and wholly unacceptable. I hope you will agree that I have not been impatient in this matter, but I find the Treasury attitude trying in the extreme.'

Had Koeppler known what else was in the offing, he would have found Treasury attitudes more trying still.

CHAPTER 13

Threat

'Threatened men live long.'
16th century proverb

'Isn't it time we had another go at getting rid of Wilton Park?' The questioner was John Boyd-Carpenter. The date was July 9, 1954, when he was still Financial Secretary to the Treasury. He moved on before expending much effort; but suspicion and hostility still surrounded what one official called 'a damned university'. On November 14, 1955, Lord John Hope gave a written answer to Captain Henry Kerby, Conservative MP for the Arundel and Shoreham Division of West Sussex, who had asked the Secretary of State for Foreign Affairs, Harold Macmillan, 'why he is keeping in being the Foreign Office establishment at Wiston House', and what it had cost in 1954. Hope's answer was bland:

> The purpose of the Wilton Park Centre is the furtherance of sound Anglo-German relations through lectures and discussions about political, economic and social problems of mutual interest, and I am satisfied that it continues to do valuable work. The total cost of the Centre during 1954 was £35,200, of which £1,450 comprised rent.

But behind the blandness there were plans. They had been laid by mid-December 1955, while Harold Macmillan had still been Foreign Secretary and before his move to become Chancellor of the Exchequer on December 22. The Foreign Office had decided to close Wilton Park.

Early in the New Year, on January 3, 1956, it fell to Macmillan's successor Selwyn Lloyd to explain the decision to Richard Winterbottom, Labour MP for the Brightside Division of Sheffield, who on December 18 had asked for it to be reconsidered:

192

I regret the necessity for closing Wilton Park, since I am aware of the valuable work which has been done there. However, I have had to take into account two main considerations: first, there is the general need for economy in the national expenditure at the present time; and secondly, a special Anglo-German Institution such as Wilton Park is becoming somewhat out of place in the developing pattern of our relationship with the Federal German Republic. The Federal German Government have expressed understanding of our point of view and have accepted our conclusion that the Institution should close in July.

Douglas Dodds-Parker, Parliamentary Under-Secretary of State for Foreign Affairs, wrote in similar vein to Richard Goold-Adams, Deputy Director of the Institutive of Directors, on January 8, 1956.

For the moment, however, the decision to close Wilton Park was known only to comparatively few. On January 2, 1956, the Head of the German Information Department in the Foreign Office, Rolland Chaput de Saintonge, wrote a private and confidential letter to Professor George Potter, a mediaevalist who was Cultural Attaché at the British Embassy in Bonn as well as a member of the Wilton Park Academic Council. 'The latest idea', said Chaput, 'is that University College, London, might possibly be used as a centre for the type of session that we have in mind as a continuation of the Wilton Park idea. I am negotiating about this but must keep everything secret.'

So secret was the whole subject that Chaput, even when writing to Peter Wilkinson in the Bonn Embassy on May 11, 1956, held back from saying that Wilton Park's demise had already been decreed:

Wilton Park is a valuable institution but it does not play the same vital role as an instrument of our information policy in Germany as the other sponsored visits. If one had to cut our numbers of visitors drastically we should consider seriously whether Wilton Park should not be first sacrificed, as it would not do to put all our eggs in the Wilton Park basket ... On the other hand, there is quite a strong lobby behind Wilton Park and it may well be that any attempt at cutting it down would arouse considerable opposition and cause a good deal of publicity ...

There may of course be a possibility of getting financial subsidies from the Germans to keep up Wilton Park. Do you think the Land or Federal Governments would either make a yearly contribution or pay for either fares or maintenance of German members? Alternatively do you think we could charge the Germans a fee for part of the accommodation or tell them they will have to pay their own fares?

Meanwhile, back at the mansion, life continued as if unaware that

Wilton Park's fate was virtually sealed. In January, John Barnes, Counsellor at the Bonn Embassy, had discussed with Chaput the 'amenities' at Wiston House. They had agreed, he wrote on January 18, 1956, that 'while we did not want to turn Wilton Park into an unduly luxurious establishment, at the same time we did not want to practise excessive austerity there'. Chaput raised the problem with Frederick Waters, the Administration Officer at Wilton Park, who in February repeated his request for single-room accommodation, defended the selection of newspapers in the Library, and went into piquant detail about the food. He summarised his remarks in a letter on March 16:

> Food is not, for very good reasons, of the variety and standard that one might find in a middle class home and someone may have expressed the view privately. For example we must purchase the cheaper cuts of meat and bacon and for most meals we serve margarine instead of butter. It could be said, perhaps, that our breakfast, which consists of porridge or cereal, a small collar or streaky rasher of bacon or one egg, is meagre and that the supper at night, which consists of soup and a 'made up dish' with an occasional sweet or biscuits and cheese is not the same as dinner at home, but taken by and large I think most of the members are well satisfied with the meals. It would, of course, be nice to lay on eggs and bacon for breakfast or serve up a baron of beef, poultry, etc., for dinner at night but this is, we realize under present economic conditions, out of the question and we accept it.

Life at Wilton Park, in fact, was continuing as it had before. There was even a minor storm, such as had once been provoked by Lady Astor. This time, its centre was Koeppler's old and volatile friend, the Left-wing Labour MP Richard Crossman. On the evening of Friday May 25, 1956, Crossman took part in a four-man Wilton Park 'Brains Trust' on the subject of 'The "Man in the Street" and Well-informed Public Opinion'. When Lord John Hope saw the programme, he 'felt that this was an unwise assignment'. His fears were confirmed when he heard – from two sources, including the German Embassy – what Crossman had said about British views of German reunification:

> He told the Germans that not one single person in England was in favour of reunification. He added something to the effect that the idea was solely in the interests of restoring equilibrium in Europe.
>
> I cannot imagine a sillier choice to make than Mr Crossman. No doubt he was chosen for his stimulating qualities, but it is one thing to enjoy the stimulus of his speeches when you are a member of a seasoned political

community; it is quite another to let him loose on a politically immature group. I am not suggesting that the Germans should not be faced with the pros and cons of reunification in terms of British opinion – far from it – but they surely ought to hear the case argued dispassionately and with at least a modicum of intellectual integrity. I do not know for how long Mr Crossman has been on Wilton Park's books, but I think that Dr Koeppler should squeeze him off the list if at all possible. There is no doubt that he is doing great harm as he is telling Germans what many of them want to hear as it reinforces the urge to make a deal with the Russians.

Lord John Hope's Minute was dated June 8, 1956. Chaput de Saintonge responded three days later:

We have tried as much as possible not to interfere with the programmes of Wilton Park so as to maintain the myth [*sic*] that Wilton Park is not a propaganda organisation. Except where there is a very pressing reason, therefore, I have refrained from giving any guidance to Dr Koeppler.

He agreed, however, to suggest that 'invitations to Mr Crossman should be "spaced out" completely'. He made no mention of 'spacing out' Wilton Park.

Shortly after Richard Crossman's 'Brains Trust', on May 29, 1956, the Academic Advisory Council met in the Foreign Office. It too seemed oblivious of any threat to the *status quo*. Chaput de Saintonge sent his apologies, as did six Council members; but Professor George Potter was there, presumably aware of the plan to close Wilton Park, yet having to keep the knowledge to himself. Proceeding as normal with routine business, the Council agreed to propose Peter Tennant, Overseas Director of the Federation of British Industry, as successor to Professor Thomas Marshall, who was leaving for UNESCO. It heard a report from Koeppler, who said that the Swiss Government's action in doubling the money for sending people to Wilton Park had encouraged the French to send (and pay the fares of) participants – an impression confirmed on a private visit to Paris on the weekend of March 17, when he had seen, among others, René Massigli, Secretary-General at the Quai d'Orsay, and Roland de Margerie, Director-General of Political Affairs.

The bomb burst – for the Academic Council – on Friday, July 6, 1956. That day, Chaput de Saintonge wrote to Robert Birley:

When we arranged for the Inspectors to visit Germany last summer and to report to us on the level of activity to be maintained in our information services there, we fully expected to be able to fix a level for our activities in

Germany for the next three years. Indeed, the recommendations of the Inspectors were intended to be carried out gradually over that period and to enable us to maintain approximately the same level of effective activity as we had had in the past.

Unfortunately the whole country has been overtaken by the need for further economy in government expenditure. [Harold Macmillan's 1956 Budget proposed cutting Government spending by £100 million.] We were first asked by the Treasury to examine very seriously the whole of our information expenditure in Germany and in particular the sum of money that was devoted to sponsored visitors and to Wilton Park. We resisted on political grounds cuts in these two activities and hoped that we would be able to ease our numbers of sponsored visits over the course of the next three years that we had planned originally.

Unfortunately developments elsewhere in the world [Nasser's assumption of power in Egypt? Britain's accession to the Baghdad Pact? The State of Emergency in Cyprus?] have created the need for emergency operations in the information field at the same time as the home economic scene called for further economy. At the urgent request of the Chancellor of the Exchequer we offered to cut down the amount of money spent on sponsored visits this year by about £7,500 which was about the sum which remained uncommitted so late in the financial year. We had, however, to examine very seriously what could be done during the next financial year.

After consultation with Derick Hoyer Millar and George Potter, we came to the conclusion that we could offer to cut down our sponsored visits programme for next year by about half. As this would not yield a sufficient sum of economies we reluctantly came to the conclusion that we should contemplate the abolition of Wilton Park.

This is a step we have fought for some time, and one which we are very loath to take, but with the development of our political relations with the Federal German Government, Wilton Park has to some extent outlived its original purpose and it is becoming increasingly difficult for us to justify the continuance of arrangements directed solely to the Germans and not to other nations. With the decreasing amount of money to be devoted to sponsored visitors, we could not in any case keep Wilton Park going, and it would be unwise to have Wilton Park as the sole activity in this sphere.

We are therefore proposing to bring Wilton Park to an end on July 31, 1957. We fixed this date partly because we think that a year's notice to the Germans would be necessary and partly because we wish to make it easier for the staff to find new jobs at the beginning of the academic year of 1957. Before we make any public announcement, I think it would be well for us to tell the Academic Council about our decision. If you agree, we would propose to call an emergency meeting as soon as possible ...

I ought perhaps to mention that Koeppler knows nothing of this development, although I have hinted to him that the future of Wilton Park was again being examined. I have written to him asking him to call in as soon as he returns from [his holiday in] Italy so that I can put him in the picture.

The Extraordinary Meeting was held in Room 195 of the Foreign Office at 4.00 p.m. on Tuesday, July 24, 1956. 'There was considerable consternation', as Chaput de Saintonge later put it: 'the members of the Council were taken aback'. The Chairman, Robert Birley, called the proposed abolition of Wilton Park 'absurd'. Lord Beveridge thought it 'the most ridiculous economy imaginable'. Dorothy Elliot was 'alarmed' to hear that matters had gone so far before the facts were put before the Council.

Chaput elaborated on the points he had put in his letter to Birley: that the Foreign Office was spending £45,000 a year on 800 sponsored visitors to and from the United Kingdom and £38,900 on 360 visitors to Wilton Park. The plan now was to reduce spending on sponsored visits to £25,000 and to close Wilton Park. This would save nearly £60,000.

Birley told the meeting that since he had heard the news he had done what he could to gauge the attitude of the Foreign Office, and had got the impression that there was little hope of preserving Wilton Park in its present form. But he believed that it would be folly to throw away a going concern that had evolved an educational technique in discussions between different nations. He had had reason to believe, he said, that there would be some support for extending Wilton Park's range to cover the NATO countries: it would be one way of fulfilling Britain's obligations under Article 2 of the Treaty.

This Article, adapted from the Brussels Treaty of 1948, declared:

The Parties will contribute towards the further development of peaceful and friendly international relations by strengthening their free institutions, by bringing about a better understanding of the principles upon which these institutions are founded and by promoting conditions of stability and well-being. They will seek to eliminate conflict in their international economic policies and will encourage economic collaboration between any or all of them.

It was a catch-all provision, included to show that NATO was not solely a military organisation; but it gave a basis for extending the scope of Wilton Park. Both Birley and Koeppler thought that the methods built up there would be suitable for NATO, and that although the problem of language was difficult, it could be overcome. Lord Beveridge proposed that the Council should approve the following Resolution:

> In the unanimous opinion of the Academic Council it will be an indefensible economy of money to throw away the established working institution as represented by Wilton Park for promoting understanding of common problems between different nations. So far from throwing this away, the Government might well consider using the machinery and experience of Wilton Park for international communication between a wider group of nations.

After some discussion, the Council agreed that Birley should write to the Prime Minister, Anthony Eden, along lines he had drafted, but should include some expression of the Council's powerful views. Meanwhile, Birley would ask the British Ambassador in Bonn, Sir Frederick Hoyer Millar, not to announce to the Consuls General the Government's intention to close Wilton Park until there had been time for the Prime Minister to consider the Council's proposal.

In the event, it was too late. On July 25, Hoyer Millar wrote to the German Foreign Minister Heinrich von Brentano regretfully announcing the Government's decision. 'It must be admitted', he said, 'that Wilton Park, with the passage of time, has become something of an anachronism, and that this particular method of strengthening Anglo–German relations and fostering a better knowledge of British institutions in Germany is perhaps not altogether compatible with the developing pattern of our relationship with the Federal Republic.' Hoyer Millar also informed the British Consuls in Germany.

On the same day, July 25, as Hoyer Millar told von Brentano about the decision to close Wilton Park, Robert Birley wrote his letter to Eden. It incorporated a slightly improved version of Beveridge's words and a long, reasoned argument for the Academic Council's new proposals for Wilton Park:

> In our view it is highly significant that there is no evidence of any feeling in Germany against it, but rather every evidence of continued German approval and support. A priori one might imagine that, now that the Federal Republic is a sovereign state, there might be resentment at the existence of such an institution in this country. But it is now a year since the German acquired this status, and yet there has been no slackening in the demand for places at Wilton Park. In fact, both the Federal and Land Governments and the German Trade Unions are prepared to pay their full salaries to their officials when they visit it, which is surely good evidence that the Germans do not consider Wilton Park to be in any way derogatory to their dignity or prestige. They certainly appreciate its usefulness.

We feel it our duty to say that we are convinced that there is still great need for the work which is carried out at Wilton Park. This is especially evident in Germany. Democracy in that country, as might be expected, has, as yet, very shallow roots; the strains and stresses of the present situation in Europe, above all the desire for re-unification of their country, make adherence to the Western world difficult for many Germans. We believe that the experience of free discussion, the meetings with prominent British public figures and the insight given to the visitors into British institutions has proved a most valuable strengthening of the democratic spirit, and of the feeling of solidarity with the West in Germany. We believe that this process should be continued and that it would be most unwise to abandon it now.

In fact, so far from closing it, we urge that the Government should consider using the machinery and experience of Wilton Park for international communication between a wider group of nations. For Wilton Park is a going concern; it has already acquired valuable educational experience and a strong educational tradition. The way in which government and administration is carried on in this country is greatly admired in many others. The difficulty is to find out how to transmit our experience to people from other lands. Ordinary visits may do much, but their effect is often superficial, and the range of experience they provide is inevitably restricted. Wilton Park has evolved a technique which enables a visitor to gain a remarkable width of experience in the British way of life in a short time ... He or she meets people of real distinction and hears their accounts of their work; he learns to appreciate their attitude towards the problems of the day. The discussions make it possible to clear away misunderstandings and often for the questions that are raised to be considered deeply.

It seems to us that there is a great opportunity here for us to carry out an obligation under Article 2 of the Treaty forming the North Atlantic Treaty Organization. Wilton Park, we believe, should become an institution dealing not only with Germany, but with all the NATO countries. To found and build up a new institution, where members of the different NATO countries could meet, and where they could be brought to understand and appreciate the British point of view and our contribution towards western civilization, would inevitably take a long time. In Wilton Park there are the means immediately to hand.

We, therefore, urge that consideration should be given to the possibility of transforming Wilton Park into an institution where members of the various NATO nations could meet, and where work should be carried on on lines similar to those followed there now.

Birley recognised that broadening Wilton Park's clientele would in some ways transform it. But for years past Koeppler had been welcoming other nationalities; and, as he had told the Academic Council, there were growing signs of interest from outside Germany. For Birley, as for Koeppler, it was better to amend Wilton Park than to end it:

> Changes, of course, there would have to be, but Wilton Park has shown itself already to possess remarkable flexibility. In fact, it has already begun to develop on the lines we have suggested. At the session at Wilton Park which begins today, there will be present among the members M. Legendre, the Head of the German Section at the Quai d'Orsay, three members of the Chamber of Deputies, two of them 'moyens ministres', and one of the two Directors of the 'Ecole Nationale d'Administration'.
>
> Simply to destroy a living organism, at a moment when work of the kind that is done there is going to prove so necessary in a larger field, would seem to us to be discarding a most valuable asset, one that has fully proved its worth.

It was not the ideal moment for approaching Anthony Eden. On July 26 1956, the day after Birley wrote his letter, the Egyptian President, Gamal Abdel Nasser, nationalised the Suez Canal. The scene was set for the Suez crisis, the Anglo-French-Israeli action against Egypt in November 1956, and Eden's own retirement in January 1957. Small wonder that the 'NATO' alternative to Wilton Park's closure was discussed inconclusively for many months of far more urgent high politics.

In any case, Anthony Eden did not of course answer Birley at once. On July 26, 1956, his Private Secretary, Neil Cairncross, wrote to John Graham, Assistant Private Secretary to Selwyn Lloyd, asking for advice on what reply Eden should make. In the Foreign Office, the parliamentary Under-Secretary of State Lord John Hope noted that 'to transform Wilton Park into a NATO meeting ground' was 'an idea that I like a lot'; while Paul Grey, Assistant Under-Secretary, was more cautious. Grey also heard, as he noted on August 1, 1956, that

> Koeppler is, as might be expected, very upset ... There is an obvious danger that, if he voices his criticisms, we may receive the backwash in the form of disgruntlement among the Germans interested in the scheme and also objections by the Members of Parliament who have personal contacts with it.

Next day, Grey wrote an apologetic and appreciative letter to Koeppler; and when on August 15 Douglas Dodds-Parker, parliamentary Under-Secretary of State for Foreign Affairs, made Grey's point (in Grey's words) to Sir Ivone Kirkpatrick, the Permanent Under-Secretary at the Foreign Office, Kirkpatrick at once agreed to see Koeppler. Largely because of the

Suez crisis, their meeting had to be postponed. Meanwhile, Koeppler certainly 'voiced his criticisms'.

'I am a little disturbed', wrote the Minister in the Bonn Embassy, Roger Allen, in a letter to Paul Grey on August 24, 1956, 'to find that Koeppler appears to be working up for something like a personal campaign against the closure of Wilton Park':

> We here already know of three letters which he has written to people in Germany. There was a letter to Stuttgart asking the Consulate-General to let him know whether certain press reports of the reasons given by the Consulate-General for the closure of Wilton Park were correct. [Koeppler's concern, as he later told Chaput de Saintonge, was prompted by letters from Germans, who thought the announcement that Wilton Park had become 'something of an anachronism' was an admission that it had been 're-educating the Germans'. If many believed that, much of Wilton Park's good work would be undone.] Secondly, Koeppler has written to [Peter] Wilkinson here enclosing some printed and duplicated material which amounts to propaganda against the recent decision to close Wilton Park and a complaint that the people at Wilton Park themselves were not consulted ... Finally, Koeppler has written personally to another member of the staff here asking in effect whether the Embassy was consulted and whether they agreed with the decision ...
>
> You may, therefore, think that a word of warning would not be out of place. I mention this because I understand that it is promised that Koeppler should come out here in September at his own expense to address a Bavarian gathering of former Wilton Park participants ... It might be well if he were warned that he must not make any remarks in Germany which might be taken as critical of the British Government's decision.

The 'duplicated material' that Koeppler had sent to Wilkinson was dated August 15, 1956. It was entitled 'The Future of Wilton Park':

> When we raised at the Foreign Office the question why Wilton Park had at no stage been brought into the discussion concerning its future, we were told that there was agreement as to its success and excellence and that nothing could have been added by Wilton Park to improve the opinions held of the work. The decision to end activities next summer was, we were assured, solely based on the paramount need for economy.
>
> In the meantime several arguments, apart from the need for economy, have been raised of which I do not know to what extent they have influenced the decision. I consider it my duty to put on record the views of Wilton Park on the three arguments which appear the most important to me.

1. The alleged increasing difficulty of recruiting participants.
We have never felt the effect of these alleged difficulties; on the contrary, there is general agreement, not only amongst the staff working here but also among those participants from other nations who make return visits after intervals of several years, that the 'weight' of the participants has increased and is increasing ...

2. The 'crest of the wave' argument.
While the work of Wilton Park is acknowledged to have been successful up till now, it is felt that conditions will change in the future and that it is therefore better to bring the work to an end before it declines. In as much as the belief that there will be a decline is based on the alleged difficulty of finding suitable people, I have dealt with it in Section 1. There is, however, a more general argument based on the assumption that the aims of Wilton Park have by now been largely achieved and that the need for it is bound to diminish. Against this argument we agree with the analysis of our task as set out in the leading article of the German newspaper 'Die Welt' of January 3, 1956 ...

That article, by the paper's Economic Editor, Dr Heinz Pentzlin, called for the West to 'achieve a consciousness of cohesion, of interdependence and community of purposes ... To achieve this ... the various partners have, first of all, really to get to know one another.' This, it continued, Wilton Park enabled them to do 'in hard discussion in which people tell each other the truth and are not afraid of making unpleasant discoveries ... It would be a good thing if Wilton Park, without necessarily being directly copied in other countries, were taken as a model.'

Koeppler's paper appended the article, and concluded the list of arguments he thought flawed:

3. The unsuitability of Wilton Park because it is a special institution.
This is an odd contention. It is acknowledged that Wilton Park has been successful, not least because it has gone different ways from those generally used in exchange programmes. To maintain that the aims of Wilton Park can now be better pursued by the old type of exchange visits appears to us surprising. It maybe that the aims of Wilton Park are best pursued by the methods and techniques developed there.

The Swiss Government appear to think so, for they have recently doubled the number of fares they are willing to pay for Swiss participants in Wilton Park and have made the grant for three years in advance. The French Government appear to think so, for they have during the current year increased both the quantity and quality of the French participants for the reasons set out in ... an article in 'Le Monde' of August 8, 1956.

This, by René Servoise, declared: 'Those in charge of Wilton Park seem particularly aware that lasting peaceful relations cannot be established in Europe on the sole basis of Anglo-German dialogue ... French participation is not yet as great as it should be, because our fellow-citizens do not know the institution and the excellence of its work.'

There were fears in the Foreign Office that Koeppler might have sent his paper to MPs and VIPs in both Britain and Germany. He had not. The official recipients had been Peter Wilkinson at the Bonn Embassy, and at the Foreign Office Chaput de Saintonge and Barbara MacLean. However, he had sent it to the members of Wilton Park's Academic Council. Since these numbered not only Robert Birley and Lord Beveridge, but also Lord Aberdare, Professor Denis Brogan, Miss H.C. Deneke, Dorothy Elliot, Sir Robert Ensor, Dr Ernest Green, Professor Agnes Headlam-Morley, Leslie S. Hunter (the Bishop of Sheffield), Sir Harold Nicolson, Professor George Potter, and J.C.V. Wray of the TUC, it was an extensive mailing-list.

Its members were also, as later events proved, extremely energetic and influential. Already on August 9, 1956, Harold Nicolson had written to the Marquess of Reading, Minister of State at the Foreign Office, enclosing a copy of Birley's letter to Anthony Eden, and adding: 'I think his idea of transforming Wilton Park into a NATO instrument is a very excellent idea. The Prime Minister knows about it and used to be favourable. But I should like you to read Birley's letter and if you get the opportunity to jog Eden's memory.' On the same day, William Shepherd, Conservative MP for the Cheadle Division of Cheshire, had written to Lord John Hope in similar vein; and on August 12 Professor Headlam-Morley wrote likewise to the Prime Minister.

Eden answered Birley on August 16, 1956 – the same day that 22 nations met in the London Conference at Lancaster House to discuss their response to Nasser's nationalisation of the Suez Canal. 'I have taken note', he wrote, 'of the interesting suggestion ... that Wilton Park should be transformed into a NATO institution. This matter has been under consideration by the Foreign Secretary, and I shall write to you again when the practical possibilities have been explored.' Replying to Professor Headlam-Morley ten days later, he again mentioned the 'possibilities' but added 'including the financial implications'. This was because the Head of the Foreign Office's Information Policy Department, Charles Stewart, in consultation with Western Organisations Department, had come to the conclusion that the Treasury would be very reluctant to grant the new money that Birley's proposal for Wilton Park would need. On the other hand, 'the idea of converting it into a NATO institution, the cost of which would be shared with other NATO countries, might later with advantage be explored through NATO: but … we should not do so until it is known how much money will be available in 1957/58 for the overseas information services.'

So matters remained in limbo – while the Suez crisis dragged slowly towards what Eden himself called 'the crunch' or armed intervention. Meanwhile, Koeppler paid his visit to Munich, calling at the Bonn Embassy on his way home, to see Hoyer Millar and Roger Allen on September 26. He assured Allen that he had 'resolutely refused' to discuss with his German friends any plans for the maintenance of Wilton Park; but when he met Paul Grey in London next day he said that 'a number of Germans were mobilising subscriptions' in the hope of keeping it going. Grey commented to Allen that, depending on the circumstances, 'it might be embarrassing to receive such an offer'. Chaput de Saintonge agreed. 'It is quite likely', he noted, 'that we shall be faced with an offer of subsidy from the German side. The B.DI. (*Bundesverband Deutsche Industrie*) may join in an offer. All this would prove embarrassing if it was so substantial as to make it seem churlish for us not to spend £10,000 or so to keep W.P. going.'

The Germans made no secret of their disquiet. George Brown, the Labour MP and future Foreign Secretary, who was visiting Germany that October, told the British Ambassador in Bonn, Sir Frederick Hoyer Millar, 'that he had been much struck by the expressions of regret about the closing of Wilton Park which he had heard from many Germans he had met when in Berlin and Hamburg'. When the German Foreign Minister, Heinrich von Brentano, wrote on October 8 to thank Hoyer Millar for informing him of the decision, he was careful not to embarrass the British Government by seeming to question its judgment. But he paid Wilton Park, Koeppler, and its staff an evidently heartfelt tribute:

> May I take this opportunity to express to your Government the special thanks of the Federal Government for the great work carried out by Wilton Park and for the hospitality offered there to thousands of Germans over the years since 1945. May I also ask you to transmit these thanks to those who devoted to Wilton Park much of their life's work, and in particular to Dr Koeppler and his colleagues.
>
> Wilton Park will undoubtedly have a special place in the history of Anglo-German relations. Its work has notably contributed to the re-awakening and strengthening of the democratic idea among the German people …
>
> It will perhaps please you to hear that the news of the forthcoming closure of Wilton Park has aroused vigorous reactions in Germany. The Foreign Ministry has received many letters, whose authors express not only their regrets but also their gratitude.

13. From left to right, Richard Crossman, (centre front unknown), Denis Healey and Heinz Koeppler at Wilton Park, 1950s.

14. Conference on The Basis of British Policy in November 1953 – front row (left to right) Anthony Nutting MP, Mrs. H. Gaitskell, Frau Christine Tensch and The Right Hon. Hugh Gaitskell MP.

15. Werner Lauermann with participants outside the front of Wiston House in June 1955.

16. Wilton Park Academic Staff member George Roundell Greene (left) with Lord Beveridge (centre) at a conference in June 1956.

17. Dinner at Wilton Park during the 11th European Conference in March 1959.

18. Heinz Koeppler, 1960s.

19. HRH The Duke of Edinburgh arrives at Wilton Park for the 100th
Conference in March 1968.

20. Heinz Koeppler addressing Wilton Park, conference, 1970s.

21. Shirley Williams MP, at Wilton Park on the 25th Anniversary of its foundation, 12 January 1971. Assisting with the cutting of the cake are Chefs, G. Gander and Mr. Handerer.

22. The Right Hon. Edward Heath, Prime Minister, arriving by helicopter for the Jubilee Conference in June 1971.

23. Robert D. J. Gibson who retired from Wilton Park in 1976 at the end of 30 years' service.

24. Heinz Koeppler planting a memorial copper beech tree on his retirement 30 June 1977.

25. The last picture taken of Heinz Koeppler in Ashley Gardens, London, circa 1979.

After referring to the visits and exchanges that Britain proposed to pursue further, Brentano concluded: 'Finally, may I once more express my wish that everything should be done to make the spirit of Wilton Park live on. I am always at your disposal for a discussion of practical measures which may serve this aim.' It was about as far as he could go towards suggesting that Wilton Park itself should live on.

On October 19, at a Foreign Office party, John Moore of the German Information Department met Sigismund von Braun of the German Embassy. Von Braun said that the Germans were disappointed about the closure of Wilton Park, and asked whether a financial contribution from the German side would make the British reconsider the decision. He said he had heard there was some talk in Bonn of the Germans offering a contribution, but was inclined to think that, even if that were so, it would not amount to much more than an offer to pay fares. He intended to ask Bonn for further details.

They came two days later – in a report by the Bonn Correspondent of *The Sunday Times*, Antony Terry:

An appeal for £12,000 to prevent the closing of Wilton Park ... is being launched this weekend by West German Government officials.

The provincial Premiers of the nine West German Länder are to meet next month to discuss the allocation of official funds to help finance its continuation. Nearly 4,000 'Old Wiltonians' – Germans who have attended Wilton Park courses, most of whom now hold leading posts in the administration, trade unions and industry – are being invited to join a Wilton Park 'Old Boys' Association' in the interests of Anglo-German relations ...

Many Germans who have attended its courses during the past 11 years wear the 'Old Wiltonian tie' ...

The total cost of Wilton Park is around £36,000 a year. The Germans are hoping that if they can raise annually a third of this sum to cover the cost of travel and maintenance of the participants at future Anglo-German courses at Wilton Park they will induce the Foreign Office to reverse its decision to close it.

Two days later, on Tuesday October 23, 1956, *The Times* published a report summarising the state of play so far, and quoted an unnamed Foreign Office official, commenting on the proposal that NATO should use Wilton Park as a civilian college:

He added that if the N.A.T.O countries agreed to the proposal and agreed to share the cost of such a venture, the British Government might reconsider their decision to close it. 'But it would depend on the degree of public support in the various countries', he said.

That afternoon, the Wilton Park Academic Council met in the Foreign Office with Harold Nicolson in the Chair, deputising for Robert Birley, who was in the United States. Before the meeting, he met Heinz Koeppler at the Travellers' Club, and afterwards wrote in his diary:

I have to break to him that the F.O. stick to their decision to close down Wilton Park. The Council, Nicolson continued, 'are incensed' ... But how, in a phase of economy, can we really justify spending £41,000 yearly in giving Germans a holiday in Sussex? Chaput warns us that in the next five years Western Germany is going to be put to a final test of choice between East and West.

This last remark was not mentioned in the minutes of the council meeting. They reported Koeppler as saying that he had received 'a great many' letters from Old Wiltonians deploring the decision to close Wilton Park. Most proposed action to offer German help for its continuation. It appeared, he said, that steps were being taken in Germany. 'The Bavarian Parliament and, in particular, the Federal Upper Chamber are discussing during this week the possibility of offering a regular financial contribution for Wilton Park ... Several Committees of Old Wiltonians have been formed in Germany with the same object in mind.' The meeting in Bavaria, which he had attended, had discussed concrete proposals of support. Before the Government's decision had been made known, there had also been two other Old Wiltonian weekend conferences – one in North Rhine Westphalia, the other organised jointly by Lower Saxony, Hamburg, and Schleswig-Holstein.

Koeppler added that he had been asked by Members of Parliament of both parties whether they should raise the matter in the House. He had advised against it – no doubt for fear that a parliamentary question might elicit a negative reply which would be hard to retract. Chaput de Saintonge, for the Foreign Office, said that Sir Frank Medlicott, National Liberal and Conservative MP for Norfolk Central, would be bringing up the matter in the Commons: apropos of Antony Terry's *Sunday Times* article, he wanted to know if the Germans were going to give money to Wilton Park. Chaput thought that the answer to Medlicott's question 'would not be a slamming of doors'.

As it eventually turned out, the question that Medlicott put on October 29 was different and more pointed; and answer, while not slamming the doors, hardly left them ajar. Would the Secretary of State for Foreign Affairs reconsider the decision to close Wilton Park? Lord John Hope replied:

No. Her Majesty's Government recognise the value of the work done by Wilton Park and are indebted to its staff and to all others who have in various ways contributed to its success. In deciding to close Wilton Park they have borne in mind not only the need for economy but also the way in which Anglo-German relationships have evolved since the centre was established ten years ago.

But if the Foreign Office was for the moment unwilling to move from its set position, to expect otherwise at that moment would have been naïf. Selwyn Lloyd had just returned from his clandestine trip to Sèvres to discuss the Suez operation; the Cabinet had met on October 25 to hear the Anglo-French plan to intervene when – supposedly only *if* – Israel attacked Egypt; and Israeli forces were on the brink of mobilisation. It was not the moment to put less momentous policies into reverse.

Yet the pressure to rethink the fate of Wilton Park must have seemed to busy, distracted officials annoyingly persistent. On October 24, the day after the Academic Council's meeting, the British Ambassador to Switzerland, Sir Lionel Lamb, wrote to Paul Grey from peaceful Berne:

The other day at a musical reception at the United States Embassy George Littlejohn Cook [Chargé d'Affaires] and Patricia Hutchinson [First Secretary] happened to meet two Swiss, Dr [Hans] Zbinden of the 'Schweizer Vortragsdienst für kulturelle Arbeit im Ausland' and Monsieur [Ernst] Mörgeli, both of whom took the opportunity to introduce the subject of Wilton Park and to express the opinion that in view of the value of its activities it was a very great pity that its closure should now be proposed even as part of the present national campaign for economy in government expenditure. Dr Zbinden demonstrated particularly strong feelings on the subject and said that he would like to call on me on my return from leave to put before me the views of those Swiss who, as he put it, had been privileged to attend a Wilton Park course.

Not long afterwards, following my return to Berne, I was singled out during a social function (actually given by the Minister of Thailand on October 16) by the Federal Councillor in charge of Foreign Affairs, Monsieur Petitpierre, for a few words in private. Monsieur Petitpierre explained that he had been asked by several prominent Swiss to approach me officially with the request that the decision to close Wilton Park might be reconsidered. These persons had strongly represented to him, as the competent member of the Swiss Government, the value attached by them from the Swiss point of view to these courses, which they regarded as imaginative and constructive. M. Petitpierre had replied that he could not properly intervene officially in a matter which was an internal concern of Her Majesty's Government, but that in view of their insistence he was prepared to mention their representations to me in an unofficial manner. He was fully conscious of the fact that he had no locus standi insofar as any formal request for the continuation of the Wilton Park programme was concerned, but he wanted me to know that the Swiss Federal Council entirely endorsed the high opinion regarding the valuable service performed by the Wilton Park courses and would therefore welcome their survival ...

By chance, in the meanwhile, we have just seen the article in the first page of the 'Sunday Times' of October 21 entitled 'Bonn Effort to Save Wilton Park' which is most timely and topical. It may well be that Dr Zbinden may be contemplating some similar suggestion for a Swiss contribution towards the rescue of an institution, the demise of which he and his friends so gratifyingly and spontaneously deprecate. Anyhow in view of this unsolicited and high level testimony by our Swiss friends, now echoed moreover by responsible German circles, it would surely be short-sighted and even politically unwise to jettison such an evidently valuable international asset for a comparatively minor domestic economy. I therefore sincerely hope that you can submit these new factors for consideration and that the decision to close the Wilton Park scheme may be reviewed and rescinded in compliance with this revelation of its valuation by foreign participants.

The Berne Chancery forwarded to the Foreign Office, with reference to the Ambassador's letter, an article from the *Neue Zürcher Zeitung* of October 7, 1956, describing the work of Wilton Park in glowing terms and clearly first-hand detail.

In public, the Foreign Office continued to stonewall. In private, officials toyed with alternatives. The NATO college option was one. Another, suggested by Douglas Dodds-Parker, the Parliamentary Under-Secretary of State for Foreign Affairs, was a link with a university college, perhaps University College, London, perhaps St Anthony's, Oxford. A third, put to Dodds-Parker by Peter Smithers, Conservative MP for Winchester and Parliamentary Private Secretary to the Colonial Secretary, Alan Lennox-Boyd, was some form of association with the Council of Europe or with the College of Europe in Bruges.

Meanwhile, outside pressure was mounting. Sigismund von Braun of the German Embassy in London, who had already buttonholed John Moore at a Foreign Office reception, asked Dodds-Parker point blank: 'What would you say if the German Government offered to make a contribution to enable Wilton Park to continue?' Dodds-Parker reported this encounter on October 24, 1956. On the following day, the Permanent Under-Secretary, Sir Ivone Kirkpatrick, minuted that the German

Ambassador, Hans Herwarth von Bittenfeld, had raised the subject of Wilton Park with him, 'quite unofficially and without instructions':

> He said that he had been much struck by the attitude of the members of the last V.I.P. course who had emphasised the value of Wilton Park and the damage which would be caused to Anglo–German relations by its liquidation. The Ambassador went on to say that old Wiltonians in Germany were now a corporate body who exercised a perceptible influence on German thought and German evolution. He himself had been to Wilton Park and never hesitated to invoke the assistance of any other old Wiltonian in a matter of Anglo–German relations.
>
> Having said all this, the Ambassador then called my attention to reports that the Germans were making an effort to drum up money for the continuation of Wilton Park.
>
> I told the Ambassador that I had recently seen Dr Koeppler, whose work I much admired. But I had pointed out to Dr Koeppler that countries never stand still and that a time must come sooner or later when Wilton Park no longer fitted into the pattern of Anglo–German cultural and political exchanges. Consequently I thought it was better policy to cut off Wilton Park whilst it was still appreciated rather than to wait until it had outlived its purpose.

Kirkpatrick added, diplomatically: 'Nevertheless, if Germany collected money for the perpetuation of Wilton Park and made representations to us in favour of the continuation of the work there, I had no doubt that the Government would be prepared to reconsider the matter.' The sting, equally diplomatic, was in the tail: 'But of course I could not say what the result of reconsideration might be.'

That same day, October 25, 1956, Reuter reported from Munich that an all-party group of eight deputies in the Bavarian *Land* Parliament had introduced a motion to help keep Wilton Park in existence. The motion called on the *Land* Government to ask the Federal Government in Bonn to pay for the trips of Germans going to Wilton Park.

Next morning, *The Times* carried a letter from Professor William Rose of the London School of Economics and Political Science, an occasional lecturer at Wilton Park, expressing 'some dismay' at the Foreign Office's decision to close 'this unique institution':

> Its establishment was one of those brilliant strokes of initiative which Britain can always be relied upon to launch in an emergency, and students of German affairs and German ways of thought are only too well aware that the emergency still exists.

The administration by Dr Koeppler and his staff of keen, well-informed tutors has helped to compensate for the muddle over our attempt at restoring a sense of humane values which has done so much to bewilder Germans of the Federal Republic, and particularly to cloud the minds of the younger generation. The changes in our policy and propaganda since the early idealistic days of 're-education' by the Control Commission have fostered the suspicion that we are allowing expediency to override principle in our exhortations to the German people ...

I would wish to urge that this invaluable centre for the meeting of minds and the generation of good will should not be allowed to disappear on the grounds of economy. The Exchequer may save £36,000 a year, but we shall have lost a continuing opportunity for studying German ways of thought and feeling such as is to be found nowhere else, not even in our universities. It may be no less vital to comprehend the Germans in the future than it has been in the past, and our earlier deficiencies in this respect have been plain for all to see. We have not yet reached the stage of understanding when we can afford to abolish Wilton Park.

The same day, October 26, 1956, Dr Hans Zbinden of Berne wrote formally to the British Ambassador there, Sir Lionel Lamb, over the signature of 91 Swiss colleagues:

to inform Her Britannic Majesty's Government how deeply the undersigned Swiss citizens would regret seeing Wilton Park, with all its far-reaching consequences, a thing of the past. We, for our part, would be willing, if necessary, to contribute to the cost of residence of our participants.

Within the Foreign Office, Douglas Dodds-Parker was still casting about for ways to keep alive the Wilton Park idea. Also on October 26, he minuted Paul Grey, with copies to the Minister of State, Anthony Nutting, and to Sir Ivone Kirkpatrick:

In view of the growing interest in this, may I have an approximate estimate of the cost of continuing 'Wilton Park' as follows.
Our aims should be:
(1) to maintain and extend the Wilton Park type of course to include other European countries;
(2) to locate any course in a centre where existing facilities can be utilised; and
(3) to save certain overheads which were justified in the past but must be saved now.

To implement these aims we would need:

(a) to maintain Dr Koeppler and his staff on a more permanent basis. This might be done by a direct Foreign Office grant or through the British Council. But it would I believe best be carried out by linking them to some academic body like St Anthony's College; and

(b) to organise these courses to take place in some permanent centre such as an Oxford College when term is down, or on a peripatetic basis, using such centres as other Universities, Ashridge, Swinton, or a public school like Eton which has rooms for visitors. The administration of such courses could be on the same basis as the Foreign Office courses held in Oxford.

Such courses might remain predominantly German and German speaking as a start, but could be spread to French and other languages as occasion required.

If we could reach agreement on the desirability of such a re-organisa-tion, and could keep the overhead finance within a reasonable limit, we might offer this as our contribution and notify Council of Europe Governments in due course of the existence of the courses, for each of which there would be a set fee, while they could pay the fares of their nominees.

Even this cautious, complicated compromise met a guarded response. 'I have spoken', noted Paul Grey, 'to Mr Dodds-Parker, who agrees that whatever we achieve in the way of special courses, we should not represent them as a "continuation" of Wilton Park; and that we should think in terms of ad hoc courses and not of a permanent establishment with a staff and a building. We could employ Dr Koeppler and others on these tempo-rary courses if we wanted them and they were willing.'

To how much of Grey's gloss Dodds-Parker actually agreed is uncer-tain. What rapidly became clear was that many others were now paying attention. On Tuesday October 30 – the day after Israeli forces crossed the Egyptian desert border, and the day of the Anglo-French ultimatum to Israel and Egypt – *The Times* published another knowledgeable letter. Its author was Dorothy M. Broome, formerly Chief Women's Affairs Officer in North Rhine Westphalia. Its plea was that, if Wilton Park continued, 'one woman of senior rank and experience' should be added to its 'permanent tutorial staff'. That same day, Bill (later Lord) Rodgers, then General Secretary of the Fabian Society, wrote privately 'as someone who has been interested in the excellent work' done at Wilton Park to ask Selwyn Lloyd why it was being closed. Lord Pakenham was the next inquirer. On October 31 – the day that Anglo-French air forces attacked Egyptian airfields – he put down a Parliamentary Question asking if the

Government would 'consider the continuance of this most successful Institution on a wider European basis'. Next day, Jacques Viot, Second Secretary at the French Embassy in London, reminded Clive Rose in the Foreign Office that before going on leave he had asked what plans there were for the future of Wilton Park. Rose answered that there were none at present. Early that evening – at 7.17 p.m. on Thursday, November 1, 1956 – Pakenham rose to ask his own question in the Lords. He apologised for doing so: he had put it down 'before I knew we were going to have this debate of first importance [on Suez]'. He had tried to withdraw the question, 'but for one reason or another that did not come about, and therefore I will not, if the House will forgive me, deploy my main arguments on this subject this evening'. Even without them, Pakenham was backed both by Lord Astor, who called Wilton Park a 'magnificent institution', and by the Liberal Lord Ogmore, who added that 'other noble Lords on this side of the House and I feel strongly on the subject'. Lord Reading, the Minister of State for Foreign Affairs, gave a cautiously open-ended reply:

> We have had a number of suggestions from different sources as to possible variants on the Anglo-German theme in the method in which we can use Wilton Park in future. The examination of those various suggestions is still in a not very advanced state, and frankly I am not sure at this stage whether, for financial and perhaps other reasons, it will be possible to carry out any new proposal on those lines.

It was non-committal: but it was more than the government had conceded before. And the call for change went on, some of it in the press. On November 2, the centre-left *News Chronicle* declared: 'To close Wilton Park would be a false economy. It should carry on and its work be extended and imitated.'

But newspaper editorialising was not the only pressure on those in the Foreign Office who had to deal with Wilton Park. Apart from the Suez crisis, now on a virtual war footing, there was also a very practical question asked on November 1 by the Ministry of Works. It had been negotiating with representatives of the Goring family for a new lease on Wiston House. The proposed rent was £700 per annum, first reviewable in March 1962. Since the Foreign Office was giving up the house next July, the Ministry of Works would no longer be responsible for it, even if Wiston became a civilian NATO college. So it proposed to negotiate on the basis that the house could be surrendered when the Foreign Office left. The Ministry's question caused a flurry of memoranda within the Foreign Office, as well as telephone calls with the Ministry, which in turn was being pressed by the Goring family's representative. It was a genuine dilemma. Almost a month elapsed before Brigadier Charles Steel, Head of the Conference and Supply Department at the Foreign Office, wrote a formal answer to the Ministry of Supply on November 28; and even then he had to ask, apologetically, for a week's or ten days' delay. After alluding to the NATO college proposal, he went on: 'This scheme depends very much, of course, on financial considerations, and at the moment it does not look as though it will be a practical proposition from this point of view.' Inconclusive though this was, the question it failed to answer had given added urgency to the Foreign Office debate about Wilton Park.

Already, on November 2, 1956, John Moore of the German Information Department had briskly reviewed the options so far mooted. He rejected the first, which was to carry on Wilton Park as before. The second was to use it for projecting the British point of view to visitors from all NATO countries – his interpretation of Robert Birley's proposal to the Prime Minister. Since this would be purely British, it would have to be wholly British-funded, and was ruled out on grounds of expense. The third option was Dodds-Parker's – *ad hoc* courses and lectures elsewhere: this Moore costed at between £14,500 and £26,500 a year, with a likely intermediate estimate of £16,500. The most economical solution, which Moore recommended for study by Information Policy Department, was to offer Wilton Park to NATO or the Council of Europe 'as a going Institution, for which we are prepared to pay overheads [about £11,000 a year] if they provide running costs'.

Moore's preference had had a mixed reception from his colleagues. Charles Stewart, the Head of Information Policy Department was sceptical about the cost: 'the £11,000 ... will be difficult, if not impossible, to find in 1957/58, and succeeding years', Patrick Hancock, the Head of Western Department, preferred NATO to the Council of Europe, but wondered if the funds would be forthcoming. Paul Grey, the Assistant Under-Secretary, wondered whether Dodds-Parker's proposal had been 'got straight' and stressed that 'I am opposed to any elaborate or permanent institution being established to take the place of Wilton Park' – no doubt for fear of Treasury opposition. The possibility of a NATO Civilian College, however, 'would have something to commend it if we can afford the money'.

Lord Reading's Private Secretary, Peregrine Rhodes, summarised the state of play for him on November 14:

> It was agreed that Wilton Park's present activities should be ceased as a measure of economy; any arrangements for the future must therefore be on a completely new basis and will involve the insertion of a new item in the

estimate for the Foreign Office Vote for 1957/58. The financial position is at present in flux, largely because of the Middle East crisis which has caused a radical revision of plans for the information budget.

By this time, in fact, the Suez crisis was passing into the hands of the United Nations. Ten days earlier, on November 4, Nasser had blocked the Canal, while in Budapest Soviet troops had overthrown the Hungarian Government. November 5 had seen the first landings of British and French paratroops at Port Saïd and Port Fuad, followed next day by a sea-borne assault, which ended in a midnight cease-fire. On November 7, the UN General Assembly had agreed to set up a UN police force, and its first contingents were due in Egypt on November 15.

Rhodes went on to summarise the Dodds–Parker suggestion and the NATO college plan for Wilton Park, and said that a submission on the recommended proposal would be prepared shortly. 'The next stage will then be to argue out with the Treasury whether any substitute arrangement can be accepted.'

Paul Grey remained unconvinced. On November 21 he minuted Dodds–Parker:

> It seems to me a great mistake to go back on our position, whatever attacks individual supporters of Wilton Park may make on us ...
>
> I would, therefore, urge that we forget about these schemes unless or until we have some evidence that we shall be granted in the next budget enough money to do even half of the urgent work required in areas to which we have agreed that the highest priorities should be given.

Dodds–Parker annotated this:

> I agree.
> 1) 'Wilton Park' is dead
> 2) From its ashes could be made a useful institution, on a wider and different scale, including Germans. This would be a NEW proposal.

Grey's 'individual supporters of Wilton Park' might have been cheered if they had seen Dodds–Parker's handwritten comments. They did not; and their 'attacks' continued. The next, and best concerted, was a collective letter to *The Times* on Saturday December 1, 1956. Its twelve signatories were impressive: Earl Attlee, the former Labour Prime Minister; Vic Feather, Assistant Secretary of the TUC; Charles Fletcher-Cooke, the Conservative MP; the Rt Hon. Hugh Gaitskell MP, former Labour Chancellor of the Exchequer; Richard Goold-Adams, Deputy

Director-General of the Institute of Directors and former Assistant Editor of *The Economist*; the Rt Hon. Jo Grimond, MP, Leader of the Parliamentary Liberal Party; Major-General Cyril Lloyd, Director-General of the City and Guilds of London Institute and Chairman of the British Association for Commercial and Industrial Education; Gilbert Longden, Conservative MP for South-West Hertfordshire and former UK Representative to the Council of Europe; Gilbert Murray, Regius Professor of Greek at Oxford; Hugh Seton-Watson, Head of the Department of History at the University of London's School of Slavonic and East European Studies; George Scott, Editor of *Truth*; and the Rt Hon. Kenneth Younger, MP, former Labour Minister of State at the Foreign Office. They wrote:

> We believe that the aims and achievements of Wilton are important to the national interest, and that the present decision should not be implemented without the public having an opportunity of considering what is at stake.
>
> Although an understandable measure of Government economy, this decision implies several things. First, it would bring to an end something of proven value to the new German democracy; 'Old Wiltonians' in the Federal Republic are now doing all in their power to help keep Wilton open, even to the extent of offering finance. Moreover, a volume of experience and expertise has been accumulated by the staff at Wilton which could not readily be recreated if they were dispersed.
>
> Secondly, the closing would remove a valuable link between British and German opinion at the very moment when confidence has been severely shaken by events in Egypt, and when it was never more important to consolidate western unity in face of the sharp changes and convulsions which are now taking place in Russian policy. Certainly it is a false economy to increase British propaganda to the Middle East at the expense of reducing our ability to explain ourselves to our allies in Europe.
>
> Thirdly, if this very successful institution is closed now, a great opportunity will be missed to widen its scope so that others, in addition to Germans, may attend the courses. In recent months a few French, Dutch, Swiss, and others have been there. Our view is that consideration should be given to developing this trend, so that other North Atlantic Treaty Organization countries may be included as well.
>
> For all these reasons we sincerely hope that this unwise decision to close Wilton Park will be reconsidered.

The Foreign Office was now receiving a small glut of letters about Wilton Park. On December 3, 1956, Peter Smithers wrote to Douglas Dodds-Parker enclosing an inquiry from a constituent and repeating his view that 'some kind of broader based institution should be established at

Oxford or Cambridge'. The idea of using a university was one that Rolland Chaput de Saintonge, the Head of German Information Department in the Foreign and Commonwealth Office, had long been discussing confidentially with Professor R.C. Fitzgerald, Dean of Laws and Professor of English Law at University College, London; but although they had further talks in the New Year, the suggestion made little final headway.

On Tuesday December 4, the Reverend William Wynn Simpson, General Secretary of the Council of Christians and Jews, wrote to the Foreign Secretary, Selwyn Lloyd, to express 'deep concern' at the intention to close Wilton Park. The Council's Executive Committee, meeting on November 28, had unanimously resolved to make its views known:

> The Committee believes that there is a greater need today than at any time since the end of the second World War for closer understanding between the peoples of Western Europe as a basis for more effective co-operation in their resistance to forces which threaten the very foundations of our European culture. There could be no more impressive confirmation of the importance of this consideration than the events of the past few weeks in Central Europe and in particular in Hungary.

Two days later, on December 6, 1956, William Vane, MP, wrote to David Ormsby Gore, Parliamentary Under-Secretary of State for Foreign Affairs, putting a similar case: 'I think you know that I have been a supporter of Wilton Park, not least in the hope that it would one day widen its function and become more international. Now when it seems we have a bigger job than ever in putting across British views to other countries surely we ought not to suppress Wilton Park, but rather widen its scope in order to attract responsible people of all the countries in Western Europe.'

Next day, December 7, Sir Lionel Lamb wrote again from Berne to Paul Grey, 'disappointed' that Wilton Park was still doomed, and reporting further representations from Dr Zbinden and one of his colleagues:

> My Swiss visitors made a good point, it seemed to me, inter alios when they suggested that the Wilton Park programme afforded a valuable and voluntary forum for illustrating to influential and intelligent foreigners the true character of the British people and the objectives of British policy. This picture of Britain, seen with the visitors' own eyes and analysed by their own sense of observation, had the virtue of avoiding any suspicion of propaganda.

He in turn made a good point – and one that proved prescient – when he remarked that 'from the Swiss angle ... the conversion of Wilton Park into a civilian College for N.A.T.O countries would bring little comfort to the Swiss who would presumably be <u>ipso facto</u> excluded'.

On the following Monday morning, December 10, 1956, *The Daily Telegraph* published a letter from Düsseldorf by Lilo Milchsack of the Anglo-German Society, saying that the 'friends of Wilton Park' in Germany were 'endeavouring to find public funds with which to finance the fare and stay of German participants in the future'. They would give their support also if 'the members were to be recruited from a greater number of European countries or on a N.A.T.O. basis – an expansion which would certainly be welcomed in Germany'. That same evening, Douglas Dodds-Parker received a deputation led by the Conservative MP the Rt Hon. Walter Elliot, and consisting of Lord Pakenham, the Conservative MP for Farnham Godfrey Nicholson, the Liberal leader Jo Grimond, and the Labour MP for Leeds East, Denis Healey. They called it 'criminal folly' to close Wilton Park. Again, Dodds-Parker held out little hope of rescinding the decision, but promised to keep his visitors informed as plans for 'an alternative scheme' developed. He gave much the same answer two days later to Peter Smithers; but within the Foreign Office he asked for a meeting to discuss the whole matter. Originally scheduled for before Christmas, this had to be postponed until the Foreign Office knew how much money would be available for its information efforts in 1957/58.

Meanwhile, the pressure from outside continued. On December 12, Kenneth Younger put a Parliamentary Question to David Ormsby Gore, only to get a stone-walling reply. Six days later, Professor George Potter, the Cultural Attaché in Bonn, reported to John Moore that his Ambassador had asked him 'to press for an answer from the Department about the whole subject of Wilton Park'. He added: 'But from what you told me I do not think that you need any pressure from this end'.

He was right. As Christmas and New Year approached, there was no lull in the flow of questions and complaints. On December 18, the Sheffield Labour MP Richard Winterbottom wrote to Selwyn Lloyd on behalf of the Anglo-German Group in the House of Commons to ask him to reconsider the closing of Wilton Park, which he described as 'a tremendous mistake'. On December 19, Richard Goold-Adams wrote a long letter to Dodds-Parker. He stressed, first, that 'the most worthwhile element in Germany, namely those who know the facts, is very keen to keep Wilton going'. Secondly, not only was 'the German problem' still 'unique': the inclusion of French, Dutch, Swiss and others 'could and should be pushed considerably further'. Thirdly, he had doubts about Wilton Park's becoming 'primarily Nato' because in that case 'some of the control and direction would have to be removed from purely British hands'. Also on

December 19, the Unionist MP for North Belfast, H. Montgomery Hyde, put a Parliamentary Question to the Foreign Secretary: would he 'continue the establishment at Wilton Park, at least for a limited period?' The answer, given by Dodds-Parker, was 'No'.

So matters stood, officially, as 1956 turned into 1957. But the New Year had barely dawned before the pressure began again. Even R.A. Butler, the Lord Privy Seal, was drawn into the argument, when Lord Davidson pleaded with him 'that Wilton Park be kept open'. On January 2, 1957, John Biggs-Davison, Conservative MP for Chigwell, Essex, wrote to Douglas Dodds-Parker picking up on his answer to Montgomery Hyde. 'I am told', he said:

> that various plans have been discussed to transform Wilton Park into something wider and to seek financial support from countries other than Great Britain and Germany. If so, I hope that the opportunity will be taken of forming under primarily British auspices an institution which will encourage the European spirit and I feel that the Council of Europe and/or Western European Union might be appropriate bodies to consult.

That same day, Robert Birley called on Dodds-Parker and Ormsby Gore. He told them that the *Land* Presidents in Germany would be meeting in the middle of the month and would submit to the Foreign Minister, Heinrich von Brentano, financial proposals aimed at contributing to Wilton Park's survival. He thought the Academic Council should be asked to submit suggestions for a 'wider' Wilton Park; but he disagreed with Dodds-Parker's idea of using university colleges: 'he believed that the continuity of one building was almost as important as the permanent staff'. Privately and not for quotation, he added that it would be better to keep Wilton Park going by saving an equivalent amount on the cultural staff in Germany.

When Rolland Chaput de Saintonge read Dodds-Parker's account of meeting Birley, he disagreed with most of Birley's arguments. He was still exploring with University College, London, the possibility of its 'taking over Wilton Park as a going institution'. He thought it would be 'dangerous' to ask the Academic Council to make concrete suggestions; and he deprecated the idea of Britain's changing its mind under pressure from outside with the promise of some financial help. What was more, he declared: 'We have received no report that the *Land* Minister-Presidents will in mid-January make financial proposals to support Wilton Park. Mr Birley no doubt heard this from Dr Koeppler who must have been in direct communication with the people concerned.'

In public, at least, Koeppler had been keeping a low profile throughout these anxious months. On the assumption that Wilton Park would indeed close in July 1957, he had suggested that Session 85 – the last course – should be converted into a short 25-person VIP conference lasting from July 10 to July 24. But he was undoubtedly in touch with sympathisers in Germany as well as in Britain. On Saturday January 26, 1957, he saw Paul Grey, the Assistant Under-Secretary of State at the Foreign Office, and spoke of 'the "Old Wiltonians" who have almost embarrassed us with the active interest they are taking in Wilton Park'. One of them was the rough equivalent of a Deputy Under-Secretary in the Federal German Ministry of Justice, a Dr Richter, who had written to Koeppler on January 23. Writing to Grey on Monday, January 28, Koeppler included a translation of part of Richter's letter:

> He (the Head of the Cultural Relations Department of the German Foreign Office, Herr von Trützschler) appeared surprised that people in England were waiting for action by the German Government. But he declared his readiness to enquire at a suitable occasion from his British colleague (Professor Potter) how things are developing and to use the occasion to stress once again that Germany would be willing to participate in a European or Atlantic institution. The Federal Parliament would not, in my opinion, refuse to provide the necessary funds.

After quoting Richter's letter, Koeppler told Grey: 'This, together with the letter from the member of the Federal Parliament which I left with you appears at last to put the German position almost on the same footing as the Swiss and the French who have officially told the Office of their readiness, should the British Government desire it, to participate financially in a "new" Wilton Park.'

It was still difficult, even in Whitehall, to determine what the British Government desired. Anthony Eden had resigned as Prime Minister on the evening of January 9, 1957, to be succeeded after some uncertainty by Harold Macmillan. Selwyn Lloyd remained Foreign Secretary; and Peter Thorneycroft became Chancellor of the Exchequer. But on Wilton Park the Treasury had not been consulted; the Cabinet had not decided; and the Foreign Office itself was divided and uncertain. As Paul Grey assured Sir Lionel Lamb in Berne on January 17, 1957: 'At the moment, we are considering various alternative possibilities for the maintenance and extension of the Wilton Park type of session on a wider European basis, not necessarily confined to NATO countries. But it is still too soon to say whether anything will come of these ideas.'

By now, this had become the standard response, slightly more encouraging than the flat statement that Wilton Park was to close and that more visits were to take its place. One recipient of the negative answer, the Reverend William Wynn Simpson of the Council of Christians and Jews, was still dissatisfied. On February 8, 1957, he wrote to Lord Hore-Belisha:

> I have discussed the matter with various people, including the German Ambassador, who feel strongly that it would be a very great misfortune if Wilton Park were in fact to be closed down – but it would be doubly unfortunate if it were allowed to happen by default!

Nevertheless, there were signs of movement within the Foreign Office. Here too, January 1957 had seen ministerial changes. David Ormsby Gore had been promoted from Parliamentary Under-Secretary of State to replace Lord Reading as Minister of State; while Ian Harvey, who like Selwyn Lloyd was an old Fettesian, had become a Parliamentary Under-Secretary of State in succession to Douglas Dodds-Parker. Shortly afterwards, on February 4, 1957, Sir Frederick Hoyer Millar moved from Bonn to replace Sir Ivone Kirkpatrick as Permanent Under-Secretary.

All this time, the Head of the German Information Department, Rolland Chaput de Saintonge, had been intermittently discussing with University College, London, Dodds-Parker's pet project for a College like it to take over Wilton Park. Professor R.C. Fitzgerald, the Dean of Laws and Professor of English Law at the College, had spoken about it to Professor George Keaton, who was Chairman of the University of London's Extra-Mural Delegacy, to see if the University might support the idea. But the mills of academe grind slowly. On the evening of February 20, 1957, Chaput told Fitzgerald that while he appreciated that the University authorities had had 'comparatively little time to consider the proposal thoroughly ... we must very soon take a decision and ... could not place the whole plan in jeopardy by too long a delay'. Just under two weeks later, on Monday, March 4, Chaput saw Fitzgerald again and, in his own words, 'prepared the position for a withdrawal' and for the possibility of 'a European Wilton Park run under Foreign Office auspices'. Commenting two days later on Chaput's minute, Hoyer Millar said: 'the first thing to do seems to be to get a decision from Ministers whether Wilton Park is to go on on any basis. When can we expect this decision?'

The answer came on the following Monday, March 11, 1957, when John Moore told Hoyer Millar's Private Secretary: 'As a result of discussions which he has had with Mr Ormsby Gore and Mr Ian Harvey, the Secretary of State has now said that he is convinced that Wilton Park should be continued in a reconstituted European form. He has agreed to

write to the Chancellor of the Exchequer putting forward a case for this.'
Selwyn Lloyd promptly wrote to Peter Thorneycroft on Friday, March 15.
He proposed that Britain should offer up to £25,000 a year as its contribution to funds into which other governments would pay too.

It looked like a happy ending. To Wilton Park's supporters it would no
doubt have seemed so – if they had heard the news. Instead, they continued their pressure. On March 11, indeed, the Conservative MP for South
Buckinghamshire, Ronald Bell, wrote to Ian Harvey praising Wilton Park's
'good sensible work' and hoping that it could be 'carried on substantially
unchanged for almost nothing' if European Governments paid fees. On
March 12, Kenneth Younger wrote to Selwyn Lloyd hoping that he would
enable 'this work to continue on a European basis'. On March 19, *The
Times* published a letter from Karl Weishäupl, State Secretary in the
Bavarian Ministry of State for Labour and Social Services, announcing
that German Old Wiltonians had formed the *Verein zur Förderung von
Wilton Park* or Wilton Park Society, of which he was chairman, and that
the Bavarian State Parliament had pressed the Federal government to
contribute to the costs. 'This will show you', he concluded, 'how anxious
we are that Wilton Park should be continued'. At dinner on March 25,
Sigismund von Braun of the German Embassy in London stressed to
Chaput 'the urgency of a fairly rapid approach to the German
Government if we wanted them to make any financial contribution' since
the present Parliament would be dissolved in July.

Still thus goaded from without, the Foreign Office now had to face the
paymaster within. It was not an easy encounter, or a swift one. On April 8,
1957, three weeks after Selwyn Lloyd's proposal to the Treasury, the
Chancellor Peter Thorneycroft wrote him a terse, unyielding reply:

> Dodds-Parker agreed on your behalf in July 1956 that Wilton Park should
> close in the coming August. Following this agreement arrangements were
> put in hand to dispose of the property. I understand that these arrangements (particularly with regard to the lease of the house) have now got too
> far to be put into reverse. For this reason, coupled with the economic
> factors involved, which are as relevant today as they were last July, I
> consider that the original decision must stand.

Faced with such intransigence, Selwyn Lloyd tried again, asking
Thorneycroft to have another look at the papers on Wilton Park. 'I have
done this', came the answer on April 11, 'and I remain convinced that the
decision taken last year should stand.'

That left Selwyn Lloyd one last, risky option. He told Thorneycroft:

I am afraid that I cannot accept your decision. I have had a word with the Prime Minister and he wishes it to be brought to the Cabinet.

I am sorry to be a nuisance but I feel I must have some latitude in how the monies devoted to Information Services are used.

The Cabinet was due to meet on Monday April 15. On Friday April 12 Selwyn Lloyd submitted a paper to the Cabinet Office, restating the nature and cost of Wilton Park and recalling the decision to close it. He went on:

As a result of the review of information activity which has been carried out in the Foreign Office, and in the light of more recent developments in Europe it is considered desirable to reverse this decision.

It is proposed to retain Wilton Park and to establish it as a European College for the benefit of all European countries.

The evidence of the influence that Wilton Park has had over leading Germans, which has been reinforced by the reaction that has occurred since the decision to close Wilton Park was known, indicates that this is an establishment through which unparalleled opportunities exist to influence opinion in European countries by means of important contact points.

There is little doubt that a contribution to the running of the College would be obtained in future from the Germans and further contributions may well be obtained from other European countries concerned. Under such considerations the estimated liability would be £25,000 a year. It would, however, be wiser in the absence of any firm agreement to budget for the full total (£41,000).

There was a touch of acid in Selwyn Lloyd's conclusion:

I regret having to bring what is seemingly a small matter before my colleagues. I have had to do so because the Chancellor of the Exchequer is disinclined to sanction the required financial adjustment.

I take the view that this action is justified by considerations of foreign policy with particular reference to our immediate relationships with Europe as a whole and Germany in particular.

'Immediate relationships with Europe as a whole' meant mainly Britain's position vis-à-vis the six countries – Belgium, France, Germany, Italy, Luxembourg, and the Netherlands – which, on March 25, 1957, had just signed the Rome Treaties establishing Euratom and the Common Market, embryos of the future European Union. The previous July, with strong British backing, the Organisation for European Economic Co-operation had set up a working party to study the possibility of a Free Trade Area around the Common Market of the Six. The working party had reported in January 1957, and officials were even now negotiating what looked to some like a great move to gather Western Europe together, and to others a nefarious attempt to dissolve the Common Market and its would-be economic union, as one cynic put it, 'like a lump of sugar in a British cup of tea'. In the debate, Germany's position was important and potentially changeable: the Federal Chancellor, Konrad Adenauer, was believed to be wary of the proposed Free Trade Area, while his Economics Minister, Ludwig Erhard, was known to be cool about economic union but a devotee of free trade.

On Saturday, April 13, Thorneycroft submitted the Treasury's case. Selwyn Lloyd's officials scrutinised its arguments, especially as regards the lease of Wiston House. The Ministry of Works had indeed been pressing for a decision, since they were being pressed by the owner. Strictly speaking, the deadline for a decision was Friday April 12, but a weekend's leeway, at least, was possible. Early on Monday, John Moore supplied some additional points to Ormsby Gore, who was to be at the Cabinet that day. He stressed Wilton Park's 'name and reputation' and finally dismissed the idea of running courses elsewhere. While Ministers deliberated, Wilton Park's champions held their breath.

It took a little time: but as Selwyn Lloyd had said, Wilton Park was 'seemingly a small matter'. After some debate, the Cabinet reached a decision.

Typically, it was a compromise, and it was provisional. 'The Wilton Park Institution' should continue in operation for a further year, i.e. until July 1958, pending a review by the Committee chaired by Dr Charles Hill, the BBC's wartime 'Radio Doctor', now MP for Luton and Chancellor of the Duchy of Lancaster. His task was 'to examine Britain's Cultural and Information Services as a whole'. 'In other words', as John Moore noted, 'a case for the continuation of Wilton Park after July 1958 has to be submitted to the Hill Committee'.

It was a reprieve as much as a rescue. 'I fear', said Rolland Chaput de Saintonge, 'the new Wilton Park will always lead a hand-to-mouth existence'. In due course the Radio Doctor gave Wilton Park a clean bill of health. But Chaput's words were relevant for a long time to come.

CHAPTER 14

New Look

'New *Presbyter* is but old *Priest* writ large.'
John Milton, 'On the New Forces of Conscience
under the Long Parliament', 1646

It suited everyone to refer to 'the new Wilton Park'. The Foreign Office could feel it had not wholly reversed the decision to close the old one. The Treasury was mollified by this and by the possibility of funds from abroad. Heinz Koeppler was glad to accept the new look, knowing it was a development rather than a volte-face. 'The great decision has been made', he wrote in a letter on May 16, 1957; 'Wilton Park is to be continued'. Continued – not transformed. After all, Koeppler had long ago encouraged participants other than Germans; and he was convinced that his existing methods needed no radical change.

He described them to Robert Birley late in 1956, when Wilton Park seemed to be hanging by a thread:

> Four ingredients appear to me to make up the specific Wilton Park formula. The first is the mixture of all influential sectors in the community which form the membership of its sessions. Of course, it is a good thing when members of some professional group from different countries come together to talk about their common professional problems. One must, however, be careful not to indulge in the illusion that such gatherings improve the international atmosphere at the political level. Thus, to have representatives of different social and economic interests together in one session makes for greater political realism by cutting out professional 'shop'; and it increases the practical use of their meeting in making an impact on the whole public opinion of their country.

The second is the curriculum, which concentrates on the discussion of those problems which have created difficulties in the past between our nations; on establishing the causes of misunderstanding, and on helping to remove them. Such difficult tasks can only be achieved in frank discussions in which people are not afraid of telling each other what they believe to be the truth. If the free peoples are to pursue their joint interests jointly, they must understand first where the interests of each of them lie.

The third is the method of work which, while not neglecting visits to institutions which are typical of Britain today, centres in discussions in small groups. This alone prevents the false impressions inseparable from the usual short visit which is all that important people can find time for today.

Finally, Wilton Park has not shut its eyes to the fact, however incomprehensible it may appear to some of us, that even the leaders of public opinion abroad cannot be expected to speak and understand English well enough for serious discussion.

This last consideration may make it appear difficult to extend the work of Wilton Park beyond the Anglo-German framework in which it started. However, some progress has already been made in this direction by the increasing participation of people from other countries. French has been made an equal medium with English and German. There will be difficulties in adapting the procedure of Wilton Park work to the use of the third language but they can be overcome. It should be possible with the help of those three languages to serve a 'European' or 'Atlantic' membership of Wilton Park sessions.

There were, however, latent contradictions. During the battle to save Wilton Park, even its champions in the Foreign Office had had to defend it as part of Britain's information effort, projecting UK policies or, at the very least, UK ways of life and thought. On June 11, 1956, Rolland Chaput de Saintonge, Head of the German Information Department, had referred in an internal minute to 'the myth [*sic*] that Wilton Park is not a propaganda organisation'. When trying to justify Wilton Park to the Treasury, or to other branches of Government, this was perhaps understandable. But as a concept it was doubly flawed.

First, and fundamentally, to regard Wilton Park as an instrument of British propaganda was to ignore both its history and its potential. When Koeppler began Wilton Park, its aim was not to promote Britain or British policies, but to spread democracy. Britain's methods and institutions were seen as imperfect examples of democracy in action that could inspire a country emerging from dictatorship. They were not vaunted as paragons, still less embodiments of that dreaded phrase, 'the line to take'. And what had been true of the Anglo-German Wilton Park was no less true for the

future. It had been, and continued to be, a forum for the peaceful, dispassionate synthesis of conflicting points of view. Koeppler felt the need to
stress this point in his first formal description of 'The New Wilton Park',
published in the December 1958 issue of the *Wilton Park Journal*.

On a lower, more cynical level, any official tendency to see Wilton Park
as a 'propaganda organisation' risked undermining its effectiveness in that
very role. As Koeppler readily conceded, the best propaganda was 'warts
and all'. Wilton Park embodied British self-criticism and tolerance of
conflicting viewpoints; and it demonstrated the Foreign Office's refusal to
meddle, allowing and encouraging the academic freedom symbolised and
ensured by the independent Advisory Council.

There was tension between these two views; but at best it was creative,
drawing synthesis from potential conflict. Koeppler explained the
apparent paradox in the *Wilton Park Journal* in December 1959:

Some have asked whether the purpose of Wilton Park is what has become
known in the international jargon of cultural relations as 'the projection of
Britain', or whether its purpose is to provide a platform for the discussion
of common European problems. If the question is put in that way there is
no doubt of our answer: Wilton Park exists to provide a forum for
Europeans who are concerned with the well-being of their country and the
wider community to which we all belong. It may be worthwhile, however,
to look at the definition of Wilton Park's purpose a little more closely ...

A definition of the two labels which are often used to describe our
purpose may not come amiss. Projection of Britain: an explanation of the
way of life, the machinery of government, the customs of the natives. A
platform for discussion of common problems: the social structure of our
various nations, the great debate between the liberal and the communist
societies, the cohesion of these liberal societies, the form their cooperation
is to take.

Put in this way there seem indeed to be two different tasks. But anyone
who has participated in our work knows that this is an abstract distinction
which does not correspond to the facts of political life. For no country has
a view on international political, economic, military and social questions
which is independent of its own history, its own traditions, its own governmental machinery, its own habits of thought, its own emotional
predilections and antipathies. Thus in order to have a matter of fact, down
to earth, realistic discussion between nations, there must be amongst the
partners in the discussion a certain minimum of common knowledge of the
basic presuppositions from which each partner starts. Quite a few participants in our work have such knowledge but many more are ready to admit
that they do not. And since Wilton Park is a British institution, the hosts
have an obligation to provide their visitors with that sort of background so

far as this country is concerned. This is perhaps more necessary in the case of Britain for she is even today very largely 'an unknown island' [an allusion to the title of a book by Paul Cohen-Portheim, translated in 1930 by Alan Harris as *England, the Unknown Isle*]. In saying this we do not forget that many leading representatives of British public life know even less of the background of our continental allies. The assumption is too glibly made that Europe is all one, and that because we have the same fears and the same ideals we have also got the same background of thought and the same presuppositions for political action.

And thus the apparent dichotomy in the work of Wilton Park between 'projection of Britain' and 'a European forum' is in practice found not to exist. To be a realistic forum for the discussion of problems common to thoughtful and responsible Europeans, a certain minimum of background must be provided to help our friends understand the oddities of British political thought and action, just as our continental participants have both the duty and the opportunity to render the same service to our British participants and speakers.

These general reflections on our work are clear today. It would not be right to pretend that when Wilton Park started in January 1946 they had all been thought out. But there is really no doubt that they have been under-lying the work from its 1st to its 100th session and that they have provided a continuity of action for those who work here ...

The ten years which passed between [the] ... first international partic-ipation and the official opening of Wilton Park as an institution for nationals of all countries which are members of O.E.E.C. have given us sufficient experience to be optimistic and to believe that the 'new' Wilton Park is a viable and practicable concept.

If the problem of Wilton Park's dual aims could thus be solved in practice, it remained bewildering to some overseas visitors and irritating to some British officials. Koeppler returned to it, more succinctly, in the *Wilton Park Journal* in January 1966:

Most countries have a proverb equivalent to the English 'He who pays the piper calls the tune.' The British Government, through the Foreign Office, pays for Wilton Park. Does it call the tune? Yes and no. The Foreign Office have set our tasks. One of these is to make the Wilton Park conferences a British contribution to western solidarity by providing a platform for the free and frank exchange of views on vital international issues, however contentious and sensitive they may be. The other is for Wilton Park to ensure the presentation of a true and adequate picture of British policy ... As one of our members once put it, Great Britain is the sort of country which believes in the value of having an institution like Wilton Park.

> The essence of this institution is its academic freedom. And here the Foreign Office does not call the tune; on the contrary, it has imposed on itself a self-denying ordinance. We receive no directives on what issue we should discuss, nor who should be asked to come and speak here. This academic freedom, symbolically expressed in our crest, is indeed the only possible basis for our work ... Thus, it is not high-minded idealism but down-to-earth enlightened self-interest which has given us this precious privilege. It has been experienced by our members for 20 years now and we know from their reaction that it is the keystone of our success.

There was a slight exaggeration here. The Foreign Office had put pressure on Koeppler to drop Richard Crossman as a guest speaker. In vain: Crossman spoke at Wilton Park on July 27, 1957. But, as time went on, its programmes were discussed more and more with Whitehall. How much discussion influenced decision was a matter for successive incumbents; but the price of the hands-off policy that Koeppler celebrated was eternal vigilance by those at Wilton Park.

Relations with the Foreign Office were mildly troubled very soon after the Cabinet's decision of April 15, 1957. On May 6, John Barnes of the Bonn Embassy wrote to Chaput de Saintonge that two of the Wilton Park tutors, Robert Gibson and Cecil de Sausmarez, had recently been lecturing on a course at Marienberg 'without the formal notification of us first'. When questioned about this, Koeppler explained that they had been invited privately, were travelling in their vacation and paying their own fares, and were not giving public lectures but talking to closed groups in small courses on civics. Werner Lauermann, he added, was also to be in Germany during his summer leave. He had asked them to inform the local British consuls, and he was sure that they had.

There was also a contretemps about the news that Wilton Park was to continue. Several weeks elapsed between the Cabinet's decision and its public announcement. Koeppler knew about it by April 23, when he mentioned it in a letter to Edward Peck, Deputy Commandant of the British Sector in Berlin. But as late as May 9 he had still had no written confirmation from the Foreign Office. At last, on May 27, 1957, Sir Frank Medlicott put an 'inspired' (i.e. pre-arranged) Parliamentary Question to the Secretary of State for Foreign Affairs, asking for further news. Even then, the answer by Ian Harvey, the Joint Parliamentary Under-Secretary of State, was distinctly guarded:

> Her Majesty's Government have examined the possibility of continuing Wilton Park in a wider European forum. This depends, however, on the interest and support of other European Governments. These

Governments are being approached. In the meantime, Wilton Park is being continued for another year on as broad a basis as the support received justifies.

Two weeks later, on June 12, 1957, the Foreign Office requested its posts in the other OEEC member states to ask the governments concerned how far they would be interested in participating in the future work of Wilton Park. It sent copies of the request to posts in Washington, Madrid, and Belgrade, and to the Commonwealth Relations Office for transmission to Ottawa. This too slightly jarred relations with Koeppler, who had been given no copy of the background briefing on Wilton Park that had gone to posts, still less been consulted about its drafting. He would have been still more disturbed had he known that Ralph Murray, Under-Secretary of State at the Foreign Office, was wondering 'whether we can make a success of the European concept of Wilton Park if we keep the naturalised German Dr Koeppler as Warden'. He later minuted to Ian Harvey on July 3: 'We probably can, but we cannot commit ourselves to doing so.' This was odd: two weeks earlier, Koeppler had been awarded the OBE.

When the Wilton Park Academic Council met on June 24, 1957, Koeppler thanked it and its Chairman Robert Birley for their help in enabling Wilton Park to survive. Now, first and foremost, it must not become 'just one of the many European talking shops'. In the past it had succeeded partly because its discussions were not vague and general. It had never sought to 'project Britain' as that phrase was generally understood. True, its discussions had normally begun with a description of the British position; but they had always broadened to cover similar problems in other countries, on which everyone could make a contribution. Sir Harold Nicolson agreed: he felt that 'one must have a string on which to put one's beans'. Koeppler admitted that now there might be exceptional subjects, such as Algeria, where a visitor should start the discussion; but this too was not a total novelty. In general, 'there would be no need ... to change the approach to our work for the new Wilton Park'.

The Council agreed with Koeppler's suggestions that the existing tutors should be maintained, and that the year's courses should provisionally be planned on the basis of eight sessions of three weeks each, starting on a Monday and ending on a Friday, plus two VIP sessions of about ten days each. Simultaneous interpretation, and a French-speaking interpreter, would be needed to cope with the influx of further nationalities. The Council concluded with agreement, in some cases reluctant, that its members should resign so that the Foreign Secretary could appoint a new Council to match the new circumstances. It expressed the hope that continuity would be maintained and that the new Council would include people who in Agnes Headlam-Morley's words, 'knew all about Wilton Park'.

At the Academic Council meeting, Sir Harold Nicolson had remarked: 'Wilton Park is an impossible thing to explain. Nobody can explain it unless they have been there.' It was with this in mind that Koeppler wrote to Ralph Murray on July 17, 1957:

> These are early days yet and we may find replies, and favourable replies, coming in with a rush. But I would like to suggest that you may consider, later on, if we find the response is rather luke-warm in some countries, whether I should not be sent to see our missions, at any rate, in the more centrally situated members of O.E.E.C. I need not tell you how many odd and phoney 'European' schemes there are about at the moment, and both our missions abroad and the governments to whom they talk may be forgiven if they do not at once see the difference between such schemes and Wilton Park.

The Foreign Office's message to posts had foreseen this difficulty. After explaining that it hoped governments would be prepared to pay participants' fares and a small contribution (£10 per week) to the cost of their maintenance, it added:

> However in fairness to countries which have no previous knowledge of the workings of this institution it is proposed that there should be a course probably in the second half of October which would be in the nature of a 'trial run' and for which Her Majesty's Government would meet all expenses except the fares of those attending.

The immediate response was mixed. Some countries were initially unable to participate in Wilton Park courses. Others, like Turkey and the Netherlands, could send to the pilot meeting only an official from their London Embassy. Some – like France and Switzerland – were eager, but had to limit their future participation on budgetary grounds. A question-mark hung for a time over Franco's Spain, not yet a full member of OEEC; but it finally sent a delegation.

The 'pilot course' or introductory conference took place from October 21 to November 2, 1957. All the full and associate European States of OEEC were represented, including Spain, but with the exceptions of Denmark, Greece, Iceland, Ireland, and Portugal. Most of those who came were serving diplomats. A few – from Austria, Belgium, and the Netherlands – were unable to stay for more than a few days.

Koeppler sent Ralph Murray an interim report on October 29. He quoted most visitors as urging that follow-up negotiations be started very quickly, and at the highest level. There was general support for governments footing travel costs, for which most Foreign Offices had funds and discretion, but 'a good deal of hesitation on the additional charge of £10 per person per week'. The visitors appreciated Wilton Park for several reasons: the chance to hear the arguments for British policies and their background – and the view of the Opposition; the ability to concentrate on issues, and to focus on political, economic, and social questions rather than the arts; and especially the opportunity to cross-examine speakers and to express their own point of view. 'As one of them put it', said Koeppler, '"You can't question a pamphlet".'

Koeppler's report reflected his own preoccupations. Foreign Office concerns dominated two separate reports sent to Charles Stewart, Head of the Information Policy Department, by a young official from Berlin, Stanley Black. 'The question of finance', he wrote after his first week with the visitors, 'bulked large in their minds, more so than I had expected'. What was more, 'their ideas extend well beyond the immediate objectives [*sic*] of learning about British policy and institutions ... and ... they are firmly attached to the concept of a wider European exchange'. Some urged that there should be authoritative speakers from other countries than Britain, and courses on a single theme, not necessarily one with which Britain was primarily concerned. Black himself felt that the number of plenary sessions might be reduced to one, or occasionally two, per day; and he was troubled by the fact that the Labour speakers seemed of higher calibre than the Conservatives.

The last day of the conference, to which Black devoted his second report, discussed future organisation and methods. It agreed with him on wanting fewer plenary and more tutorial sessions, and – *pace* Koeppler – endorsed a French proposal for special courses on special subjects. The French also suggested that, especially in these cases, written briefs prepared beforehand might help focus the discussion more quickly – an idea taken up many years later.

Above all, however, the final day's discussion reinforced Black's initial impression of the kind of Wilton Park the visitors wanted. It would not be primarily to promote Britain, and it would have an international advisory committee:

It is quite clear that the majority of participants were interested in the new Wilton Park primarily as a medium for a wider European exchange of views on problems of common concern and only secondarily as a means for learning about British policies and institutions. This I believe is the opposite of our intentions and, as it worked out in practice, of the experience of the present course.

It is only on this basis that any government will agree to contribute a share of the cost ... For all except the Germans (who have 12 years' experience to go on), some form of international committee, even if largely formal and meeting only at infrequent intervals, is a sine qua non.

This idea – which, Koeppler controversially told the conference, 'was under active consideration' – was certainly not new. It had been broached in the previous May by the British Ambassador in Bonn, Sir Christopher Steel. In a letter on May 15 to Viscount Hood, Assistant Under-Secretary of State, he had argued:

I don't think that we can ask foreign countries to contribute without giving them some say in the management, and I think it would help if I could tell the Germans that we propose to set up a governing body on which participating Governments could be represented.

At the time, Foreign Office reactions had been cautious. Hood had replied coolly:

We do not think any practical purpose could be served by such a body and it would become unwieldy and embarrassing at any time we decided to close down the institution. It is for this reason that we do not propose to ask Governments for any direct contribution to the Park, but only to pay part of their nominees' accommodation costs and the cost of travel to the United Kingdom.

Advising Hood, Rolland Chaput de Saintonge, Head of German Information Department, had warned darkly that, if such an entity were formed, 'some busybody might try to use it to pass resolutions and give advice'. Later, on October 11, 1957, Chaput wrote to Peter Wilkinson, Counsellor at the Bonn Embassy, with a still more alarming thought:

The suggestion of some sort of international committee of ambassadors was in fact started by Koeppler himself and I think he discussed it with the German Ambassador in London, among others. What he was looking for was an international pressure group which would make it very difficult politically to abolish Wilton Park in the future. An international committee of this kind could only be an embarrassment. Either they would do nothing, or they would intervene in the administration and planning of the courses in such a way as to make it difficult for us to control the expenditure of money on Wilton Park. For our part, we would not favour such a committee. We intend however to maintain an academic council of some sort for Wilton Park ... We shall try to appoint ... an entirely British committee which would in any case have to accept the decisions of the Minister without raising awkward diplomatic questions.

Recent experience should perhaps have told Chaput that Wilton Park's Academic Council was no rubber stamp. It would certainly not be in the future. Nor was the Foreign Office able to ward off the creation of an international council.

On November 11, 1957, Ralph Murray wrote to Ian Harvey, Joint Parliamentary Under-Secretary of State, with somewhat unwelcome news:

The results of the pilot course on an international basis at Wilton Park show:

(a) it is most improbable that Governments will agree to support an international Wilton Park if they have to pay for the subsistence of their visitors; if we pay it means another £10,000 per annum on the bill;

(b) although the visitors were favourably impressed by the course, the more intelligent of them have emphasised that their Treasuries will be difficult to convince of the value of a purely British institution and they have shown interest in Wilton Park as a potential 'European forum' rather than as a means of learning about British policies and institutions; this would be a new enterprise;

(c) we shall have to allow the formation of some sort of international committee to advise on subjects to be discussed and persons to be invited, even though we do not necessarily take their advice, as a sop to this internationalist approach. Such a committee would be a nuisance, but it is a price which, if there is a chance of Wilton Park continuing, we shall have to pay. The next step is for us to approach the Governments on the basis of the Cabinet decision, i.e. inviting them to participate entirely at their own expense, fares and subsistence. If we do so, and as seems very probable, fail to obtain adequate support, we can either:

    (i) increase the budget of Wilton Park from £25,000 to £35,000 a year; or

    (ii) abolish Wilton Park and spend an extra £25,000 a year on visits and tours, attempting to infiltrate some of the intellectual content of a Wilton Park course into such visits.

Alternatively we might approach the Treasury now, after due reference to Ministers, to obtain the extra £10,000. If we did so, however, we should be invited to show a saving under some other heading. I am by no means convinced that this is advisable, quite apart from the difficulty of finding a heading from which to effect the saving, apart from the first year and possibly the second. Whatever the value of Wilton Park in the educative period of our relations with Germany there is some doubt whether its present rather cumbrous structure, involving a resident Warden and tutors and the hire of a large mansion, is really suited to the international task we envisage for it.

Murray recommended that the Foreign Office put the proposal to the OEEC Governments concerned, and that if it failed to obtain support it should close Wilton Park down. But he added a prudent proviso:

Before actually issuing instructions to Missions, however, I would be grateful to know that, with an eye to possible Parliamentary and press agitation in favour of Wilton Park, Ministers will be prepared to face its possible elimination.

Ian Harvey agreed, and passed the question up to the Minister of State for Foreign Affairs, David Ormsby Gore. The upshot was that on November 22, 1957, Charles Stewart, Head of the Information Policy Department, wrote to posts asking for their host Governments' reactions. His circular despatch made two – or one-and-a-half – concessions to the views expressed at the pilot conference. Although maintaining that 'from Her Majesty's Government's point of view the most important aim will remain that of promoting understanding of British problems and policies', it also recalled that 'one of the objectives of Wilton Park is to develop a greater appreciation of European problems'. More significantly, Stewart wrote: 'I am prepared to contemplate an advisory body which we could consult in London as to persons who might be invited to attend and also the subjects which might be most usefully introduced into the courses.' This was the body that became the Wilton Park International Advisory Council, consisting mainly of the London ambassadors of the countries concerned, and meeting once a year.

Replies from UK embassies in continental Western Europe trickled back to London over the next few weeks. The earliest news, on November 28, 1957, came from Bonn, whence Peter Wilkinson quoted a meeting that he and Koeppler – in Germany for an 'old Wiltonians' meeting – had had as early as November 22 with Dr von Trützschler, Head of the Cultural Department in the German Foreign Office. 'Trützschler said that he did not think there would be any great difficulty in finding funds for a German team to attend the courses next year, and he was sure that if this matter was ever raised in the Bundestag it would receive great support.'

Writing from Luxembourg on December 5, the Ambassador Harold Freese-Pennefather foresaw no financial problems, but a dearth of candidates 'in this small country'. Five days later, the Ambassador in Stockholm, Sir Robert Hankey, reported that 'the Swedish authorities would find it most useful to continue to send representatives to Wilton Park' but could not pay for their upkeep 'since any such payment, however relatively insignificant, would have to be separately shown in the budget of the Ministry for Foreign Affairs and might have to be justified before the Swedish Parliament'. They could, however, pay travelling expenses, since these came under a general heading in the ministry's budget. From Berne on December 16, the Chargé d'Affaires, George Littlejohn Cook, described a meeting with Dr Hans Zbinden, President of the *Schweizer Vortragsdienst* or Swiss Lecture Service, three of whose members had attended the pilot conference. 'They were all convinced that it had proved a satisfactory basis for future progress.' The organisation was very willing to go on paying travel expenses 'and also, if necessary, the £10 a week per person on which H.M.G. were insisting'. From The Hague, the Ambassador, Sir Paul Mason, wrote on December 19 that the report received from the member of the Netherlands Embassy in London who had attended the pilot conference had been 'very favourable' and that the Netherlands government were anxious that suitably selected Dutch people should take part in future courses. Candidates might be unwilling to pay £10 a week, but the Dutch Foreign Ministry might possibly be persuaded to produce some kind of subsidy. From Madrid, the Ambassador, Sir Ivo Mallet, wrote on December 20 that he had talked with both the Spanish delegates on the pilot course: 'our impression is that they have reported favourably to the Ministry'.

One of the few discouraging replies came on December 11 from Copenhagen, where the British Chargé d'Affaires ad interim, Anthony Lincoln, thought it unlikely that the Danish government would change its mind and accept. Otherwise, the responses were favourable enough for the 'European Wilton Park' to be launched in the spring of 1958.

As had been suggested at the pilot conference, each meeting now engaged with a specific subject. The first, from May 4 to 17, considered 'Political and economic problems of the Common Market and the Free Trade Area'. This was highly topical. On January 1, 1958, the EEC Treaty had come into force, and negotiations were proceeding in OEEC 'to determine ways and means on the basis of which' a Free Trade Area could be established around the Common Market of the Six. Although Walter Hallstein, President of the EEC Commission, then believed that the proposed Free Trade Area was 'a necessary supplement to the Common Market', the OEEC's cautious wording reflected the difficulty of the negotiators' task, and some governments' scepticism about their objective. The second week of the Wilton Park conference, moreover, saw dramatic events in Paris and Algiers. At 3.00 p.m. on Tuesday, May 13, 1958, Pierre Pflimlin rose in the National Assembly to make his investiture speech as the new Prime Minister of France; two hours later, rioters determined to keep Algeria French invaded the Government Building in Algiers. So began the train of events that led General Charles de Gaulle back to power in France. When the Wilton Park conference dispersed on Saturday May 17, the outcome was still nervously debated; but on the evening of Sunday June 1, 1958, while people were assembling for the next Wilton Park conference, the General was voted into office in Paris to head a Government of National Safety.

For the rest of that year, the new Wilton Park covered subjects of burning relevance in a Europe shadowed by the towering figure of De Gaulle. The meeting that accompanied his inauguration was on East–West relations. The next discussed European attitudes to the new nations in Asia and Africa. Then came 'Educational Problems of a Free Society'; then 'Public Opinion and its Formation'; then 'Safeguards of Society in Western Europe: Relations Between Legislature and Executive'. In the middle of this last conference General de Gaulle's Executive dropped a diplomatic bombshell. On the evening of Friday, November 14, 1958, the French Minister of Information, Jacques Soustelle, announced: 'it has become clear to France that it is not possible to set up the Free Trade Area as wished by the British'. Unsurprisingly, six of the next ten Wilton Park conferences were devoted to the European and Atlantic issues that Gaullist policy had broached.

At the beginning of 1958 it had still been uncertain whether the new Wilton Park would survive this inaugural year. Not until the spring had the Cabinet agreed in principle that it should. The fresh deadline, as the Head of the Foreign Office's Establishment and Organisation Department, Laurence Pumphrey, told the Treasury on April 22, 1958, was 'at least until April 1, 1960'. He was writing in the hope of sorting out the salaries of the Warden and his staff, including their contribution to board and lodging. To advance this process, Bernard Thimont of the Treasury visited Wiston House on June 25, 1958, to see the place in action. He arrived late in the second week of the conference on new nations in Asia and Africa, and was duly impressed.

To begin with, Koeppler explained to Thimont how the new Wilton Park worked:

The Conferences, of which English, French and German were the official languages, were conducted on the following pattern:-

(a) lectures by eminent speakers, either English or foreign, experts in their own fields, or Brains Trusts of experts; these to be followed by a general discussion. During the lecture and discussion periods simultaneous interpretation facilities in the official languages were provided;

(b) discussion groups in the three official languages, chaired by a tutor; and

(c) discussions between small groups of participants and individual tutors or the Warden, designed to deal with particular points of interest or difficulty.

The number of participants averaged some 25 a Conference and the Conferences occupied 20 weeks in the year with an additional 20 weeks devoted to preparatory and post-mortem work.

The Warden was entirely responsible for the running of Wilton Park both on the academic and administrative/financial sides.

On the academic side, he had to plan, in consultation with the tutors as necessary, the programme for the individual Conferences, and arrange for the necessary speakers and extra-mural activities ... It was proposed that future Conferences should be attended by suitable people from this country as participants and the Warden would be responsible for securing this. The Warden invariably took the chair at all lectures and discussions referred to at (a) above and was available for consultation by participants at most times during a Conference. Experience showed that these informal meetings usually tended to continue until a late hour (e.g. after midnight) ...

The present establishment on the tutorial side was a Dean and four tutors.

The main functions of the tutors related to duties under (a) and (b) above, and the provisional of simultaneous translations during lectures and plenary discussions ...

In discussing the work and problems of the tutors with them, they made the following points:-

(a) discussion groups in which foreigners from a number of countries participated were more difficult to conduct than those comprised [*sic*] entirely of Germans since it was necessary:-

(i) to have an understanding of the various national points of view on topics of current interest;

(ii) to have a working knowledge of those affairs and problems of the different countries which usually came up for discussion.

(b) Simultaneous translation in the context of specialised subjects presented considerable difficulty in that a more literal translation would often obscure the true meaning of an important point.

I listened to group discussions in English and French and I was impressed by the extent to which the tutor was required to participate and the amount of basic knowledge on a range of subjects which he was expected to possess. The Warden informed me that, in future, as an additional qualification a tutor would be required to be bilingual in either French or German ...

Dr Koeppler is, undoubtedly, a man of outstanding ability and personality; without a Warden of his calibre it is difficult to imagine Wilton Park being able to carry out its present role with any measure of success. The change in the role of Wilton Park has clearly laid emphasis on the difficulties of heading an establishment catering for people of many different nationalities and temperaments, the majority of whom are of standing in their own countries.

Bernard Thimont's report aptly illustrated the new situation of Wilton Park. But it remained a Treasury assessment. On the status appropriate to the Warden's 'outstanding ability and personality', it observed: 'Nevertheless, the exceptional personal qualities of Dr Koeppler cannot be allowed to influence the grading of the post.'

In the end, the Treasury allowed the Foreign Office a relatively modest increase in Koeppler's salary; but the number of tutors on the staff remained in dispute. On October 25, 1958, Laurence Pumphrey wrote to Antony Peck, Assistant Secretary in the Treasury:

> You asked us to use our best efforts to reduce the number of tutors from 5 to 4. We have discussed this proposal with Koeppler at some length. We agree with you that for purely tutorial purposes, an establishment of four tutors is adequate. But, as Thimont noted in his report, one of the tutors' main functions is the provision of simultaneous translation into and from French and German during lectures and plenary discussion. Formerly, the translations were done consecutively. Simultaneous translation is not only more difficult intellectually but also much more strenuous (I am told that at United Nations meetings no simultaneous translator works for longer than ten minutes at a stretch). It appears that the recent resignation of three Wilton Park tutors after 12 and 8 years' service was in part due to the increased demands made on them for translation – an added burden which is not compensated by the reduction of numbers in the tutorial groups. An establishment of 5 people capable of simultaneous interpretation is therefore absolutely necessary during conferences.

In fact, Alec Glasfurd had given up full-time tutoring on July 5, 1958; George Greene had gone on August 31; while David Balfour and Cecil de Sausmarez were both to leave Wilton Park in December, 1958. The *ad hoc* hiring of professional interpreters – which the Treasury recommended – was expensive. Pumphrey continued:

Fortunately the intellectual content of the tutor's job seems to have some attraction for linguists who could undoubtedly earn more money as pure interpreters: we are thus able, by recruiting tutors with outstanding linguistic ability, to satisfy our requirements on the cheap ... We may, of course, not be able to find a fifth tutor, in which case we shall carry out your recommendations perforce – but at a greater cost to Her Majesty's Government.

Some non-British speakers prided themselves on their command of English, with occasionally eccentric results. Dexter Keezer, in his study of Wilton Park, reported several instances:

There is the ... case of the German-speaking Swiss who was so confident of his English that he elected to make his 'intervention' in that language. 'The fleshpots of the West and the desert of the East' came out as 'the meat dishes of the West and the dessert course of the East'. A German, speaking confidently in English and wishing to identify his role as an educator, is recalled to have explained, 'I am a teacher of adultery education ... There is also a ... recollection of still another German participant who, being identified as a teacher, made a stern correction, 'I am not a teacher. I am a university professor' ...

Alec Glasfurd recalls, 'The most impressive-sounding job I held in the war (though only briefly) was Acting Director of Manpower in the Fortress of Gibraltar. Encouraged by the Warden, as so many sonorous achievements were being rolled out during the introductory session of a VIP Conference, I mentioned this in self-defence. But my *stellvertretender Direktor der Manneskräfte in der Festung Gibraltar* delighted the Germans because it meant Director of 'virility'. I should have said '*Arbeitskräfte*'.

Graver than linguistic howlers were Wilton Park's personnel problems. Immediate concerns, mainly about the rent and other fees to be paid by staff, rumbled on well into the following year. Salaries and tenure caused recurrent grievances for years to come, largely because the institution could not fit into a pre-existing official category.

Yet, despite disputes, the new Wilton Park prospered. It continued to deal with obviously urgent topics: 'Free Europe and the United States', 'The Cohesion of the Western Alliance', 'European Economic Unity', 'Britain, Europe and the Commonwealth', 'Britain and Europe', 'The Present State of European Economic Co-operation', 'The Essence of the Threat to the West'. But Koeppler also found time for more general subjects. One that was central to his deepest concerns was discussed in the following spring, from April 26 to May 9, 1959. This was 'National Stereotypes: what do the countries of Europe know of each other?'

As Heinz Koeppler wrote soon afterwards:

The superficial similarities of life in the countries of the West often conceals wide differences of experience, or tradition, and in the basic assumptions of public life. In moments of crisis or tension between allies and neighbours these differences suddenly come to light and often assume more threatening proportions than reality justifies, simply because public opinion is not prepared for them. What Her Majesty the Queen said, speaking to an American audience, is applicable to the countries of Western Europe:

'We have so much in common that at times there is a risk that we may take each other for granted. We may believe that we understand each other without troubling to make sure that we really do; without making the necessary conscious effort to appreciate the different factors, whether social, political or economic, which underlie the other's actions and govern the other's problems.'

Her Majesty was not the only authority that Koeppler called in aid of his policy when describing and defending the new Wilton Park. Another was the Milanese and national newspaper *Il Corriere della Sera*, in which 'an Italian participant in Wilton Park work' had written:

Political conversation in Wilton Park has become an art. This is indeed the most interesting aspect of the institution; the discussions centre on problems of a European character, but the spirit of this initiative remains English, and this is a good thing, for Europe is not an abstract entity. Europe is a group of nations, and a European union does not mean the abolition of the various nationalities; rather does it imply the closest possible co-operation amongst them. Hence it is desirable that each people should maintain its typical qualities and make them known to others.

A further witness cited by Koeppler at the same time was a Swiss journalist, who had written: 'Wilton Park must not become a meeting place of experts, but, to use an expression of the Warden's, of "amateurs éclairés" who are capable of seeing things whole.' A German Minister's comment completed the European trio: 'The value of Wilton Park is that it is an unofficial meeting of public personalities.'

Koeppler himself continually stressed the word 'unofficial'. The distinctive feature of Wilton Park conferences, he declared:

has come to be the frank and civilised discussion of vexatious problems in an atmosphere affording the maximum of informality. Although most members hold positions of public responsibility, neither they nor the speakers who open the discussion speak for anyone but themselves. The proceedings are strictly in private. Although members are at liberty to make use of the information gained during the discussion they must not make direct attributions ...

For the success of such discussions two factors are essential. One is an ingredient in all successful international meetings: a readiness to understand, even if this means that beliefs hitherto unquestioned have to be treated as questionable in the light of the opinions of others. The second is the determination to discuss those questions which potentially might be dangerous for the unity of the free world, and to discuss them in a spirit of goodwill, even if, or precisely because, they touch upon sensitive points. Friendliness and politeness are laudable in themselves, but too high a price is paid for them if they lead to difficult, contentious and even delicate issues remaining untreated.

It was a point that Wilton Park was to rediscover many years later when it hosted visitors from the People's Republic of China.

At this time, however, Wilton Park remained principally Western – and, for the moment, predominantly European. Koeppler continued:

British and continental speakers, invited to address plenary sessions, reflect all shades of opinion. No attempt is made to put across an official point of view; everything that is said is a personal opinion for which the speaker alone is responsible.

The value of this method is that it allows the real problems to be freely discussed, makes it easier to understand those rarely formulated assumptions which underlie national attitudes, and shows how particular national or political groups appear through the eyes of others.

Looking back later on the early years of the new Wilton Park, Koeppler took stock of the changes that its broader catchment had brought. Partly at French prompting, each conference now covered a special subject, on which it issued a general, anonymous report. The conferences were shorter – at most two working weeks – to accommodate busy people from all walks of life and many countries.

This great variety of professionals and nations makes Wilton Park a livelier and, I hope, a more useful forum. It encourages 'cross-fertilisation'. Members do not only study the British position, they learn from their fellows about developments in all the other countries represented. In this field direct exchanges matter more than reading books. People realise that the same international problem may look quite different not only to members of other nations but to two people from the same nation but with different backgrounds; the 'European' view does not exist ...

Simultaneous translation is perhaps the most obvious example of the many changes that Wilton Park has undergone ... There are others. The outward and visible sign of our internationalisation is the Wilton Park Advisory Council. Ten Ambassadors [it had begun with eight, and was soon to number sixteen] accredited to the Court of St James's form this body which serves to keep participating nations informed of what we are doing. We are grateful for their advice on various aspects of our work, quite in particular for their help in devising the best methods of selecting participants.

So the new Wilton Park had new features to match its new size. But, as all the rest of Koeppler's comments made clear, the vision that had created it was still the same: 'With all these necessary changes and welcome improvements over the years, the outstanding fact in Wilton Park's history remains that its aims and methods have stood the test of time.'

CHAPTER 15

New World

'America is a nation created by all the hopeful wanderers of Europe, not out of geography and genetics, but out of purpose.'
Theodore H. White, *The Making of the President*, 1960

The United States had been politically interlocked with Europe since 1917 and beyond. In World War II, the Normandy beaches became as much a part of American history as Pearl Harbor. After that war, American Marshall Aid – the European Recovery Program – brought Europe grants and credits totalling $13,150 million, some five percent of America's national income. The precondition of such aid was that the Europeans work together on their recovery plans. The institution they set up for the purpose was the Organisation for European Economic Co-operation (OEEC), established on April 16, 1948, with Canada and the United States becoming associate members in June 1950.

Contrary to America's original hopes, OEEC had not developed into a customs union, but remained a forum for co-operation between sovereign states. When the Six – Belgium, France, Germany, Italy, Luxembourg and the Netherlands – launched first the European Coal and Steel Community (1951), then Euratom and the Common Market (1957), Britain proposed the Europe-wide Free Trade Area that was finally spurned in 1958 by General de Gaulle. The British response was the seven-nation EFTA or European Free Trade Association, comprising the United Kingdom, Austria, Denmark, Norway, Portugal, Sweden and Switzerland – swiftly labelled 'the outer Seven' and giving rise to remarks about 'Europe at Sixes and Sevens'.

The gibe was accurate. Especially outside the Six, feelings had been soured by De Gaulle's abrupt action, and there was rivalry and latent

243

hostility between the two groups. It was partly in response to this that the United States – under two very Europe-oriented Presidents, Dwight D. Eisenhower and John F. Kennedy – decided to take an active part in the debate. It helped to organise, with West European statesmen, a special meeting in Paris in January 1960, from whose deliberations emerged the transformation of OEEC. This was remodelled into OECD, the Organisation for Economic Co-operation and Development, established on September 30, 1961.

The changes to the title were doubly significant. The addition of 'Development', now that Europe was on its feet again, stressed the member states' responsibility towards developing countries. The omission of 'European' broadened the focus of economic co-operation to take the heat off intra-European conflict between the Six and the Seven, by including the United States and Canada as full members instead of just observers. This had implications for Wilton Park.

Americans had already attended its sessions. Even in the early days at Beaconsfield, there had been American speakers; by 1953 there had been about a dozen. Ordinary American participants had been far fewer. One of them, James H. McFarland, US Consul in Hannover, had taken part in a Wilton Park course from July 10 to 24, 1957, during his annual leave, and paying his own travel costs. On August 2, he had reported to the US Consul General in Hamburg:

> The opportunity for uninterrupted discussions in an informal, relaxed atmosphere is especially welcome ... Should the United States Government be invited to participate regularly in the Wilton Park conferences by sending one or two Foreign Service Officers to each conference and furnishing speakers from time to time, the reporting officer recommends that the US Government give favourable consideration to associating itself with this worthy effort. He has rarely seen such a well-planned and well-directed conference program in which anyone who asked a reasonable question was assured of a reasonable answer. The writer is convinced that the excellent staff of Wilton Park is well equipped to contribute in large measure to increased European understanding and would welcome formal association with this institution.

In the following year, two Americans had been included; in 1959 just one; in 1960, three. Unlike Europeans, American citizens had no government or other help with their travel costs, which naturally inhibited their coming from the United States. On September 30, 1960, however, the Ford Foundation announced a grant of $100,000 to Wilton Park, to be used over a 5-year period, primarily to cover the expenses of US visitors, though up to 25 per cent of it might be used by Europeans. From 1961 onwards, Americans began to come in what Dexter Keezer called 'a steady and expanding stream'.

Dexter Keezer was one of them. He described himself as 'an economist, with experience in journalism, business, and government who spent eight errant years as the president of an American college of liberal arts and sciences' – Reed College, Portland, Oregon. Like most of his compatriots, Keezer succumbed to the spell of Wilton Park, its historic setting, its intellectual atmosphere, and its Warden:

> To get to Wilton Park, you go to the beautiful medieval market town of Steyning, a few miles north of the English Channel and not far from Brighton. A reminder of Steyning's venerability is to be found in the fact that Athelwulf, father of the greatest of the Saxon Kings, Alfred (849–99?), was buried in the yard of the Norman church, now used by the town parish, until his remains were removed to Winchester Cathedral.
>
> The shortest route to Wilton Park from Steyning is along Mouse Lane. As befits a mouse lane, it is very narrow and a veritable tunnel part of the way, completely arched over by trees and worn almost to ravine depth by travel and erosion during the centuries. In about a mile Mouse Lane leads into a beautiful rolling park which has as a backdrop a section of England's South Downs, crowned by the Chanctonbury Ring of great beech trees. It is country which Rudyard Kipling, who had a home base not far away for his travels over much of the world, thought some of the most beautiful he had ever seen.

A later American visitor, Professor John A. Ziegler of Hendrix College, Conway, Arkansas, took a longer route, by taxi, but was equally enchanted:

> I shared the cab with a friendly middle-aged resident of Steyning who was returning home from London. Since I had never been that way before, I peppered him with questions about the area but especially about the Wiston House Conference Centre and the work of Wilton Park there which were virtually unknown to me at that time. To my surprise my companion related that the 'mysterious work at Wiston House' – as he put it – was also little known in Steyning as well ...
>
> As the taxi turned off the principal road from Steyning and entered the main gate to the farmlands of Wiston Park, as the old manor is called, the house could not be seen. The thick foliage of trees and bushes near the lane produced an almost impenetrable darkness that intensified the growing mystery of it all. However, after a short ride, the foliage quickly parted like a stage curtain on opening night, and straight ahead in the sunlight on a low, flat hill that was almost barren of trees was the massive pile, Wiston

House. What a magnificent entrance! What a magnificent setting! Which was further enhanced by the tree-covered South Downs that served as a backdrop behind the house. The autumn colours – the reds, yellows, browns, and fading greens – added to the splendour of the view.

Within this splendid setting, as other US visitors testified, Koeppler was a gracious host:

We met him first in his apartment, the first night of our visit to Wilton Park, and were immediately embraced with that special brand of pride and hospitality that so distinctly marked the Warden. Our Texas ways seemed diminished and absorbed into the giant flow of our host's personality as he made us welcome and part of such luminaries as guests from Oxford, and Sweden and France.

For Elizabeth and Samuel Calderon, as they said, 'The enchantment had begun.' It was felt no less keenly by their Texas colleague, John S. Belew, College Dean and Assistant Vice-President at the College of Arts and Sciences, Baylor University:

I first met Heinz in November, 1976, at Wilton Park. There I learned why he was so respected throughout the Western world for his ability to cause people to face problems with a broader vision. He was a realist who simultaneously had the hopes of an idealist; his goal for all was perfection and yet he was willing to settle for the 'denting of one's prejudices', one of his favourite expressions.

'I shall never forget', wrote another Baylor visitor, Loyal Gould of the Department of Journalism, 'how many years ago he took a green, young American foreign correspondent in hand and did marvels in helping broaden his perspective and develop his sensitivity to the plight of others'. And William G. Toland, Baylor's Graduate Dean and Assistant Vice President for Academic Services, also an alumnus of Wilton Park, wrote: 'He made me feel at home in another country.'

A further index of how Wilton Park beguiled and impressed its United States visitors was their determination to form their own alumni association, The American Friends of Wilton Park. They organised it nationally, with nine regional groups across the country. Beside arranging seminars that were much more than reunions, the American Friends helped to recommend – and in some cases subsidise – further US participants. Baylor, the University of Missouri, and Iowa State University all established awards to enable faculty members to attend Wilton Park; and three more – Indiana, Wisconsin, and Ohio State – forged informal links with it.

In July 1972, the American Friends went further. Their first President, Dr William Olson, Director of the Rockefeller Foundation at Bellagio, got together with like-minded colleagues to organise a two-day Wilton Park style conference at Wingspread, Racine, Wisconsin, the home of the Johnson Foundation, which helped defray the cost. One of the Foundation's Trustees was Dr John C. Weaver, President of the University of Wisconsin and an Old Wiltonian. The other prime movers included Dean Peter F. Krogh of the School of Foreign Service of Georgetown University; Robert Rankin, Vice-President of the Danforth Foundation of St Louis, Missouri; Congressman Charles Mosher; the current President of the American Friends, Zygmunt Nagorski, Director of Programs for the Council on Foreign Relations; and Dr Paul R. Schratz, Director of the Office of International Studies at the University of Missouri, and later President of the American Friends with headquarters at Baylor University's Department of Journalism. Heinz Koeppler attended both this meeting and a follow-up, reassured that plans to launch 'an American Wilton Park' would not detract from the Friends' first priority – 'assuring', as their by-laws laid down, 'participation by qualified persons in the Wilton Park Conferences' in Britain.

So enthusiastic were American Wiltonians that by 1971 the number of Americans who had attended Wilton Park – 610 all told – was outstripped only by the Germans, with 1,061. The UK had sent only 462, Austria 373, France 300, Italy 296, and Switzerland 294. These were followed by Spain (143), Norway (139), Denmark (135), the Netherlands (116), Belgium (84), Sweden (84), Finland (79), Turkey (72), non-OECD countries (35), international organisations (27), Yugoslavia (26), Luxembourg (19), Greece (18), Portugal (17), Iceland (3), and Ireland (2).

'The intrinsic value of American participation,' wrote Robert Sturrock, who had joined the academic staff in 1959, 'is self-evident. Conferences claiming to reflect informed Western opinion, but without American representation are, in the Warden's phrase, indeed "Hamlet without the Prince of Denmark".' His remarks appeared in the December 1960 issue of the *Wilton Park Journal*. And the new American presence was reflected in many of the conferences now planned. 'European Attitudes to the New Nations in Asia and Africa', a perennial of three previous sessions, in 1961 became 'Western Attitudes to Developments in Asia and Africa'. 'Economic Co-operation in Europe', a veteran of two, was replaced by 'Economic Co-operation – European or Atlantic?' 'Great Britain and Europe', also twice before on the agenda, became 'Great Britain and the Continent of Europe – an Atlantic solution?' The same year, 1961, saw meetings on 'The Two Sides of the Atlantic Community – North America and Europe' as well as 'The Western Alliance and Competitive Co-existence'. In 1962, four of these themes recurred in only slightly different guise, while two more were added: 'The Defence of the West – Military, Economic, and Social Aspects' and 'Common Issues in Western Economic and Defence Policy – How Much Sovereignty is Retained by Individual Members of OECD and NATO?'

Yet, as Sturrock added: 'In recognising that the world must be its sphere, Wilton Park has not ... lost sight of the fact that Europe must remain the centre of its work. 'The Common Market and the World Outside', which figured in the 1962 programme while Britain was negotiating to join the European Community, took on new significance in 1963, when General de Gaulle's veto had killed the talks: in that year, Wilton Park dealt with the same subject twice. 'Europe Without Great Britain?' was the slightly plaintive title of a conference in 1964, when again two meetings were devoted to the same urgent theme: 'British Relations with the United States, Europe and the Commonwealth' – a subject that recurred on the programme in both 1965 and 1966. 'The Atlantic Community and the Integration of Europe' was another recurrent topic, in 1965, 1966, 1967, 1968, and 1969, when it appeared in the new and apter guise of 'Atlantic Partnership and European Integration', to be followed in 1970 by 'The United States and Europe – Political, Economic and Defence Issues'. When Wilton Park touched on Vietnam, in 1966, it was primarily to assess the impact on NATO and the Alliance in general.

Continuity of this sort did not preclude alertness to less geopolitical issues. Already in the new Wilton Park's very first year, one meeting had considered relations between scientists and humanists. Education had figured in that conference and in the programme every year from 1962 to 1970; development aid every year from 1962 onwards.

Patrick Ground, an aspiring barrister who joined the academic staff in 1958, made it part of his job to build up contacts within Britain with business, banking, industry and the mass communications media. Within a year, he had secured participants from such firms as British American Tobacco, Dunlop Rubber, Esso Petroleum, Mobil Oil, Rolls Royce, and Unilever, as well as from the press and the BBC. When Ground left to take up his profession in the law, George Baird came from the Colonial Service to pursue the same efforts. Appropriately enough, the impact of foreign affairs on business management was on the agenda in 1959; leadership in a democracy in 1960; industrial relations in 1960, 1961 and 1963; the welfare state in 1961; and automation in 1967.

No less appropriately, 1968 – the year of 'les événements' in Paris – saw

a conference entitled 'A Panorama of Social Issues – Urban Renewal;
Regional Planning; Drugs, Crime and the Offender; the Role of
Television; the Population Crisis'. Protest and dissent, as well as the
environment and ecology, figured in 1969, 1970, and 1971.

So Wilton Park continued to shadow events and preoccupations outside
its traditional scope, and to keep in touch with its contacts overseas, not
only on the continent and in the United States, but also in Canada and
Australia, whose first participant attended a conference on 'Great Britain
and the continent of Europe' in October 1961. Old Wiltonians returned on
both official and private visits, while in the summers of 1960 and 1962 the
German Wilton Park Association held its annual reunion conferences at
Wiston House instead of in Germany. Members of the academic staff,
vacationing abroad, were glad to attend similar reunions and to meet individual Wiltonians in Austria, France, Germany, Italy, the Netherlands,
Spain, and Switzerland. Koeppler in particular took advantage of such
meetings to discuss the perennial problems of selection; and in the winter
of 1960-61 he took up an invitation to be Visiting Professor of Political
Science at his old University of Heidelberg, returning in March 1961. It
was not Koeppler's only sabbatical term. As well as acting as a Consultant
to the Ford Foundation in 1961, he was Visiting Distinguished Professor
at Ohio State University in 1966, and Visiting Professor of West-European
Studies at Indiana University, Bloomington, in 1970.

Koeppler liked landmarks. In 1959 he looked back with satisfaction on
'A hundred sessions held at Wilton Park':

> This is certainly more than the original team of Wilton Park expected but,
> to be quite frank, it is no more than we then hoped for. For whatever may
> have been in the public mind at the time the experiment started, those who
> decided at the end of the war to throw in their lot with what has become
> known as the Wilton Park idea, and to devote their lives to it, did so in the
> belief that the principles on which this new experiment was based
> answered genuine needs of our society and were in tune with the intellec-
> tual situation of our times.

Seven years later, Koeppler pointed to another milestone:

> To reflect on 20 years of Wilton Park is an agreeable task ...
>
> Looking back on these 20 years, one is struck by three facts. First, that
> Wilton Park should be 20 years old; second, that it should have changed so
> much; and, in apparent contrast, third, that its inspiration, principles, and
> methods should have survived all these changes.

Not long after he wrote these words, Heinz Koeppler was given a further British honour beyond his OBE. On January 1, 1967, he was named as an Ordinary Commander of the Civil Division of the Order of the British Empire – a CBE.

But an even better occasion for celebration came in 1971 – the twenty-fifth anniversary of Wilton Park. In Europe, there was new hope of progress. In France, Georges Pompidou had succeeded General de Gaulle, and Britain had resumed negotiations to join the European Communities. On expert level, they had proved technical and sticky: but, from February 1971 onwards, confidential Anglo-French contacts had begun to oil the wheels. At Wilton Park, it was the ideal time to hold a Jubilee Conference. It took place in the early summer, from June 20 to July 3, 1971 – and Koeppler excelled himself. He designed the Conference partly – but not only – to reflect Wilton Park's history and his own.

Who should open the inaugural session but the Prime Minister, Edward Heath? He had been associated with Wilton Park since its early days, and had spoken at several of its conferences. A convinced European, he had led Britain's EEC negotiations in 1961–63, thwarted by De Gaulle's veto. In late May, 1971, shortly before the Jubilee Conference, he had had a long summit meeting with Pompidou in Paris – so long that he could not be back in time to skipper *Morning Cloud* in an evening yacht race. 'It would be unreasonable now', Pompidou told the ensuing press conference, 'to believe that an agreement will not be reached in June'. In fact, Heath's chief negotiator Geoffrey Rippon returned to London with the terms of the agreement while the Wilton Park Jubilee was still in full swing.

Next day, three distinguished continentals opened the discussions. Léo Hamon, President Pompidou's Secretary of State, spoke on 'Europe in the Seventies'; Helmut Schmidt, Federal German Minister of Defence, on 'European Security Problems in the Twenty-Five Years Since World War II'; and General Manuel Diez-Alegria, Chief of the Spanish Defence Staff, on 'European Partnership and Atlantic Alliance'. Schmidt took the opportunity to digress:

> The twenty-five years to which Wilton Park is looking back today mark at the same time a critical period of German history and a most significant chapter in the development of Anglo-German relations. Wilton Park had its ample share in both of them. Specifically in the first decade of this quarter of a century, the rural seclusion of the South Downs gave birth to many ideas which became a political reality in Germany in the years to come. Almost a whole generation of German politicians defined their concept of and attitude towards Britain and the British on the basis of the

impressions they received at Wilton Park. At a time when Anglo-German relations were under less favourable auspices than they are today, Wilton Park formed one of the links between our two nations which could be really relied upon.

Historians of the future will perhaps give an account of the contribution rendered by Wilton Park to political developments in post-war Germany. I do not want to pre-empt their analysis. It might have been a 'ruse of history' that a historian such as Heinz Koeppler was called upon to work at Wilton Park just in the nick of time – or was it, rather, the artful historian who realised that his time had come to write a few letters in the book of history?

There were many other prominent speakers at the Jubilee Conference. They included: Jeremy Thorpe, Leader of the Liberal Party; Brigadier W.F.K. Thompson, Defence Correspondent of *The Daily Telegraph*; Dr Leo Mates, former Yugoslav Ambassador to the United States; Vic Feather, General Secretary of the Trades Union Congress; Roy Jenkins, Deputy Leader of the Labour Party and former Chancellor of the Exchequer; Sir William Armstrong, Head of the Home Civil Service; Professor Esmond Wright of the University of London, and former Conservative MP; Poul Hartling, Danish Minister of Foreign Affairs; Dr Joseph Luns, Foreign Minister of the Netherlands; and Sir Denis Greenhill, Head of the UK Diplomatic Service.

Equally notable were those who might later have been dubbed 'the usual suspects' – people closely associated with Koeppler and with Wilton Park. Sir Frank Roberts spoke on the future of NATO; Professor Max Beloff on the Commonwealth; Sir Robert Birley, still Chairman of Wilton Park's Academic Council, on nationalism; the Rt Rev. Roger Plumpton Wilson, Bishop of Chichester, on the cultural scene; Kenneth Younger, Director of the Royal Institute of International Affairs, on British policy; and – veteran of potentially blackballed veterans – Richard Crossman, on the media and public opinion.

There were two 'extra-mural visits'. On a day in London during the first week, Douglas Dodds-Parker presided over a luncheon in the House of Commons, and Lord Lothian hosted a reception at Lancaster House. Halfway through the Conference – and no doubt most cherished by Koeppler – there was an overnight visit to Oxford. It ended in a Celebration Luncheon at Koeppler's *alma mater*, Magdalen College, with speeches by its President Dr James Griffiths and by Sir William Hayter, Vice-Chairman of the Wilton Park Academic Council.

In these respects, then, the Jubilee Conference had traces of nostalgia. The subjects allotted to some of its speakers – Diez-Alegria, Mates, Beloff,

Birley, Roy Jenkins, Armstrong, Younger, Luns – were surveys of the past twenty-five years. But all used the past as a vantage-point for scanning the years to come. In effect, that was everyone's essential remit. And, most notably, two of those who opened its discussions embodied the new Wilton Park's even newer status as a transatlantic institution. One was Dr A.W.R. Carrothers, President and Vice-Chancellor of the University of Calgary, Alberta, Canada. The other was Dr William Olson, Vice-President of the Rockefeller Foundation, Director of the Villa Serbelloni at Bellagio, and Chairman of the Board of the American Friends of Wilton Park. On the very first day of the Jubilee Conference, the President of the American Friends, had given the library a collection of books by American authors, and presented an illuminated scroll. It read:

A TRIBUTE TO WILTON PARK

On the occasion of the Twenty-fifth Anniversary
of the establishment of the Wilton Park Conferences,
where scholarship and fellowship have combined to
advance the great goal of North Atlantic Community,
the American Friends of Wilton Park wish to express
their gratitude and appreciation.
In this setting – so evocative of the common heritage
and ideas shared by the peoples of the North Atlantic
World – reasoned and candid dialogue has demonstrated
that our problems, perils, and destiny are inseparable.
May this Community swiftly grow, a generous and
responsive partner in the World Community, and may
Wilton Park flourish as its companion.

So the Jubilee Conference, as Koeppler had always planned it, was not simply a milestone, but a springboard for the future. Yet even Heinz Koeppler could hardly have foreseen the fresh vicissitudes in store for Wilton Park.

CHAPTER 16

Democracy in Aristocratic Dress

> 'One still strong man in a blatant land,
> Whatever they call him, what care I,
> Aristocrat, democrat, autocrat – one
> Who can rule and dare not lie.'
> **Alfred, Lord Tennyson**, *Maud*, 1855

In his opening speech at Wilton Park's Jubilee Conference on June 20, 1971, Heinz Koeppler had tackled head-on the problem of 'élites'. Reminding his audience that 'Our work is private, privileged, and off the record', he admitted that this had meant 'a sacrifice which in many ways is quite serious':

> If, since 1946, we had recorded all our discussions we would now have a most useful and revealing archive of the evolution of, and changes in Western public opinion since the end of the war. What glorious material for untold doctoral theses! However, the price for this source of knowledge would have been too high in the perspective of Wilton Park's aims, for, given that so many of our members are in official and often in sensitive positions, the fact that records were being taken would, inevitably, have restricted their freedom of expression. And Wilton Park values above all an honest, free and frank discussion amongst people who, because of their functions, know what they are talking about ...
>
> Free government will not continue, will indeed perish from this earth, unless we have in all our countries at least an active minority which does accept the implications of having as the ultimate basis of government lay decisions, and which is prepared to do something about it. But if there exists such a minority of sufficient size, then, I believe, we have a guarantee for what the American Declaration of Independence calls the pursuit of happiness.
>
> I am not afraid to call this minority the political élite of our countries.

The term 'élite' has often a nasty connotation in politics not least amongst some of the younger generation of today. However, it will be clear from what I have said that this political élite is indeed an open-ended one, that everyone who wants to may join quite irrespective of his position in our society. It is in this sense that Wilton Park is dedicated to the political élite of all the countries participating in our work. In other words, we provide meetings between people who are – or shortly will be – in key positions in their various specialist occupations and who do understand, often perhaps only subconsciously, that societies, in order to be free, must ultimately be based on lay decisions.

Bland though his words might sound, Koeppler was right to call Wilton Park, in the same speech, 'an heretical institution'. 'Private' – 'privileged' – 'off the record': for some, such terms were as contentious as 'political élite'. Equally, the notion that 'lay decisions', however 'élitist', should be the basis of, say, foreign policy could seem an affront to jealous professionals. In the words of Professor Ziegler's taxi-sharing companion, there was indeed 'mysterious work at Wiston House'.

Academic freedom and independence – frank talking, in secrecy, with no reports – a privileged life in a country mansion: no wonder that a Swiss journalist, Gustav Lang, writing in the Berne *Der Bund* on April 5, 1973, described Wilton Park, as 'Democracy in aristocratic dress'. He applies the same phrase to Great Britain itself; but it may have been the 'aristocratic' aspect of Wilton Park that chiefly aroused perplexity, suspicion and jealousy. In certain sections of Whitehall – not to mention the Treasury's headquarters in Great George Street – it seemed to provoke positive hostility.

This was partly why, for so long, Wilton Park had led a hand-to-mouth existence. In 1958 its lease of life had been extended 'at least until April 1, 1960'. Early in 1960, the Academic Council had declared that 'to work on a year-to-year basis' would be 'intolerable' and had recommended 'establishing Wilton Park on at least a five-year basis in the future'. Later in that year, the Foreign Office had recommended extension until March 3, 1963, with a review a year before the deadline. In 1962, a further extension had been granted until March 1968, and in 1967 another until March 1973.

There was also, of course, a material reason for this grudging approach. At the 1971 Jubilee Conference, Koeppler had admitted it: 'Almost 90% of our budget comes from Foreign Office funds.'

In cash terms, the full cost of Wilton Park for the fiscal year 1971/72 was some £92,000. Of total government expenditure, the net cost of Wilton Park was about six ten-thousandths of 1 per cent. But the daily government subsidy to each participant was some £20 – which at that time would have secured bed and board at a very comfortable hotel.

Treasury pressure to reduce these costs – and even to eliminate Wilton Park altogether – began again barely a month after Koeppler's Jubilee Conference, almost as if it had never been held. On August 5, 1971, Ian Rich of the Treasury wrote to remind Miss Debbie Betts (of the FCO's Information Administration Department) that the authorisation to continue Wilton Park was due to expire in about eighteen months' time. He had understood, he said, that when the question had last been raised the most important factor in the Foreign Office's recommendation 'to continue the work for a further period' had been its assessment of 'the adverse effect of closure in Britain's policy on the EEC'.

> This consideration will not, of course, apply on this occasion [by which time Britain was likely to have joined the Community] and we shall need to be convinced that the work of the centre (if it is to continue) is of vital and indispensable importance to British interests.

Rich had spent two days at the Wilton Park conference following the Jubilee: it had been devoted to 'Problems of Democratic Control – the Relevance of Political Parties, Interest Groups and the Mass Media'.

> My own impression was that the calibre of both speakers and participants, and the level of the discussions, were extremely high, but it was arguable whether HMG received any 'pay-off' (as an American visitor described it to me) from the operation which now costs the taxpayer about £74,000 a year.

The cost of actually running Wilton Park in 1971/72 was £73,896. The Treasury could clearly have quoted a higher figure had it included upkeep and maintenance. But, for the moment, political considerations held sway. On September 10, 1971, Miss Betts answered Rich by quoting from the Chairman of the Inter-departmental Study on Anglo–French Cultural Relations: 'The Prime Minister (Mr Heath) accepts that Wilton Park satisfactorily fulfils the role of our European Centre and should continue as such.' She added that he had opened the Jubilee Conference 'and made particularly warm remarks about the establishment and its Warden'. A few months later, in February 1972, the Government allowed another five-year extension, with a review in 1978, but with an assurance that this did not imply closure in that year.

Meanwhile, before the end of 1971, matters had been complicated by a fresh idea. Ministers had instructed the Foreign Office to examine 'the possibility of setting up a new European Discussion Centre at Wiston

House which would organise conferences separate from the Wilton Park sessions'. This was the brain-child of Edward Heath and Georges Pompidou, and intended as a contribution to building the enlarged European Community, all of whose member States were to be invited to join. As the Belgian writer Paul M.G. Levy put it later, writing in *Le Soir* on August 11–12, 1974, *'Le grand problème n'est pas de parler la même langue mais bien de parler le même langage.'* Such was the essential task of the European Discussion Centre. Work to establish it continued while the enlargement negotiations drew to a close, culminating in the Accession Treaties signed on January 22 1972. These were quickly ratified by the parliaments of the existing member States and of all the new members except Norway, which held a referendum in which the Accession Treaty was rejected by the narrow majority of 53 per cent. The way was now clear for Denmark, Ireland, and the United Kingdom to join the Community, which they did on January 1, 1973.

The European Discussion Centre (EDC) began life in Wiston House soon afterwards, with a provisional budget of £40,000 for 1973/74, all of it borne by the Foreign and Commonwealth Office, although the Centre was academically independent, like Wilton Park.

The EDC, in fact, was Wilton Park in miniature. Heinz Koeppler was its Warden, assisted by two multilingual Deputy Wardens: the Resistance historian Michael (M.R.D.) Foot and the Director of Programmes Alan Hughes, an experienced multi-national businessman, from Oxford and Cambridge respectively. Open to people with what Koeppler called 'senior distinguished positions in their countries or within the institutions of the Community', it planned to hold ten short round-table conferences each year, when Wilton Park was not in session. Its own meetings lasted two and a half days each, from Monday night until Thursday lunchtime, to avoid too much disruption of busy people's work. Each day involved three structured sessions, the remainder unstructured, each lasting no more than two hours. Like Wilton Park, it insisted on privacy, privilege, and candour. To guarantee its independence, it had a council, chaired by Sir Con O'Neill. Like Wilton Park's International Council, this consisted of the London Ambassadors of the countries concerned; like Wilton Park's Academic Council, it also included representatives of industry, the trade unions, the universities, the Foreign Office, the European Movement, and the three main political parties. Later, representing the European Commission in London, I attended the Council myself and found its discussions lively, constructive, and uninhibited.

The EDC held its first Conference from April 9 to 12, 1973, discussing 'The First Three Months of the Enlarged Community'. Subsequent conferences during the year discussed 'Steps Towards a Common Foreign Policy', 'Bureaucracy versus Democracy in the Community', 'The Three Europes: Community Relations with the Rest of Western Europe and with the Eastern European Countries', 'The Relationship Between Monetary Unity and Economic Unity', and 'Common Agricultural Policy and Common Regional Policy within the Community'. The addition of the EDC to Wilton Park placed extra burdens on Koeppler. That summer, a Foreign and Commonwealth Office Inspector, Douglas Brown, visited Wiston House to consider the Warden's official grading. His report, on July 12, 1973, recommended a Diplomatic Service [DS] Grade 3, plus – if there were no upgrading – a 'responsibility allowance' in view of the Warden's additional role with the EDC. He commented:

> Although I have recommended a grading in DS terms (which is all a DS Inspector is competent to do), I am bound to say that I am doubtful whether a DS grading reflects what is required of the Warden. On the other hand nor would a Home Civil Service grading be any more appropriate, nor would equation with an academic official – the Warden of Wilton Park and his institution are unique.

Unique they certainly were – not least in their escalating costs. In 1972/73, the total net expenditure on the EDC and Wilton Park combined was £114,941. In 1973/74 it was £147,389. In 1974/75 it was £168,100; and the projected figure for 1975/76 was £182,000. In 1976/77 it threatened to reach £223,700.

It was hardly surprising that questions began to be asked in Whitehall. Although Wilton Park had been warmly endorsed by Edward Heath, he had ceased to be Prime Minister in February 1974; and his successor Harold Wilson was less familiar with it. On June 12, 1975, the FCO's Planning Committee met to discuss, among other things, the situation of Wiston House as the home of both Wilton Park and the EDC. 'It was generally agreed', the minutes recorded, 'that we could no longer afford to maintain it, that it should come to an end in March 1978 when the lease would terminate'. This was not everyone's view. On June 24, the Director General of British Information Services and Deputy Consul-General (Information) in New York wrote to London disagreeing with his own ambassador, who had cast doubt on the effectiveness of Wilton Park. In a letter to the head of the FCO's Cultural Relations Department, he declared:

> There can be no doubt that the tiny sums invested by HMG in Wilton Park have had an immense multiplier effect and yielded enormous dividends across the US.

I am concerned lest the view of HM Ambassador, based on the comments of miscellaneous Consuls-General around the US (many of whom know little or nothing about the institution in West Sussex) should work its way through the ... machinery and have a greater impact than it deserves.

For the present, the Planning Committee took no action on its own negative opinion; and, later in the summer of 1975, another FCO Inspector said of Wilton Park: 'It remains a very good investment.' What also remained was the perpetual question-mark over its survival.

In the New Year, the latent threat became doubly explicit. On January 6, 1976, the Planning Committee circulated its report. It recalled its decision of the previous June, and pointed out that in 1976/77 the combined cost of Wilton Park and the EDC would rise to £184,700, plus repairs and maintenance expenditure of £30,000. What was more, the European Cultural Programme funds (known as 'Rippon Money' after Geoffrey Rippon, the chief negotiator of Britain's EEC membership) would expire on March 31, 1977. The committee therefore repeated its advice against renewing the lease on Wiston House when it came to an end in 1978.

Some ten days later, on Sunday and Monday, January 18–19, the FCO's Under-Secretary of State gave Heinz Koeppler some still less welcome news. The Government 'think tank', the Central Policy Review Staff or CPRS, which was due to examine the Foreign and Commonwealth Office and its posts abroad, would be including Wilton Park within its remit. Koeppler 'accepted this', the Under-Secretary noted, 'though very reluctantly'.

Typically, however, the wind blew hot and cold. On Thursday January 21, 1976, the PUS's Planning Committee met again – and changed its mind about Wilton Park. 'The Committee generally agreed', said the minutes, 'that it would be a mistake now to take a definite decision to close it down'. Instead, it should seek economies.

As before when under siege, Koeppler began to stockpile ammunition. On March 1, he wrote to the FCO's Information Administration Department (IAD): 'We are at present surveying the careers of some of the people who had been participants over the past 30 years. We were endeavouring to show how many had reached positions of eminence in politics, or in any other specialist field.' In the Foreign Office itself, the Head of the IAD came to Koeppler's aid. Writing on April 9, he referred to the founding of a Los Angeles branch of the American Friends of Wilton Park, and quoted what Lord Goronwy-Roberts, Minister of State for Foreign

Affairs, had said on that occasion: 'It is a further proof of the efficacy of Wilton Park, and it is impossible to quantify its influence. It is unique in quality, considerable in extent, and of increasing significance.'

On the very same day, as if to show how official opinion was divided, the Head of the FCO's Policy Planning Staff, Brian Crowe, wrote to the Private Secretary to the new PUS, Sir Michael Palliser: 'I have never been to Wilton Park and so have no first-hand impression of it. I am, however, personally persuaded that we should not continue with Wilton Park.' It was costly and outdated, he thought, and there was difficulty in getting VIPs to attend. Nevertheless, any action either way would have to await the report of the CPRS.

Koeppler continued to stock his arsenal. On April 13, 1976, he sent to the FCO an appreciative piece about Wilton Park published by Elio Fazzalavi in the Rome daily *Il Tempo* of March 13; and it was from Koeppler, no doubt, that the FCO received a similar article by A.C.W. van der Vet in the Dutch *Algemeen Dagblad* of February 10, which he sent on to Ronald Scrivener on April 22.

May 10, 1976 saw another piece of ordnance wheeled on to the battlements, at the annual meeting of Wilton Park's International Advisory Council. On the initiative of Karl-Günther von Hase, the Federal German Ambassador in London, the members of the Council voted a unanimous tribute to 'Professor Heinz Koeppler':

> They want to express their gratitude to him and at the same time to the British Government for making the work of Wilton Park in its present scope and form possible. They want to express their appreciation for the valuable contribution to mutual understanding in Europe and with Australia, Canada, Japan and the United States which Great Britain makes through Wilton Park.

Koeppler was also pleased to note another tribute received that month, from Dr Rupert Stettner of the University of Augsburg, who had attended one of the EDC conferences:

> I must thank you once again for the invitation from your Government to attend at Wiston House; let me assure you that it made a strong and lasting impression on me. I am convinced that with this institution Great Britain is making a substantial contribution to the integration of the European Community and is furthering the process of mutual understanding between the peoples of Europe in a significant fashion.

A few days later, on May 18, 1976, Koeppler sent the FCO the results of a survey he had conducted, listing the Old Wiltonian associations overseas. The first, in Germany, had been founded in 1957, the second, in Washington in 1966, had given birth in 1967 to the American Friends of Wilton Park, followed by the Canadian Friends in 1970. Austrian Old Wiltonians had held their first conference in 1967; in the same year, the French based had founded an association which had led in 1968 to a broader Franco-Belgian-Swiss *Société internationale des amis de Wilton Park de langue française*. From the first, this had had some Italian members; then the Italian Ambassador in London, Roberto Ducci, had initiated moves towards an Italian counterpart, chaired by Egidio Ortona, former Italian Ambassador to the USA. Spain, too had been influenced by the *Société Internationale*, and had held its first purely Spanish meeting, under official auspices, in 1973. In Switzerland, the semi-official *Vortragsdienst* had originally sent participants to Wilton Park in liaison with the German association; it had been succeeded by the Swiss Committee for Wilton Park and then in 1974–75 by the Association of Swiss Friends of Wilton Park. Finland had no formal association but strong links with Wilton Park, while Swedish old Wiltonians had an informal network. In Norway, the parliament had voted money for Wilton Park and the Foreign Ministry had sent participants; in Denmark, they had been sent by both. Yugoslavia had sent visitors to Wilton Park since December 1961.

Koeppler included with these data a translated excerpt from the message that Helmut Schmidt, who was now Federal German Chancellor, had sent to a meeting of German, Austrian, and Swiss Old Wiltonians in Bad Godesberg in May 1975: 'Although I look forward with confidence to further developments in Europe and on the Atlantic partnership, I must nevertheless underline how very necessary the contributions to this end are, which Wilton Park makes.'

Finally, Koeppler reminded the FCO of a letter that the Information Officer at the British Embassy in Berne had written to IAD on March 24, 1975:

Herr W. Schenk, Editor of the weekend magazine published with Switzerland's second biggest daily, *Tages Anzeiger*, was at the 169th Conference [February 2–15, 1975, on 'Industrial Relations at a Time of Inflation']. There is an amusing account of how the various foreign participants lectured the British on their problems, then a recital of British problems and shortcomings, and finally a remarkably warm tribute to British tolerance and relaxed way of life.

260

For all its adverse criticism this article has done us good; furthermore its author, whom we have always found very difficult to deal with, is suddenly a changed man where the British are concerned. He has even belatedly apologised for a damaging article on Northern Ireland which he published last year, whereas previously he had stuck to his guns in the face of all argument.

On May 26, moreover, the Head of the FCO News Department in London, formerly of the British Information Services in New York, weighed in with another compliment to Wilton Park:

> I know of no other institution which has at such modest cost won us so many worthwhile friends ... I am strongly of the view that the institution should be kept going ... If it is a question of economies, let us cut some of our tail (e.g. within the FCO) rather than one of our teeth.

IAD, meanwhile, had been conducting their own survey of attitudes to Wilton Park among overseas embassies. On June 30, 1976, they reported: 'Ten posts are broadly in favour of continuing the Centre; four are lukewarm; and three are opposed to its continuation.'

A good case seemed to be building; but, as always, the process took time. On Friday July 9, 1976, the PUS Sir Michael Palliser chaired a meeting to discuss Wilton Park's future. There was still no sign of the CPRS's 'think tank' report. On Friday, July 16, FCO officials had to admit to the Academic Council that they were not expecting it until January or February of 1977. However, on August 19, 1976, IAD received weighty backing from the newly appointed Head of the FCO's Guidance and Information Policy Department (later known simply as the Information Policy Department). This was the 42-year-old Nicholas Barrington, who had risen rapidly through the Foreign Office and was destined to play an important role in Wilton Park's preservation and development.

Barrington admitted that it could give better value. In this he was not alone. An Assistant Under-Secretary of State at the Ministry of Defence complained on November 2 that a two-week Conference he had attended 'could have been squeezed into a period of seven days':

> Three days were spent in sight-seeing – the term is hardly too strong. The hours of work were also somewhat eccentric, in as much as the morning session did not start until 11.15, the afternoon was left free and the second and third sessions started at 1700 hours and 20.15 hours respectively.

The Head of the FCO's North America Department, writing on

December 3, was also critical of Wilton Park 'in its present form': 'I think it would be a pity if Wilton Park were to disappear partly as the result of yet another economy drive. But clearly something must be done to improve its present effectiveness.' Already in the summer Nicholas Barrington had had ideas about what could be done – running slightly shorter conferences, using interpreters more flexibly, selecting better UK participants with more from industry and commerce, and conducting more systematic follow-up. But he was convinced that:

> The FCO would be very unwise to give up Wiston House, with its special beauty and good facilities within reasonable reach of London. We should also be foolish to kill off the institution of Wilton Park, with its high repu-tation and wide network of contacts throughout the developed world.

It was left to Sir Robert Birley, Chairman of the Academic Council, to raise the defence of Wilton Park from official to political level. On August 24, 1976, he wrote to Evan Luard, Parliamentary Under-Secretary of State at the FCO:

> I have known Wilton Park for thirty years ... [From the beginning] I was at once struck by the way in which the British position was put across, not by preaching it, but by encouraging frank discussion when it would be listened to. I can see just the same thing now. In a way which it is almost impossible to define and quite impossible to measure it has, I believe, done splendid service for this country.

Fortified by all this testimony, IAD prepared a short paper about Wiston House on October 26. Its annual cost (for Wilton Park and the EDC combined, including repairs and maintenance) was now £230,000. It held nine Wilton Park Conferences and 8 EDC conferences every year. Seven of the Wilton Park meetings lasted for two weeks, two for one week only; each of the EDC conferences was for three days. IAD later confirmed the cost figure, adding that this was 'not an excessive price' and that it was 'not worth trying to find an alternative location'.

But the pressure for economy persisted. On November 4, 1976, Evan Luard had a meeting with Heinz Koeppler. He had been struck, he said, by what he thought was the excessive number of staff – ten or a dozen – in attendance at the conference held on Wilton Park's thirtieth anniversary. Considering that Wiston House housed the EDC as well as Wilton Park, it was reasonable enough. In fact, changes in staffing levels had been agreed nearly a year before, on November 11, 1975, by the FCO's Personnel Policy Department. His conclusion was that there should be one Deputy

Warden, who would be Chairman of Sessions and also carry out the duties of Director of Programmes. The existing post of Dean was to be abolished, and the Director of Participation was to take over the general directing of the administrative staff, then to assume the title of Dean when its existing incumbent, Robert Gibson, retired on December 31, 1975.

The years 1975 and 1976, in fact, had seen a fair turnover of staff at Wiston House. Michael (M.R.D.) Foot had left. Len Verreck had joined on January 1, 1975; Martin Hansford on January 2, 1975; Tim Slack on February 1, 1975; Valerie Seward on October 1, 1975; Jim Starkey on January 1, 1976. With Alan Hughes, Oliver Hayward and others already in place Koeppler had a largely new team, and a good one.

With Heinz Koeppler's 'trumpets' evidence, the FCO's figures, and Personnel's agreement on staff, there was surely now ample material on Wilton Park and the EDC for the Central Policy Review Staff 'think tank' to reach a conclusion on their future. But there were also delaying factors. Some were administrative and relatively minor. Some arose from the high politics of the day.

The first was the heavy burden on the Central Policy Review Staff itself. Set up originally by Edward Heath's Government to audit – in the broadest sense – the administration, it had made itself unpopular early on by attacking entrenched privileges, customs, and habits. Now, increasingly, there were calls for it to do more.

As inflation had grown in the early months of 1975, the Treasury had presented a large package of proposed spending cuts. Tony Crosland, then in charge of the Department of the Environment, thereupon wrote what officials thought an unprecedented letter to the Prime Minister, Harold Wilson. Why, Crosland asked, could Ministers not stop thinking purely in terms of their own departments? When there was more economic pressure, it was even more crucial to take an overall view and choose priorities. The CPRS, he concluded, should be put to work on co-ordination, even if one's own department got less as a result.

It was a call for what was later nicknamed 'joined-up government'. But the CPRS already had too much on its plate. Even its Report on the Foreign and Commonwealth Office had so broad a remit that members of the 'think tank' had too little time to visit Wiston House. It was a serious omission, but it was not the only reason for the Report's delay.

If 1975 and 1976 saw personnel changes at Wiston House, 1976 and the early months of 1977 saw bigger changes at Westminster. On March 16, 1976, Harold Wilson had announced to a stunned Cabinet his decision to resign as Prime Minister. On Monday April 5, after a brisk leadership contest, the Foreign Secretary James Callaghan had been elected to succeed him; and on Thursday April 8 Tony Crosland had become Foreign Secretary.

One change at the top of the Foreign Office was enough to multiply official minutes, Ministerial briefings, and what looked like bureaucratic delays. Two at least doubled the commotion. And on February 18, 1977, Tony Crosland died. His successor was the Minister of State, Dr David Owen, a comparatively unknown quantity. 'I had the feeling', wrote Sir Con O'Neill, 'that Owen, while not hostile to Wilton Park, is a bit rattled by the pressures on him to reduce expenditure. I don't suppose the pressure is much less than that experienced by at least 9 of his predecessors, but they all spared Wilton Park.'

O'Neill's note was addressed to Heinz Koeppler on July 16, 1977. But by that time something else had changed. On June 30, 1977, Koeppler had celebrated his sixty-fifth birthday, and formally retired as Warden of Wilton Park. On the birthday evening, there was a reception for nearly a hundred past and present colleagues and their wives in the Great Hall, with a speech and tributes from all over the world. The longest serving member of staff, the chef, Albert Handerer, presented Koeppler with an early 19th-century Old Sheffield candelabra, and Len Verreck handed him a tankard in memory of the Chanctonbury Ring Club. Koeppler then planted a memorial copper beech tree on the verge of the avenue. A group photograph was taken; a birthday cake was cut; and champagne was drunk. Koeppler then unveiled the final birthday gift – his portrait – which he at once agreed to leave on permanent loan at Wiston House.

It was a memorable occasion. But as an ending it was untidy. Appropriately, Koeppler stayed on, to preside in July over the last conference of the summer season. And, although the omens were promising, the fate of Wilton Park was still in the balance. Partly for this reason, a new Warden had not yet been formally chosen. That was no fault of Koeppler's. He had prepared for his departure long in advance.

CHAPTER 17

Headhunting

'Ask, and it shall be given you; seek, and ye shall find.'
St Matthew, *Gospel*, Chapter 7, Verse 7

On June 30, 1975, Heinz Koeppler had been sixty-three. Most Foreign Office officials would at that age have been retired for three years. Many academics, in Britain at least, would have only two more years to serve. Several of his friends had urged him to write his memoirs; but, as he told one of them, a professor at Heidelberg: 'I am a slow writer' and 'to make such memoirs worth reading, I would have to breach the essential confidentiality of our work.' Yet with his abundant energy, he was reluctant to contemplate an idle retirement. 'I shall certainly not be sitting in the depths of Sussex in my cottage. I might keep it, but I am quite determined to move into the very centre of London, to profit from all that is going on there.' In the event, he took a flat in Ashley Gardens, Westminster. Meanwhile, he was alert for a possible successor. As he wrote to Lord Gladwyn – a leading member of the Wilton Park Academic Council – on October 13, 1975:

> Although I shall not disappear until the last day of June in 1977, what with finding the person, allowing him, or her, to give notice, and to have an overlap with me here, it will not be too soon to start moving early in the new year. My point now is to alert our friends, since people are apt to hear of possible candidates quite accidentally.

Long before the fatal date, in fact, Koeppler even approached me, very tactfully, to see whether I might be among the candidates to succeed him. I was flattered, but otherwise engaged and very busy: more to the point, I rightly doubted whether I could be anything but the proverbial carthorse following Koeppler's Lord Mayor's Show.

He had also made discreet inquiries in Brussels, notably approaching Michael Shanks, who as well as being a member of Wilton Park's Academic Council was also at that time Director-General for Social Affairs in the European Commission. On May 22, 1975, Shanks promised to 'think about possible successors', but added that 'my immediate reaction is that one should not be in too much of a hurry to look for people because I should frankly hope that an internal appointment could be made'.

Quite properly, Koeppler also approached the Foreign and Commonwealth Office. On October 7, 1975, a senior official replied:

I think I can now summarise the Office's position on the following lines.

1. Firstly of course we want to have the best possible person; and we are of course required to consider women as well as men.
2. On tenure, the Chief Inspector recommended that 'the new Warden should be appointed for an initial period of 5 years, with the expectation that ... he should occupy the post for about 10'.

This, the FCO stressed, was 'subject to a decision on the future of Wiston House', about which there was 'still unresolved uncertainty', likely to last, he thought, for 'several more weeks'.

Koeppler agreed that the chairmen of the Wilton Park and the EDC Councils, Sir Robert Birley and Sir Con O'Neill, should be consulted on the succession, although the post would have to be publicly advertised. Meeting in London on January 27, 1976, the Wilton Park Academic Council set up a search committee, headed by Kenneth Younger, to advise on Koeppler's successor: its other members were Frank Giles, Foreign Editor of *The Sunday Times*, Sir Con O'Neill, Michael Shanks, Andrew Shonfield, Director of the Royal Institute of International Affairs (Chatham House), and John Whitehorn, Deputy Director of the Confederation of British Industry (CBI). It was joined by two FCO officials from IAD. The Committee held its first meeting at Chatham House a week after the Academic Council, and met there again on March 22. Among the many names it mooted were the writer and journalist François Duchêne of the University of Sussex, former Director of the International Institute for Strategic Studies (IISS); Charles Hargrove of *The Times*; and George Wedell of the European Commission. Kenneth Younger also proposed to ask advice from David Astor, Director of *The Observer*, and Ralf Dahrendorf, Director of the London School of Economics (LSE), as well as Alan Bullock, Founding Master of St Catherine's College Oxford, Asa Briggs, Provost of Worcester College, Oxford, Huw Wheldon of the BBC, and Sir Frank Roberts of the Foreign Office.

The CBI, as Whitehorn wrote to the Foreign Office on March 15, 1976, had heard from several possible candidates: a former MP, Rafton Pounder; a former Ambassador, Denis Laskey; and Lieutenant-Commander G.C. Hollingworth, RN. One who was soon to emerge from the Foreign Office itself was the 56-year-old Robin Edmonds, Assistant Under-Secretary of State for North, Central, and South American questions, who had recently been a Visiting Fellow at Glasgow University. On April 2, 1976, he wrote to the PUS's Private Secretary, John Kerr, with his impressions on visiting Wilton Park for the first time:

> Until Sunday evening I had not met Dr Koeppler since the early days of the war at Oxford. What he has done is more than empire-building; it is a remarkable achievement. He must have a lot of friends and supporters in this country, quite apart from Old Wiltonians abroad. A decision to close Wilton Park is therefore bound to provoke criticism and to lose some accumulated goodwill, the extent of which should not be underestimated. It would do us more damage than – e.g. – closing missions in Central America, I think.
>
> This said, I also believe that Wilton Park should not continue in its present form. Its principal and characteristic activity – conferences lasting a fortnight, in their present form and with their present kind and level of participants – no longer corresponds to the needs of the late 1970s.
>
> My suggestion is that Wilton Park should be converted into a high quality, high level centre for international discussion. It would remain under the aegis of the FCO, but it would maintain close links with universities such as Sussex, as well as with Chatham House and perhaps with the IISS. Participation in conferences at Wilton Park should no longer be confined to the OECD countries ...
>
> At a Wilton Park reformed on these lines it would be essential to ensure a stringent standard of intellectual rigour.
>
> The ultimate intention of these changes would be radical, but their introduction should be gradual. The new Warden should exercise flexibility in regulating the pace of the wind of change. But in any event, space would probably have to be kept in the annual programme for one or two traditional Wilton Park fortnight-long conferences in order to retain Old Wiltonian 'goodwill': an exercise in diplomacy.
>
> If this suggestion were adopted, more money would probably be needed. On the assumption that this could not be obtained from the FCO Vote it would be necessary to get it from industry and from the Foundations. Judging from my experience so far on the Finance Committee of Chatham House, the Foundations still have money available for a good cause; and industry might be persuaded to contribute if Wilton Park were to pay more attention to economic subjects. (I had great diffi-

culty during the time that I spent at the current conference in persuading anyone to talk about the economic aspects of the Transatlantic Relationship) ... Finally, if Wilton Park were reorganised on these lines it should stay where it is, both because of its setting, which is extremely important, and also because of the considerable asset represented by the people who are already working there.

Much of this tallied with ideas that were already in Nicholas Barrington's mind. At the same time, Edmonds's note reads in retrospect like a personal election manifesto. But his hat was not yet in the ring.

One June 10, 1976, the Vice-Chancellor of the University of Bath, Lord Rotherham, wrote to John Moore suggesting another candidate: Dr Kenneth Humphreys, Director of the University's Centre for Adult Studies. His name was one of many discussed by the Academic Council when it met at Wiston House on July 16: they now included Professor Roger Morgan of Loughborough University and Christopher Cope, a former diplomat now Overseas Director of the CBI. On behalf of the Council, Sir Robert Birley paid tribute to Kenneth Younger and Alastair Buchan, two colleagues who had recently died. Sir Con O'Neill agreed to take Younger's place on the search committee.

The council also discussed a draft job description. It was a daunting task. In most people's minds, the true description would have been a character-sketch of Heinz Koeppler, with some of his abrasiveness removed. As it was, the council based its draft on a report by the Foreign Office Inspector:

1. The successful applicant will be a person of sufficient learning and intellectual stature to be acceptable to and respected by the participants in Wilton Park and European Discussion Centre conferences. He or she must have a sufficiently informed interest in, and grasp of, public and international affairs to enable him or her to deal easily with politicians, Ministers, and other distinguished figures in public life.
2. In addition the person will be capable on his or her own, though within general guide lines laid down by the FCO, of running the Conference Centre and working out ways of achieving its aims. He or she will possess a capacity for managing a disparate staff, for organising conferences, and for handling high-level meetings, together with an ability to meet the representational requirements of the post.
3. The person appointed ought to be able to converse on matters of substance in either French or German and to understand a discussion in the other language without the use of interpreters.
4. The appointment would be for a period of five years in the first instance and would at current levels attract a salary in the range of £10–12,000 p.a.

At the same meeting of the Academic Council, the Foreign Office revealed that they would soon be putting forward their own candidate. It was, of course, Robin Edmonds. The council agreed that he was a strong contender. As one of its members, the former diplomat Sir Peter Tennant, wrote privately to Koeppler two days after the meeting, 'we must see the F.C.O. man'. But he added: 'I never put my faith in princes and suspect ulterior motives as far as the F.C.O. is concerned.' However, another former diplomat, the Hon. Henry Hankey, wrote to Koeppler on January 21, 1977, that Edmonds 'really fitted well, as a most worthy successor to yourself. Quick-witted, immediately likeable, a little panache but not too much (a few extra years and the experiences in his present job have had their effect) – a blend not too far from yourself if I may [say] so – even if so different in many ways.' Koeppler replied, circumspectly, on January 28, 1977: 'The all important thing, particularly for Robin as a member of the Diplomatic Service, is that we can establish a selection board on which, not only the Foreign and Commonwealth Office and the Civil Service Department, but the chairmen of our Academic Councils, are represented. I cannot think of any single act which will help him more to make his academic independence credible to our participants.'

By this time, a further possible candidate from government employment had emerged. He had attended the October 1976 Conference at Wilton Park and made a very good impression: one of his fellow-members let it be known that he would be interested in the Wardenship, and an American participant told Koeppler 'that he would make a splendid successor'. Given Koeppler's problems with the military in the very early days of Wilton Park, the new aspirant was unusual. He was David Crichton Alexander, a Major General in the Royal Marines. Born on November 28, 1926, he was on the point of fifty. During his service he had been an adviser to the Shah of Iran, an equerry to the Duke of Edinburgh, and an ADC to the Queen. Now, on the brink of retirement, he was in charge of all Royal Marine training. 'I talked with him over a meal yesterday', Koeppler wrote to Birley on November 12, 1976, 'as a result of which I am passing on his CV. I would not do so if he corresponded in any way to the usual caricature of Generals and Marines.' Sir Patrick Nairne, the Head of the DHSS and a former pupil of Koeppler's, who had known Alexander when he had been concerned with defence, wrote on November 22, 1976, that he was impressed by 'his intelligence, vigour, charm, and general good sense ... My general feeling is that he would run Wilton Park very well; he has always seemed to me to know how to organise, and to handle people, with the minimum fuss and maximum reliability. What I am less able to assess from my limited experience is his width of knowledge of the international scene and his intellectual cutting edge. He may be better than any other competitor on both counts ... I am certainly ready to confirm, without qualification, that he will make a good candidate for consideration.' Nairne's verdict was seconded on December 2, 1976 by Arthur Hockaday, Deputy Under-Secretary of State at the Ministry of Defence. Koeppler passed these endorsements on to the search committee, and advised Alexander – and anyone else who was interested – to make an official application once the advertisement appeared.

Before it did so, another General had appeared on the candidates' scene. This was the 55-year-old Lieutenant-General Sir James Wilson, GOC South East District, a staff officer and writer of wide experience, and Association Football Correspondent of *The Sunday Times* since 1957. He visited Wiston House in March 1977, as did Professor George Wedell from the European Commission in Brussels. Wedell withdrew his candidature for the post because the terms were 'such that I can't afford to take it at present. I hope the F.C.O. find a successor who will do justice to your splendid work.'

It was, of course, up to the FCO. As Koeppler wrote to General Wilson: 'In the best – or worst – traditions of British universities, the outgoing man is firmly kept away from decision-making.' The selection board was chaired by the then Head of the Personnel Policy Department at the FCO, which was in charge of screening candidates. These were not all outsiders. As early as May 1975, in his letter to Koeppler, Michael Shanks had written from Brussels: 'I should frankly hope that an internal appointment could be made and the obvious candidate needs, I imagine, more time to prove his worth.' That October, in his letter to Gladwyn, Koeppler had added a handwritten footnote: 'Of course, the successor might be on the staff already!' He was.

His name was Timothy Willatt Slack, and he had joined the staff at Wiston House as Koeppler's Deputy on February 1, 1975, at the age of 46.

Born on April 18, 1928, Tim Slack was the younger brother of William Willatt Slack, Surgeon to the Queen. Both brothers had been educated at Winchester and New College, Oxford; but their academic paths had diverged. Tim had read PPE (Philosophy, Politics and Economics) at Oxford and gone on to be an assistant at the *Lycée de Rennes* in France, followed by an assistant mastership at the Salem School in Baden, Germany. From 1953 to 1959 he had taught at Repton, then been Headmaster of Kambawsa College, Taunggyi, Shan State, Burma. In 1962 he had been appointed Headmaster of Bedales School, where he stayed for twelve years, including a two-year stint as Chairman of the Society of Headmasters of Independent Schools and two campaigns, in February and

October 1974, as Liberal parliamentary candidate for neighbouring Petersfield.

Koeppler had suggested Tim Slack as a possible successor in the Spring of 1976. It was discussed, briefly, at the Academic Council meeting on July 16, 1976; and two days later Sir Peter Tennant wrote to Koeppler: 'My mind is made up and I am quite sure Tim Slack is the man. The same with John Whitehorn.'

Nicholas Barrington was more cautious. Writing to John Moore on August 19, 1976, he faced the fact that no possible successor was likely to match Heinz Koeppler:

> There can be no doubt that Herr Koeppler's personality, of course, imposes itself upon any conference. He can be somewhat intimidating but everyone feels that they are in the presence of a big man in all senses of the word. In particular I think he does an excellent information job in putting over a sympathetic view of Britain. The way he emphasizes the peculiarly tolerant and enlightened qualities of the British establishment which allow him to have complete academic freedom is very telling.
>
> No-one could fail to like Mr Slack, the Deputy Warden ... He is intelligent and balanced, but ... he gives an impression of being a slightly smaller man ... I think this is a pity because of course Deputy Warden is really not a sufficiently good job for anyone of Mr Slack's experience and talents ... I doubt whether in fact with a new Warden you would need both a Director of Studies and a Deputy Warden ...
>
> The only criticism I might have of Herr Koeppler is that his style is somewhat too Olympian. The special invitations to dine or lunch up in his rooms are a bit like a summons to the headmaster's study.

But if Koeppler's was a hard act to follow, Tim Slack was very much a front runner. On September 14, 1976, John Moore wrote to Sir Con O'Neill: 'Frank Roberts has told me that he can think of no one better than Tim Slack.' And when the search committee met again on September 30, it had before it a short list of three: Slack, Robin Edmonds, and Roger Morgan. By October 9, the list had shrunk to two: O'Neill wrote to Moore that Roger Morgan, 'after a couple of days' reflection' had decided 'that he would not wish to be a candidate'.

This was potentially embarrassing – and not simply because the two remaining candidates, in their different ways, were rather evenly matched. The Foreign and Commonwealth Office was naturally attracted to its own man. The PUS, Sir Michael Palliser, told Evan Luard on November 1, 1976: 'I have no hesitation in regarding Mr Edmonds as the stronger candidate.' But, as one senior FCO official had pointed out to Palliser a few days earlier, on October 28: 'I do not think it would do us or Mr Edmonds any good to impose his candidature.' While the Civil Service Department had no role in the selection and would be involved only if the Foreign Office asked the Civil Service Commission to decide, the Academic Council was another matter: for fear of political trouble, it had to have a say. Evan Luard told Palliser on November 5: 'If one of the candidates already known ... is chosen, it should not appear to be a put up job: either in the sense of a deputy automatically succeeding or the FCO putting in its own nominee.'

Significantly, Luard had talked with Koeppler the day before. The Warden had very firm views about his successor. On November 30, 1976, he wrote to an American friend – Dr A.G. Unklesbay, Vice-President for Administration at the University of Missouri – accepting his invitation to nominate a colleague for a visit there:

> I have given the matter good thought and, without hesitation, I would recommend that your invitation be extended to Tim Slack, my Deputy and our Chairman of Sessions. I am quite sure he deserves the trip and would profit from it. I know he would particularly enjoy it if his wife could come with him. She is not only very good-looking, but a lively and highly intelligent person.
>
> To take you further into my thoughts for nominating Tim: he is, as you know, a candidate for my job. I judge him to be a very strong candidate, but the decision is not mine and the full field will not be known until the advertisement in the late spring (!) of next year. If he gets the job, it will be a marvellous opportunity for the new Warden to be introduced to the heartland of the US. If he does not get it, it will be a well merited consolation prize for the Deputy Warden.

In the end, no consolation prize was needed. There was more discussion, and more to-ing and fro-ing by the remaining candidates – including Roger Morgan, who in February 1977 paid a visit to Wiston House and expressed renewed interest. But over the whole process hung the perennial question: would Wilton Park be allowed to survive? No answer was forthcoming by the time of Koeppler's retirement on June 30, 1977.

From that date, the Foreign and Commonwealth Office formally designated Tim Slack. But with so much uncertainty he could not be appointed Warden of Wilton Park. It was as Deputy Warden that he made the opening speech at Koeppler's birthday party: it was as 'Acting Warden' that he took up the reins on August 6, 1977. Meanwhile, Heinz Koeppler was off to fresh woods and pastures new.

CHAPTER 18

Warden Emeritus

'There must be no retirement.'
Earl Haig, *Order to British Troops*, April 12, 1918

Even during his time at Wilton Park, Heinz Koeppler had received many official honours. On June 13, 1957, he had been awarded an OBE, and on January 1, 1967, a CBE. In 1960–61, he had been a Visiting Professor at the University of Heidelberg, and in 1961 Consultant to the Ford Foundation. In 1966 he had been Distinguished Mershon Professor at Ohio State University. In 1970 he had been Visiting Professor of West European Studies at Indiana University. In 1974, he had received from Wisconsin University the President's Medallion for service to international education. In 1975 he had been promoted Assistant Under Secretary of State at the Foreign and Commonwealth Office. He was a Fellow of the Royal Historical Society. And in January 1977, he was made a Knight Bachelor. That October he received the Joseph Bech Gold Medal, created by the Hamburg *Stiftung FVS* in memory of the Luxembourg statesman and pioneer of European union.

This was shortly after Koeppler's departure from Wilton Park: 'retirement' was a notion he shunned. On that occasion he quoted a line from John Milton's *Samson Agonistes*: 'Nothing is here for tears.' It applied, he said, to his leave-taking

> after 32 difficult and splendid years, from 'Year Zero' in Germany and from the beginning of Britain's realisation that victory in war was no guarantee of wellbeing. The founder and first Warden of Wilton Park is unlikely to live for ever; so it's good to leave while Old Wiltonians, colleagues, and even the Foreign Office ... still regret one's departure, rather than asking themselves 'When on earth will he finally go?'

273

It was a question unasked because firmly answered by Koeppler himself. In the autumn of 1976 he had signed the contract for a London flat in Ashley Gardens, near Westminster Cathedral. It was a short distance from his club, the Athenaeum, and almost midway between the Houses of Parliament and Buckingham Palace – convenient, as he said, 'for the Queen to drop in for tea'. He was especially pleased that his telephone number there was 828 2828. But as early as October 1975 he had told an American friend: 'It now looks as if I shall spend the academic year 1978–79 in the States.'

He did. In August 1978, he went to Baylor University at Waco, Texas, roughly midway between Austin and either Dallas or Fort Worth. Baylor, founded in 1845, is one of a number of private universities in Texas, and the only survivor of the five established during the ten-year period of the Republic, between 1836, when the Texans had thrown off Mexican rule, and 1846, when they had voted to join the USA. Its contacts with Koeppler dated back at least as far as 1967, when Baylor had been represented at a Wilton Park Conference. It now welcomed Heinz Koeppler as Visiting Professor in International Politics, as well as Founder and first Director of the Institute for the Study of the Interaction of Foreign and Domestic Affairs.

The Institute's title reflected Koeppler's awareness of what had come to be called 'interdependence'. He had already discussed this at Wilton Park with Dr John S. Belew, Vice-President for Academic Affairs at Baylor, in the autumn of 1976. War, trade, technology, and European integration had made it obvious that frontiers were no longer – if they had ever been – impregnable castle walls. Aircraft and ballistic missiles flew over national boundaries; pollution ignored them; so did modern communications. And if what had once been foreign affairs now deeply affected national life and were influenced by it, so supposedly domestic factors were increasingly matters of international concern. At one time, for instance, customs tariffs had been regarded as purely domestic: now, they were routinely negotiated with other countries. How long would it be before violations of human rights, like crimes against humanity, would be seen as deserving punishment that broke the old taboo on 'outside interference in the internal affairs' of a UN member State?

In their 1976 conversation, Belew had explained to Koeppler 'the desire of Baylor to provide an added dimension to our students' experience'. Koeppler supplied it from the first. 'He immediately entered into campus activities just like the rest of us, as if he had always been here ... Students would follow him to his office to continue a discussion that had begun in the classroom. There is no question about it; he stimulated the thinking of all of us.'

So said the Chairman of Baylor's Sociology, Anthropology and Social Work Department, Charles M. Tolbert. A graduate student in the Department of Journalism, Tommy Holmes, was equally impressed by

the constant stimulus he provided for students and faculty to think seriously about the impact of world events on our lives and to consider how our future is being shaped. His unique experience and intellectual abilities opened up new avenues of thinking for us and created a new awareness of world events. Sir Heinz's concern that people have a well-rounded understanding of the arts, different cultures, social sciences and sciences should have a long-lasting influence on those who knew him.

A faculty member of the same Department, Basil C. Raffety, already had memories of Koeppler at Wilton Park, with his red rose buttonhole, his cigar, and his trilingual conversation. He recalled the visiting professor's arrival at Baylor:

I remember his first days on this campus when he and I had a private lunch and he quizzed me in great detail about the customs of this community, and his concerns lest his own customs might somehow not fit in. And I remember urging him not to change his ways or his habits, but to let this community – students and faculty alike – come to know him as we, his friends, knew him ...

I remember the rush of students whom I serve as academic adviser, to my office during the first few days of his classes, trying to find out what manner of man they were up against – a teacher who gave no tests and required no term papers. But I noticed, and I am sure they did too, that after only a few days when they attended one of the public seminars which he presented as part of his work at Baylor, he addressed them by name – often by given name – when they had questions to ask or comments to make. I remember also that after a few days this rush of students to my office subsided and instead they dropped by to tell me something he had said or something he had talked about in his class.

Some of them were fascinated by his treatment of students who took up class time with wordy but meaningless discussions. He would simply lower his head and 'blow air', which is the way this generation of students describes that Americanism which was known in my time as 'the Bronx cheer'.

I remember the almost machiavellian look of glee on his face when such large crowds turned out for afternoon or evening seminars that he was forced to move the crowd en masse to a larger room ...

I remember the reports of his Sunday afternoons just talking with students who wanted to visit with him more than class encounters would permit. Some even called it 'Sir Heinz's Sunday School' – but they never missed a session.

I remember the way the students in nearby apartments scrambled to lure him to their quarters to have dinner and how sometimes the best comment he could manage after being subjected to some of the less than perfect male cookery he was confronted with was to say the cuisine was 'interesting'.

Everyone at Baylor found Koeppler approachable, 'winning new friends, new admirers with each day', as Raffety put it. 'Soon after the opening of the school year in August, 1978,' wrote Mrs Jean F. Tolbert of the university's Moody Memorial Library,

> Sir Heinz called the library and asked to speak with me ... He was calling to make an appointment ... I was delighted, because I had read of his coming to Baylor and had hoped I could meet him – also – I was very frightened because of who he was ... The time came for our appointment. Suddenly, I was walking through four floors of books, offices, microfilm reading rooms and people with this giant person. Not once was I made to feel ill at ease, he was so gracious and so easy to talk with. After our orientation session he never forgot me. With all the people he met at Baylor and in Waco, it would have been easy to forget me, a librarian, but each time we met, he would smile, call my name, and say 'I must get back over to the library soon.'

A student waitress at the faculty restaurant, the Harrington House, said that on working days she waited

> for the moment when Mr Koeppler, the man with the funny accent, would come in ... Many teachers couldn't care less how much time of day they gave to the students waiting at table, but not Mr Koeppler. Here he would come walking through the door and speaking to all he knew in that neat accented voice of his. And then he would sit with his four or five plates spread all over his table while he was intensely absorbed in reading the latest magazine on world affairs. But as soon as someone joined him, then he was all for making that person feel welcome at his table while he gradually would draw them in on some interesting topic ...

'Mr' Koeppler's knighthood caused no less a stir than his stature and his accent. A colleague at Baylor recalled how Koeppler bought a large car, and took him for a trial drive – verging on 100 miles an hour. The colleague reminded him of the local speed limit, but Koeppler merely shrugged – until a motor-cycle patrolman flagged him down. Koeppler handed over his driving licence and his British passport. The policeman studied both. 'Say – are you a Knight? I must tell my wife: I stopped a real British Knight!' And he waved them on.

Driving together, sharing meals, going to the theatre, and endlessly debating: these were what Koeppler's Baylor students remembered. 'The thing that I treasure most,' wrote one of them, 'was our friendship ... We laughed together, and even played around like kids together ... I remember him singing in the first of spring with no refrain on a clear day just because it was a happy day. He was wise, but he was just a youth inside.' To another student, 'he was almost like a very close grandfather'. 'I'll always remember him', said a third, a woman student of journalism, 'with a brandy in his hand and a glint in his eye, talking about his greatest love, Great Britain.' Another added: 'I can picture him very clearly at one of our public lectures, leaning forward in his chair, cigar in mouth, eyes twinkling with delight as one of his students asked a question.' She concluded: 'I will always cherish the memory of him because I think he is a symbol of all that is good about academia: never-ending curiosity, brilliance, grace, and a willingness to accept new ideas.'

The Chairman of Baylor's Department of English, Robert G. Collmer, put it crisply: 'Sir Heinz Koeppler walked tall and saw far. He taught us to look at humanity beyond the barriers of region and language. He made us see the shape of the future through the eyes of the past. His brief stay with us has brought strength to our task of forging the bonds of humanity for a world where people try to understand one another.'

Collmer's lapidary prose betrays its origin – in a collection of tributes to Koeppler compiled for his family by Baylor colleagues immediately after his death in the early hours of Sunday, April 1, 1979. For Koeppler, death was sudden, and unexpected. Long before the end of his first semester, he had been making plans for the next. And as late as Wednesday March 28, 1979 he entertained his students for dinner and went with them to the annual campus event known as 'the University Sing'. There, he sang favourite arias with his office staff, ending with 'A mighty fortress is our God' – followed by a late snack of pizza. It was his last public appearance. On Saturday March 31, 1979 he suffered a massive heart attack. He was rushed to hospital. But he lingered only briefly.

On that same Saturday night he was visited by Loyal and Ilse Gould, who had first met him at Wilton Park in 1967:

My wife and I were the last of his many friends to see him alive – during a late night visit to the hospital room in which he died a few hours later. Although he had been ordered by his physician not to talk, he tried to cheer me up with his humour, as always gentle. As I bent down to wipe the perspiration off his brow, I told the Warden I would be in early the following morning, Sunday, to see him. On hearing that, he wagged his right forefinger at me while admonishing me jokingly: 'But don't miss church because of me.'

That was typical. He thought more of others than he did of himself.

Heinz Koeppler was mourned in the old world as deeply as in the new. On Thursday May 17, 1979, the Federal German Chancellor Helmut Schmidt awarded him the *Grosse Verdienstkreuz mit Stern*. One week later, on Thursday May 24, 1979, a Memorial Service at St Martin-in-the-Fields, Trafalgar Square assembled some 125 family and friends from across the globe. They included the Minister of State at the FCO; the ambassadors of Germany and Luxembourg, and many other senior diplomats, British and foreign; representatives of overseas Wilton Park associations; members of both Houses of Parliament; the Director of the Royal Institute of International Affairs; and distinguished individuals ranging from Enoch Powell and John Birt to Max Beloff and Esmond Wright. In his address as Chairman of the Wilton Park Academic Council, Sir Robert Birley recalled being 'absolutely astonished' by what he saw in Wilton Park's very early days:

> The people there were German prisoners-of-war, awaiting the time when they would return to their own country. They were not preached at and told how disgracefully their country had behaved, as might so easily have happened then. They were persuaded to think about the problems that would face them when they returned and to discuss them, and to recognise their personal responsibility. There was nothing 'patronising' about it ...
>
> I often think of two remarks made to me, which made a deep impression on me. One was in 1936, when Birley had gone from Berlin to Prague. There he had told a Professor of Philosophy how horrible he found the position in Hitlerite Germany. 'Yes, yes, I know,' he said, 'of course, Hitler is a devil. But remember he walked into an empty room.' That was what Heinz knew. He was preparing these young men to return to their country and then that they should ensure that the room would not be 'empty' ...
>
> The second remark was made to me by a young Dutch lady. She was one of a group of young Dutch people, all of whom had been in the Resistance. She herself had been arrested and had suffered terribly. This group was engaged in spending their spare time going over into Germany to help in various ways the Evangelical Church in that country. And, standing one summer evening in the garden of the house I had in Germany then, near Osnabrück and not far from the Dutch frontier, this young lady said to me, 'The last war was the kind of war that one can only win after one has won it.'

And that, I think, was what Heinz Koeppler was doing for the rest of his life.

The St-Martin-in-the-Fields service – whose final hymn was 'A mighty fortress is our God' – was followed by a reception in the India Office Council Chamber of the Foreign and Commonwealth Office. It had been preceded, on Friday April 6, 1979, by a simpler but no less international funeral service in Sussex. There, Tim Slack – now at last officially 'Director' of Wiston House – gave a simple address. Among other things, he said:

> We all have our own memories of Heinz. My own is centred on his unceasing vitality and enthusiasm. Every Wilton Park conference was prepared and carried through as though it were the first. Every participant was made to feel central to the success of the venture; his faith in mankind was not selective. And very much part of this enthusiasm was his distrust of the bogus, and his utter rejection of political oppression. Underneath this lay, without any cloying sentimentality, a passionate belief in his work.

It was a passionate belief that Tim Slack shared. For nearly two and a half years, he had worked alongside Koeppler. For nearly two years since then, he had headed Wilton Park himself. Without the giant figure of its founder, he had faced old uncertainties and new challenges, to defend and develop what the Warden had begun.

CHAPTER 19

New Regime

'Es ist eine alte Geschichte,
Doch bleibt sie immer neu.'
Heinrich Heine, *Lyrisches Intermezzo* (1823), No 39

Tim Slack had begun his first two years at the head of Wilton Park as only 'Interim Warden'. The reason was that the institution's future had still hung in the balance. At the time of Slack's appointment, on June 30, 1977, the lease of Wiston House had only nine months more to run: it was due to expire on March 25, 1978. Would the Foreign and Commonwealth Office renew it? On what terms? And with what expectations?

Despite a change of Prime Minister, two changes of Foreign Secretary, and delay to the Central Policy Review Staff's long-awaited report on the FCO, debate about Wilton Park at official level had continued unchecked. In particular, the Head of the FCO's Guidance and Information Policy (later Information Policy) Department, Nicholas Barrington, worked out in more detail his thoughts from the summer of 1976. The ensuing paper he entitled 'A New Look for Wilton Park'.

The EDC, Barrington considered, was 'worth maintaining'; but there were flaws in the operation of Wilton Park:

> The generalist approach and unstructured form of the conferences … makes the discussions themselves undemanding and at times superficial …
> We propose that a new series of conferences be started which would be more intensive, of shorter duration, and limited in size.

He echoed a number of critics in thinking that one week was the right length for a conference; and he personally favoured limiting the number on each to about 35.

The approach would be more rigorous and participants will [*sic*] be required to put more effort in the conferences ... There would be no major extramural programmes ... and the discussions will [*sic*] be more closely focussed [and] would be expected to lead to useful conclusions on specific topics.

Participants should come, Barrington thought, from a much wider range of countries, including the Third World and the Communist bloc.

Under this new more specialised approach and with the wider participation envisaged it will [*sic*] be possible to develop the range of subjects, some of which can be specifically related to Britain's current foreign policy and domestic preoccupations.

Some of Barrington's proposals, as in the last paragraph, might have skewed Wilton Park in the direction of propaganda and away from free discussion; some would have reduced its work from the expansion of experience to exchanges among experts. But his long hard look was timely; and several of his thoughts were prescient – notably on work with developing and Communist countries, which was to be pursued successfully in later years.

On July 14, 1977, he sent a confidential copy of it to Tim Slack; and on August 19 he circulated it to Britain's embassies in the OECD countries, asking for their comments.

Tim Slack read Barrington's paper with care and some concern. Before formally commenting, he made private notes of his own. How soon, he wondered, would it be possible to modify the pattern of conferences? To what extent could Wiston House expand its role as a venue for fee-paying use by other suitable bodies? It should not become just 'a hotel centre'; and its staff salaries should be related to those at 'other similar establishments'. Above all, Wilton Park must remain a full-time institution.

He responded formally, promptly and at length to Barrington's paper, writing him a confidential note as soon as August 23,1977. It was based, he said, not only on the FCO document but also on 'limited discussions (without Heinz Koeppler)' among the staff at Wiston House and on 'selected views of other interested persons', including his own:

Though this [Barrington's] memorandum is entitled 'A New Look for Wilton Park' (for it is in that area where change is most needed) it is important to calculate the new structure of Wilton Park within the wider possibilities and demands of all that happens, or could happen, at Wiston House.

These, of course, included both European Discussion Centre (EDC) conferences and specialist meetings, as well as those organised by outside bodies. As regards EDC conferences:

> The length and content of these Conferences is right. The recruitment of participants from the other 8 countries of the EEC works well on the whole.
>
> The deficiencies in UK participation are similar in some respects to the deficiencies in UK participation at Wilton Park. There is scope for widening the range of British participants, for aiming more at those who are neither committed pro or anti Europeans, and for increasing the actual numbers of British, providing the Conferences do not lose the essential Community feel ...
>
> Wiston House provides a suitable location and atmosphere for a variety of FCO sponsored seminars and specialist Conferences. The staff at Wiston House would welcome the wider use of the building in this way and would be glad to be drawn in to helping with such Conferences where their skills could be of assistance ...
>
> Isolated comments by Community officials attending EDC Conferences have suggested that Wiston House could provide a valuable venue for Community sponsored Conferences ...

Tim Slack's note then dealt with the heart of the matter – Wilton Park:

> The time is overdue for a new definition of countries entitled to participate. OECD may have been right for 1957. It is too narrow for 1977. There must be flexibility to allow participation of significant developing and underdeveloped countries.
>
> Even if OECD were to remain the criterion for participation, there are glaring imbalances in countries represented. These imbalances arise from a variety of causes including the early history of Wilton Park, the weakness of recruiting bodies in most countries and the lack of finance to bring Southern Europe to Wiston House in much quantity.
>
> Wider and better recruitment of participants requires more and better recruiters. At present the recruitment at Wiston House is covered by one person only who has to spend much time on other matters. This is woefully inadequate. If we are to gain a desirable extra control over which individuals come to us we must also receive more help from embassies and consulates abroad.
>
> Without the recruitment of participants by overseas Wilton Park Associations it would be hard at present to have a viable number at the Conferences. But, though it would be desirable to monitor more effectively those who come to us via these Associations, the problems of achieving

such a control are considerable.

There are possibilities for closer liaison with bodies organising sponsored visits to the United Kingdom and our activities at Wilton Park. Such possibilities would be enhanced if the Conferences became shorter ...

There are many good reasons for moving to shorter Conferences. There has, in any case, been a decision taken to hold 4 rather than 2 one-weekers in 1978.

Shorter Conferences should approach the more intensive style of the EDC. But, though long excursions to distant parts of the country would cease, careful building-in of 'extra-mural' activities would remain an important ingredient.

Whilst over-large numbers at Conferences are expensive to the taxpayer and detract from the effectiveness of the Conference, it could be a false economy to have numbers that could only be accommodated within the present accommodation of Wiston House. There is a case for putting into action a small building plan which has been under consideration for some time ...

Simultaneous interpretation is a highly costly exercise. But the elimination of this service would limit the participation of some of the categories of persons and nationalities most desired at Wilton Park.

The word 'generalist' as used at Wilton Park is an uncertain term. But it remains a sound principle in our approach to selection of themes. It is vital to retain a good mixing of professions, nationalities and political attitudes at the Conferences. But there is scope for handling the Conference themes in a more specialist way.

Tim Slack finally turned to the problems of costs and staffing, both of which had haunted his previous private considerations:

It is entirely reasonable to press for a reduction in staffing in the present economic climate. It is my personal view that some economy is possible under present circumstances. But a 'new look' Wilton Park could bring about greater requirements. In particular, better recruitment and the raising of finance from Trusts and industry would require much extra staff time.

It is important that the Staff should not be members of the Diplomatic Service. Our BBC style of independence is a major factor in building up and maintaining credibility overseas. But a happy conclusion to current negotiations on the terms of recruitment of staff to Wiston House is important and urgent ...

Any finance from outside sources must limit to some extent the freedom of action of the FCO. But such limitation could be minimal and yet give a much needed boost to more effective recruitment.

He went on to propose a concerted plan of action to solicit funding from sources in Germany and the United States and the European Commission. Extra revenue could come from commercial lettings. But he warned against increases in fees.

Some 24 hours after writing his note, Slack left for his scheduled visit to the United States. He returned on Sunday, September 18, 1977, with the impression that there were 'reasonable prospects for fund-raising'.

On the following Wednesday evening, September 21, he had a long talk with the Superintending Under-Secretary of State at the Information Policy Department of the FCO. They mainly discussed staffing and conditions of service. It was important, as Slack wrote in a follow-up letter on Tuesday, September 27, 'to move as fast as possible towards having a satisfactory solution ready for the moment when the future of this institution is secure'. If the worst came to the worst, and if Wilton Park did have to close, 'I would like to think that for all concerned here ... the effective final date of service should be August 31, 1978. Such a date would allow those whose future might be related to work in the academic field to carry through to future employment without a break.' He added: 'I know that you and I do not believe that there is any serious danger of there being an abrupt cessation of the activities of Wiston House, but I feel that so long as uncertainty exists, it is right to put such points in front of Personnel Services Department for sympathetic consideration.'

Tim Slack followed this letter with a full staff meeting at Wiston House on Wednesday September 28, 1977, at which he explained his own thinking. Some ten days later, Nicholas Barrington agreed that his own July memorandum could be shown to the academic staff, in preparation for his visiting Wiston House on Wednesday, October 19. Unfortunately, the proposed visit had to be delayed when Barrington succumbed to 'flu.

In the Foreign and Commonwealth Office, nevertheless, matters were moving ahead. On October 14, Evan Luard, Parliamentary Under-Secretary of State, sent Barrington's memorandum to the Foreign Secretary, Dr David Owen. Luard proposed that expenditure on Wiston House be cut by some £32,000 a year, reducing the budget to about £135,000. But his essential recommendation was positive: both Wilton Park and EDC should be retained:

I think it may be right that a decision to close Wilton Park (and the European Discussion Centre) now might be attributed to a general anti-EEC or anti-foreign trend in our policy. It would certainly be taken, both at home and abroad, as a sign of an increasingly insular approach and perhaps as an acceptance of a decline in our world role which I do not believe that we do, or should, acknowledge. I therefore recommend that we should keep Wilton Park going on the new basis proposed in the attached paper.

On Wednesday, December 7, Tim Slack had met FCO officials in London to go into detail about the Wilton Park and EDC calendar for 1978. The new schedule was needed for the EDC Advisory Council, due to meet on December 13, the Wilton Park Academic Council, set for January 5, and an official FCO inspection provisionally booked for March or April, 1978. But it also amounted to a tacit acknowledgement that Wilton Park would go on.

When the EDC Council met, in fact, the FCO was able to announce that Dr Owen had decided that Wilton Park should continue, with a new look taken at the organisation of its conferences, some of which would be more specific.

So the New Year began in what those who give titles to conference subjects might have called 'Continuity and Change'. For Tim Slack personally, however, 'continuity' had an unfortunate ulterior meaning. Announcing his definitive appointment, at the Wilton Park Academic Council meeting on January 5, the FCO had had to make a damaging admission.

When the competition for the new Warden had been arranged, the FCO had told the Civil Service Commission (CSC). The CSC had confirmed that since the FCO was not planning to offer an appointment for more than five years, there was no need for the Commission to be involved. There had therefore seemed no reason why the FCO should not offer the successful candidate (Tim Slack) a so-called 'period appointment' of up to five years. The selection procedure – advertisement in the press, sifting of entries by the Academic Council and the final Selection Board – had been modelled on that used for selection in which the CSC was involved. Only after the appointment did the CSC drop its procedural bombshell. It then decreed that, although the Wardenship was a new post for Tim Slack, his previous service as Deputy Warden to Heinz Koeppler must be counted as part of the five years to which he was now being appointed – meaning that he could hold the post for only two years.

On hearing this, the Academic Council was incensed. Max Beloff called the decision 'appalling'. Was it an attempt, he asked, to view Wilton Park 'simply as a branch of government?' After the meeting, on January 10, 1978, Robert Birley wrote to Sir Michael Palliser, the Permanent Under-Secretary at the Foreign and Commonwealth Office, saying that the Academic Council was 'really indignant'. He also wrote to the First Civil

Service Commissioner, asking for a meeting to discuss the CSD's ruling. The Commissioner replied on the following day. He saw no point in meeting, because 'this is not a matter on which I intend to change my mind'.

Among other things, the CSD was not convinced that the selection procedure had been both fair and sufficiently high-level. It therefore proposed that Tim Slack take part in a new open competition for a five-year appointment, either straight away or near the end of his (truncated) term of office. He considered the matter, and soon decided to take the plunge. So the appointment procedure was set in train once more.

The new job advertisement, published in early March, was for five years which 'may be extended beyond the period of five years'. This meant, as the FCO told Slack on February 10, 1978, that:

> there should be no difficulty in authorising extensions of the Limited Period Certificate which they would issue to you if you were appointed. Such extensions would normally be, by mutual agreement, for periods of 2 to 3 years at a time and could be continued, if necessary, beyond the nominal 10 year ceiling set for period appointments.

It was an interpretation that caused problems later.

The new selection committee met on April 21, 1978. It consisted of Birley, Sir William Hayter (former Warden of New College, Oxford), Sir Peter Tennant, and Oliver Forster (Assistant Under-Secretary and Deputy Chief Clerk at the FCO). Unsurprisingly, it also included the First Civil Service Commissioner, Dr Fergus Allen. Equally unsurprisingly, it decided to appoint Tim Slack. At last, on May 25, 1978, the Head of the FCO's Personnel Policy Department formally offered Slack the job he had been doing in practice since Heinz Koeppler's retirement on June 30 of the previous year: 'Your appointment will be for a limited period of 5 years from 24 May 1978 but there may be prospects for an extension beyond this period.' Again, there were to be problems later on.

Meanwhile, the Government had been negotiating for a new lease on Wiston House, ideally for three years with an option for three years more. It had encountered problems as early as February 1978. The old lease had cost £4,000 a year including a service charge. Now, the landlord's agent was asking for £14,000, with a service charge on top of that. The Property Services Agency (PSA) had refused, preferring to go to arbitration; and a court hearing had been scheduled for March 20. As the weeks went by, the costs went up; but the court advised both parties to resolve matters between them. The talks dragged on, month after month, and were still unresolved by the end of the year. Eventually, on January 26, 1979, Alan Hughes had a long, informal talk with John Goring. From this it emerged that Goring wanted the Foreign and Commonwealth Office to stay on and was in principle happy about repairs and refurbishment; but he would prefer a tribunal to settle the rent and service charge. This was encouraging; but it still delayed any refurbishment, because the PSA was understandably unwilling to start work until the new lease was signed. Nor was a new short lease a sensible prospect. As the PSA wrote on April 19, 1978, to the Head of the FCO's Information Policy Department:

> Your use of this building goes back over a term of some 28 years. During this long period we have never been free to negotiate a lease for a period longer than 3 years as that has apparently been as far forward as you can see a use for the property. This is against all the principles of good Estate Management ...
>
> We are under pressure from the Treasury to get value for money and this is impossible under the present arrangement whereby we only move forward in 3 year periods.

In the three years 1975/78, maintenance and minor new work at Wiston House had cost more than £70,000. So: 'We shall have to press you for a longer lease. After 28 years it looks like something reasonably permanent to us.'

The dilemma was a good example of 'unjoined-up government'. The Treasury was pressing for economies; but it had also been pressing for the abolition of Wilton Park – which prevented the FCO from looking ahead. Coupled with pressure from the Goring estate, this made rational planning virtually impossible. On May 4, the FCO replied to the PSA with a compromise: that the PSA negotiate for a five-year instead of a three-year lease. Even so, the negotiations were not concluded until January 25, 1980 – more than two years after they had begun. The term of the lease was for five years, from March 25, 1978, at £10,000 a year.

On Wednesday July 12, 1978, the Wilton Park Academic Council had held its summer meeting at Wiston House. Next day Birley had met the academic staff. All of them assured him that interpretation was 'essential'; and all wanted greater security of employment. Urged on by both Birley and Tim Slack, the FCO debated how to respond to this very reasonable concern. At length, on October 19, Personnel Policy Department wrote to the Civil Service Department. Their proposal was that the academic staff on 'period appointments' should enter into open competition, and that those who were successful should become established civil servants. By the time of the next Academic Council meeting, in London on November 24, 1978, Tim Slack was able to announce that this had been accepted, and that the successful candidates would be informed by February 1979. When the Academic Council next met, on July 9, 1979, at Wiston House, Slack had even better news: all the tutors were now established – although he himself was not.

In all these ways, Wilton Park was becoming consolidated in its post-Koeppler form. With the new lease of Wiston House, it now had the prospect of surviving until at least March 1983. The FCO had approved Nicholas Barrington's blueprint for future development. Tim Slack had been appointed, at last, for five years – taking the title of Director rather than 'Warden'. The academic staff had acquired the security of tenure as established civil servants. After an Assistant Under-Secretary of State at the FCO visited Wiston House in early March, 1980, he wrote to Tim Slack: 'I was impressed by the spirit and enthusiasm of the staff.' Soon afterwards, similar praise came from Sydney, Australia, where on July 30, 1980, A.H. Spire wrote from the British Consulate-General to a member of the FCO Training Department:

> Notwithstanding the very strong and successful personal direction that Heinz Koeppler imposed on Wilton Park, I think that the present Director, Tim Slack, and his Deputy, Alan Hughes, have achieved a remarkable success in taking over from a man who many must have thought irreplaceable. Wilton Park is alive and well and very ably managed. Indeed, it was my impression that the administration is, if anything, better than it was on the occasion of my last visit in 1973 ...
>
> So far as winning friends and influencing people is concerned – and that, I submit, is the name of the game – Wilton Park continues to perform a valuable, if not unique, role.

As a senior official concluded: 'Wilton Park seems to have survived the last round of cuts in good shape, and I am happy to say that I know of no present pressure to close it down.'

As always, however, there were loose ends. One of them, although serious, was internal. It concerned a member of staff. On December 5, 1978, an official from the Internal Audit Section of the FCO's Finance Department had written to Alan Hughes to point out that: 'During our recent audit inspection of Wiston House we were unable to reconcile the bank balance on the date of our check of the account against the cash book balance figure.' On the face of it, this was not a major problem. There had been discrepancies in the past, partly owing to unfamiliarity with the Foreign Office's accounting system. Accordingly, on January 11, 1979, the

Internal Audit Section recommended that the Wiston House accountant should attend a special accountancy training course. On April 19, 1979, officials visited Wiston House again. According to the Head of the Internal Audit Section:

> He could find no copy receipts for payments to staff in November for meals, coffee, and tea, and was told by the accountant that an intruder had entered the offices and taken a receipt book and one or two other documents.
>
> A page of the November bank statement was in typescript rather than the normal computer print. The accountant thought that the statement 'may' have been removed by the intruder, and he 'may' have asked the Bank for a duplicate.

This clearly raised a security problem. There had been a previous intruder, in April 1977. But if another had broken in now, his choice of booty had been strange: his predecessor had merely left marks on the safe. On April 24, 1979, without making accusations, the Internal Audit Section again recommended training for the Wiston House accountant. By now, the Finance Department at the FCO was seriously concerned. On June 19, 1979, it asked Tim Slack for the Wiston House accounts up to the end of March, and proposed sending one of its staff to help the accountant.

Help was certainly needed. The cuts that the Foreign Office had mentioned were still sore. The Bursar, John Forsyth, had been ill, and although the duties of Sub-accounting Officer formally devolved on Alan Hughes, as Tim Slack's Deputy and Chief Administrative Officer, his other tasks on the academic staff, including recruiting, took up more than a normal working week. Moreover, as the FCO's Deputy Finance Officer noted on June 20, 1980:

> Partly because of the personality of the present Accountant, and partly because of the Bursar's recent spell of ill health, the accountant has been encouraged to take on the role of a Conference Officer to the detriment of his accounting and administration duties.

Far worse was to come. On the resignation of the accountant in July 1980, Alan Hughes, wondering at his unexpected departure, checked the month-end cash balances in exceptional detail and unearthed an almost undetectable 'rolling balance' embezzlement. He found that £2,415, representing 22 conference fees, were missing. To recoup them, Alan Hughes wrote to all the 22 participants who seemed not to have paid. One of them was slow to reply; seven responded by apologising and paying up; but fourteen protested that they had paid already. This left a deficit of £1,485, of which £1,285 was ultimately recovered. Alan Hughes, as Sub–accounting Officer for Wilton Park, voluntarily reimbursed the final £200 from his own pocket, to the grateful surprise of the FCO (which was thus spared a board of enquiry to seek authority to write off the loss). The matter was referred to the police. On November 17 the case came to trial. After a plea of guilty, the court issued an order for repayment by May 28 of the following year.

Soon after the court hearing, on November 26, 1980, the FCO Inspectorate submitted its draft report. Noting 'a failure of communication in administrative matters' at Wiston House, it declared:

> Our major conclusion is that the administration does need strengthening, and that this can only be achieved by the employment of a part-time Conference Officer (at CO level) on a contract basis ... The extra cost might be partially offset by adding a surcharge to Wilton Park fees.

So previous cuts had been counter-productive. But more might well be needed. The running cost of Wiston House in 1979/80 was £339,000. In 1980/81, Tim Slack told the Foreign Office on December 17, 1980, it would be £360,000. This made it all the more important to secure whatever revenue might be available from outside. One possible source had already been discussed at the Wilton Park Academic Council meeting held at Wiston House in the late afternoon and early evening of Monday 9, 1979. On that occasion, two lawyers had been invited in to brief the Council on the progress – or lack of it – in enabling Wilton Park to benefit from Heinz Koeppler's Will. This was another of the loose ends to be dealt with under Wilton Park's new régime. It took a long, hazardous, and expensive time.

CHAPTER 20

Where There's a Will

'Grammatici certant et adhuc subiudice lis est.
[Scholars dispute, and the case is still before the courts.]'
Horace (Quintus Horatius Flaccus, *Ars Poetica* 1.78.

Speaking at Heinz Koeppler's funeral service in Sussex on Friday April 6, 1979, Tim Slack had said: 'Just three hours ago I was told by his family that he has left the major part of his estate to the Academic Council of Wilton Park to use as they see fit in the furtherance of the aims and objects of Wilton Park. We are enormously grateful for this final act of generosity.'

Generous it undoubtedly was. But, before it bore fruit, Heinz Koeppler's Will involved serious and costly headaches for those he intended it to benefit.

Koeppler had made his Will, dated January 12, 1972, with the help of a Brighton firm of solicitors, Messrs J.E. Dell and Loader, with Barclays Bank Trust Company to be its executor and trustee. Most of its provisions were straightforward. Its first bequest was of £1,000 to his closest friend, Erhard Dornberg, who had been on the very first Wilton Park course. Koeppler then directed all his net assets to be held in trust by Barclays and used, first, to pay his mother Gertrud a £500 annuity and, secondly, to divide among various legatees. In the event, Koeppler's mother predeceased him. His estate was then to be divided into 36 parts. Ten parts were to go to his sister Hanni and (in the event of her death) to be divided between Koeppler's niece Judith Capper and his nephew Nicholas Frederick Capper, each of whom was in any case to receive a further three parts of the estate. That left twenty thirty-sixth parts – amounting in total to some £125,000. It was the Will's provisions for this section of the estate that led to what Wilton Park's Deputy Director Alan Hughes later called, very mildly, 'considerable legal complications'.

The ensuing roller-coaster ride went on for six anxious years. It raised hopes, then dashed them. Disappointment sparked stubborn anger. Persistence paid off, only to be thwarted. Defeat seemed definitive – but would it prove final? As minutes, days, months, and years ticked by, the cost steadily mounted. Could two hundred words in a Will have really caused so much expensive strife?

Koeppler's intention had been that the £125,000 or so in question should go to Wilton Park. But if Wilton Park had ceased to exist or been very drastically altered during his lifetime, the money was to pass to Magdalen College, Oxford, to help refugee students like Koeppler himself. The idea seemed clear enough. Unfortunately, Koeppler appears to have insisted on his own wording of the relevant clause. Did he know the 19th-century proverb, 'A man who is his own lawyer has a fool for his client'? Koeppler was no fool, and may have felt that the proverb was professional propaganda. At all events, Clause 6 (i) of his Will ran:

> Subject as aforesaid the Company [Barclays Bank Trust Company Limited, executor and trustee] shall hold the Trust Fund upon the following trusts, that is to say: (i) As to twenty thirty-sixth parts of both capital and income thereof for the Warden and the Chairman of the Academic Advisory Council for the time being of the institution known as Wilton Park, now housed at Wiston House, Steyning, Sussex, of which I am the Founder Director, for the benefit at their discretion of the said institution as long as Wilton Park remains a British contribution to the formation of an informed international public opinion and to the promotion of greater co-operation in Europe and the West in general, but in the event of the said institution having ceased to exist in such form at the date of my death the Company shall hold the legacy upon trust for the President and Scholars of the College of St Mary Magdalen in the University of Oxford.

Koeppler's intentions seemed obvious. Barclays Bank Trust Company (Barclaytrust) had no difficulty in accepting that Wilton Park existed in the desired form at Sir Heinz Koeppler's death. This should have meant that Magdalen College, Oxford, was out of the running. But there were at least two possible snags, sharpened if anything by the wording of the Will: 'the Warden and the Chairman of the Academic Advisory Council for the time being'.

First – and this was something that Koeppler had foreseen – *although* the legacy was bequeathed in perpetuity, it could continue only if Wilton Park continued in the desired form. Secondly, under English law and jurisprudence – and this Koeppler seems not to have realised – just *because* the Will bequeathed the legacy in perpetuity, the beneficiary itself needed a guarantee of future existence in perpetuity, best assured by gaining charitable status.

The Assistant Legal Adviser to the Foreign and Commonwealth Office, suggested that Wilton Park obtain Counsel's Opinion to clarify its charitable status, register itself as a charity, and set up a properly constituted Trust. Sir Robert Birley, Chairman of Wilton Park's Academic Advisory Council, Tim Slack, and Alan Hughes agreed to proceed on these lines. On November 14, 1979, they held a meeting in London with two representatives from Barclaytrust; also present were their own lawyer and an FCO Adviser on Trusts, Foundations and Voluntary Organisations, Michael Cullis, plus two further potential trustees – Koeppler's doctor, Alec Frank, and the Vice-Chairman of the Wilton Park Academic Council, Sir Peter Tennant. Barclaytrust had some slightly disappointing news: with expenses paid, the net bequest to Wilton Park was now expected to be some £105,400. However, the lawyer hoped to have Counsel's Opinion – from the eminent QC Mr Leolin Price, later to be well-known as a 'Eurosceptic' – by the end of November 1979. Thereafter, he estimated, it would take three to five months to draw up the trust deed, have it accepted by the Charity Commissioners, and set up the Trust.

As so often, the forecast proved optimistic. Meanwhile, a further question arose. Earlier discussions with the FCO had encouraged Birley, Slack, and Hughes to proceed independently, other than maintaining contact and seeking FCO advice. But on February 1, 1980, the FCO wrote to say that its Finance Department and the Treasury were worried about the independent initiatives taken so far. Both would want a say in how the funds were administered, and the Treasury even seemed to be laying claim to them for itself. Tennant, Slack, Hughes, and their lawyer discussed this rather alarming possibility at a meeting in London on February 13. But there was little they could do until they had received Counsel's Opinion. It arrived six weeks later, dated April 3, 1980. Counsel confirmed that it was essential for Wilton Park to be deemed charitable. 'Unless Wilton Park is charitable, the bequest cannot in my opinion take effect ... A gift on trust to the officers of an unincorporated association, not as a gift to its members for the time being, but on trust to carry out the non-charitable purposes of the association, must fail for want of a beneficiary.' Koeppler's Will had set up no tightly defined procedure to ensure that the money be applied for all time to the purpose for which it was bequeathed, and with no alternative legatee or procedure for handling the money should Wilton Park cease to exist or change its form. So Barclaytrust would be wrong to hand over the money until Wilton Park's charitable status was recognised by creating a registered charitable Trust. To speed matters up, Leolin Price enclosed a draft Declaration of Trust with his Opinion.

Armed with these, Tennant, Slack, Hughes and their lawyers met officials from the FCO on April 29, 1980, and managed to overcome the misgivings on both sides. A week later, the FCO's Assistant Head of Information, who had attended the meeting, wrote to approve the creation of an independent Trust, subject to certain conditions. On May 15, 1980, Slack and Hughes briefed Sir Robert Birley on developments so far, and won his approval both for what had been done and for the next steps. On July 2, 1980, their lawyer met with Leolin Price's junior Counsel to propose a formal approach to the Charity Commission. Two days later, the Wilton Park Academic Council met to endorse the proceedings: it formally approved the names of Sir Robert Birley, Sir Peter Tennant, Tim Slack, Dr Alan Frank, and Alan Hughes as Trustees of the proposed Sir Heinz Koeppler Trust. On July 28, 1980, Counsel issued a fresh Joint Opinion, and drafted a letter for submission to the Charity Commissioners. Advisedly, this fell short of a formal application for registration as a charity, but more cautiously asked for a reaction to the intended application, backed by the draft Trust Deed and full documentary evidence. The Wilton Park legatees' lawyers sent the letter on August 21, 1980.

It was now well over a year since Heinz Koeppler had died. All his legatees, understandably, were eager to see his estate settled and the bulk of the inheritance handed over. But complications continued to dog the process. One irritant was the FCO's insistence – to satisfy the Treasury – on minor changes to the draft Trust Deed. These were finally agreed at a meeting of all the interested parties in Leolin Price's chambers on February 13, 1981. There had been no reaction from the Charity Commission. April 1, 1981, marked the second anniversary of Koeppler's death. Yet the estate was still not wound up.

At last, on April 13, 1981, came a response from the Charity Commission. Eagerly opened, it amounted to a rebuff. Theoretically, there were four criteria for determining charitable status: the organisation concerned could be religious, for the relief of poverty, educational, or for the public good. The Wilton Park legatees firmly believed that the last two criteria were relevant in their case; their Counsel Leolin Price inclined towards the 'educational' role. The Charity Commission disagreed.

Wilton Park was not 'educational', the Commission argued, because participation at its conferences was too limited. Participants were carefully selected, as much for what they could contribute as for what they could learn. There was no original professional research, and little of the proceedings was later disseminated. Nor, in the Charity Commission's preliminary view, did Wilton Park qualify on the grounds of 'public good'. It might well have contributed to better international understanding, the

furtherance of peace, and the development of democracy in other countries. But, laudable though this was, it did not make Wilton Park charitable
in a British context: jurisprudence had already excluded international
friendship societies from registration as charities.

It was a heavy blow. But the Wilton Park legatees were more indignant
than discouraged. The Charity Commission's reaction – still merely
advisory and therefore not disallowing a formal application – seemed to
them to misinterpret the spirit and object of Wilton Park. Leolin Price
agreed. He advised making a further approach to the Commission, restating the case and adducing fresh evidence. Meanwhile, on June 18,
1981, Sir Peter Tennant wrote to the Chief Charity Commissioner,
answering the Commission's objections and proposing a meeting to
discuss the whole affair.

The Chief Commissioner's response was reassuringly prompt. He
wrote back less than a week later, on June 23, 1981. He criticised some of
Tennant's arguments on points of law, and seemed not to appreciate that
the initial approach had hoped to elicit an off-the-record reaction to the
proposal and advice on the wording of the draft Trust Deed. However, the
previous, negative Charity Commission letter of April 13, 1981, had been
written by a junior member, and did not preclude a formal approach now.
Indeed, the Chief Commissioner's answer to Sir Peter Tennant, while
making clear that no further off-the-record advice was on offer, did suggest
that a formal submission be made for registration, supported by a definitive Trust Deed.

On July 2, 1981, Leolin Price gave a further Opinion, restating the case
for charitable status. At a meeting in his Chambers, preparations were
made for a formal application. Tim Slack and Alan Hughes assembled
additional background and documentary evidence, writing in August 1981
to some thirty or forty people who had attended Wilton Park and asking
them for supporting letters to Sir Robert Birley, Chairman of the Wilton
Park Academic Council. One of these was a further endorsement from the
British Consul-General in Sydney, Australia, on September 4, 1981:

Those who, like me, knew Heinz Koeppler can well understand how, characteristically, he wished to endow the institution of which he was the
Founder Director. The original purpose of Wilton Park was to assist in the
rehabilitation of democracy in Germany after the War. Few would deny the
success achieved. Self-evidently, Wilton Park proved to be not only educational but a powerful influence for the public good, both in Britain and
Western Europe.

The development of the Wilton Park concept in later years attracted enthusiastic support in many countries and those who have been privileged to participate in Wilton Park conferences have almost invariably become devotees of the wider aims of the organization. Wilton Park is certainly not a tool of the Foreign and Commonwealth Office; indeed, I have always found it gratifying that, over the years, financial support from the FCO has been forthcoming for a body which has much broader aims than the furtherance of one country's foreign policy. A broad range of individuals of differing intellectual attainments, widely diverse backgrounds and often conflicting political opinions have come together most successfully in an unorthodox educational environment, which has been the model for similar institutions subsequently founded in other countries.

To common sense, these arguments sounded convincing; but the legal minefield remained, ill-charted by previous case law. Even Leolin Price's Opinions had reservations about the likely success of Wilton Park's application for charitable status. And the Charity Commission was still unconvinced: it inclined to the view that Wilton Park was 'political', but would not commit itself either way. To try to clarify matters, the Commission consulted the Attorney General, Sir Michael Havers; but this too took time. While still awaiting a decision, the Wilton Park legatees and their advisers drew up a Declaration of Trust, made by Sir Robert Birley, signed by all the five Trustees (Birley, Slack, Tennant, Frank, and Hughes), and executed on May 22, 1982.

They were not the only interested parties who were growing impatient. Heinz Koeppler's sister Hanni and her two children Nicholas and Judith (to whom she made over her own legacy) were together due to receive sixteen thirty-sixths of what Koeppler left. Barclaytrust had already advanced much of their legacy; but if Wilton Park's bid failed, they would receive a further twenty thirty-sixths. But although that prospect might be tempting, their real concerns were the continuing uncertainty and long delay – not to mention the growing cost of trying to settle matters, which was likely to be a charge on the whole estate. Accordingly, they asked Barclaytrust to seek some way of cutting the Gordian knot. As executor and trustee, Barclaytrust was equally keen to reach a settlement. Eventually, in 1983, it decided to seek a judgement in the High Court. By now, four years had gone by since Heinz Koeppler's death; and the value of the putative legacy to Wilton Park, prudently invested, had risen from £105,000 to £140,000.

Shortly afterwards, Sir Michael Havers, the Attorney General, gave his Opinion as requested by the Charity Commission. He concluded that Wilton Park *was* charitable, after all. But it was too late to halt the process: Barclaytrust felt that its High Court action must still go ahead.

In preparation for it, the Wilton Park Trustees' Counsel, Hubert Picarda, from Leolin Price's chambers, secured five supporting affidavits. The first, from Tim Slack, described Wilton Park and its working methods, backed by a number of its programmes and participants' lists. Another, from Alan Hughes, evoked Heinz Koeppler's formative years. Three eminent academics – Lord [Max] Beloff, Dr Richard Hoggart, and Professor Hugh Seton Watson, testified to Wilton Park's educational credentials.

'The Koeppler bequest', wrote Max Beloff, 'seems to me … , if I as a historian may be pardoned for saying so, thoroughly in line as to its essential charitable purpose with the long tradition of English charitable bequests going back to the founding of Magdalen College itself and beyond.' Richard Hoggart pointed out that the key to Wilton Park's success and international reputation was its intellectual independence. 'This makes its atmosphere more like that of a university college composed almost wholly of senior members.' Hugh Seton Watson ended his own affidavit, with heavy irony: 'I can only say, on the limited basis of thirty-two years as a full professor, that if the work of Wilton Park was not "educational", I do not know what education is.'

The most touching of all the affidavits came from Hanni Capper. If the legacy to Wilton Park failed, she and her family would obviously gain. Even if they had to pay tax on the bequest, their share would still be considerable. It was difficult, therefore, to testify for either side. 'I am advised', she said, that there were doubts about the Trust Deed and that whether Wilton Park's work was 'educational, as used in the law of charities' was a matter for the court. But she prefaced these remarks with a declaration making very clear where she really stood:

> I should state at the outset that, whatever the merits of the particular point, I do not accept the role of arguing against the validity of that bequest with any great enthusiasm. I am fully aware that Wilton Park represented my brother's life's work and, if the bequest is invalid, it is my present intention to use the moneys thereby devolving on me to honour my brother's memory in some other way. I understand that doubts have been expressed as to the charitable nature of Wilton Park by the Charity Commissioners and that, as a result of such doubts, the Capital Taxes office will not accept the validity of the bequest until the matter has been determined by this Honourable Court. Accordingly, I propose to do no more than present such arguments as may properly be presented against the validity of the bequest in the hope that the decision will be accepted by all the relevant authorities who are not parties to these proceedings.

The hearing in the High Court began on November 16, 1983, before Mr Justice [Sir] Peter Gibson. The Plaintiff was Barclaytrust. Sir Robert Birley having died in June 1982, the four defendants were: Tim Slack (represented by Alan Hughes, since by this time Slack had left Wilton Park); Magdalen College, Oxford; Koeppler's sister Mrs Hanni Capper; and the Attorney General. The case lasted four days. One month later, on December 21, 1983, Mr Justice Gibson gave his judgment. It was an unpleasant Christmas present for Wilton Park.

Thanks perhaps to Beloff's, Hoggart's and Seton Watson's affidavits, the judge fully accepted that Wilton Park was 'educational' and ignored its connection with the Foreign and Commonwealth Office. But, as the Charity Commission had earlier indicated, he considered that the Wilton Park purpose and process had 'political' ends. Relying on earlier case-law, he gave judgment against both Wilton Park and Magdalen College, and – under intestacy laws – awarded to Hanni Capper the twenty thirty-sixths of Koeppler's estate that he had sought to leave to Wilton Park. All costs – estimated at over £30,000 – were to be charged to the estate.

This left the Wilton Park Trustees nonplussed. Their first impulse was to lodge notice of an appeal, as Tim Slack did; but with no legacy, there were no funds to finance it, so it was dropped by consent on October 1, 1984. By this time, however, Sir Michael Havers had come to the rescue. As Attorney General, he saw serious and damaging implications in the present judgment for charitably registered international affairs institutions such as the Ditchley Foundation or Chatham House. To clarify the law, he decided to appeal against the key part of Mr Justice Peter Gibson's High Court Judgement. He agreed with Hanni Capper, however, that whoever finally received the bequest – herself or Wilton Park – should pay both parties' costs, which in the event totalled more than £7,000. Magdalen College, meanwhile, quietly withdrew from the proceedings.

The grounds for appeal were that the learned judge had erred in law on ten separate counts. Although couched in technical language, their essence was: that the purposes of Koeppler's bequest and of Wilton Park were exclusively charitable; that Wilton Park, although lacking a legal identity, was neither vague nor uncertain in its operation; and that the purpose of the bequest was educational whether or not it had an ultimate (not a short-term or party) political aim. Notice of Appeal, seeking a declaration that Koeppler's bequest to Wilton Park was a valid charitable gift, was lodged on May 24, 1984.

The Notice of Appeal formally read: 'TAKE NOTICE that the Court of Appeal will be moved so soon as Counsel can be heard.' In effect, this meant some ten months later. Finally, the hearing opened on April 1, 1985, at Court 19 in the Law Courts in the Strand.

It took place before three Lords Justices: Sir Patrick O'Connor, Sir Christopher Slade, elder brother of the author and composer Julian Slade, and Sir Robert Goff.

At length, on May 15, 1985, the Court of Appeal delivered its judgment. Unanimously, the three Lords Justices allowed the Appeal by the Attorney General – i.e. in favour of the Wilton Park trustees. In giving judgment, Mr Justice Slade declared that when Wilton Park activities touched on political matters, they were 'no more than genuine attempts to ascertain and disseminate the truth'. All in all, the work of Wilton Park was both 'admirable and worthwhile'.

It was a belated triumph. And administrative tidying-up remained to be done – fees to be allocated and settled, the Sir Heinz Koeppler Trust Deed to be registered with the Charity Commission, and the Koeppler estate to be finally wound up: this was expected to be finished by July 1986 – more than seven years after Heinz Koeppler's death. In the end, the Trust received some £100,000, having lost nearly £75,000 in legal costs.

CHAPTER 21

Most Unkindest Cuts

'Economy is going without something you do want in case you should, some day, want something you probably won't want.'
Anthony Hope (Hawkins), *The Dolly Dialogues* (1894), No 12

While the Koeppler bequest wound its way through the law courts, work at Wilton Park continued as usual – in two senses. In Sussex, within the walls and grounds of Wiston House, it remained intensive and tightly packed, though outward-looking and wide-ranging. Some fifty miles to the north, in Whitehall and Westminster, Wilton Park's future still hung in the balance, with renewed threats of budgetary cuts or worse. A new Government had come to power in May 1979. It was headed by Margaret Thatcher.

Routine at Wilton Park was well established. At the introductory session for each conference, participants were welcomed and introduced to the staff. The programme was explained, with a reminder that detailed timetables would be posted every day in the Great Hall passage. At the plenary sessions, speakers' names and biographies would be circulated; talks would last for 25 minutes, with 75 minutes for discussion. They would be interspersed with small discussion groups. Other gaps in the day would be reserved for silent work, meals, and socialising in general. Extramural visits would offer a change of scene and contacts outside the ivory tower. Participants would be reminded why they were here, as individuals on a mini-sabbatical at Wilton Park. It was partly to escape the daily grind and recharge their batteries without interruption. It was partly to meet a range of nationalities, professions, age groups and political persuasions. It was partly to enable experts and generalists to engage with each other, outside their specialist fields, and experience the inter-relation of political, social, economic, technical and defence problems. No one was at Wilton Park as a representative of a country, a firm, an institution, or an employer: all spoke for themselves alone. Everything said – opening statements, comments, questions, answers – was off the record. Participants could write generally about the discussions, but they must not attribute remarks to individuals. General reports of the meetings, and (if speakers agreed) texts of talks, might appear in the *Wilton Park Journal*, which went to more than 2,000 Old Wiltonians worldwide.

Behind the scenes of this presentation to participants as they gathered in their tranquil country-house setting, there was incessant activity. It was not just a matter of catering for the current visitors. Future conference programmes had to be planned, confirmed, and printed several weeks in advance. Participants had to be recruited from a score of countries. Promotional material, and next year's conference calendar, had to be agreed, printed, and circulated in several languages. Conferences by outside bodies (including FCO and other training courses) had to be booked, accommodated, and sometimes organised. Papers had to be prepared for the Academic and International Councils. Links with overseas contacts had to be sustained. The library had to be kept up to date. Wiston House itself had to be maintained, refurbished, and modernised, partly to improve the visitors' accommodation. Personnel problems had to be settled with the staff. Above all, budgets had to be agreed with the FCO and the Treasury.

On December 17, 1980, when Tim Slack told the Foreign and Commonwealth Office that the overall net cost of running Wiston House for 1981/82 was estimated at £360,000, against £330,000 in the current year, he was responding to a request (on November 27) for 'some thoughts about possible areas for savings ... for the financial year beginning April 1982'. This was quite a while ahead. In its first two years, Mrs Thatcher's Government included some moderates, rather disparagingly known as 'wets'. But its hope of curbing public expenditure was already manifest; and the Foreign and Commonwealth Office, like other departments, was already preparing its 'options-for-cuts exercise'.

The options mooted by Tim Slack were tentative and sceptical. They covered both Wilton Park and the European Discussion Centre:

Wilton Park

Minimal savings would arise from cutting down from the existing 10 Wilton Park conferences a year. The conference fee of £130 for a week is geared to cover all running costs (board and lodging, speakers' fees, etc). In theory, any Wilton Park conferences displaced could be replaced by hosting outside conferences, but outside conferences (see below) do not bring in large profits ...

Wilton Park income should amount to £54,000 during the current financial year. Therefore a doubling of fees would produce, in theory, a saving of £54,000. But any increase in fees beyond inflation could lead to a dangerous narrowing and reduction in numbers of participants. This is an issue which has been raised on previous occasions, and has been set aside each time in view of the likely harmful outcome ...

I am assuming that I am not called upon to consider the complete cessation of Wilton Park in this letter. Obviously, such a step would mean the end of Wiston House in its present form. As I told you when we talked in London, any threat to the existence of Wilton Park would be met by a major outcry from influential circles in the United Kingdom and many other countries. There was such an outcry in 1957 – and it was effective. A similar one started to emerge in 1977 at the last period of uncertainty.

European Discussion Centre

Given the existence of the Wilton Park conferences and the attendant over-heads, the marginal cost of running EDC is about £40,000 during the current financial year. No fees are charged, and participants are here as guests of Her Majesty's Government ...

A third alternative could arise from European Community funds being used to finance EDC activities. There is a history of some funds being received already and there are other possibilities worth investigating during my forthcoming visit to Brussels in March ...

Outside Conferences

The net contribution to our overheads from running six Outside Conferences in the current financial year is likely to be £5,000 – £6,000. Therefore the possible two extra outside conferences resulting from the cessation of EDC would bring in an extra £1,500 – £2,000.

I must stress that any extra addition of Outside Conferences in the current empty slots in the calendar could not be done without extra staffing. It was the inability of the FCO to appreciate this in 1978 which contributed to the recent administration problems with which you are familiar.

Within the Foreign and Commonwealth Office, the Information Department continued to debate these ideas and found a formula that seemed to meet Tim Slack's doubts. The proposal was to merge the European Discussion Centre and Wilton Park, which they thought could be done at the end of the year.

This looked very like a euphemism for closing EDC down. But, as a senior FCO official later explained to the European Commission's representative in London, 'As the years have passed and circumstances have changed, the EDC's role has increasingly overlapped with that of Wilton Park.' In practice, the FCO envisaged expanding Wilton Park's programme from ten to twelve conferences a year, and focussing four of the twelve on European themes instead of one out of the ten. Writing to the FCO on March 11, 1981, Tim Slack pointed out that 'If it is the wish of the FCO to stop EDC in its present form extreme care must be taken over how the decision is presented.' He also offered a new estimate of the money it might save:

> The savings arising from the cessation of EDC in its present form but with its absorption into a revised Wilton Park programme would give annual savings of approximately £25,000. This would represent a 7% reduction in the overall net cost of running Wiston House ... The staff would be reduced by one Grade 5 officer ...
>
> My main concern must always be to run first-rate conferences. If it is justifiable to stop EDC in its present form, the new structure of Wilton Park must be carried on in strengthened form. Wilton Park will only continue to attract so long as it remains a highly successful enterprise.
>
> I shall look forward to discussing possible reorganisation with senior staff at Wiston House as soon as possible.

As soon as he did, he found that the staff were uneasy. They feared, as Slack explained on April 1, 1981, that the proposed reorganisation might be 'the thin end of the wedge'. Feared or not, it was accepted by the Lord Privy Seal, Sir Ian Gilmour, on April 6, and was to be announced at the next Wilton Park Academic Council meeting. But it was indeed a wedge. On May 1, a good month before the Council was to be told of the merger plan, the Foreign Secretary, Lord Carrington, chaired a meeting of officials in his office to consider the 'options for cuts' required by Mrs Thatcher's Cabinet. The cuts were to range from 3 to 7.5 per cent of planned expenditure for 1982/83. 'It is inescapable', the Head of the FCO's Information Department wrote on May 20, 1981, 'that one option must be the elimination of Wiston House or reductions in expenditure on the centre'.

Wiston House was still unpopular in parts of the Treasury and the FCO itself. 'I would cheerfully see it closed down!' wrote one official on May 20. Another had declared two days earlier:

> I do not think ... that in the present economic climate (with further five

per cent cuts), we could guarantee the future of Wiston House until 1990 [as requested by the PSA, anxious to negotiate a new lease for seven years after its expiry in March 1983] ... I personally think that Wiston House in its present state does not project a positive or dynamic image of Britain and that it would take considerable investment to convert it into a conference centre likely to attract the type of participant which HMG should be aiming to influence. Indeed, running Wiston House seems an expensive way of influencing the middle-range civil servants who seem to form the majority of the participants in Wilton Park conferences at present.

But even this assessment was not all negative:

On the other hand, the objective of the Wilton Park conferences (according to the 1978 Inspection Report) is 'to win friends for Britain and understanding for British policies among the rising generation in OECD countries by attracting good people to residential conferences on generalised political subjects. The independent status of Wiston House is an important element in this.'

The Head of Information Department himself assumed that there was no intention to abolish it. He recommended that HMG should go on subsidising Wiston House at 80 per cent and meet the fares and accommodation costs of those who could not otherwise afford it. He was uncertain whether European Community nationals should be exempted from fees – as they had been for EDC conferences – after the merger with Wilton Park. A senior official endorsed this general conclusion:

The activities of Wiston House must be considered as an integral part of our overall, and unquantifiable, overseas information effort ... I do not believe it makes sense to think in terms of lopping one of them off altogether, quite apart from the Parliamentary row that would result.

Even so, some Ministers were as critical of Wilton Park as were some civil servants. On June 3, 1981, the Assistant Private Secretary to Nicholas Ridley – Minister of State at the FCO and soon to become Financial Secretary to the Treasury – minuted that his master wanted the full costs and accounts: 'He suspects that Wiston House might be very badly run; he wonders if it should instead be in the private sector, or some sort of Trust, with perhaps a small FCO grant. He feels we need a complete restructuring to save £400,000.' In fact, the net cost of Wiston House for 1981/82 was some £448,000; but the cost per participant was £1,000 as against the cost per ordinary Sponsored Visitor, which was £1,500. On June 11, 1978, the FCO assured Ridley's Private Secretary that it was well run, adding:

'We keep as close an eye on it as we can.' On June 15, the FCO warned Tim Slack that the Treasury had asked the FCO to do 'an internal exercise on FCO expenditure', and that the Information Department was having to 'analyse' Wilton Park. To this end, it had begun to ask overseas posts for their views. History was repeating itself.

Replies came in quickly. The first, on June 12, was from the Permanent Representative to OECD, who had been at Wilton Park three times, in 1975, 1979, and 1981:

> I think there has been an immense improvement since 1975. Reducing the length of the courses from 2 weeks to 1 week has involved little loss. Koeppler's extreme tendency to generalise and avoid detail has been corrected. There has been an improvement in the academic and intellectual level (a tendency which in my view could still be pushed further with advantage).

From Berne on June 16, the British Ambassador wrote that Wilton Park's country-house atmosphere – also stressed by many others – was 'more important than the number or the frequency of the conferences'. HM Ambassador in Paris replied on June 17 that the place was 'useful if it is there but not essential'. The British Ambassador to Norway declared on June 18 that Wilton Park was 'much more cost-effective than Sponsored Visits'. On June 24, HM Ambassador in Madrid wrote that ending it 'would be a pity but would not seriously affect our interests in Spain'; and, from Helsinki, on June 29, the Ambassador affirmed: 'I regard Wilton Park as an essential part of British influence in Finland. I would view its end as an absurdity.' Britain's Minister in Bonn added on June 30: 'The abolition of Wilton Park would be seen as further evidence of British insularity.'

An FCO official summed up these reactions on August 7, 1981:

> Half the posts concerned, including most, but not all, of the major ones, considered that Wilton Park was positively helpful to their effort to influence opinion-formers in their countries. Other majority views favoured the 'country-house' atmosphere, restricting fee increases, shorter and fewer conferences, and acceptance of the burden on our posts' staff. 'Old Wiltonian' organisations exist in a number of countries (e.g. Germany, France, Belgium, Italy, Switzerland, Canada and the USA) which help with recruitment, sometimes financially. Some governments (e.g. Norwegian, Dutch, and Swiss) provide funds for Wilton Park participation from their countries. On the other hand, most posts agreed that the COI/FCO Sponsored Visits were more useful (though they cost three

times as much per man-day) and that the abolition of Wilton Park would not seriously damage British interests ...

The estimated net cost of running Wiston House in 1981/82, allowing for participants' fees, is £450,000, which represents just over 80% subsidy of the total cost of the programme.

Back-up for arguments in favour of Wilton Park was provided, as always, by listing distinguished Old Wiltonians. From Britain they included: The Duke of Edinburgh, Earl Attlee, Edward Heath, James Callaghan, Roy Jenkins, David Steel, Jeremy Thorpe, Lord Carrington, Vic Feather, John Freeman, Sir Shridath Rampal (Secretary-General of the Commonwealth) and ... Margaret Thatcher. German participants had included Helmut Schmidt, Ralf Dahrendorf, Rainer Barzel, and Lilo Milchsack. From France had come Raymond Aron, Jean André François-Poncet, Claude Cheysson, Jules Moch, Antoine Pinay, and Jean-François Deniau; from Belgium, Paul-Henri Spaak and Leo Tindemans (later Prime Minister); from Denmark, Per Federspiel and Knut B. Andersen (President of the Folketing); from Austria, Chancellor Bruno Kreisky and Deputy Chancellor Hannes Androsch; from the Netherlands Joop den Uyl (later Prime Minister); from Norway Knut Friedenlund (later Foreign Minister); from the United States, Zbigniew Brzezinski and Stansfield Turner (former head of the CIA).

Wilton Park was again going to need all the support it could muster. On July 30, 1981, the Head of the FCO's Finance Department had placed a *caveat* on these favourable opinions. The Assistant Under-Secretary of State, Deputy Chief Clerk and Chief Inspector, HM Diplomatic Service, urged Information Department not to 'put a ring fence' round Wilton Park in response to calls for budget cuts: 'I do think we have to ask ourselves whether in this day and age the price of maintaining a "country house" atmosphere is worth the closure of one or two Posts overseas.' No wonder that on August 7 the Head of Information Department explained to Tim Slack 'fairly frankly the threats to Wilton Park inherent in this autumn's options-for-cuts exercise'.

One of the options debated at this time as an alternative to Wiston House was that of using an hotel, possibly in London. Some officials believed that to use hotels could halve the current cost. Tim Slack disagreed.

Retaining the present number and length of conferences and retaining a small permanent secretariat close to the hotel would bring savings of approximately 26% over the cost of a Wiston House based programme adjusted to take account of the absorption of the European Discussion Centre ... If the savings created by reducing the two 2-week conferences to two 1-week conferences (£17,000) and the absorption of the secretariat into the FCO (£14,000) were added, the total savings would increase to 34%. No calculation has been made for the idea of using several hotels in different regions of Britain, but the costs would, of course, be greater. I find your calculation that 40–50% savings would be achieved by using a hotel not realistic.

Given the appropriate staffing and facilities it would be technically possible to run Wilton Park Conferences in a hotel or hotels. But their nature would change markedly and I calculate that the result would be most harmful ...

Above all we are trying through our conferences to make a lasting impression on our participants ... I cannot imagine being able to create such impressions in the necessarily more clinical and impersonal atmosphere of a hotel – especially if the conferences were very short. The quality of private hospitality and the provision of a residence which allows a specifically British flavour cannot be provided in a hotel. I cannot visualise Ditchley Park [the Anglo-American Conference Centre] surviving in the Randolph Hotel, Oxford. I doubt whether Ambassadors would feel that hospitality could be effective through living in a flat and holding their receptions and parties in a hotel ...

It is not only that at Wiston House we can get people to loosen up and talk freely. We can show the human face of bureaucracy. We can be highly efficient and temper it with warm informality. We can demonstrate British character and characteristics in a way which we could not do, were we acting as impresarios in a hotel.

If it should be found essential to save up to £200,000 a year, I would ask for two other avenues to be explored before the idea of hotel based conferences is taken further.

(a) We should approach trusts and industry at home and abroad for financial assistance. The Ford Foundation made a grant of 100,000 dollars in 1960 but no serious attempt has been made since then to raise money.

(b) A suitable conference organisation should be invited to take over the lease of Wiston House with the FCO being absolved of all financial and administrative responsibility for staffing and running the building. The FCO would negotiate with the conference organisation to hold Wilton Park Conferences at Wiston House. It is unlikely that the charges per day would be above that of a hotel and the reduced secretariat could remain in the same place. At a time when pressure for further cuts in public expenditure looks inevitable it would be unrealistic for us to believe we should not have our position closely examined. But I would find it hard to support savings which damaged our effectiveness. Unless we remain very good we will quickly die.

If the Treasury had had its way, Wilton Park would certainly have died. On September 29, 1981, a senior Treasury official wrote to the FCO pointing out that whereas the Civil Service College at Sunningdale held courses for 46 weeks out of the year, Wiston House was in use for only 25:

> We would therefore like to explore with you the possibility of closing this establishment down, not in the context of our immediate public expenditure exercise, but with a view to securing savings in the longer term by cutting marginal activities.

Some senior FCO officials seemed rather to agree, and certainly favoured the hotel option. One wrote on October 8:

> My own experience of Wilton Park suggests that the original philosophy behind it is now out of date ... I also believe that those who would lament the loss of the 'country house' atmosphere might be outnumbered by those who would welcome the increased conference, business, and social opportunities of meeting in London.

The hotel option remained on the cards for some time. But the last word belonged to Richard Luce, the MP for Shoreham, who was predictably against any move from Wiston House. As he wrote on October 20, 1981, to Lord Trefgarne, Parliamentary Under-Secretary of State at the FCO: 'I have no doubt whatsoever that the whole concept of the Wilton Park conferences would immediately be destroyed if the operations were to be moved to an hotel.'

By this time, indeed, there were signs that what might have been called 'the Auld Alliance' (between Wilton Park and Germany) was swinging into action, at least to prevent outright abolition. On October 9, 1981, the Federal German Foreign Ministry sent the FCO the draft of the joint communiqué it hoped to issue at the close of the Anglo-German 'summit' meeting between Mrs Thatcher and Chancellor Helmut Schmidt in Bonn on November 18. The draft praised 'the International Conference Centre, Wilton Park, which has brought German and British people together in the European spirit since 1946 and has developed into a strong and durable instrument of Anglo-German understanding.' By the time of the summit, after amendment and re-translation, the draft had been watered down. It now said that the two leaders 'commended the contribution made by the international conference centre at Wilton Park, which began as an Anglo-German initiative and developed into an international meeting-place.' Feeble as it now was, this text remained significant. Having publicly praised Wilton Park in an Anglo-German communiqué, even Mrs

Thatcher would find it more difficult to decree its closure. Furthermore, as the Consul-General in Munich had already pointed out on October 28, a decision to close Wilton Park at this point would be awkward anyway. Next April, its 25th jubilee was to be celebrated in Munich, with 200 delegates, a speech by the Prime Minister of Bavaria, Franz Josef Strauss, and visits by the British Ambassador and the German Foreign Minister, Hans-Dietrich Genscher.

At length, on Friday December 4, 1981, the new Lord Privy Seal, Humphrey Atkins, held a large-scale meeting involving Ministers and senior officials in his office to discuss Wilton Park. The Foreign Office put the case for Wilton Park's value, but admitted that the last report by the Comptroller and Auditor General had been critical. Atkins wondered whether it could charge more in fees. FCO officials agreed that the overheads were huge, although Training Department planned to make more use of Wiston House in the future, taking up 28 or 29 weeks in 1982 and 33 or 34 in 1983. They also argued that it would be damaging to close Wilton Park in view of its forthcoming merger with EDC. To dismantle it, suggested one sympathiser, 'would be another example of paying a heavy political price for minimal financial saving, like students' fees and the BBC ... Parliamentary reaction on both sides would be very sharp.'

The upshot was a recommendation that the FCO Inspectorate should report by the end of January 1982 on:

> How to maximise the benefit to HMG of Wilton Park and reduce the existing net costs by a minimum of 25% (£115,000) by 1983/84 so as to justify renewing the Wiston House lease in March 1983; and to propose alternative courses of action if this is not possible.

Two days before Christmas, as if on cue, Wilton Park's sternest traditional critic resurrected its own favoured alternative. Leon Brittan, Chief Secretary to the Treasury, wrote to the Foreign Secretary Lord Carrington: 'I very much hope you can agree ... that we should discontinue the Wilton Park conferences which I believe have now outlived their usefulness.' It looked as if austerity would have to be the alternative to oblivion.

When the Wilton Park Academic Council met in the Foreign and Commonwealth Office on Wednesday, January 13, 1982, the FCO announced the terms of reference of the Inspectorate's Review. It added that:

> In the attempt to reduce costs a number of options would be examined including raising fees or charging the same fees for shorter conferences,

privatisation, eliminating marginal activities, increasing the number of outside conferences, ending extra-mural visits, seeking outside finance, sharing facilities at Wiston House with kindred organisations, inviting the landlord to reduce the present rent to a peppercorn and, as a last resort, moving from Wiston House to an hotel or another conference centre where no substantial overheads would arise.

A normal FCO inspection of Wiston House, the FCO explained, had been due later in 1982. But the Review now in train was intended to be both broader in scope and more radical. It would be conducted, they explained, in close consultation with the Director and his senior staff. As well as an accountant and an office systems expert from the FCO, the Inspector had called on an outside firm of consultants to assist him. He was being 'encouraged' to produce his report by the end of January. It would be shown promptly to Ministers, and then presented to the Academic Council for their comments.

The prospective Inspector, who was present at the Council, answered questions from its members. One FCO official reported privately afterwards:

> The roughest was Mr [David] Watt, Director of Chatham House. He asked if the 25% figure was one which Ministers had simply pulled out of a hat, insinuating that the Review might merely camouflage an intention to abolish Wilton Park altogether. He asked what the views were of Ministers of Wilton Park, implying (this is a hobby horse of his) that Ministers have no sense of priorities as far as their work in the information/cultural field was concerned. He announced darkly that Wilton Park had a very strong lobby behind it.

Information Department assured Watt that 25 per cent was considered a reasonable figure to aim at, and one which would be defensible against possible criticism from the Public Accounts Committee. It also said that there was no magic behind the 25 per cent figure, and that it had not been seized upon to placate the Public Accounts Committee. It also said there was no magic behind the 25 per cent figure and that it had not been seized upon to placate the Public Accounts Committee. Nor had it been selected by Ministers as an unattainable figure. If the target seemed on the high side, it was an indication of the radical nature of the Review intended by Ministers. As to the underlying feeling about Wilton Park, no one should doubt that the FCO greatly valued it.

'Of the others', an official reported, 'Lord Beloff ... was constructive. He saw no reason why Wilton Park should be wedded to its present location at Wiston House.' If it were to stay there, Beloff wondered whether Wilton House staff could shed 'hotel' responsibilities. He also proposed dropping simultaneous interpretation and possibly extra-mural visits; and he hoped that the Review would look also at Ditchley Park. Had a merger been considered? The Inspector confirmed that he planned to visit Ditchley.

But it was Michael Shanks, the former journalist and Eurocrat, who posed what later proved to be the key question. Was it really essential for the Inspectorate's report to be presented by the end of January? This was little more than two weeks away. Given the complexities of the Review, time constraints could seriously harm its value.

Senior officials acknowledged the difficulties, but thought it best to stick to the time-limit. The Inspector, for his part, said that he aimed to do so.

'The Review', wrote the Inspector on January 29, 'got off to an uncertain start'. This, he claimed, was partly because Tim Slack 'did not share Ministers' enthusiasm for cutting costs at Wiston House'. But he went on: 'I found that the Wilton Park conferences are successfully conducted with quiet efficiency. By contrast, the administration of Wiston House is a shambles. Outside conference time there is a tremendous waste of human and physical resources.' He pointed out the need for a new Bursar when John Forsyth retired on reaching the age of 65 later in the year. He also called for conferences to be of 5 days or less, with no extra-mural visits, the *Wilton Park Journal* to be abolished, and the academic staff to be cut from five (Oliver Hayward, Valerie Seward, David Spence, Jim Starkey, and Robert Sturrock) to four. He further recommended that the post of Deputy Director be abolished, and that of the Director be down-graded from DS 3 (Under Secretary) to DS 4 (Assistant Secretary).

Tim Slack received the draft of the Inspectorate's report on Thursday, February 4, 1982, on the second day of an experimental four-day Wilton Park conference on 'The Politics and Economics of an Enlarged European Community'. It was the first he had heard of any proposal about the staff. He worked over the weekend to produce his comments on the draft. He agreed with some of it. But he questioned much else. He strongly criticised one of the administrative suggestions – moving the offices to the top floor – which he thought would complicate life unnecessarily; and he firmly opposed dropping extra-mural visits, abolishing the *Journal*, and making such drastic changes to the academic staff. His comments reached the Inspectorate on Tuesday, February 9, but the next day he was told that it was too late to discuss the report.

This being the case, Slack decided to address the Academic Council direct. On February 26 he wrote to each of its members setting out in detail, on the major issues, where he agreed and where he disagreed with the Review. Underlying most of the disagreements was a lack of consultation and discussion, which he left the careful reader to discern.

THE ACCEPTABLE PROPOSALS

1. Wilton Park to remain at Wiston House ...
2. <u>Fuller utilisation of Wiston House throughout the year</u> ...
I believe the Review is too cautious and that the building could be used for even more than the 42 weeks proposed ...
3. <u>Better organisation on the domestic and catering front</u> ...
I am pleased that Management Consultants have now been brought in. Without discussion I am unable to comment on the validity of some of their recommendations regarding catering, accounting systems, and domestic staffing levels. As they were only able to be here for 3 days there are some aspects of the domestic side of our operations which they cannot be expected to have investigated or understood fully. The final decisions will have to be explained carefully to a loyal workforce who are going to have to face up to some radical changes. Having brought in professional experts, they should be retained to help implement and subsequently monitor the decisions ...
4. I accept the proposal to cut out the remaining two two-week conferences and replace them with four one-week conferences ...

There are several other objections to the proposal. These would have been put to the Inspectors if they had discussed their proposal with me or anyone else who has to work at Wiston House ...

<u>The proposal for reduced Secretarial staffing levels</u>
... Until these proposals are worked out carefully with me and others responsible for running the administration, I cannot agree to them as they stand ...

<u>The proposal for the removal of the post of Deputy Director and a member of the Academic Staff</u>
My strong objection to this proposal is based on my contention that all the senior staff are fully employed doing essential work ...

As there has been no discussion with the Inspector on this question of staffing I do not know the calculations and reasoning which lie behind his proposal.

There is much more I could add about this matter of staffing ...

There was. It was also to create considerable turmoil and anger, both now and in future years. The same was true of:

<u>The proposal to downgrade the Director and the Deputy Director</u>
I do not know if there is a precedent for downgrading existing holders of
posts other than for cases of misconduct. Looking also towards future
holders of these posts, I would deplore the downgrading proposed. I have
long felt that the responsibilities, intellectual strength and personal qualities of a Deputy Director are equivalent to an Assistant Secretary rather
than the existing level of Senior Principal. I would not have accepted the
post of Director of Wilton Park if the post had not had the rank of Under
Secretary. It is not only a question of status and salary. The Director needs
to liaise inside and outside the FCO supported with the necessary authority. Ditchley Park feels it necessary to appoint an ex-diplomat of Grade I
level. Wilton Park is at least as important and influential as Ditchley. The
Academic Council and FCO should give serious consideration to whether
a future Director of the required calibre would be attracted by the level of
Assistant Secretary – or indeed a Deputy Director by the level of Senior
Principal.

Sadly, behind the proposal, it will be assumed that HMG considers the
work of Wilton Park to be of reduced importance.
<u>The proposal to cut out Extra-Mural Visits combined with the proposal to
reduce the length of the conference to four full working days and the
related proposal to increase thereby fees by 42%</u>
I object to all three strands of these proposals and feel that all of them,
whether individually or combined, would seriously damage our effectiveness ...
<u>The proposal to cease publishing the Journal</u>
The Wilton Park Journal is an important link with former participants and
part of the process of making a stay at Wilton Park a lasting experience. We
have just received over 700 renewal slips from our latest mailing and they
are still coming in. But I suggest that we charge a small renewal subscrip-
tion ...

Recent articles in the *Journal*, as Slack might have specified, had
included one based on the speech that Dr Bruno Kreisky, the Austrian
Federal Chancellor, had made at a meeting of the Old Wiltonian
Association in Vienna in May 1980. Its subject was 'Europe and the Near
East', and it appeared in the first of two issues whose costs and timing
Hughes had earlier quoted to the FCO. The same number (No. 61, Winter
1980) published a piece based on a talk given at Wilton Park on February
20, 1980, by John Birt, then of London Weekend Television, on
'Television and Democracy'. As well as the usual 'Notes on [or news of]
Wilton Park', there were also contributions by Dr Paul R. Schratz of the
US Defense Department, on 'Prospects for Détente', and Hung Hyon
Kim, Director of the Korean Traders Association, Düsseldorf, on 'The

Newly Industrialised Countries: Is There a Challenge' – an early and prescient glimpse of 'globalisation'.

Given such rich variety in the *Wilton Park Journal*, it was natural for Tim Slack and his team to defend it, and to believe that its recipients would be willing to pay.

Although I cannot accept all the proposals, I quantify the effect of what I accept or oppose as follows:

	Savings proposed in review (%)	by Director (%)
Reduction and regrading of senior staff	10	0
Rationalisation of administrative and secretarial staff structure	2	0.25
Discontinuing extra-mural visits	4	1.5
Domestic staff savings	8	7
Increased utilisation of Wiston House as conference centre	8	8
Merger of European Discussion Centre with Wilton Park	7	7
Increased fees for Wilton Park Conferences	3	3
Other savings	2	1
TOTAL SAVINGS PROPOSED	44	28

Primed with Tim Slack's proposals, the Wilton Park Academic Council held a private meeting at Chatham House on Wednesday, March 3, 1982. Its members were divided. Some approved of the Review's recommendations. Others became what one observer called 'quite heated', arguing that cuts of 44 per cent were too much, objecting to the lack of communication about proposed staff changes, and insisting that Tim Slack should retain his grade.

The Council aired these grievances in the presence of officials in the Foreign and Commonwealth Office when it held an Extraordinary

Meeting there on Wednesday March 17, 1982. Sir Peter Tennant, in the chair because Sir Robert Birley was ill, began by complaining that consultations between the Inspector and the Wilton Park Director and staff 'had not been all that close'. Tim Slack asked when he would be able to discuss the reasoning behind the recommendations on staff. If there had not been 'an adequate dialogue in the past', suggested a senior official, he and Tim Slack 'would sit down together and thrash out with precision the points Mr Slack wanted to put across'. When the Review was submitted to Ministers, Tim Slack's proposals and the views of the Academic Council would also be put to them.

Ministers had already asked for 'outhouse options' to Wiston House – i.e. possible alternative sites for Wilton Park conferences – to be studied in greater detail. So FCO officials were preparing a report on suitable places within two hours' drive of Heathrow or Gatwick. They visited: Minster Lovell Mill, near Oxford; Madingley Hall, near Cambridge; Elvetham Hall, Hartley Wintney, Hants; Farnham Castle, Hants; Easthampstead Park, Wokingham, Berks; Brocket Hall, Welwyn, Herts; Cumberland Lodge, Windsor; St George's House, Windsor Castle; Roffey Park, Horsham, Sussex; The White House, Haywards Heath, Sussex; Castle Priory, Wallingford, Berks; and Nuneham Park, near Oxford. Of all these, the most suitable was Elvetham Hall, described as 'Well run, comfortable'. Its possible net overall cost was estimated at £356,100 – not very different from that of Wiston House. The Review had plumped for no change of venue; and so did the Academic Council. With that, the 'outhouse option', like the 'hotel option', quietly faded.

The Council's main discussion centred on the question of staff. Sir Peter Tennant pointed out that the Director had been recruited in his present grade, and he had not known of anyone being downgraded *in situ*. The time to downgrade the post of Director would be when the present Director was replaced, and he hoped that would not be for a long time yet. He said that the Council felt very strongly on this point. Michael Shanks added that the role of the Deputy Director was equally important – at which Alan Hughes intervened 'to state unequivocally that he would not accept a downgrading of his job'.

On April 6, 1982, Tennant wrote to Lord Trefgarne, Parliamentary Under Secretary of State at the Foreign Office (who had been among those pressing for the 'outhouse option') with the Academic Council's comments on the Review. It was, he said, 'concerned with lack of consultation on certain aspects of the review' but pleased by proposals to improve the administration and use space capacity.

Our preference would be for Wilton Park to remain at Wiston House in spite of the very marginal savings which might be achieved by an alternative site, and we therefore welcome the fact that these proposals, even though they will call for some additional initial expenditure [£35,110 for improving Wiston House, according to the consultants], combine with other proposals to produce, within a very short time, savings which come close to achieving the basis target of 25% ...

The Council strongly opposes the downgrading of the post of Director and the abolition of the post of Deputy Director ... Likewise, the Council strongly opposes the proposal to reduce by one the Academic Staff ...

We feel most strongly that if economies much beyond the basis target of about 25% are to be sought there is a serious danger of throwing out the baby with the bathwater.

Tim Slack wrote to Trefgarne on the same day. In doing so, he went back to basics in a style reminiscent of Heinz Koeppler:

Wilton Park provides a unique forum for free discussion amongst influential international groups on problems of deep concern to all. By its very non-propagandist nature it can have a more marked and lasting pro-British effect on important sections of foreign opinion than any overt attempt at conversion.

Wilton Park gives those who speak and participate here the chance to hear the views of a whole series of well-informed foreigners on topical issues and to compare their own position with them. This process of debate is, in both senses of the adjective, a vital one which lets visitors in positions of importance in a range of professions and countries know what are the significant currents of thought here in Britain.

Wilton Park also plays a worthwhile role in giving the lie to damaging notions, quite common even amongst intelligent foreigners, regarding Britain today. It is a living refutation of misconceptions such as British insularity, bland unconcern and ignorance about others' approaches to common problems, and the apparent self-obsession of our press. The whole conference experience is designed, discreetly yet indisputably, to underline our continued ability to organise with the highest efficiency and to think positively. Participants leave better informed and describing Wilton Park as a uniquely useful experience ...

There is no reason why another house could not, over some years, provide what Wiston House does so well at present. But the peculiar combination of superb countryside, relationship to the small town of Steyning, distance from London and, above all, informal British hospitality in a private home, bring Wiston House close to perfection. However pleasing someone else's conference centre may be, it cannot offer the relaxed yet purposeful personal touch which springs from working at one's own base. And the British Government benefits likewise by the implied prestige that it is their own centre – and not someone else's. Thus I support the Inspector's recommendation that Wilton Park remains at Wiston House. I note that [the] supplementary review only produces a marginal cost benefit in moving elsewhere.

There is nothing sacrosanct about the present content, style and length of Wilton Park conferences ... However, when sights are set on financial savings, there is a danger that quantitative cuts will produce severe qualitative cuts too. The present pattern of participants arriving on a Sunday evening and leaving the following Saturday morning produces a fine combination of quality of participants and effectiveness of discussion ... Indeed, some believe that two-week conferences do this even more effectively.

Four main ingredients cause success. First, the good mix of people under the same roof; this demands the time and staffing to recruit effectively... Secondly, good session-speakers; this, and the related activities of building a programme, demand talent, judgement and adequate time on the part of the programme coordinators. Thirdly, ... the extra dimension afforded through the midweek visits ... Fourthly, the right style in the right atmosphere; for this we are dependent on the quality of staff.

Wilton Park is highly labour intensive; it is understandably tempting to save large sums by cutting staff. But this current review is not the first that advocates such cuts. In 1976, a Principal's post was eliminated with no reduction in workload. In 1978, my promotion to Director left my previous post of Deputy Director (one of two) unfilled. The 1981 Management Review subsequently commented on the overload borne by the Director and Deputy Director. The Inspector also recommended the new appointment of a part-time Conference Assistant. In 1975 the Chief Inspector carefully assessed the workload of all senior staff. He did the same in 1978. His 1978 recommendations gave the present team of four Wilton Park 'front-of-stage' Principals duties which have led on to their present workload and pattern of work. My detailed calculations show their present commitments to be greater than in 1978, but they are bearable. The absorption of the European Discussion Centre (EDC) into Wilton Park justifiably eliminated one Principal post, but the second Principal (only partly concerned with EDC) is now giving much needed help with recruitment for the larger number of Wilton Park conferences. Every year the help which can be given by posts abroad has to be reduced. I contend strongly that Wilton Park cannot be effectively run with fewer senior staff than at present.

Likewise, I cannot accept the proposed reduction on the Secretarial side ...

Related to the level of staffing is the importance of the post of Deputy Director and the grading of the post of Director. The Wilton Park

Academic Council have given their views on this issue. I only add that I would not have accepted my present post at a lower grade, and that I believe the responsibilities of the job demand leadership and judgement which do not equate with the level of Assistant Secretary. Ditchley Park has former Grade I Ambassadors in command ...

Tim Slack went on to adumbrate other possible economies and sources of finance. He concluded by quoting the joint communiqué issued in Bonn on November 18, 1981, by Margaret Thatcher and Helmut Schmidt and added a quotation from the speech that Mrs Thatcher had made the same day in Bad Godesberg:

> Our problem today in a way is how to communicate these things which have come to mean so much to us by virtue of our experience to the present and future generations who have come to live for so long under the flags of liberty that they have come to take it for granted and they have never known what it would be like to lose it. That is the great positive job of communication that we have ... I don't know quite how we do communicate it except by constantly talking about it.

'I believe', added Tim Slack, 'that Wilton Park is an effective instrument in the vital field of communication between nations.'

The less technical tone of this letter reflected the fact that the debate was now shifting to the political level. The defenders of Wilton Park, in fact, were preparing to mobilise the parliamentary and other support that had proved effective in earlier battles. On Thursday, April 22, Tim Slack and Sir Peter Tennant met with Richard Luce, Conservative MP for Shoreham, who planned to approach Lord Belstead, Minister of State at the FCO, and possibly Malcolm Rifkind, FCO Parliamentary Under-Secretary.

On May 1, Belstead received another letter, from Sir Peter Tennant as Acting Chairman of the Council, seeking a meeting to discuss the cuts. He answered on May 12 and agreed to see Tennant, with Lord Beloff and David Watt, on Thursday May 27. After the meeting, also attended by senior FCO officials, Belstead decided that a reasonable savings target would be 30 per cent and that the PSA should be asked to negotiate for a 7-year lease. He planned to visit Wiston House himself on Wednesday, June 9, during an experimental four-day conference on 'Protectionism versus a Free-Trade World'. By the end of the following week, on June 18, he was in a position to announce the Government's decisions to the members of the Advisory Council prior to their next meeting on June 25. 'Certain detailed points,' he wrote, 'still require study':

We agree with the Review's conclusions subject to the modifications mentioned below. In particular we agree that 'Wilton Park conferences are a unique and successful information activity. They are efficiently conducted'. After further in depth study we also agree that 'Any move from Wiston House would imply a considerable risk of damaging the effectiveness of the Wilton Park operation.' To demonstrate our confidence in Wilton Park we have therefore proposed that the Wiston House lease be renewed for a further seven years. The Review proposed savings amounting to some 44%. After allowing for amortisation of the new capital expenditure also proposed, this becomes 42%. After very careful consideration [familiar phrase!] we believe the following modifications should be made:

(a) the Deputy Director's post should be retained and (subject to review after one year) that of his Secretary. After further consultation we are satisfied that an important role remains to be filled as the Director's understudy and senior colleague who plays a vital part in the recruitment of participants – a field rendered harder by the decline in information staff in FCO posts abroad;

(b) the Director should have discretion to include Extra-Mural Visits in half the proposed 14 conferences; these could then continue to be 6 night conferences as at present, with the balance being 5 night conferences (as proposed in the Review) or of shorter duration;

(c) whilst as much as possible of the proposed £37,000 saving on domestic staff and overtime should be sought, we consider that £33,000 would be a more reasonable target, at least in the first full financial year;

(d) a working group should be set up, to include at the outset the consultants who helped in the Review, to reconsider the consultants' proposed rearrangement of office and bedroom accommodation in the light of alternative proposals prepared by the Director.

After allowing for these modifications savings would principally come from the following:

(i) The Wilton Park – European Discussion Centre merger which took place at the beginning of this year.

(ii) Reduction of 1 Academic Staff, 1 Secretary and 2 or 3 Domestic staff plus overtime.

(iii) Regrading of certain posts, including replacement of 2 part-time staff by a new DS9 Administration Assistant.

(iv) Ending half the Extra-Mural Visits and the Wilton Park Journal.

(v) Ending out-housing of participants in hotels.

(vi) Securing 16 weeks of outside conferences.

(vii) Raising fees …

Whilst stressing that any estimates can only be very approximate given the many unpredictable elements, particularly (vi) above, we calculate that the overall net saving which should result from these changes would be about 30%.

Francis Pym [the Foreign Secretary] and I attach the greatest importance to ensuring that Wiston House is fully cost-effective. The consultants' proposals for improved accounting and catering will need to be pursued vigorously. The Bursar and his new Assistant will need full training in organising both Wilton Park and outside conferences.

Belstead gave some satisfaction to Tim Slack and the Academic Council. He confirmed the continued existence of Wilton Park. He maintained it at Wiston House, with the lease to be renewed for seven years. He reduced the proposed cuts from 44 per cent to some 30 per cent. He reinstated the posts of the Deputy Director and his Secretary; he restored half the Extra-Mural Visits; he moderated the reduction of the domestic staff; and he offered consultation on the rearrangement of bedrooms and offices.

But unpalatable features remained. All of them provoked strong reactions when the Wilton Park Academic Council met at Wiston House on Friday, June 25, 1982. Sir Peter Tennant was in the chair owing to Sir Robert Birley's continued illness. Only five other members were present: Lord Beloff, Edmund Dell, Hugo Herbert-Jones (late of the Diplomatic Service, now with the CBI), Dr Roger Morgan, and Professor Peter Nailor of the Royal Naval College, Greenwich. Also present were Tim Slack and Alan Hughes, as well as officials from the FCO. Although the meeting was small, it lasted more than two hours. It began relatively calmly.

Tim Slack reported on staff changes, including the replacement as Bursar of John Forsyth by Derek Jackson. Numbers attending Wilton Park were up, especially from France and southern Europe; so were requests by outside bodies to use Wiston House.

The meeting then turned to the Review of Wilton Park and Lord Belstead's letter. Sir Peter Tennant began by recalling that the Council had been deeply shocked by the original minimum target for savings of 25 per cent. It had been still more affronted by the Review's proposal to make cuts of 44 per cent. Now members were told that because of their own and the Director's representations the cuts were to be 30 per cent. A number of worrying details militated against what the Council stood for – to see that the quality of the operation was maintained. If the Council gave way to the Treasury it would be doing the wrong thing as far as information policy was concerned.

Tim Slack challenged very strongly the authority and quality of the Review. He had not been consulted, he said, about major aspects of it, and he was concerned that the figure of 44 per cent had been given unjustifiable status because it had been circulated to the Treasury and to FCO departments. FCO officials reported that the 30 per cent figure of savings was actually 23 per cent since seven percentage points had been saved already by the merger of EDC with Wilton Park.

Peter Nailor was indignant about the proposals to end the *Wilton Park Journal* and halve the number of the Extra-Mural Visits (EMVs). In this, he said, the FCO seemed to be usurping the functions of the Director. As in the shortening of conferences, it was interfering in the academic affairs of Wilton Park, supposedly free from government control. Nailor preferred the Director's judgement as to the value of these operations. Tim Slack said that the present pattern of 6-night conferences including EMVs had proved very successful: EMVs were an integral part of them. Ending the *Journal* would save only £3,000; he had proposed charging for subscriptions, which would save £1,500. Edmund Dell suggested that instead of making small savings on these items they should forego the concessions on fees mentioned at the end of Lord Belstead's letter. Officials, however, argued that all these savings were part of a closely interdependent package. For instance, there were hidden staff costs in producing the *Journal* and arranging EMVs. The FCO had already untied some of the package: to untie more would risk seriously reducing the total savings.

If FCO officials had difficulty with the Academic Council over these details, they faced a storm over staffing.

On the proposed reduction of Academic Staff from five to four, Slack said that at first he had thought this might be feasible. But on reconsideration he had concluded that the Review had not properly assessed the workload. For example, the Academic Staff would have to help with some of the outside conferences. One of the present five was engaged largely on recruiting participants – an increasing task; the other four would now have to prepare (and find speakers for) 14 one-week conferences instead of 12 covering 14 weeks. Their workload would be reduced if simultaneous interpretation were dropped, but there had been criticism of a one-off experimental English-only Conference, from which a Swiss who spoke four other languages had had to withdraw. In view of this, said Tennant, there seemed to be grave objections to the proposed cut.

But the gravest objections were still to come. It was Peter Nailor, again, who raised the most contentious issue. What was meant, he asked, by Lord Belstead's reference in his letter to 'regrading of certain posts'? If this referred to the downgrading of the Director's post to DS 4 it should say so clearly. Such a change was quite unacceptable. Lord Beloff said that the proposal reflected very adversely on the status of Wilton Park. If it was persisted with he did not think he could continue to serve on the Council. The Director of Ditchley Park was a DS 1 Ambassador. From the Chair, Sir Peter Tennant also expressed serious doubts. Though apparently 30 British Ambassadors were DS 4, the status of the Wilton Park Director was higher than theirs. He had understood that the initial uncertainties over Tim Slack's appointment had been resolved by an assurance that he would remain as DS 3.

Roger Morgan asked if this had been made clear in the Director's letter of appointment. Slack answered that it had not been put in writing. His memory may have played him false. In reality, the FCO had assured him, on February 10, 1978:

> There should be no difficulty in authorising extensions of the Limited Period Certificate which they would issue to you if you were appointed. Such extensions would normally be, by mutual agreement, for periods of 2 to 3 years at a time and could be continued, if necessary, beyond the nominal 10 year ceiling set for such appointments.

This had been echoed, more cautiously, by the Head of the FCO's Personnel Policy Department in his letter of appointment on May 25, 1978: 'Your appointment will be for a limited period of 5 years from 24 May 1978 but there may be prospects for an extension beyond this period.'

There had been no promise that the extension would be at the same grade, but equally no threat that it might be at a lower. To the Council Slack pointed out, however, that he was in the unique position of being on a fixed 5 year contract which meant he could secure no compensation.

Edmund Dell remarked that the Review gave no reasons for this extraordinary downgrading. What were they? Officials replied that FCO Inspectors were constantly reviewing gradings which sometimes went up and sometimes went down, depending on certain standards which applied across the Diplomatic Service. There was a downward trend in the number of DS 3 posts available. The Director's post had been at D 4 level until the creation of the European Discussion Centre (EDC) in 1973, and EDC had now been merged with Wilton Park. The FCO had a high regard for the present Director who they hoped would continue after his contract ended in May 1983. The Ditchley Director was a retired officer whose salary was half that of the Wilton Park Director [although the retired officer presumably had a pension as well]. It was the FCO's hope that no publicity need be given to the change, which was why it was not spelt out in sub-paragraph (iii) of Lord Belstead's letter.

These explanations failed to satisfy Edmund Dell. It was not the quantity of EDC conferences that mattered, he said, but the quality. The merger had been accepted on the understanding that there would still be some Europe-oriented conferences. Peter Nailor protested that the FCO was taking advantage of the fact that Tim Slack's contract was nearing its end, so that a new contract could be at a lower grade and he could in effect be downgraded during his tenure, if he stayed on. And the downgrading was bound to become widely known. Hugo Herbert-Jones thought that the saving of £2,000 hardly seemed worthwhile.

Sir Peter Tennant concluded by saying that the Council was agreed in opposing this implied reduction in Wilton Park's status. He asked whether Ministers' decisions were final. Officials answered by referring to the text of Lord Belstead's letter, which spoke of 'decisions' and 'conclusions': he added that the FCO had received ten written questions from the Public Accounts Committee, to which it was replying.

As the long debate ended, Sir Peter Tennant said he would convene a private meeting of the Academic Council so that those absent today could attend. It would then decide what action to take. He asked that the strong view of the present meeting be conveyed to them in the minutes.

The senior FCO official who had attended the Council also conveyed them, three days later, to his superior in the Office. The FCO had no inkling of the ructions that lay ahead.

CHAPTER 22

Ructions and Resignations

'Il faut toujours être botté et prêt à partir.'
Michel Eyquem de Montaigne, *Essais* (1580), Book I, Chapter 2

The downgrading of the Director's post at Wilton Park, proposed by the Inspectorate's Review and endorsed by Lord Belstead, had had still more senior backing. On March 8, 1982, the Foreign Secretary himself, Lord Carrington, had declared: 'I intend to downgrade from Under-Secretary to Assistant Secretary the job of the Chief Economic Adviser in the Diplomatic Wing and that of the Director of Wilton Park.' After Carrington had resigned – over the Falklands invasion – on April 6, 1982, Lord Belstead told his successor Francis Pym of this decision, which had been taken in the context of 'economies in Civil Service manpower'. After Belstead's meeting on May 27 with Sir Peter Tennant, Lord Beloff, and David Watt, he had sought advice on how to 'soften the blow' to Tim Slack when his contract expired in May 1983. But as well as seeking to soften the blow, the FCO had been trying to make sure that it could not be legally parried. Already on May 17, legal advisers had seen no objection to extending Tim Slack's appointment for a further period but at a lower rate of pay. His terms of appointment would be being varied. His consent would therefore be needed. If he gave it, there was no problem. If not, there seemed equally to be no legal problem, since he would not get his appointment extended, but that would give him no basis for complaining to an industrial tribunal since he had no legal right to an extension after the expiry of his existing appointment in 1983. There would then have to be a new competition for what would in effect be a new job, on new terms.

If this seemed devious or even heartless, the FCO deserved credit for also trying to make sure that downgrading would involve few – or no –

financial penalties. On June 17, 1982, a good week before the Academic Council meeting at Wiston House, officials suggested making a special approach to the Treasury to enable Tim Slack to receive 'mark time pay' – a continuation of his present (DS 3) salary until the DS 4 rate caught up with it.

Whether the Treasury would be sympathetic remained uncertain. As Lord Belstead wrote to Francis Pym on July 1, 1982:

> Leon Brittan and the Treasury have their eye on Wilton Park in the context of public expenditure cuts, and the 30% economy measures we are propos-ing are partly designed to get Wilton Park on a firm and defensible basis for the future and preserve it from a worse fate.

On the same day, more support came from Parliament. The Foreign Affairs Committee of the House of Commons issued a statement on Wilton Park recommending 'that no steps be taken which would jeopardise the future of this valuable and internationally respected institution'. The fact that MPs were becoming involved in the debate, prompted partly by the Academic Council and partly by the Director, was already causing irri-tation in Whitehall. On July 2, a senior FCO official wrote that:

> At a meeting earlier this week with Lord Belstead it was decided that the Chief Clerk might summon Mr Slack in due course to remind him that his lobbying activity was incompatible with his status as an employee of the FCO ... We are all agreed that Mr Slack must be brought into line in the near future.

Irritation was increased when David Watt warned Information Department that the whole Academic Council might resign 'because of a high-handed FCO 30 per cent cut'. The FCO retorted that it was not a cut but a 30 per cent saving, and that in any case this was a reduction of only 15 per cent because of 7 per cent economy achieved already by merging EDC with Wilton Park, and the 8 per cent contribution expected from more outside conferences. But Watt remained unconvinced.

When Watt hosted the Wilton Park Academic Council's one-and-a-half-hour private meeting in Chatham House on Wednesday morning, July 7, 1982, Tim Slack confirmed that he had indeed been talking about the current problems with Members of Parliament. A member of the Public Accounts Committee had told him that the Committee was no longer planning to call the FCO in front of it: a few weeks later, in fact, its chairman Joel Barnett declared himself happy with the 30 per cent cuts. Other MPs had said that, should there be trouble, there should be no hesitation about getting in touch with them. There were certain backbenchers from all parties who would be very concerned about the degree of cuts. Eldon Griffiths, Conservative MP for Bury St Edmunds and a member of the Foreign Affairs Committee, had recently been to Wilton Park, and had suggested both that the whole Committee should do likewise, and that the Ministries of Defence and Trade should also become aware of it. There might be scope for following up on this, perhaps with a letter to *The Times*. Sir Peter Tennant, still in the chair owing to Sir Robert Birley's illness, suggested that he should write to both Eldon Griffiths and Sir Anthony Kershaw, who would be prepared to do whatever they could.

On the substantive issues, the Academic Council went over familiar ground. Tim Slack felt that the Review had been handled irregularly. The arguments against Extra-Mural Visits and the *Wilton Park Journal* had been based on bogus evidence. No member of Information Department in the FCO had been on an Extra-Mural Visit until after the Review came out. The FCO had claimed that it had included an inspection; but the procedures of an inspection had not been carried out. He had not been consulted about staffing levels and no evidence at all had been produced to justify cutting staff, as had always been the case on previous inspections. The Institution of Professional Civil Servants (IPCS) was also concerned by this.

Several members of the Council thought that the Director should have more latitude, for example to negotiate charges for outside conferences. Tim Slack agreed, but said that it all came back to the need to have enough staff to do a proper job. He personally was more concerned by this than by his own grade and status.

Nevertheless, it was the proposal to downgrade the Director that most exercised the Council. The only explicit dissenter was Lord (Hugh) Thomas who had written to Sir Peter Tennant before the meeting:

> I regret that I cannot be present on Wednesday to put my views personally ... My own feeling is that the Government's proposals as expressed in John Belstead's letter of June 18 are about right. The cuts will surely enable a most interesting institution to survive if at a lower level of dignity. I cannot believe that this lower level would prevent a determined and imaginative director from making a major contribution. Many ambassadors do a good job at the level of DS 4, as all of us know who travel in Latin America.

Frank Giles, Editor of the *Sunday Times*, also thought that the Council should make the best of an imperfect job, although expressing disapproval at the way the Review had been conducted. But he thought that the Director's status was something that affected the standing of Wilton Park as a whole. Could it perhaps be 'fiddled'? Edmund Dell believed that it was the only matter of substance that the FCO was likely to concede, and he was therefore prepared to press that one point. When EDC had been merged with Wilton Park there had been no suggestion that this would affect the status of the Director. Hugo Herbert-Jones wondered whether a solution to the problem might not be to remove the Director's post from the orthodox, mainstream civil service rules, ill-adapted to Wilton Park.

Lord Beloff thought that the FCO was taking unjust advantage of Slack's contract's coming to an end. Tim Slack explained that the reason he had been left as contract member of staff was that as a DS 3 he could not be transferred sideways within the civil service. He believed that a dishonourable advantage was now being taken of a contract instituted for that very different reason.

If the Academic Council thought that the FCO was interfering in management affairs by seeking to fix Wilton Park fees, it would have been more indignant still if it had seen a minute that Leon Brittan, Financial Secretary to the Treasury, wrote on July 9, 1982, to Malcolm Rifkind, Parliamentary Under-Secretary of State at the FCO. Urging that the fees be put up, he commented on the Review:

> You will not be surprised to learn that I regret the narrow mandate given to those conducting this review. I accept that you do not share the view that Wilton Park conferences have outlived their usefulness. Nevertheless, we would have been more reassured by a report which actually considered whether they had a continued raison d'être.

On July 26, Belstead replied to this, since Wilton Park was now his responsibility:

> The Inspector's Review ... considered the raison d'être ... [and said that] 'A recent survey of OECD posts provides support for the proposition that Wilton Park is indeed effective in winning friends and influencing the right sort of people.' All the evidence we have shows that it is an invaluable part of Britain's overseas information armoury.

Lord Belstead was indeed between two fires. Less than two weeks after his exchange with the Treasury, at 11.00 a.m. on Thursday August 5, 1982, he faced Sir Peter Tennant, chairman of the Academic Council in succession to Sir Robert Birley, who had died after his long illness on July 22. Tennant warned Belstead that 'there would be a row, including letters to *The Times*, and that the German Chancellor Helmut Schmidt might get involved, bearing in mind the passage on Wilton Park in his and the Prime

Minister's summit communiqué of last November'. This skirmish was the beginning of a long battle of words.

That same day, Belstead wrote formally to the Academic Council arguing that:

> Some of the points raised ... seem to go rather beyond the normal areas of academic interest on which the Council has traditionally offered advice ...
>
> I regret that it would not be possible for the Director to be free to modify elements of our carefully balanced package within an agreed total.
>
> Wilton Park is not like those bodies to whom we give Grants-in-Aid approved by Parliament. It must remain subject to central control like our Embassies and other FCO units.

If the FCO's tone was growing firmer, there was also growing impatience with what it regarded as Tim Slack's 'lobbying'. As one official noted, 'Mr Slack has had over 7 months to feed in his views, which he has done at all levels and at great length.' In one respect, at least, this had been less effective than Koeppler's similar action in the past. When on August 12 a senior official explained FCO's position to the German Chargé d'Affaires, he was told that the Director's grade was 'of no importance to the German Government and in no way affected its high opinion of Wilton Park'.

Meanwhile, however, the suggestion of last June that Tim Slack might receive a 'mark time salary' had been considered by the Treasury, and on August 25 Leon Brittan gave it his approval. In one sense, this was encouraging: but in another it may have helped harden the FCO's determination to proceed with the downgrading of the Director's post. On September 8, Tim Slack had several meetings at the FCO. Though officials were disappointed that the Director seemed not 'to have fully hoisted in the point that he must now stop arguing and carry out Ministers' decisions', Slack, for his part, was also disappointed. 'Coming back from my meetings with you yesterday', he wrote to the FCO on August 9, 'I think I felt more gloomy about the future than I have done throughout the crisis'.

Sir Peter Tennant may well have felt the same. After the August break, on September 10, 1982, he replied on behalf of the Academic Council to Lord Belstead's earlier letter:

> My colleagues and I on the Wilton Park Academic Council have noted your letter of August 5 and are disturbed by its tone and by the FCO's evident intent to hold Wilton Park on an ever-tighter rein by intervening in the day-to-day management of the centre. We are concerned at the reference to Wilton Park being equated to Embassies in terms of central control;

such a view strikes at the vital academic independence of the institution ... Your letter reprimands us for not minding our own business, which in fact is to maintain this freedom and high academic standards. We do not hold that Whitehall knows best and would wish to remind you that we are unpaid volunteers of some standing and with a wide experience of the realities of life and the day-to-day realities of Wilton Park. It is irksome to us to see an operation of good repute and improving standards emasculated for an insubstantial and ephemeral advantage.

As if to belie tales of lobbying, Richard Luce told Lord Belstead on October 5 that 'Mr Slack had played a particularly responsible role recently in restraining the more dissident members of the Council.' But this by no means prevented the onset of political protests. On October 18, Eldon Griffiths wrote to Belstead saying that he was 'deeply disturbed' about the cuts at Wilton Park and that there was 'real danger of something very valuable being damaged'. 'This we must not allow!' he exclaimed. A week later, on October 25, Lord Beloff wrote an article in *The Times* on the subject under the headline 'THE FO: SOFT SOAP, BUT NO HARD SELL'. It complained about what Beloff called 'the myopia of officialdom'. On the specific issue of Wilton Park he spoke for himself and his colleagues:

> It is now common knowledge that the Academic Council of Wilton Park, the FCO discussion centre, is at odds with the FCO about the effect of the economies imposed on it in the latest round of cuts. It is the view of the Council that the scale and nature of these cuts make it impossible to underwrite the quality of an institution which has won respect and admiration throughout the Western world and beyond.

Sir Peter Tennant wrote to *The Times* in similar vein on the following day. And on October 29, braving the lioness's mouth, Tim Slack wrote to Sir Anthony Parsons, who had returned from being UK Permanent Representative to the United Nations in New York and was now at No. 10 Downing Street as Special Adviser on foreign affairs to the Prime Minister. Parsons's daughter had been at Bedales when Slack had been its headmaster; and as well as congratulating him on his new post he felt able to raise the question of Wilton Park.

On the same day, *The Times* published a letter from the Pro-Vice-Chancellor of the University of Surrey, Otto Pick, which concluded:

> It is particularly serious that the economies proposed by the FCO for Wilton Park represent a serious threat to that institution's standards.

> Wilton Park has succeeded in combining objectivity with academic excellence to a high degree, and it is this mix which has created its unique reputation and which has served this country so well over the years. The FCO should think again before it is too late.

This was followed on November 3 by another letter from Sir Peter Tennant, who pointed out that the total annual cost of Wilton Park was just under £500, or 0.1 per cent of the FCO budget. Some 15,000 people had been there. The original target for cuts had been 25 per cent; the Inspector had recommended 44 per cent. The compromise offered by the FCO was 30 per cent. 'The Council believes', said Tennant, 'that this condemns Wilton Park to a lingering death and undermines its academic freedom'.

The Foreign and Commonwealth Office, as well as *The Times*, was bombarded with mail. On Friday, November 5, William Waldegrave, Conservative MP for Bristol West and Parliamentary Under-Secretary of State at the Department of Education and Science, wrote to the Foreign Secretary, Francis Pym, urging him to 'maintain a reasonable level of support for Wilton Park', which he described as 'an extremely useful institution'. On the same day, Sir Julian Ridsdale, the Conservative MP for Harwich with long experience of Japan, wrote to Cranley Onslow, Minister of State at the FCO, enclosing a letter on Wilton Park which Sir Peter Tennant had distributed fairly widely. It complained, among other things, that the FCO Inspector had failed to discuss Tim Slack's workload with him, and in 75 minutes with Alan Hughes had spent only two on the workload question – although 14 months earlier an FCO Management Review had said both were overworked. On Monday, November 8, Sir Geoffrey Johnson Smith wrote to Pym supporting Tennant and Beloff, and Professor Hugh Seton-Watson of the University of London wrote to *The Times* deploring Wilton Park's 'imminent emasculation or demise'.

That week and the next saw a further angry flurry. On Tuesday, November 9, Max Beloff told the House of Lords, in the debate on the Address, that the proposed cuts would 'damage the potential of Wilton Park'. Next day, David Alton, the Liberal MP for Edge Hill, Liverpool, sent Francis Pym a cutting from *The Times* of November 3 and in his covering letter warned of a 'disaster': 'I think it would be tragic if any proposed cuts were made and, as a consequence, the quality of the work done by, and at, Wilton Park were severely impacted.'

Nor did the postbag's contents come only from London. Also on November 10, the Chancellor Emeritus of California State University and President of the Institute for Contemporary Studies, Glenn Dumke, wrote to Francis Pym pleading on behalf of Wilton Park. On Thursday, November 11, Agnes Headlam-Morley, Professor of International Relations at Oxford University, sent a letter to *The Times* endorsing what Seton-Watson had written earlier in the week. Giles Radice, Labour MP for Chester-le-Street, wrote on the same day to Douglas Hurd, then Minister of State at the Home Office: 'I was appalled to hear of the proposed cuts in the Wilton Park budget.' The next day, Friday November 12, Eldon Griffiths wrote to Sir Anthony Parsons, suggesting that Wilton Park might be helped by cash from outside.

On the following Monday, November 15, another United States Professor Emeritus, John C. Weaver of the University of Wisconsin, begged Francis Pym to spare Wilton Park. But by now the Foreign Office had begun to riposte in public. That morning, *The Times* carried a letter from Lord Belstead himself defending the FCO's policy. 'There is no question,' he wrote, 'of damaging, much less abolishing, this excellent institution':

> The Government fully recognise Wilton Park's contribution to under-standing of British and overseas institutions and attitudes. To show our confidence in its future, the lease on Wiston House is being renewed for seven years, compared with the existing five-year lease ...
>
> The savings we now aim to achieve, after taking into account the suggestions of the Academic Council, amount to a reduction of only 15 per cent in current resources ...
>
> These measures will not, in any way, affect Wilton Park's academic freedom, which we are determined to safeguard. They are designed to strengthen Wilton Park's long-term future and I am confident that, with the co-operation of all concerned, its high reputation will be fully preserved.

That evening Malcolm Rifkind, Under-Secretary of State for Foreign and Commonwealth Affairs, replied to an Adjournment Debate on Wilton Park in the House of Commons. Cyril Townsend, Conservative MP for Bexleyheath, opened the discussion, at 11.03 p.m., by quoting recent contributions to *The Times*, and instancing such distinguished speakers at Wilton Park as Helmut Schmidt, Bruno Kreisky, and Leo Tindemans. Chris Patten, Conservative MP for Bath and a member of the Academic Council, broke in to remind the House of Schmidt's joint communiqué with Mrs Thatcher at their 1981 Bonn 'summit'. Townsend continued:

> Our EEC partners were promised that the merger of the European Discussion Centre with Wilton Park earlier in the year would not diminish our commitment to the Community.

Much of the success of Wilton Park has been due to the knowledge of the participants that, although the Foreign and Commonwealth Office provides the overwhelming share of the budget, Wilton Park is run on the basis of academic freedom. Wilton Park has not been seen as the mouthpiece of the British Government of the day. This independence has made an essential contribution in attracting for more than 30 years men and women for whom officially inspired discussions would have little or no appeal. I regret to inform the House that this self-denying ordnance by the Foreign and Commonwealth Office has become less obvious in recent months. It cannot be right that an old and tried British tradition should give way to what has become a form of direct rule. Civil servants, however capable they may be, should not become the managers of Wilton Park – that is the task of the Director and his staff.

Townsend then told the story of the Review and its recommendation of 'massive cuts' which, the Academic Council warned, 'might seriously damage the whole operation'. He described the FCO's compromise figure of 30%, which was being implemented:

The majority of the Council is of the considered opinion that this will undermine the centre's academic freedom and condemn it to a slow but sure decline. Two particular and highly damaging decisions have been made by the Foreign and Commonwealth Office.

First, it decided, wrongly, to downgrade the post of the Director. Ministers concluded that the job belonged rather more in grade four than in grade three. As the post is a contract post, the Director has reduced pension rights, and he is not provided with accommodation. Secondly, it has reduced the academic staff from five to four at a time when, in the view of those directly concerned, the burden of work is being increased ...

Those last two decisions appear to me and many others to be a downgrading of the centre itself.

What is the point of assuring the centre of its future with a seven-year lease if its reputation is to be undermined in that clumsy way? The sum of money involved is an unbelievable £23,000. I am grateful to the Minister for coming to the House to reply to the debate. Why has he allowed the crazy row to simmer for so many months for such a paltry sum? The row has been of sufficient importance for the Select Committee on Foreign Affairs, of which I am a member, to carry out an investigation ...

Richard Luce, Conservative MP for Shoreham followed by attesting that:

Wilton Park is in the heart of my constituency. It has made a distinctive contribution to the greater international understanding of the United Kingdom and international relations as a whole since the war ... It is diffi-

26. Sir Robert Birley, Chairman of the Wilton
Park Academic Council (1950–1982).

27. Dr Bruno Kreisky,
    Federal Chancellor
    of Austria, opened the
    221st Wilton Park
    Conference in
    September 1980.

28. The Rt Hon. Sir Geoffrey Howe, British Foreign Secretary, attending the conference on USA and Europe in March 1984.

29. Alan Hughes, Deputy Director (1972–1984), in 1984.

30. Group photograph of the Employment Crisis conference in November 1986. Participants included Gordon Brown, as a backbench Member of Parliament, seated next to Geoffrey Denton, Director of Wilton Park (1983–1993).

31. Sir Geoffrey Howe and Geoffrey Denton admire the 1576 ceiling of Wiston House's Great Hall during the March 1984 conference.

32. Tim Slack, Director of
Wilton Park 1977–1983.

33. Richard Langhorne, Director of Wilton Park, (1993–1996).

34. HRH The Prince of Wales signing the Golden Book at
Wilton Park's 50th Anniversary Conference 1996.

35. Harry Goring (right) welcomes the Prince of Wales to Wiston
House with (left to right) John Knight (High Sheriff of West
Sussex) and Sir John Coles (Permanent Secretary of the FCO).

36. Colin Jennings,
    Chief Executive of Wilton
    Park (1996–).

37. Richard Latter, Director
    Wilton Park (1987–)

38. Nicholas Hopkinson, Deputy
    Director, Wilton Park
    (1987–)

39. Peter Hain, Minister of State for Foreign and
Commonwealth Affairs (centre) with Senator Khairat
Abdu-Razaq, Senator for the Federal Capital Territory
Nigeria (left) and Olatunji Abayomi, Chairman, Human
Rights Africa, Nigeria, at the conference on Challenges
for Governance in Africa, September 1999.

40. Hanni Kapper, right,
(sister of Heinz
Koeppler) with Dr.
Hedwig Theisen
attending the Wilton
Park 50th Anniversary
of the first Wilton Park
conference at Wiston
House in January 2001.
Dr. Theisen was a
participant in 1951.

41. Dr. Rainer Barzel (right), former Chairman of the CDU and speaker at
the January 2001 Event with (centre) Lode Willems the Belgium
Ambassador to the UK and Tim Slack.

42. Lord Hurd of Westwell shaking hands with
    Bel Anda, Deputy Spokesman Office of the
    German Federal Government at the annual
    British German Forum in July 2001.

43. (left to right) Esperanza Aguirre, President of the Senate, Jose Maria Anzar,
    Prime Minister, and Colin Jennings, at the Economic Reform in Europe
    conference in El Escorial, Spain, in February 2002.

cult to quantify these matters, but Wilton Park is irreplaceable. Now, more than ever, there is an international requirement for dialogue and cross-fertilisation of views across the international spectrum ...

As for the grading of the Director, I have always believed that the graded director should be decoupled from the Foreign Office system. There is no point in having him graded with ambassadors. It is a distinctive post and it should be graded as such.

Robert Rhodes James, Conservative MP for Cambridge, sounded an initially sceptical note:

I have had some doubts about the direction of Wilton Park. I have also had some doubts about the value by themselves of international conferences. However, Wilton Park, in my experience, is one of the most important facilities for international dialogue in the United Kingdom.

Eldon Griffiths recalled that, when he went to the United States every year, he spoke to audiences from politics, business, industry and the academic world:

I find that Wilton Park is admired and appreciated everywhere. The Foreign Office and the Academic Council are separated by the equivalent of the salary of one Assistant Secretary in the Foreign Office. That is perhaps £23,000 a year.

I tell my Friend the Under-Secretary of State that that sum can be raised, and would be raised, from the private sector and from our friends in the United States and Germany, if only the Foreign Office would allow the Academic Council time to bring it about.

The debate had been in progress for little more than fifteen minutes when Malcolm Rifkind rose to wind it up:

The Government recognises the great value of the Wilton Park conferences, which are a British contribution to the creation of informed international public opinion. They help to promote an understanding of British and overseas institutions and attitudes ...

Rifkind gave no ground, however, on extra-mural visits or the *Wilton Park Journal* – nor on the grading of the Director and the reduction in the Academic Staff. On the percentage cuts, he said:

The net reduction in current resources is only 15%, as 7% of the saving has already been achieved by the merger of Wilton Park and the European Discussion Centre last January. A further 8% should come from additional revenue from the extra outside conferences ...

And he reaffirmed: 'We have no wish to interfere with the Director's autonomy in the choice of conference themes, speakers and participants, nor with Wilton Park's renowned academic freedom.'

For the champions of Wilton Park, the outcome of the debate was disappointing. On the following day, Tuesday November 16, 1982, Eldon Griffiths wrote to Lord Belstead, reiterating the point about private capital that he had made the night before:

> It astonishes me that Conservative Ministers should be supporting the FCO bureaucracy's resistance to mobilizing the available – and continuing – opportunity to supplement the FCO's own grant for this uniquely valuable institution.

Similar mail continued to pour in during the weeks leading up to Christmas, 1982, often enclosing letters from Sir Peter Tennant.

Unlike previous lobbying, little of this led to second thoughts in the Foreign and Commonwealth Office. Instead, it seemed to spark irritation. As early as November 23, 1982, at least one senior FCO official was growing critical of Tim Slack's complaints, especially about having been hustled over the Review: 'His actions seem to me to have destroyed the basis of confidence upon which I, Information Department, or our successors, would require to work with him in the future.'

At a meeting with Slack two days later, he warned the Director that:

> there would be a further round of cuts. I said that no one had suggested wishing these on Wilton Park, but the possibility could not be excluded. It was even possible that someone would think of suggesting that Wilton Park be abolished altogether.

One feature of it had been abolished already. This was the *Wilton Park Journal*. By a curious anomaly, however, it managed one last issue – No 65, Winter 1982 – before it finally expired. David Spence had prepared the text before the fate of the *Journal* was confirmed, and he argued successfully that to cancel at so late a stage would be uneconomic. So, just after Christmas, readers received a plump 66-page edition. On the cover was a pale grey photograph of Wilton Park's long-standing friend, patron, and defender, the late Sir Robert Birley, Chairman of the Academic Council from 1950 until his death on July 22, 1982. His narrowed eyes shrewd but friendly, his long, lined face on the brink of a smile, his buttoned suit jacket hopelessly crumpled, he looked just about to intervene with some penetrating remark. What he might have said at the present juncture was unguessable: he had seldom taken the obvious or orthodox line. The

Journal reprinted part of Sir Peter Tennant's tribute to him, originally published in *The Times*:

> Leading international figures in politics, management and unions, academic life and journalism have met at Wilton Park and remained in touch under the wise chairmanship of Robert Birley, who not only lectured and summed up at many of the conferences but guided the Directors of Wilton Park in the planning of their programmes. As an historian he was always able to illuminate current problems with apt anecdotes which never lapsed into anecdotage.
>
> His support of the activities of Wilton Park was backed up by old pupils friends and colleagues from his many incarnations in the world of education, who rallied to him whenever the future of the centre was at risk. His contribution through Wilton Park to the understanding of this country and the understanding of international problems by future leaders of the Western world has been outstanding. And many thousands of Britishers and foreigners will remember their debt to this wise and humorous scholar.

In this final edition, David Spence's stocktaking suited the *Journal*'s valedictory issue. So did his reprinted article by Heinz Koeppler which he quoted, on 'A Hundred Wilton Park Sessions', written for its 22nd number in December 1959. But Spence nowhere alluded to the journal's demise. He published articles by such diverse authors as Henry Birdseye Weil of Pugh Roberts Associates, François Simon of *Le Monde*, the Minister of State for Trade Peter Rees, Jonathan Holmes of BBC Panorama, and Neil Kinnock, Opposition Spokesman on Education. He described the recent travels of Wilton Park staff members and staff changes at Wiston House itself; and he printed the full programme of 14 conferences to run from January 16 through December 16, 1983. He made no mention of the current crisis. He could not, of course, have predicted the repercussions it would have in the coming months.

The New Year began amicably enough, but with some hardening of positions. On January 5, 1983, Sir Peter Tennant saw Lord Belstead. He broached the question that Eldon Griffiths had put in last November's Adjournment Debate: could the Academic Council not raise money for Wilton Park? Belstead answered that the Foreign and Commonwealth Office would have no objection to that – provided that any such funds were not used to pay the staff. This brought them back to the sticking point of the Director's downgrading in situ. It looked, said Tennant, 'as though he were being punished for some wickedness'. Belstead repeated the familiar FCO argument; and they parted without a further meeting of minds. At the same time, Tennant and his colleagues lost a potential ally in the dispute when Sir Anthony Parsons wrote from No 10 Downing Street: 'I do not want to become embroiled.' On January 11, a senior official recalled that Leon Brittan had told FCO Ministers that Wilton Park was 'the kind of marginal activity which he believed should be ended in the context of the Government's expenditure cuts'.

But its defenders had not given up hope. Giles Radice, who had already tackled Douglas Hurd on the subject, wrote to Malcolm Rifkind's private secretary, also on January 11, to say that he felt 'very strongly' that the FCO's treatment of Wilton Park and its Director was 'a very mistaken economy'.

It was more than that. For Tim Slack, it was 'the third time since I came to Wiston House in February 1975 that I have been the victim of ill-faith or mistakes'. In a memo on January 12, he rehearsed the occasions: starting at the bottom of his grade in 1975 despite assurances that he would start near the top; having to go through the selection process a second time in 1977 because the Civil Service Department had insisted on subtracting his previous years as Deputy Warden from his five-year appointment as Director; being downgraded, now, despite 'a clear understanding on the part of ... the Selection Board that a second contract would respect the conditions of the first. Only the special nature of Wilton Park prevented the Director being established in 1978 like everyone else.' This had implications not only for his salary, but for his pension.

By now, indeed, the downgrading of the Director had become the only major bone of contention between the FCO and the Academic Council. On January 13, the Council empowered Sir Peter Tennant to write to Lord Belstead accepting the reduction of the Academic Staff from five to four. But on the Director's status it was adamant. So was Tennant's letter the next day: 'We request you to re-examine your decision. If you are unable to revise this the Council is unanimous in insisting on outside arbitration.'

Shortly afterwards, on January 17, 1983, the Foreign Affairs Committee of the House of Commons issued a report on Wilton Park opting for neither the FCO plan nor the Academic Council's. Noting that the Council believed that it could raise funds for several years to cover an annual gap of £23,000, the report concluded:

> We repeat our view that no step should be taken which would jeopardise Wilton Park's future. We very much hope that agreement can be reached between the FCO and the Wilton Park authorities to secure the future of the Wilton Park conferences and their valuable contribution to understanding and co-operation between the OECD countries.

Meanwhile, preparations for awarding a new contract, whether or not to Tim Slack, had had to begin. On January 25 the post was advertised in *The Times*. For Slack himself, it was becoming urgent to decide his future. On January 27, he visited the FCO and its Personnel Policy Department to discuss the post and its possibilities. Sensing the possibility that he might accept a downgraded contract, officials were agreeably open to ways of softening the financial blow. The Head of Information Department told him that the Treasury was agreeable to his buying back added years for his pension and that he might be allowed to top up his salary by acting as Secretary to the Heinz Koeppler Trust. This, Slack said, he was unlikely to accept. But there was also the possibility of a 'mark time' salary in his old grade until that in the lower grade caught up with it.

On February 3 he told both Belstead and the FCO's Chief Clerk that he did not wish to accept a new contract when the present one expired on May 24, 1983. 'The FCO has not treated me honourably', he wrote to Belstead.

The FCO News Department had the story by February 7. Next day, Edmund Dell resigned from the Academic Council. He was the first of many: Lord Beloff and Sir Peter Tennant on February 9; Roger Morgan on February 10; Frank Giles on February 12; John Birt and Rosalyn Higgins on February 14; David Watt on February 18; Richard Goold-Adams and Sir Denys Wilkinson, Vice-Chancellor of the University of Sussex, who considered the affair 'intolerable and dishonourable', on February 21; Eric Heffer, Labour MP for Walton, Liverpool, on February 22; Russell Johnston, Liberal MP for Inverness, on March 4 'with sadness and anger'.

These were emotions widely shared. 'I am outraged', wrote the Liberal Party leader David Steel on February 9 to Francis Pym:

at the way in which I have been treated, not just because of our own Select Committee's report but also because I was instrumental in securing the availability of Tim Slack in the first place [in 1975].

It seems that penny-pinching is being allowed to ruin an excellent institution.

On February 11, the Lord of Appeal in Ordinary Lord Scarman, who had been an undergraduate at Oxford with Heinz Koeppler, asked Lord Belstead to reconsider his decision: 'I would like to say that I regard Wilton Park as one of the finest European and international initiatives ever taken officially by this country.' On February 17, Richard Needham wrote to Lord Belstead of his distress: 'at your refusal to reconsider the downgrading of Tim Slack. I really think that the Foreign Office decision is abominable.'

Such were some of the 44 letters on the subject before the end of February 1983, from 14 MPs (9 Conservatives, 3 Labour, 2 Liberal), three peers (2 Conservative, 1 Independent), two US academics, and two foreign Friends of Wilton Park. There had also been five letters in *The Times*, and a number of eloquent broadsides from Sir Peter Tennant.

It was hardly surprising that tempers began to fray in the FCO. 'Sir Peter Tennant', wrote a senior official on February 9, 'does not seem to have learned that rude letters don't get results'. Nor, as it turned out, did ambitious demands. On February 8, Lord Belstead inquired of his officials when Alan Hughes would normally retire – no doubt as a preliminary to asking him to be Acting Director at Wilton Park in the interim between Tim Slack's departure and the arrival of his successor. But on February 18 Alan Hughes wrote to Information Department with a series of requests that amounted to asking for nearly all the FCO's economy plan to be scrapped. Information Department found Hughes's letter 'somewhat high-handed', and other senior officials were 'appalled'. Its 'tone and content', they thought, indicated 'a total lack of understanding of the relationship between Wilton Park, the FCO, and HMG'. Did they? Heinz Koeppler might not have thought so. He might well have been 'appalled' had he read a manuscript comment from one official: 'I consider Mr Hughes should be given no leeway whatsoever; he must do as he is told.' Not for nothing had Roger Morgan, in his letter of resignation from the Academic Council on February 10, complained that FCO control over the running of Wilton Park had now 'become unacceptably tight'. Tim Slack believed that it had all begun some three years before, at the time of the accountant's misbehaviour. But, in his view, Information Department had lately tended to exert more control over the administration of Wiston House, as distinct from its finance.

What annoyed the FCO, however, was that its control was being challenged – in public, and by its own paid employees. On March 9, an official noted that:

> The letters by the former Acting Chairman of the Council, Sir Peter Tennant, to MPs, *The Times*, and overseas Wilton Park Associations were typed at Wiston House and owe much to Mr Slack's input. He himself gave oral evidence to the Foreign Affairs Committee last October in which he challenged our 30% saving goal and said it should be 25%.

On the same day, another wrote of Slack that:

I think it is true to say that he has effectively destroyed any basis for a future harmonious working relationship between the FCO and himself in future, if ever this was still on the cards ... He must have spent very many hundreds of man hours working up a Parliamentary lobby against our proposals.

In fact it was Michael Shanks, not Tim Slack and Alan Hughes, who had convened the March 8 meeting of the remaining nine members of the once 21-strong Academic Council. Lord (Hugh) Thomas and Derek Gladwyn were unable to attend. Those who did were Agnes Headlam-Morley, Hugo Herbert-Jones, Peter Nailor, Chris Patten, George Scott of the EEC Commission, Shanks himself, and Ernest Wistrich of the European Movement. In a letter to Lord Belstead the next day they confirmed:

We share the views of our colleagues who have resigned. We have grave doubts whether in present circumstances we have a useful continuing role ...

We would not wish to be associated with the selection process for a new Director until the relationship between the FCO and Wilton Park, which in our view has been radically altered by recent events, can be clarified.

Despite the cooling of relations, Tim Slack went to see the PUS on Friday, March 11, 1983. Morale at Wiston House, he said, was 'very bad'. As the next Director, he added: 'Don't appoint a diplomat!' He also spoke with Information Department, who on the following Monday, March 14, reported:

I understand from Mr Slack that this [the Academic Council's concern about FCO control] related to whether the FCO have the right to lay down the length and frequency of conferences, whether they include EMVs, and whether the *Wilton Park Journal* should continue. I have explained that all these points were part of the independent Review package designed to achieve 30% savings, but that there might be room for adjustment (e.g. fewer but longer conferences) provided we could be certain those 30% savings were achieved.

If this was an olive branch, or twig, hostilities continued elsewhere. Wednesday's Guardian newspaper carried an article about the cuts. It contained a quotation from Sir Peter Tennant: 'For the price of installing a new bathroom at Wilton Park they could allow the Director to carry on at his own level.'

The Guardian article was a curtain-raiser to an Unstarred Question

Debate that evening, March 16, in the House of Lords. Seven speakers from all the main parties criticised the FCO's action. They included Lords Beloff, Ezra, Hooson, Walston and Gladwyn, who called for a Bill to rectify matters. Only two – Lord Belstead and Lord Greenhill of Harrow, a former FCO Permanent Under-Secretary – defended the cuts.

On the following day, in a further attempt to resolve the dispute, FCO officials suggested that Tim Slack, Alan Hughes, and the members of the Academic Council should debate the whole affair with senior FCO officials. A meeting was scheduled for April 20, 1983.

Meanwhile, Richard Luce and Chris Patten began to discuss a more radical approach which might free Wilton Park from dependency and red tape. On Thursday, March 24, they wrote to the Foreign Secretary, Francis Pym:

> We think that the time has come for taking a totally fresh look at the matter and for considering what might crudely be called the Tadworth [Hospital] solution, that is re-establishing Wilton Park on a quasi-autonomous basis with a guarantee of a Government grant over a number of years to which the institution would be able to add those funds that it was able to attract from other sources.

If this notion seemed conciliatory, Patten remained firm on the subject of Tim Slack's grade. 'How many Foreign Office posts of Under-Secretary rank', he asked Lord Belstead on March 28, 'have been downgraded while the occupant has actually been in post?'

The question remained unanswered two days later when Patten and Luce went to see Francis Pym. They had the backing of a lot of MPs, they said, but had resisted forming an all-party delegation. The Tadworth solution, a mixture of public and private finance, would enable the Director to be paid out of private funds and thereby avoid the problem of civil service grading. The public funds could take the form of an FCO grant-in-aid.

The immediate response was only partly encouraging. Lord Belstead pointed out that Wilton Park's record of financial management in the past had been 'frankly poor'; and legislation would probably be needed for public-private finance. Finance Department in the FCO was against such a solution; Personnel Policy Department advised delaying it until after the 1984 Review. There was no objection in principle, however, to raising outside funds. The danger was that the Treasury might use them as a pretext for reducing any grant-in-aid, thereby restoring the unsatisfactory status quo. Years later, the Luce/Patten proposals would look remarkably prescient. But their moment had not yet arrived; and the machinery for seeking a new Director was already beginning to move. The post was advertised on March 31.

On Wednesday April 13, the Head of the FCO Finance Department – one of whose hobbies, as he said in *Who's Who*, was laughter – went down to Wiston House to talk with Tim Slack and Alan Hughes about a Discussion Paper that the FCO was preparing for the Academic Council's meeting in London on April 20. Essentially, it was a welcome and encouraging attempt to respond to the Council's request for Wilton Park and its Director to be given more independence. It at once took the bull by the horns:

FCO Relations with Wiston House management:

1. The Director has a free hand in academic matters subject to taking into account suggestions from the Wilton Park Academic Council and the International Advisory Council. In particular he is ultimately responsible for the choice of themes, speakers and participants though he should make full use of the advice available in the FCO and Diplomatic Service posts.

The Discussion Paper went on:

2. On the administrative and financial side the Director is sub-accounting officer responsible to the Permanent Under-Secretary, as Accounting Officer, for all expenditure and receipts relating to Wiston House. The responsibilities can be divided into three sections:
(a) The FCO will decide the staff establishment and the cost of basic salaries and national insurance, including the notional cost of headquarters staff in the FCO. The FCO will also decide on all accommodation related expenditure now the responsibility of the PSA.
(b) For all other expenditure an overall ceiling will be laid down for each financial year and individual ceilings will be set for specific items, e.g. food and drink, housekeeping, travel and transport, laundry, books, newspapers and miscellaneous items, all of which needs to be in Vote 5 – as well as casual labour, overtime and telephones, telex, postage (old Vote 1 items). Subject to consultation with the FCO the Director may switch expenditure between these items within the overall ceiling.

(Why, asked Hughes, must the Director consult the FCO on such switching so long as he remained within the annual budget? 'This is no devolution of financial management.')

(c) As regards receipts, the FCO in consultation with the Director will decide on fees for Wilton Park and outside conferences, including those

run by FCO Training Department and other Government departments plus spouses' fees in such a way as to cover marginal costs and to
make a sufficient contribution towards overheads to fit in with the
annual FCO subsidy to Wiston House; the target for this subsidy (this
is net annual expenditure) will be a figure yielding savings over
1981/82 estimated net expenditure as close as possible to 30%.
Charges for staff rent and meals will be set so as to cover marginal costs.

(This, said Hughes, again implied detailed control. The Director must be
free to reduce or increase fees, or waive them altogether, so as to maximum
earnings and occupancy, and generally ensure the quantity and quality of
participants.) The paper concluded:

3. In all matters affecting Wiston House, the FCO will consult the management as closely as possible.

Despite Alan Hughes's strictures and suspicions, the Discussion Paper
was a move in the direction of '*patti chiari, amicizia lunga*'. On Wednesday
April 20, four members of the Academic Council – Michael Shanks, Agnes
Headlam-Morley, Hugh Thomas, and Ernest Wistrich – went to Lord
Belstead's office to talk it over with him. Three of the members called for
Tim Slack to stay on as Director of Wilton Park; only Lord Thomas
argued that a new person was needed. The FCO officials explained that
the recruitment procedure had already begun for a Director at DS 4 grade;
so that if Slack applied he might forfeit any special personal concessions.
The Council members promised to let Belstead have their considered reactions to the Discussion Paper as soon as possible.

On the following Tuesday, April 26, Tim Slack went at his own request
to the FCO to discuss the new guidelines. The next day, they talked again.
Having slept on the matter, Tim Slack said that, in the light of the new
ideas about financial devolution and management flexibility, he now saw
the way open for him to renew his contract and for the absent members of
the Academic Council to withdraw their resignations. The Heinz
Koeppler Trust was 'almost there', and might supply the much-needed
extra funds.

FCO officials seemed somewhat taken aback by this change of mind.
They pointed out, as before, that the current job advertisement was for a
DS 4 post, without the special terms that had been considered for Tim
Slack's personal situation. There had now been nearly 100 applicants.

Two days later, on the afternoon of Friday, 29 April, Michael Shanks,
Agnes Headlam-Morley, Hugo Herbert-Jones, and Ernest Wistrich met in

London with Tim Slack and Alan Hughes to finalise their reactions to the FCO Discussion Paper and hear Slack's report on his talks with the FCO. 'In general terms,' they wrote: 'we draw encouragement from the tenor and contents of the discussion paper in that it goes some considerable way to allowing a looser machinery and considerable degree of devolution for Wiston House management.'

To clarify matters further and to seek reactions to their proposed amendments, the Council members agreed that Patten and Shanks should seek an early interview with Lord Belstead.

The meeting took place on Tuesday May 10, 1983. Patten and Shanks handed over the Council members' brief response to the Discussion Paper, including the proposed amendments. They said that the Council members would be willing to take part in the Selection Board for the Wilton Park Director if their conditions were met. Belstead and his officials said that Lord Thomas had already offered to do so, and to help sift applications: the FCO had gladly accepted. Patten and Shanks protested vehemently. Thomas, they pointed out, was in a minority of one on the Academic Council and did not represent its general thinking.

They were unaware that on the previous Friday, May 6, Francis Pym had met Belstead and senior FCO officials who had told him they believed it was too late to stop the recruitment process and offer Tim Slack the special terms that had previously been devised. On the same day as the meeting with Patten and Shanks, the FCO gave the bad news to Slack. It was, they said, too difficult to stop the selection process; but he was welcome to submit his candidature along with the other candidates. Slack answered that he was not prepared to justify himself a second time to a selection board when his past record spoke for itself and when the FCO admitted that, in extremis, the selection procedure could be stopped. He therefore decided finally to leave when his contract expired on May 24, 1983. It was a bitter moment. But Tim Slack still had much to contribute to the work of Wilton Park.

It was no doubt pure coincidence that on the very day of his formal departure from Wiston House, the Treasury renewed its Thirty Years' War of attrition. Information Department had, on May 10, sent a copy of the Discussion Paper to the Treasury, which on May 25 commented in writing that:

We do not think that an adequate case has been made out for continuing indefinitely the present level of subsidy for Wiston House. We think that the fees, as currently charged, could be increased to a level which would cover the cost of running Wiston House, while keeping the Wilton Park conferences intact.

In line with this hope, it added:

> We can see no reason why private finance should be barred from contributing to the ordinary running of Wiston House, although ... any long-term outside finance designed to meet regular basic expenditure would result in a compensating reduction of the subsidy provided from public funds.

To the FCO, any prospect of phasing out the subsidy to Wiston House sounded unrealistic. As one FCO official explained to the Treasury's Aid and Overseas Services Division, 'at no stage in Wilton Park's 37-year history have fees been able to cover more than a quarter of total costs'. The Treasury riposted on June 24 that 'departments should normally recover the full cost of any service they provide' – perhaps forgetting that Wilton Park was providing a service to the Government. The Head of the FCO Finance Department commented four days later. If laughter was among his hobbies, it must this time have been sardonic. The Treasury's letter, he wrote, was 'wretchedly negative':

> It highlights our difficulties with the current Treasury mentality ... *The Economist* was right earlier this year to say (disparagingly) that 'the Defence and Foreign policies of this country are being run on the lines of high street business'.
>
> I think we must go back very robustly here. We have perhaps accepted too readily in the recent past that the Treasury have the right to be so negative with us and to interfere in this sort of way with, e.g., the management of our Information programme. Particularly when they patently do not understand (or care about) its aims ...
>
> We are not 'providing a service': we are seeking to influence people. Influencing people costs money.

Further amendments to the Discussion Paper had helped to clarify still more the demarcation lines between Wiston House and the FCO. Writing to Alan Hughes, now Acting Director, on June 3, Information Department accepted the three points made by the Academic Council members, with the proviso that, if the Director had his pay supplemented as secretary of the future Trust, this should not interfere with his duties as an FCO employee or raise any conflict of interest. It added further adjustments of wording to make the text more flexible in response to Hughes's concerns. 'I think', the FCO concluded, 'we have gone a very long way to meeting the wishes of the Academic Council'.

The Council, like Wilton Park, was itself somewhat in flux. Already in April, FCO officials had discussed reshaping it after the dozen resignations that had left it so small. As one official noted: 'It would be nice to have back Professor [Rosalyn] Higgins and Mr [John] Birt, and one or two others, but some have been so critical of the FCO that it would be unwise to encourage their return.' On April 25, the FCO suggested that the Council members should be fewer and politically balanced, with the FCO represented at their discussions. This was the case when the Council held its next ordinary meeting at the FCO on Monday July 18, 1983, with three FCO officials sitting in.

Michael Shanks presided as Acting Chairman, and welcomed two new members: William Wallace from Chatham House, and Roderick Cavaliero from the British Council, deputising for Sir John Burgh. Both Wilton Park and its Council, said Shanks, were almost back to normal. Although there was no Director of Wilton Park, Alan Hughes had in the meanwhile taken on the role 'manfully' and was doing very well.

In the meantime, Shanks continued, a Board had been held for a new Director, and the candidate provisionally selected was Professor David Greenwood of Aberdeen University. A senior FCO official explained that there was a slight delay in the appointment, since Professor Greenwood wanted to know the rules on living in London, continuing personal research and publishing articles, while the FCO wanted to be sure that such outside activities were compatible with the post of Director at Wilton Park. In the end, after three months' debate, Greenwood withdrew.

Alan Hughes reported that between May 1982 and April 1983 attendance at Wilton Park had been lower than in 1981/82. In terms of sheer numbers, the first two conferences in 1983 had been 'rather disastrous'. The subjects – 'Destructive divisions in modern society: class, race, and access to work' and 'The political seismology of the Middle East and Gulf' – might not have been attractive; it was a bad time of year for travelling; some governments were cutting back expenditure. But since March numbers had gone up, especially, with FCO help, from non-OECD countries. He was also trying, fairly successfully, to get more participants from southern Europe. There was an increasing tendency, he noted, for Wilton Park to attract specialists. This doubtless reflected the more targeted nature of the conference themes. He was trying to balance the specialists with more generalist UK participants. The reduction in conference staff meant that savings would have to be made, probably for the present in simultaneous interpretation. When the fifth member of the Academic Staff had to go, it was hoped that he or she might find an alternative post in the FCO. A name had been put forward, but the final decision was up to the new Director.

When Michael Shanks had said that the Council and Wilton Park were 'almost back to normal', the word 'almost' had had point. As regards the Council, new members were needed to fill the gaps. As regards Wilton Park, much depended on the meaning of 'normal'. For the FCO, normality was now defined by the Discussion Paper. For Alan Hughes and his colleagues, it meant the greater autonomy, real or apparent, enjoyed by Heinz Koeppler. Amendments to the Discussion Paper had nudged it in that direction, giving Wilton Park slightly more latitude. And the Conference Calendar for 1984, which Alan Hughes outlined to the Council and circulated ten days later, tended to test the limits of that extra scope.

It proposed twelve conferences, two of them of five days each and co-sponsored, nine of them of one week each, and one of them of two weeks. All save the five-day conferences were to include extra-mural visits, probably full-day. Simultaneous interpretation was to be limited, and conference fees were to be raised by an unspecified amount.

The FCO reaction was mild but critical. On August 5 1983 the FCO wrote to Alan Hughes noting 'an interesting range of subjects' and presuming that it contained 'some flexibility ... to enable the new Director to feed in any of his own thoughts'. On the question of fees, they asked how they had been reached, and added that they would of course have to be agreed with the Treasury. The letter went on:

> This said, there are a few aspects of the 1984 Calendar which we find disappointing ...
> I think we should have no illusions about the likelihood of further questions from the Public Accounts Committee in due course.
> He cited the small number of conferences – 10 down from 14 in the current year, the re-insertion of two-week conferences, and the introduction of an Extra Mural Visit.

The FCO's letter arrived at Wiston House while Alan Hughes was on leave. When he replied on September 13, 1983, his only real disagreements in principle were on two-week conferences and extra-mural visits:

> Two-week conferences do scare people off at first sight – most notably, in my experience, our posts abroad. They also positively attract others. I know one Frenchman, who I am keen to get to a conference, who has told me he will only come for a fortnight or not at all. Several reactions so far received to my circular letter of 28 July also welcome the reinstatement of the two-week conference ... Also many participants who come from further away (e.g. US West Coast) feel their long journeys only justified by a full fortnight here. Unquestionably the effect on participants is more than double that of a one-weeker ...

EMVs must be relevant to the conference theme and not just a mid-week breather. But this does not weaken our conviction, strongly supported by evidence, of the intrinsic value of EMVs ... We are sure that extra conferences without an EMV would be of lower value.

Hughes concluded:

I believe that departures from the original Reviewer's recommendations, if well considered and based on our own practical experience and judgement, will not offend the Public Accounts Committee; indeed, knowing some of its members I think some of our ideas and proposals may well find favour.

Both Hughes and the FCO agreed that decisions taken in the interregnum could not easily be definitive. True, 1984 conference dates and themes had to be fixed now; but the new Director would naturally be able, said Hughes, to influence the detailed programming of individual conferences not already published. Likewise, it would be up to him to decide what to do in 1985 and after, but Hughes believed that he should certainly have the chance of experiencing one two-week conference himself in 1984.

Ironically, when that two-week conference began, in July 15, 1983, the new Director was to be away for two weeks in Germany. But by then there had been considerable changes at Wiston House. Some of them were painful. Some were overdue.

CHAPTER 23

New Broom

'Management that wants to change an institution must first show it loves that institution.'

John Tusa, *The Observer*, February 27, 1994

Wilton Park's new Director was appointed on Monday October 17, 1983. It was Geoffrey Denton. He had read PPE at Oxford, had been Reader in Economics at the University of Reading, Head of Economics at the College of Europe in Bruges, Director of the Federal Trust, and Special Adviser to the House of Lords European Communities Committee. His own childhood had been disrupted by World War II. His wife, Marika, was a Hungarian Jew whose father had died on the Eastern Front, had herself been in hiding from the Nazis and their Hungarian collaborators, and had taken refuge in Britain after the 1956 revolution. So, though of a later generation than Heinz Koeppler, Denton shared with him a strong commitment to international understanding, and was a keen supporter of European integration and the ending of the East-West divide.

Denton knew Wilton Park well. He had been impressed by the quality of its international and inter-professional discussions; but already at his interview in June 1983 he had proposed a number of possible reforms. Soon after taking up his post at Wilton Park, he had talks with the FCO. He took with him a draft policy paper on Wilton Park. This identified several signs of strain in the system: the difficulty of recruiting top-class participants, the lack of 'product' in the sense of reports and other documents, and constant pressure from the Treasury. Denton wondered whether conferences could be shorter, whether there could be more sponsored, outside and special meetings, and whether more participants could come from London, including the FCO. Notably on publications and shorter meetings, Denton's views contrasted with those of Heinz Koeppler, who had discouraged written reports and defended longer conferences. Sooner or later, he seemed likely to clash with custodians of the Koeppler tradition.

The FCO accepted that during his first six months Denton needed one day each week to fulfil his outstanding teaching commitment at Reading University, and that he would continue to live in London and commute to Wilton Park. When he arrived at Wiston House, he was greeted by Alan Hughes as an old acquaintance. 'His first remark', said Hughes later, 'boded well: "You have worked tremendously hard to keep Wilton Park going and as Acting Director you have run it for five months; I can well understand you may resent my coming in now above you." I thanked him for his thoughtfulness' Hughes went on, 'and told him I looked forward positively to working with him; I asked only that he respect the great conference experience accumulated by the Wilton Park staff and that before making changes he should seek our views and advice. It seemed a good start.'

Geoffrey Denton was less sanguine. He sat in on the first conference under his Directorship; and while impressed by the quality of the discussions, he had other misgivings. As he said afterwards, he found the chairman and the speaker enthroned on chairs, as Koeppler had been, while the participants were in low armchairs, 'almost lying on the floor and very uncomfortable. They were ranged in several rows in a semi-circle, most looking at the head of the person in front, and unable to see anyone speaking from behind them.' He determined in future to replace the armchairs with upright chairs placed around a table, to give everyone equal status with the chairman and speakers. This, he thought, would facilitate face-to-face discussion, and also the taking of notes.

Many of the tutors, too, had been recruited as interpreters, not primarily conference organisers, and were not expected to turn up except when their linguistic skills were needed. One tutor had a cottage in the grounds, where he gave private English lessons. Another spent much of his time in Paris. Yet interpretation from English into French and German had already been abandoned, and Denton suspected that within a few years interpretation into English would also prove unnecessary. If he managed to broaden Wilton Park's geographical scope, then Spanish, Russian, and Chinese would be more relevant than French and German; and interpreters for these languages could be hired when they were needed. As soon as he could, he insisted that the tutors be more than just interpreters, however brilliant, and that they organise and attend the conferences.

The participants, in line with Koeppler's policy, tended to be 'generalists', sometimes of poor quality and advanced age, and the conferences were not, to his taste, specialised or specific enough. Instead of a predominance of academics, officials, and journalists, Denton hoped to recruit more scientists, business people, and experts to exchange their particular insights. This also pointed to a need to shorten and intensify the conferences to suit busy people, leaving weekends free to hire out Wiston House.

Denton's reforms were radical, challenging, and unpopular: they took four years to carry out in full. By the autumn of 1987, all but one of the tutors who had been on the staff in October 1983 had left and been replaced. One, Valerie Seward, strongly supported the changes, and stayed on. Another, David Spence, agreed that the reforms were essential, but personally preferred to move in 1985 to a post at the Civil Service College. Broadly, however, the secretarial, administrative, and domestic staff saw reform as essential for the survival of Wilton Park and of their employment there.

Geoffrey Denton presented his policy proposals to the Wilton Park Academic Council when he met them for the first time on Wednesday morning, November 23, 1983, at the Foreign Office. The members broadly approved. As well as Roderick Cavaliero, George Scott, Professor Hugh Seton-Watson, William Wallace and Ernest Wistrich, several new members were present: Barbara Beck, Secretary-General of the Anglo-German Foundation for the Study of Industrial Society; Sir Geoffrey Chandler, late of Shell and the National Economic Development Office; David Dilks, Professor of International History at the University of Leeds; Peter Hordern, Conservative MP for Horsham; John Pinder of the Federal Trust and the European Movement; and Edward Rowlands, Labour MP for Merthyr Tydfil. The FCO was also represented. In the absence of Michael Shanks, who was ill, Peter Nailor took the chair.

After the meeting, Barbara Beck wrote to Ray Whitney, Parliamentary Under-Secretary of State at the FCO, giving her impressions of the Council meeting:

> I was much heartened by the down-to-earth, practical nature of this morning's discussion. In my view Wilton Park is and remains an excellent idea, but had become a little complacent; there now seems a good chance that it will update itself, try out promising new ideas and become better value for money.

There was certainly briskness in the air. There was also brusquerie. For all his considerable virtues – intelligence, expertise, and organising ability – Geoffrey Denton was not the most patient of men. He believed that

Wilton Park could not afford to waste time. After nine weeks trying to impose his will at Wiston House he was both critical and cross. He spoke very frankly of his impressions when he telephoned an FCO official on December 19. His strictures – not always tactfully expressed – had gone down badly with the tutors, and things were approaching 'the crunch'. 'The Academic Staff', the official reported Denton as saying,

> had been allowed to develop into a small introverted body (he actually called them at one stage 'a disorganised rabble'!) and they were determined to continue with past practices. They were resisting strongly the implementation of the policy programme which Mr Denton had devised and the Academic Council had approved. The Academic Staff were holding meetings of their trade union and a confrontation seemed inevitable ... They were unwilling to take on the tasks of preparing background briefs for conferences and to report on the outcome of conferences. They also objected to working on co-sponsored conferences, on the grounds that the FCO would then say that the staff were not sufficiently occupied if they had time to devote to such conferences. Mr Denton said that one member of the Academic Staff ... was however co-operating fully and had advised him to join the staff trade union, in order to avoid a clash with the union, if it should come to that.

On the following day, Denton went to the FCO. He was still indignant – and determined. He complained that the main resistance to change in general, and to his policy proposals in particular, came from the Convenor of the Wilton Park branch of the Institute of Professional Civil Servants, Jim Starkey, and from the former Acting Director, Alan Hughes, whom he described on a later, less tense occasion as 'a workaholic devoted to Wilton Park'. Hughes had proposed that, as Deputy Director, he should run the conference programme and manage Wiston House, while the Director should concentrate on external relations, representing Wilton Park abroad and vis-à-vis the Foreign Office, and continuing his academic activities. This seemed to Denton like a bid to run Wilton Park. He therefore decided that he needed to spell out, in writing, what Hughes's new role in Wiston House was to be, and he sent him a letter making three points. First, Hughes was to handle the administration of foreign participation in Wilton Park conferences; secondly, he was to be responsible for drumming up 'outside' conferences; thirdly, he was to be the Accounting Officer, in charge of financial administration but not financial policy. The letter would also make it clear that he would deputise for the Director whenever the latter was absent. Denton had agreed that Hughes would have the Christmas break to mull over the terms of the letter, which he sent on December 22.

In it, Denton admitted that:

> In the course of trying to make an early impact, and above all to improve
> our credibility with the FO and elsewhere, I may well have failed to take
> the careful course of consulting well in advance and leaving time for your
> views to be taken into account. However, when I have consulted you by
> sending documents, comments have not always been forthcoming.

He had consulted staff in writing, he explained later to FCO officials, to
avoid the long and disputatious Academic Staff meetings he had witnessed
as an observer in his first week. His letter to Hughes plainly admitted that
they disagreed, and made a final appeal for co-operation:

> We have to recognise that there are important differences between us with
> regard to both style and policy (for example, relations with the FO,
> Conference Reports, chairmanship) ... My policy follows guidelines laid
> down by the Minister when offering me the appointment. The statement
> contained in my paper to the Academic Council was approved by them and
> has also been endorsed by my supervising Under-Secretary.
>
> This, therefore, is the policy on which I shall look forward to having
> your co-operation in the New Year.

Appropriately, 1984 was to be a traumatic year.

It began with a death. On Sunday, January 22, Michael Shanks died.
He was only 56. He had had a varied and distinguished career, moving
from journalism to the civil service, then to business, to academic life, to
the European Commission, and to the Academic Council of Wilton Park.
He had held together the remains of the Council after twelve resignations,
without compromising on the principles for which the twelve had
resigned. Peter Nailor was a worthy successor, as he was also to prove with
the Heinz Koeppler Trust.

At Wilton Park, Geoffrey Denton was still pressing his plans for
reform. As he told the FCO on January 30, he proposed shorter conferences, beginning at 5.00 p.m. on Mondays and ending at Friday lunchtime.
This would enable busy people to start and end their working week in their
offices, and also make room for weekend conferences at Wiston House –
such as the Federal Trust had successfully held in Denton's day. Extra-
mural visits he planned to shorten to half a day, or even drop altogether.

His zeal for change did not stop there. On Sunday, March 11, he had
the opportunity of talking with the Foreign Secretary, Geoffrey Howe.
Next day, Howe's Assistant Private Secretary reported the conversation to
Information Department. Denton would be happy, he had said, with some

staff reductions at Wilton Park. At present, there were seven Academic Staff, including the Director and Deputy Director. Some were inter-preters, with no particular academic ability. He believed that he could manage with five staff instead of seven. As an FCO noted on May 3, these proposed cuts were more drastic than those recommended in 1982 by the Inspectorate's Review, which had proposed to reduce the Academic Staff by only one.

News of impending changes inevitably leaked out to overseas friends. On March 28, René-Louis Picard, President of the *Société Internationale de Wilton Park*, wrote to Geoffrey Denton stressing the importance of simultaneous interpretation, arguing that conferences should last at least a full week, condemning 'bilateral' meetings with one partner organisation, doubting the usefulness of East European participation, and calling for the *Wilton Park Journal* to be reinstated and published in English, French, and German.

Picard, as the British Embassy in Paris confirmed, was not always the easiest of people to deal with: his *Société* consisted mainly of elderly right-wingers. And his letter, thought Denton, had a familiar – and suspicious – ring. As he told Information Department on April 3:

> It appears to represent a fundamental attack on all the new policies: inter-preting, length of conferences, so-called bilateral conferences, joint conferences, the *Wilton Park Journal*, participation of Socialist countries. We shall clearly have to find a way of heading off this kind of criticism from the Amis and the Mitglieder, while holding to the new policy. This attack could also revive opposition within the House. A show-down may be neces-sary, and even desirable, but I suppose we want the least possible fuss ...
>
> P.S. Some of the information about the new policies to which Picard's letter refers has not been communicated to him or to any others in the Friends. We can only assume he received this information from inside Wiston House.

To stem some of the speculation, Denton debated the new policies with Old Wiltonians at their reunion meeting at Linz in Austria on March 17–20, 1984.

There were financial as well as policy reasons for some of the changes Denton proposed. He spelled these out in a note to the FCO on April 17, confessing that Wilton Park was falling short of its cash targets, but claiming that staff cuts and strict austerity could save £97,000, which a few more economies could make £100,000. On May 4, Denton discussed these suggestions with senior officials face-to-face. By now, it was beginning to be clear what staff cuts he had in mind. FCO officials turned their minds to ways of softening the blow and dampening the likely explosion. The fatal decision was taken at a meeting in the Foreign and Commonwealth Office chaired by Parliamentary Under-Secretary of State Ray Whitney on Monday June 11. It was agreed, his private secretary reported a week later, to follow Geoffrey Denton's proposals to abolish the Deputy Directorship, declare Alan Hughes redundant, and (on the basis of the 1982 Report's recommendation) ask Oliver Hayward to transfer to another post. 'It was further agreed', the minute added, 'that the two individuals concerned would not be informed until after July 28 when Course 268 was due to end'.

That Course, planned in all innocence by Alan Hughes before Denton's arrival, had the all too apt theme of 'The State and the Individual in 1984: was Orwell Wholly Wrong?'

When the Academic Council held its next meeting, at Wiston House on Friday June 22, Geoffrey Denton reported on most – but not, obviously all – of the changes that were now under way. Current innovations included background notes issued before each conference to give participants more advance information, and conference reports on the main lines of the discussion. These maintained the off-the-record rule of Wilton Park, but were valuable as tangible evidence of the quality and scope of each conference. Another of his innovations – ultra-short conferences – he planned to maintain. As he said later, in a note to the Wilton Park staff on July 11, 'we should normally have the House reasonably fully occupied from Mondays to Fridays, with occasional use at weekends'. However, he told the Academic Council, if the 1984 two-week conference was a success it might be repeated.

For 1985 he planned to group 15 weeks of Wilton Park conferences under a number of themes, to host 17 weeks of FCO training courses, and to leave 16 weeks available for outsiders. If Wilton Park were successful in attracting outside conferences, he would make a case to the FCO for retaining some of the proceeds rather than simply paying it back to the Treasury and reducing the FCO subsidy. In fact, even if Wiston House were fully let for 300 nights in the year, revenue earned at £50 per room would still cover only about two-thirds of total expenditure. As it was, he planned to continue co-sponsored conferences, notably with the Japanese mission to the EEC in Brussels and with the European Commission itself, and he envisaged at least two joint conferences. Answering inquiries from Hugh Seton-Watson, Barbara Beck and John Pinder, Denton said he would like to hold up to 6 regional conferences on Eastern Europe: he hoped in any case to continue expanding participation beyond the OECD, including East Europeans. His own experience of talking with Hungarians on economics had been fruitful; and he had discussed the question with the FCO. One FCO official remarked at this point that outside the conference rooms even 'apparatchiks' might relax in the informal atmosphere of Wiston House.

Soon afterwards, Wilton Park received backing from an august source. On July 11, the Prime Minister's Private Secretary, wrote to the FCO to say that Mrs Thatcher had approved an article on 'The role of Great Britain in the Contemporary World' to be published in the Commemorative Booklet for the 10th Anniversary of the Swiss Association of the Friends of Wilton Park. Her contribution contained a passage which might have been devised as FCO protection against future Treasury attacks:

> All democratic countries have a wider responsibility for promoting round the world the values they profess. This is where Wilton Park plays such a useful role and it is no coincidence that Wilton Park has so many friends in Switzerland. They, like all Swiss, recognise that the vitality and contribution of our democratic societies depends in large part on the open, questioning approach to common problems exemplified by Wilton Park.
>
> For me, Wilton Park represents many of the virtues which modern Britain offers to the world: confidence in proven values combined with readiness to challenge doubtful assumptions; the courage to voice unpopular views but tolerance of reasoned dissent ...
>
> I know Wilton Park has played an important part in keeping our two countries close and I wish your Association of Swiss Friends of Wilton Park well for the future.

Germany, not Switzerland, was Geoffrey Denton's next port of call. He left for two weeks' leave there – and a visit to Karl Weishäupl, Chairman of the German Wilton Park Association – just as the two-week course on 'The State and the Individual: was Orwell wholly wrong?' was due to start at Wilton Park on Sunday July 15. The opening speaker that evening was Peter Hordern, Conservative MP for Horsham. Other prominent speakers included Johan Galtung (Founder and Former Director of the Oslo International Peace Research Institute), Dr Bernard Crick from Birkbeck College, University of London, Alan Beith (Liberal MP for Berwick-upon-Tweed), Professor Richard Hoggart, Professor Oscar L. Steenhaut (Rector of the Free University of Brussels), Ray Buckton (Chairman of the TUC), Lord Pitt of Hampstead, Sir James Eberle (Director of Chatham House), Gough Whitlam (former Prime Minister of Australia), and – at the closing session – Denis Healey, Opposition Spokesman on Foreign and

Commonwealth Affairs. At the end of Healey's session he said: 'What an impressive group of participants.' There were 49 of them, from 18 countries, including Australia, New Zealand, Poland, Turkey, the USA and Yugoslavia. There were two extra-mural visits: one to the Palace of Westminster, the other (lasting two days) to Bristol (for policing and child studies) and Swindon (for industrial redevelopment and information technology).

The whole conference was a timely and memorable event, in the tradition of Heinz Koeppler. Even financially, it was a success: with a highest-ever fee of £690 per person, it brought in £32,730 – the biggest single sum that Wilton Park had ever earned. It was a triumph for its main organiser, Alan Hughes. But it was also, as he discovered three days later, his swan song as Deputy Director of Wilton Park.

At 5.00 p.m. on Monday July 30, 1984, Hughes signed his thank-you letter to Denis Healey. At 5.35 p.m., when he had reached home, the telephone rang. It was an assistant in the FCO's Personnel Operations Department. He was calling to say that his post of Deputy Director at Wilton Park had been abolished, and that he must prepare himself for redundancy.

Next day, as requested, Hughes went up to London and in the afternoon saw the Head of Personnel Operations Department. He was polite and apologetic to Hughes, but had to hand over the FCO's formal letter and memorandum notifying Hughes of the decision and setting out the procedures and financial conditions. On the following morning, Wednesday August 1, Geoffrey Denton returned from leave, and 9.30 a.m. met Alan Hughes. The occasion was unpleasant for both of them. Denton did his best to explain the decision to abolish the Deputy Director's post: there had been tremendous pressure from the Treasury to cut costs. He apologised for not having told Hughes personally. His failure to do so was wide open to objection, but from his point of view it was comprehensible. To avoid long delay, he had had to seek Ministerial approval before Parliament's summer recess; but had he announced the decision when it was taken, this would have deeply blighted preparations for Hughes's triumphant George Orwell conference. No less understandably, Alan Hughes called him a coward for not having told him in person.

Similar considerations had delayed the announcement that Oliver Hayward was to go. He too heard the news after the end of the Orwell conference; but it was given more tactfully. It was also accompanied by the offer of alternative employment within the FCO. Hayward was to understudy the Head of the Translation Branch of the Library and Records Department, and succeed him when he retired in September 1985.

The fact – and the manner – of Alan Hughes's departure provoked indignation and concern. On Friday August 17, just before going off on holiday to France, Hughes had a long interview with an old colleague at the FCO. It was Nicholas Barrington. As Head of Information Policy Department, he had been responsible for Wilton Park from 1976 to 1978. 'I ... take some credit', he said, 'for its survival at that time'. Now Barrington was back (from Tehran and New York). He was now Assistant Under-Secretary of State. At this higher level, his responsibilities once again included Wilton Park. And, once again, he had inherited trouble. Alan Hughes reported afterwards: 'He was very open with me, even indiscreet, and certainly sympathetic. I have heard it said that he is upset at having to administer a decision which, had he been in his job at the time, he would not himself have taken.'

As a responsible official, Barrington had to be loyal to what had been decided. On July 31, no doubt expecting outcry, he had written to members of the Academic Council:

> Mr Denton has reached the conclusion that there is no work for a Deputy Director which cannot be performed by himself, other members of the Academic Staff, and the Bursar ...
>
> In deciding which of the five members of the Academic Staff should be asked to leave, Mr Denton had to take into account how the residual workload could best be distributed among the remaining members of staff. This meant taking into account the qualifications, experience and skills of each member of the staff including his own. Mr Denton's concern was that there should be an appropriate balance of skills on the part of the four remaining staff, and on this basis he concluded that Mr Hayward should be asked to leave.

If Barrington had expected an outcry, he had been right. On Wednesday August 8 Sir Peter Tennant wrote Barrington a frankly startled letter. Tennant was no longer on the Academic Council, but – like Tim Slack and Alan Hughes – he was a Trustee of the Heinz Koeppler Trust. He had heard by chance about how Hughes's post had been abolished, and he called it 'a devious way to go about a delicate and distasteful operation with an old and trusted servant of the Crown'. Recalling the Academic Council's partly successful resistance to the 1982 Review and its failure to prevent the downgrading of the Director's post and hence Tim Slack's decision not to renew his contract, he continued:

> In the end I and others resigned from the Council and I refused Francis Pym's invitation to become its chairman because of the FCO's inept

357

personnel policy ... To lose one director, Mr Worthing, may be regarded as a misfortune; to lose his deputy as well looks like carelessness ...

I was associated with Wilton Park for a long time and took part in recurring battles with and between the FCO and the Treasury on cutting its finances. There is always much talk of cost effectiveness but in the end the importance of cost seems to outweigh that of effectiveness, and it might be a more sensible decision to abolish Wilton Park altogether rather than continue diminishing financial support to a lame duck. But the reason for the present decision, while probably spurious, is less important than the ill-mannered and incompetent behaviour of the FCO as an employer. It is a shocking story and I am sad that you should find yourself landed with this baby. If the FCO were a good private firm the man to fire would be the head of personnel, but the privatisation of our foreign policy is an unlikely option. Nevertheless one wonders whether the tax-payer should tolerate this kind of ineptitude.

Barrington answered this letter on August 22. He pointed out that in recent years the FCO's financial support for Wilton Park had increased in real terms in spite of the public expenditure cuts. But as long as Wiston House was receiving a subsidy of over £500,000 a year, the FCO must keep its cost-effectiveness under review.

Tennant replied, on September 3, that what he feared most was that Denton might turn out to be a weak manager, and that Wilton Park might become 'a direct extension of the FCO without the illusion of independence it had before with Heinz Koeppler and Tim Slack'. This fear, as Alan Hughes noted, seemed to be confirmed by the phrasing of an FCO minute that Oliver Hayward saw that October: it said that 'the Director is putting in a lot of effort to make the conferences more relevant to the FCO's objectives'.

This was the old dilemma. Some FCO and Treasury officials – and especially their Ministers – wanted Wilton Park to prove that it was promoting not only Britain's image, but also its interests and even its policies. Again and again, such critics had to be reminded that Wilton Park was not a propaganda outfit, but a centre for enlightened debate. As such, it most effectively presented Britain as a nation democratic, self-confident and relaxed enough to tolerate and support totally free discussion of world problems, including trenchant criticism of the UK itself. It was what might be termed 'the Koepplerian synthesis' of international altruism and enlightened patriotism. Nicholas Barrington understood it in 1976-78. So, *pace* his bitterest critics, did Geoffrey Denton, with his experience of the Federal Trust. His close relations with the FCO – as became clear later – were to preserve Wilton Park's reputation and show that the Koepplerian synthesis really worked.

On Friday, September 12, 1984, Barrington paid his first visit to Wiston House since assuming his new duties. Members of the Academic Staff spoke their minds to him about Alan Hughes's plight – especially David Spence and the trade union representative Jim Starkey. As Barrington noted afterwards:

> They recognised Mr Denton's academic credentials ... and the merits of his discarding humdrum interpretation work and leaving more nuts and bolts activities to the competent secretaries. They felt that the pace at which Mr Denton now wished to drive Wilton Park was too hot, and that quality and personal contact with those attending conferences would suffer.

Hughes's union – the Institute of Professional Civil Servants – advised two courses of action: a formal appeal by Alan Hughes against his personal redundancy, and a plea to the new FCO Parliamentary Under-Secretary of State, Tim Renton, about the post of Deputy Director.

Hughes's appeal began on Monday September 24, when he appeared before the FCO Sub-Committee convened to hear his submission against redundancy and his plea for alternative employment. The FCO made twelve attempts between July and October 1984: its help included testimony from Barrington that Hughes later described as 'embarrassingly complimentary'. But the trawl found no suitable posts in either the FCO or the Home Civil Service. Hughes worked for some months in Amsterdam at the European Cultural Foundation; but although he applied to some 20 outside institutions in all, and had excellent references from his many friends, he remained on paid 'gardening leave' while his case was fought. It was concluded on November 13, 1985. On the following day he took early retirement. But, as in the case of Tim Slack, this was by no means the end of Alan Hughes's connection with – and services to – Wilton Park.

'I do not doubt Tim Renton's sincerity', Hughes wrote later, 'in insisting that I be found another good job'. On October 22, Renton listened sympathetically to Jim Starkey and representatives of the IPCS. 'We recognise', he wrote to them afterwards, 'Alan Hughes's valuable contribution to Wilton Park over the years and I am sorry that he has to leave.' But there was no real prospect of reversing the FCO's decision on the post of Deputy Director. Alan Hughes rightly described Renton as 'by all accounts a liberal and decent man ... Incidentally, as a fellow-student at Magdalen College, Oxford, he is a close friend of Erhard Dornberg, Heinz Koeppler's best German friend and ex-prisoner-of-war protégé.'

Irrespective of the Koeppler connection, Tim Renton was drawn into the discussion of Wilton Park partly in reaction to his postbag.

Much of it came from North American friends of Hughes's whom he saw on a lecture tour of the US and Canada in the second half of October 1984, paid for by the University of Missouri. When Geoffrey Denton followed, in November 1984, he indeed found the American Friends of Wilton Park 'disorganised and demoralised'.

As ever, Renton was understanding and friendly. But he had to look to the future. As he wrote to Tennant on October 9:

> I think it is inevitable that we are now going to have, under the new Director, a Wilton Park Mark III, which will be slightly different from its predecessors, but the main objectives will remain and I believe the institution will still go on doing a good job.

Geoffrey Denton took a similar evolutionary view in the essay he wrote for the Swiss Wilton Park Association's Commemorative Booklet, or *plaquette*, to which Mrs Thatcher had contributed. Published on October 24, 1984, it won congratulations from the Prime Minister: 'It bears eloquent witness to the strength and vitality of the Association and to its firm attachment to the Wilton Park ideal we all hold dear.' Denton's contribution stressed:

> In 1957 perhaps the most important threshold in the history of Wilton Park was crossed when participation was formally internationalised to the extent of covering the membership and associate membership of OEEC, later OECD, thus involving the USA and subsequently Japan. By the 1970s even the latter basis was seen to be too narrow and Wilton Park began to welcome participants from the Third World ... The latest development of membership has brought in the first participants from Eastern Europe ...
>
> Whereas the original Anglo–German sessions lasted a month or even six weeks, and the majority of conferences in the 1950s and 1960s took up a fortnight, the 1970s saw a move to a duration of one calendar week ...
>
> *Pari passu*, the nature of conference work itself has changed from the broad subject areas of earlier days to the closely targeted conference titles of today. These are in no sense technically specialist, but they do serve better the needs of contemporary Wiltonians who come to a conference from as many different professional backgrounds as ever but with a well defined special interest in the given theme.
>
> Finally, Wilton Park, while jealously guarding its own independence, has begun a fruitful process of co-operation with like-minded bodies whether official or private in two forms: co-sponsored conferences and joint conferences. The first are conferences organised by Wilton Park inte-

grally in its annual calendar but enjoying the financial and intellectual backing of co-sponsors. The second are sessions largely organised by other bodies which take place at Wiston House with meaningful involvement of Wilton Park staff in their planning.

Denton reported the recent traumas and his future plans to the Academic Council when it met on November 21, with Peter Nailor in the chair. There some disquiet over the staff changes, but with Oliver Hayward in a new job, and Alan Hughes no longer in his Wilton Park office, which he had had to vacate on November 16, the painful process had become a *fait accompli*. Further departures were to follow later. David Spence was to leave in August 1985 for a job at the Civil Service College (and was not replaced for over a year). Robert Sturrock was due to retire after 27 years' service in August 1987. In the meantime, there were five staff to run 15 conferences in 1985 – three for each one, with each featured in a single page of the Annual Report that Denton now proposed. The scheduled subjects included Technology, the European Community, the Middle East, the Pacific Basin, South Africa, and East–West Relations. For 1984/85, Denton estimated, the total expenditure would be £669,000.

Five days after the Council meeting, the *Société Internationale de Wilton Park* held its traditional end-of-year dinner at the *Cercle de l'Union Interalliée* in Paris. Geoffrey Denton was unable to be present, but Robert Sturrock was there. The British Ambassador, Sir John Fretwell, was also absent owing to the imminent Franco-British 'summit' meeting. But the UK Consul-General and Information Counsellor at the Embassy made the speech in French that Fretwell would have given. It too emphasised the evolution of Wilton Park in a rapidly evolving world:

> Wilton Park, like many other institutions which have made their mark on the contemporary political scene in Western Europe, was created by men and women whose vision of the world was enriched by the chaos and suffering of war. Those events marked for ever those who lived through them. There is little danger that they will forget the values that Wilton Park is pledged to promote.
>
> But there are now leaders and decision-makers who have not seen with their own eyes war's horrors – people of my generation, who were born during the war. And that leads to a new danger, the danger of complacency, of blind optimism, of insouciance – or in certain cases, among those who fall for our enemies' propaganda, the danger of excessive fear. In both cases, institutions like Wilton Park risk being thought of as exclusive clubs, looking not towards a dangerous future, but backwards to an epoch that to our children already seems as remote as the battle of Waterloo seemed to us. So we must be vigilant. Wilton Park must adapt if it is to still be

relevant to much of today's society.

'This speech', wrote René-Louis Picard, President of the *Société Internationale de Wilton Park*, 'was highly encouraging for our Society'. The March 1985 issue of the Society's annual *Bulletin*, in which he reprinted and praised it, echoed it in reminding readers that Wilton Park was forty years old. 'The celebration of this anniversary will take place over the weekend following the 287th Wilton Park Conference (December 9–13, 1985) on "Germany in a Divided Europe and a Divided World".' To mark the occasion, Wilton Park was looking to the future of what had been its very earliest concern.

CHAPTER 24

Forty Years On

'At twenty years of age, the will reigns; at thirty, the wit; and at forty, the judgement.'

Benjamin Franklin, *Poor Richard's Almanac* (1741) June

Geoffrey Denton began the New Year of 1985 with an official visit to North America. He spent three days in Canada (January 6–8) and four (January 9–12) in the United States. His aim was to revive, reassure and if possible rejuvenate the transatlantic Friends of Wilton Park. The American Friends were holding their Conference in Los Angeles under their new President, Professor Werner Hirsch. In London at the beginning of last August, Hirsch had confided that some US visitors to Wilton Park, 'though they may have been splendid persons, came from universities no one had ever heard of'. Many were also middle-aged or more, and worried by what they had heard of the new plans. As Nicholas Barrington told Denton on January 23, 'For a time to come there will always be some who will regard any change in the Koeppler formula as a form of *lèse-majesté.*' It was a general remark, but it applied especially to North Americans, who quite reasonably wondered whether the new short courses at Wilton Park really warranted a journey of several thousand miles. That argument – and a complaint about the FCO's cutting the budget – appeared in the American Friends' *Newsletter* in Spring, 1985.

This was only one of Geoffrey Denton's anxieties. Now that two of the Academic Staff had gone, some of their remaining colleagues were complaining of overwork. To alleviate it, Denton had suggested that his Personal Assistant become an Executive Officer and be replaced by a secretary. On March 21 the FCO's Personnel Operations Department noted: 'There are faint signs that the administration of Wilton Park is starting to crack under pressure ... It may be early days but it is worth recording that all does not seem to be well at Wilton Park.' Part of the problem was the lack of a likely replacement for David Spence, who was due to leave in August 1985. His post was 'trawled' in the FCO, but found no takers; a trawl in the home Civil Service produced only three candidates, none of them suitable. In the event, the post stayed vacant for over a year. Nor was this all. On July 5, 1985, Geoffrey Denton complained to Jim Starkey of what he called 'evidence of lack of commitment and negative attitude'. Next day, Starkey wrote to the Head of Personnel Operations Department, asking for a transfer from Wilton Park owing to 'deteriorating relations' with the Director. On July 24, another official of the Personnel Operations Department, after a meeting with Denton, described him as feeling 'isolated'. His only real supporter on the Academic Staff, he said, was the 'excellent' Valerie Seward.

There were also financial pressures. On May 13, Denton complained to the Financial Section of the FCO that, whereas he had proposed to recover 42 per cent of costs by raising the number of participants, increasing the fees charged, planning more joint and sponsored conferences, etc., the Treasury was demanding 45 per cent, which was unrealistic. The recovery achieved in 1983 had been 17 per cent.

There was one small bright hope on the horizon. On May 15, 1985, the Court of Appeal finally settled the case of Heinz Koeppler's Will. It had been a long and costly suspense drama. A week later, Geoffrey Denton told the Wilton Park International Advisory Committee that £100,000 'might accrue' to Wilton Park. It was an optimistic estimate. There were formalities to be completed – and, perhaps inevitably, further disputes.

Meanwhile, however, despite his critics, Geoffrey Denton made a speech that demonstrated not only that he understood and endorsed the Wilton Park that Heinz Koeppler had founded, but also that in the new circumstances it was still going strong. The occasion was an international colloquium organised by German Old Wiltonians at Lindau, on the Bodensee – Lake Constance – on June 14–16, 1985. In some Wilton Park conferences, said Denton, there were considerable difficulties of communication: 'The problem arose most acutely in the tripartite joint conference held in April to May 1985 with delegations from China, the US and the UK on "China, the UK and the US: an evolving relationship towards a more peaceful world".'

This conference, made possible by China's new policy of greater openness, and by the 1984 agreement on the future of Hong Kong, had been proposed as a joint venture by Ed Haddad, the Old Wiltonian Chairman of the Los Angeles World Affairs Council. As Denton reported:

About the fourth day of the seven-day meeting we openly confronted the fact that there had been misunderstandings.

There was complete difference in style of discussion. It was discovered that among Western countries there is usually an acceptance of wide basic agreement, and discussion therefore centres on problems. Chinese discussion devotes much time to expressions of agreement, while mention of a few minor problems symbolises wider areas of disagreement. Thus it was easy for the Chinese to be offended by what to them appeared a radical and even rude hostility, as Westerners criticised aspects of China's economic policies, for example. Westerners were misled by the Chinese style of discussion into thinking that the Chinese were agreeing with almost everything, whereas in fact the Chinese were attempting to indicate substantial areas of disagreement. Once this difference in methods of communication was brought out into the open there was a great relaxation of tension and the following discussions were much more fruitful.

It was exactly the kind of striving toward mutual comprehension that Koeppler had encouraged between Britons and Germans, now transposed from Europe to the wider world.

On more mundane matters, Denton gave a detailed factual report to the Academic Council when it next met, on June 21. As well as going to Lindau, the Academic Staff had travelled widely. Both Hughes and Denton had visited North America; Denton had attended the tenth anniversary of the Swiss Friends in Berne, and had gone to Finland, Stockholm, Barcelona, and Istanbul; Sturrock had attended the *Société Internationale* dinner in Paris.

Attendance at Wilton Park over the past year had dropped from 437 to 427, but was up to 511 if joint conferences were taken into account. The numbers from Australia were up from 4 to 14; from Italy, from 2 to 7; from Belgium, from 7 to 14; from the Netherlands, from 18 to 25; from Spain, from 8 to 14; from the UK, from 74 to 106; from international organisations, from 12 to 24; and from non-OECD countries, from 13 to 37. The most popular conferences were those on the Third World; the least popular, those in January and February. Conferences on the European Community seemed not to be notably attractive, especially to non-EC nationals. In 1984 the length of most conferences had been reduced to four days. While US academics preferred long courses, diplomats and businessmen preferred them to be short. Interpretation had been offered only from French and German into English since the summer of 1983.

The true cost of attending a Wilton Park conference was £2,000; the fee charged by Wilton Park was £270. The income from these fees for the whole year would probably be £130,000 – one-fifth of the budget needed to maintain Wiston House. The true cost to each participant, including travel, was about £1,000.

They were also relevant to the forthcoming 'Next Steps Report' on further cutbacks in the public sector in line with Mrs Thatcher's policy. One such 'next step' might of course be privatisation. Another might be the establishment of semi-autonomous Executive Agencies. Would such a status be suitable for Wilton Park? In preparation for the possibility, Nicholas Barrington asked Denton to draft a paper on Wilton Park's official objectives. On August 21, Barrington sent him back a rewrite of the draft. It was not an elegant document. But its emphasis on international understanding, academic independence and 'very special atmosphere' might have reassured even those most suspicious of FCO 'interference'.

The legacy of Sir Heinz Koeppler was now the responsibility of the Sir Heinz Koeppler Trust. Its members were Sir Peter Tennant, Tim Slack, Alan Hughes and Alec Frank. They held their first meeting on October 8, 1985, at the St Catherine's Foundation at Cumberland Lodge, Windsor Great Park, where – partly thanks to the FCO – Tim Slack had been made Principal after spending a year as Headmaster of the Hellenic College of London. In addition to dealing with routine administration, they appointed as their Chairman Sir Peter Tennant, and as a new Trustee Professor Peter Nailor, Chairman of the Wilton Park Academic Council.

The Trustees agreed, as they put it later in a publicity leaflet, that the Fund would be used essentially:

(a) To foster conferences or projects at Wiston House or elsewhere, to help pay the conference fees and travel costs of participants otherwise unable to attend, and to attract speakers of special interest.
(b) To promote study trips by Wilton Park staff and such activities as publishing the Journal and acquiring books and material for the Wiston House library.

Such grants, they decided, would be made out of income, leaving the Trust's capital invested. This stood at some £100,000 by the time of the Trustees' third meeting, in May 1986, yielding an annual income of about £5,000.

For the Trustees' first meeting, in October 1985, Alan Hughes had prepared a paper on 'General Policy for the Use of Funds'. This set out a number of 'criteria', reflecting Koeppler's views and philosophy, to apply in deciding what projects and activities qualified for grants from the Trust. As phrased by Alan Hughes, they looked like a last effort to row back against the tide of recent changes at Wilton Park:

(i) Avoidance of narrow specialisation – 'making experts think generally'.

(ii) Off-the-record cross-fertilisation of ideas, opinions and experiences between honest, intelligent people of widely varied nationalities, jobs/professions, political persuasions and age groups – 'denting prejudices'.

(iii) Eschewing purely academic work, professional research, and producing of reports and papers –'publish or be damned'.

(iv) Presentation of varied, even opposite, points of view with no attempt to gloss over ugly aspects, stupidities or differences of opinion, thus letting participants judge for themselves – 'the best form of propaganda is "warts and all"'.

(v) Preferring speakers to be practitioners rather than professional teachers – e.g. sessions on democracy and government to be led by Members of Parliament rather than political scientists – 'telling it how it is'.

(vi) Sheer passage of time to help participants lose inhibitions and get to know and understand each other; preferred length of conference was two weeks – 'real cost for busy people who come to Wilton Park is not money but time'.

These criteria survived verbatim into a Memorandum by the Trustees dated June 5, 1987, which was annexed to the Declaration of Trust. After some discussion, however, a further paragraph had been added:

In noting these practical criteria the Trustees also recorded as a seventh criterion Sir Heinz Koeppler's most important characteristic, namely his ability to change, such that the criteria listed above should be flexible (reflecting Sir Heinz Koeppler's own flexibility) and not exclusive.

Even with this prudent proviso, the criteria were at least a reminder of Koeppler's principles, and a moral incentive to preserve those that were still relevant. One of these was the 'Chatham House' rule of off-the-record discussion. Participants at Wilton Park conferences were at liberty to use any new information revealed there, but not to disclose its source or to attribute to any speaker whatever opinions might be expressed. Not long after Hughes had presented his paper to the Koeppler Trustees, the 'non-attributable' rule was breached by a British participant at Wilton Park. The culprit was an official from the Treasury, who on November 4, 1985, wrote a 'Note for the Record' about Wilton Park Conference No 285 (October 28 – November 1) on 'The external relations of the EEC: "Fortress Europe" or Open to the World?' Two days later, far from apologising, the Treasury added insult to injury, complaining that the conference in question had been too low-level: 'You and the organisers of such conferences might therefore like to consider whether anything can be done to improve their cost-effectiveness.' That strain again! 'A snide letter' commented one FCO official. From Wiston House on November 14, Geoffrey Denton wrote to the new Head of Information Department, that the Treasury official's 'Note for the Record' was not only in breach of Wilton Park rules, but also inaccurate. Thirty-one people had attended the conference, and from more countries than the Treasury had alleged. Fortunately, Great George Street grumbles of this sort also had a dying fall. There were no further breaches of Wilton Park rules, and fewer cavils about cost-effectiveness.

In fact, as Nicholas Barrington told Sir Peter Tennant over luncheon on Tuesday November 19, the Foreign and Commonwealth thought that Denton:

> had done a great deal for Wilton Park recently. He had made it more financially viable and thus deflected pressure for cuts. He had brought a substantive academic contribution and had shifted several of the areas of discussion to the Third World where there was most interest and demand.

Conferences on the Third World, Denton reported to the Academic Council two days later, had been very successful – unlike those on Europe, where there was heavy competition. Total participation was slightly down, from 420 in 1983/84 to 406 in 1984/85; but the quality remained high, although he would like to see more people from Ireland, Norway, Italy, and France. In 1984/85, Wiston House expected to recover 34 per cent of its total costs of £669,000, and would do better in 1985/86. Lack of flexibility by the Treasury at present limited potential earnings. Wiston House needed to be able to charge outside users more than the present statutory £65 a day.

The staff situation at Wiston House, however, continued to suggest that Geoffrey Denton might have over-estimated that cuts that were practicable. David Spence had left with effect from August 1; Jim Starkey had applied for a transfer; and Robert Sturrock was due to retire in 1987. As a temporary replacement for David Spence, there was the possibility of offering John Pinder a short-term, part-time post as Conference Adviser. The offer was eventually made in the following March, to run from April 1 to June 30, 1986.

When Robert Sturrock left in November 1987, Valerie Seward was the only member of the 1983 Academic Staff still working at Wilton Park. She specialised on the developing world, and organised with the FCO important meetings on South and Southern Africa. By the end of 1987, Geoffrey Denton was able to make significant new appointments. Previously, unlike the Director, the Academic Staff had been career civil servants with no fixed term. To avoid new recruits becoming permanent fixtures before their quality had been assessed in practice, Denton decided to follow the general trend towards fixed-term appointments. This made recruitment more difficult, especially for a post in the countryside some way from London, and outside the mainstream of the FCO. But it helped stress that special nature of Wilton Park and to attract candidates with experience in – and enthusiasm for – promoting international understanding.

Richard Latter, with a Ph.D. in International Relations from the London School of Economics, was appointed in November 1987, initially on a five-year contract, but with provision for renewal. He built a reputation both inside and outside Wilton Park, in security and defence policy, including terrorism. With the expansion of the programme, Latter was appointed in 1991 to the revived post of Deputy Director. After further expansion in the late 1990s, and the separation of the posts of Chief Executive and Director, Latter became Director.

December 1987 saw the recruitment of Nicholas Hopkinson, who had studied international relations in Canada and at the Johns Hopkins Centre in Bologna. He ran a large number of conferences every year on a wide range of topics, including European integration, East–West relations, and international trade policy. He also had his contract renewed in 1992, and in 2002 succeeded Richard Latter as Deputy Director.

In 1988 Dr John Dunn joined the staff. A linguist from Ulster, specialising in German and Russian, he had just obtained his doctorate from the University of Tübingen. Although lacking experience in international relations as such, he had travelled extensively in Eastern Europe and the Soviet Union, on which subjects he made distinguished contributions to the Wilton Park programme before moving on to a post in the European Commission in 1991.

Meanwhile, new technology altered the staff's working methods. With the academic conference organisers now using computers, secretaries were redeployed as administrative assistants. The organiser of each conference was responsible for recruitment to it, but the detailed work was done by an administrator, under the leadership of Elizabeth Harris, MBE, who worked at Wilton Park for twenty one years from 1977 to 1998.

The administration of Wiston House had previously been the responsibility of a Bursar, an FCO officer on a short-term posting, sometimes without the relevant experience to run what was in effect an hotel. In November 1987 a new Manager was recruited from the private sector.

Although he sometimes seemed abrasive to those unaccustomed to the harsher world of commercial hotel management, he successfully reorganised the domestic administration, trained and promoted junior staff, and oversaw in-house improvements such as new bedrooms and bathrooms. He was ably supported by the Housekeeper, Patricia Hanley and her assistant Joan Kingdon.

That said, the previous upheavals to the Academic Staff upheavals had left deep hurt and bitterness. Potentially, this threatened relations between Wilton Park and the Sir Heinz Koeppler Trust, manned as it was by veterans of the Koeppler era and the days before Denton. On November 19, 1985, the Trustees' Chairman, Sir Peter Tennant, discussed the problem with Nicholas Barrington of the FCO. Next day, Geoffrey Denton wrote to Tennant, inviting him to the opening dinner of the Wilton Park 40th anniversary celebrations on Friday, December 13. Neither, presumably, was superstitious. In the same note, Denton suggested that they discuss liaison between the Trust and himself. In the meantime, by telephone, they agreed to meet at 3.30 p.m. on Friday December 6. One of the questions to be decided was that of appointing more Trustees. The original Trust Deed of May 22, 1982 stipulated that: 'it is intended ... that the Trustees hereof shall at all times include the Chairman of Wilton Park's Academic Council and such other persons as have been nominated for appointment by the Council.'

The Council's Chairman, Professor Peter Nailor had already been appointed a Trustee on October 8, 1985. Two other Council members – Barbara Beck and Ernest Wistrich – were in the offing. There remained the possibility of appointing as a Trustee the Director of Wilton Park. For understandable personal reasons, Alan Hughes was opposed. But before this issue could be dealt with, a storm blew up which seriously threatened relations between the Trust and Wilton Park, potentially wary as they already were.

On Tuesday February, 11, 1986, the Trustees held their second meeting, this time at Dr Alec Frank's house in the High Street of Steyning. Among other things, they decided to approach Ernest Wistrich and Barbara Beck as possible recruits, and to commission a plaque for Wiston House in memory of Heinz Koeppler – a proposal which, subject to John Goring's consent, Nicholas Barrington thoroughly endorsed, as he told Sir Peter Tennant on February 3. But at the same meeting the Trustees made their first two grants of £500 each. Both had been suggested by Sir Frank Roberts. The first was to a proposed 'Young Königswinter' conference, the second was to an Anglo-German conference of Historians of the Second World War. Both seemed to Tennant and his fellow-Trustees fully in line with Heinz Koeppler's aims and ideals, especially as Denton had not responded to Tennant's asking for projects to finance. But neither grant was to Wilton Park.

The day after the Trustees' meeting, Tennant wrote a routine letter to Barrington announcing these decisions. There was silence for a few days. Then, on February 17, came a stinging letter from Geoffrey Denton:

Dear Peter,

I write immediately on receipt of a copy of the letter you addressed to Nicholas Barrington on 12 February 1986.

I was most surprised to learn that the Trustees had decided to make grants to two organisations, Young Königswinter and Leeds University. These are, of course, worthy institutions which one would want to support. However, it is my understanding that the Trustees received the Heinz Koeppler bequest to hold for the benefit of Wilton Park, and not for the benefit of any other institution.

I have received legal advice which firmly supports this view, by reference to both the Will and the Declaration of Trust.

The original Will is quite clear on this point: 'as to twenty thirty-sixths parts of both capital and income thereof for the Warden and the Chairman of the Academic Advisory Council for the time being of the institution known as Wilton Park ... for the benefit at their discretion of the said institution ... '.

I am further advised that the payment of grants to other institutions is in conflict with the general intention and with the wording of the Declaration of Trust. In particular, the Trustees do not appear to have acted in accordance with Clause 4 which states that the monies must be used exclusively in furtherance of Wilton Park.

I believe that if the Trustees pay part of the proceeds of the bequest to any other institution than Wilton Park, they may be in direct breach of trust and could be held personally responsible for refunding the monies thus diverted from the purpose for which the Trust was established.

As co-legatee of the Trust I therefore request an early meeting before this decision of the Trustees is implemented. In view of the urgency of this matter I am copying this letter to all members of the Wilton Park Academic Council, and delivering a copy by hand to the Trust solicitors who no doubt will ensure that copies are sent to the other Trustees.

This broadside was followed on February 20 by an equally pained but more diplomatically worded reproach to Sir Peter Tennant from Nicholas Barrington. He recalled that in his earlier letter of February 3 he had said: 'My own feeling is that the Trust funds should be devoted to Wilton Park.' Now he went on:

I am aware that as I am not a Trustee, I have no formal standing to influence the decisions of the Trust. I must nevertheless express my concern on two grounds. We agreed in our discussion of 19 November that, although not a Trustee, Geoffrey Denton should be closely associated with the deliberations of the Trust if not attending meetings in person. Clearly there has been a breakdown in communication. Secondly, although Geoffrey has not yet submitted detailed proposals for the use of the Trust Funds, he has as you know a number of positive ideas for their use in support of the Wilton Park Programme for this year which we consider should take priority over any other proposed use. The *fait accompli* with which we have been presented means that, as cheques have already been issued to Young Königswinter and the Leeds Conference, £1,000 less of the limited Koeppler Trust funds are available this year for Wilton Park's purposes.

This brings me to the legal position. We have consulted our Legal Advisers, whose preliminary assessment is at variance with Akermans, whom [a colleague] tells me you have consulted. Our lawyers believe that the Trustees' use of the Trust Funds in support of Young Königswinter and the Leeds Conference conflicts with both the wording and the intention of the Declaration of Trust, dated 22 May 1982; it is clear that the Trust was set up with the needs of Wilton Park in mind. From Point 1 in the Whereas clauses it emerges that the decision to administer the Bequest separately from Wilton Park was only a friendly arrangement, because there was no Warden/Director of Wilton Park at the time, and that there was never any intention to separate the institutions of the Koeppler Trust and Wilton Park.

Point 3 defines the powers of the Trustees and authorises them to further 'the Wilton Park Purpose', but Point 4 provides the specific powers, all in relation to the work of Wilton Park/Wiston House. In that context it is clear that the Wilton Park Purpose is to be pursued in a Wilton Park context. We are advised that where it is clear that the Trustees are executing the Trust in such a way as to move its 'centre of gravity' away from Wilton Park, they may not be acting in accordance with the Proviso to Point 4, which states that the Trustees have the powers vested in them 'in furtherance of the Wilton Park Purpose' (and for no other purpose).

I can take further advice on this, but our Legal Advisers' current assessment is that the Trustees may well have acted *ultra vires*, both in their action and in having failed to take account of Geoffrey Denton's views before disbursing Trust funds. I cannot predict the reaction of the Academic Council, but I believe that Peter Nailor, who was unfortunately unable to be present at your meeting on 11 February, is also unhappy with the use of Trust Funds for Young Königswinter and the Leeds Conference, and is concerned that cheques should have already [been] issued. I fear that a number of the other members of the Academic Council are likely to echo his view.

As you know, the last thing I want is for the Koeppler Trust to become a subject of contention between the Trustees, the FCO, Wilton Park and the Academic Council. This would certainly not be in accordance with Heinz's wishes. Above all, we must, of course, avoid litigation, which could only result in further depletion of the Trust Funds. Geoffrey Denton plans to write to you. It would be very valuable if you could discuss the whole situation with him as soon as possible.

Barrington added a manuscript PS:

I hope you won't think I'm making too much of this but all concerned here have done a lot of work to get the Trust going and we all want it to get off on the right foot. I am at your disposal if you wish to discuss further.

By the time he received this, Tennant had already – on February 22 – sent off an answer to Geoffrey Denton. 'It is a pity', he said, 'you did not give me a ring or drop in to see me for a talk on your way home instead of causing such a stir.' Tennant's house, in Haslemere, was not far off Denton's route back to London from Wiston House. After announcing that the two £500 drafts had already been paid, he reminded Denton:

We are still waiting for your application for Wilton Park itself and are holding some funds in reserve for this purpose ...

It is not the intention that this shall be in any way exclusive ...

You are mistaken in believing that the Sir Heinz Koeppler Bequest should be solely for the benefit of Wilton Park, though in most cases it would be so. The Trust is independent of Wilton Park and could have a life longer than that of Wilton Park itself. If Wilton Park were to alter its character in any way, i.e. become Party Political, a purveyor of Government policies or be dominated by vested interests, the Trustees would use the Koeppler Fund for other projects consonant with 'the Wilton Park Purpose' as defined in the Declaration of Trust (see paragraph 4 of the Declaration concerning powers under sub-paragraph (1) which refers to 'seminars and meetings at Wiston House or elsewhere').

The Declaration specifically states in Recital (I) that there being no Warden at Wilton Park, Sir Robert Birley (and I later as his successor) with the Original Trustees should administer the Koeppler Bequest ...

It is a matter for the Trustees to decide what is in accordance with the Wilton Park Purpose and on this occasion they have decided that the two applications were not only well within the scope of the Purpose, but both of them would have appealed to Sir Heinz Koeppler personally. I noted that you had some interesting literature on display on the German Resistance at the Wiston House 40th Anniversary celebration. This of course is the subject of the Leeds University Conference. Sir Heinz was also a strong supporter of Königswinter and of its junior offshoot. The young were always in his mind ...

You refer to Clause 4 of the Declaration of Trust stating that monies must be used exclusively in furtherance of Wilton Park. This is not so. The text refers throughout to the Wilton Park Purpose. You will note from paragraph 8 of the Declaration that 'none of the Trustees shall be liable or responsible for anything except his own wilful default or his own fraud'. I am not prepared to accept your accusation that we have committed a breach of trust and are liable.

At the end of your letter you refer to yourself as 'co-legatee'. This is not so, but I am always happy to meet you and talk things over, bearing in mind that the Wilton Park Purpose is concerned with peaceful understanding and not contentious misunderstanding.

Sir Peter Tennant enclosed a copy of this letter when he answered Barrington on February 25. He had heard, he said, from several members of the Academic Council:

Their reactions have ranged between bafflement and cheerful enquiries about my visiting hours in gaol. I am anxious that relations between the trustees and Wilton Park should be a friendly one. Of course we wish to associate Denton with the deliberations of the Trust.

'I do not think that we will achieve much', replied Barrington on March 6, 'by prolonging this debate by letter'. The respective lawyers were examining the position:

But I trust that this is not something that we should leave to the lawyers to sort out. I have suggested to Geoffrey Denton that he should seek an early meeting with you to try and sort out a mutually acceptable modus vivendi. I am glad to note from your letter to Geoffrey that you would welcome this. With flexibility and goodwill on both sides and with full consultation between Wiston House and the Trustees, Heinz Koeppler's money can then be put to the most productive use – support for the Wilton Park purpose as personified by Wiston House.

Reading the last five words, Tennant no doubt noted that Barrington had not forgotten the legal difference between them. The Trustees' lawyers finally concluded that the capital and interest on Koeppler's legacy itself should be applied to what came to be called 'the narrower purpose' – i.e. Wilton Park – while any outside contributions to the Fund could be used at the Trustees' discretion for 'the wider purpose' – e.g. such projects as Young Königswinter or the Leeds Conference. As a legal solution, it was neat and clear.

But the real solution, as Barrington had said, had to be practical and personal. From the Royal Naval College, Greenwich, where he was Professor of History and International Affairs, Peter Nailor poured oil on troubled waters with a long letter that he wrote on March 13 to the three semi-public protagonists – Tennant, Denton, and Barrington:

> I am prompted by the recent rounds of correspondence to write very frankly to the three of you, as friends as well as collaborators bound together. I do so under the burden of a strong feeling that, as the most obvious link between the Academic Council and the Trustees of the Koeppler Trust – the jam in this currently indigestible sandwich – I ought more than anyone else to have been sensitive to the possibilities for dissonance ... What is more important, however, is what I can do now. The requirement is to repair a position which is becoming not only unsatisfactory but unacceptably threatening, with many signs of being on the brink of developing into a tortuous, harmful and unedifying wrangle – of the sort that usually only happens when families become divided over a will ... The general proposition that I want to state is a two-fold one: the wrangling must end and the wider Wilton Park community must be assured that the Koeppler bequest is a source of additional strength rather than any cause for concern.
>
> If I were Robert Birley I would be able to have you all – us all – into the headmaster's study; but I am not, and I can only ask that we jointly determine that we seek a new start. The basic position is that the Trustees must find a *modus vivendi* with the Director and (I think this has to be said) the Director must be reassured that the basis for such a relationship exists ...
>
> I must make two issues clear. The first is that regard has to be taken of the wishes of the Trustees to make a general point, as quickly and sensibly as they could, that the Trust was – at long last – established and in business. It so happened that this coincided with the Fortieth Anniversary, and that this factor was instrumental in emphasising the Anglo-German context of Wilton Park's historical range of activities.
>
> The second issue is that, because of the way in which the bequest lingered in the Courts, a gap has occurred between what the make-up of the Trustees was intended to signify when it was first drawn up and what that make-up should now be in order to represent, fairly, the original intention. It was, of course, the duty of the original Trustees to get the show on the road as soon as they could: and this they have done. But I do not think we can now avoid considering what should be done about the anachronisms, specifically in regard to the Wilton Park representative component.
>
> I have described these issues in general terms, and see them as balancing out, if the future is to be more equable. They require concessions,

and, as well, a commonly-shared determination to make the relationship between the Trust and the Centre work ...

I do not claim that I can act in this matter as an unpartisan broker: my special interest, of reconciliation, is one however that we all share, even if my particular concern is to have the matter resolved before the next meeting of the Council in June. I do not want the Council to debate it, because it could only result in an entrenchment of positions into which we have, quite frankly, drifted.

With that in mind, I can see two possible ways forward. You may wish to reply to this letter, and I would of course welcome your views. But you might also think we could proceed to a discussion, in which case I would be happy to arrange a meeting, either here or wherever it might be convenient to you. It is conceivable that lunch under the beady eyes of George I's entire and reprehensible family might put our problem into a new perspective.

Before any lunch in the Painted Hall at Greenwich proved necessary, human contacts were resumed. On the same morning as Sir Peter received Nailor's letter, March 14, 1986, Geoffrey Denton called to see him at home. 'Our conversation', Tennant wrote to Nailor two days later, 'was perfectly amicable. He kept on protesting his friendship for me ... We have ... mended fences and should be able to work together perfectly easily. The main sticking point is that he is not a trustee. I feel that as an employee of the FCO and potential beneficiary of grants he should not be involved in their giving. Could we not allow him to see papers before meetings and even offer him the chance to attend when he has a proposal to put forward?'

That same day, Tennant wrote a brief note to Denton, recalling that the objectives of Wilton Park and the Koeppler Trust were identical. While Wilton Park was an extension of the FCO and the Trust (in order to qualify as a charity) was independent, they must work closely together. By April 25, after an exchange of suggested amendments, they had completed a joint text to circulate to the Trustees. It agreed to differ on legal niceties. It redeemed the grants to Young Königswinter and Leeds by labelling them 'in association with Wilton Park'. As befitted a 40-year old institution, wisdom had prevailed.

The way was now clear for normal relations to begin. On May 9, 1986, Geoffrey Denton submitted an ambitious schedule of the kinds of project for which Wilton Park might in future seek the Trust's help. It included: support for participation from poor countries, trade unions, workers' organisations, ethnic minorities, and young people; pump-priming of joint conferences, and staff travel. On May 20, the Trustees held their third meeting, again at Alec Frank's house in Steyning. They confirmed the distinction between 'Narrower Purpose' and 'Wider Purpose' grants, and established separate funds to handle them. Geoffrey Denton explained his schedule of potential requests. It totalled £9,460 – a figure he recognised as beyond the Trust's present resources. The Trustees agreed to make available £5,000, to be used in accordance with Denton's priorities. Finally, they handed over the ceramic plaque in memory of Heinz Koeppler, which the Goring family had agreed could be exhibited inside, but not outside Wiston House.

The Koeppler Trust's ceramic plaque had a piquant later history. For three years, it vanished from sight. When it was finally unveiled, in 1989, the Trustees were astonished to see that it had turned, as if by magic, into a brass plate. On May 9, 1989, Sir Peter Tennant wrote an indignant protest. Deeply embarrassed, Geoffrey Denton wrote to Peter Tennant on May 12:

> You are right, and I apologise. I should have come straight out long ago and explained that the plaque you commissioned was regarded as unsuitable by virtually everybody who saw it here. In trying to be diplomatic, and then finally being in a great hurry with a conference going on during the week of the meeting, I omitted to explain the position to you.

Some ten months later, on March 13, 1990, he was able to report to the Trust:

> I am pleased to confirm that the memorial plaque has now been fixed to the wall of the Conservatory, in a prominent position near the door to the garden and in full view as people enter the Conservatory from the Library.

It was an equivocal coda to an equivocal tale. But by that time Wiston House was undergoing yet another radical change.

CHAPTER 25

Luxury

'You can't feel fierce and revolutionary in a bathroom.'
Eric Linklater, *Juan in America* (1931), book 5, part 3

'Too down-at-heel' for outside conferences was how one FCO official described Wiston House on April 11, 1986. It needed private bathrooms, better bedroom furniture, better-appointed public rooms, and improved downstairs lavatories. When another official of the FCO's Management Review Staff or MRS, asked the Treasury why it made no use of Wiston House for its own training courses, the answer – in writing – was that there were not enough *en suite* bathrooms.

In the early months of 1986, in fact, soon after Wilton Park had celebrated its 40th Anniversary, it had suddenly become, once again, the focus of official scrutiny. By no means all of this was hostile. In January, the MRS official spent a day at Wiston House. After talking with those in charge, he saw that the institution found it hard to fit into the FCO's categories and rules. On February 18 he proposed to the Head of Information Department, that a Review Officer conduct an inquiry into greater flexibility for Wilton Park, beginning on Monday, March 24.

This was not the only inquiry afoot. The Treasury, always suspicious of what it still seemed to think of as 'Koeppler's College', and apparently unaware of how often and thoroughly its questions had been answered, now again asked the FCO, on February 26, whether other possible venues for Wilton Park's work had been examined. The Review Officer, meanwhile, even before his on-the-spot survey, said on March 11 that he was unhappy about Geoffrey Denton's trying to attract outside conferences: he would prefer him to host FCO training courses. Perhaps they demanded less luxury.

On April 15, FCO officials met to discuss the Reviewer's report. It showed that Wiston House was fully used for only 185 days of the year – sixty days for Wilton Park Conferences, ten for joint conferences, 70 for FCO training courses, and 45 for outside organisations. All told, the report made 56 specific recommendations. They ranged from policy issues like negotiating a longer lease, and running two training courses in parallel, to domestic matters like employing contract cleaners, replacing coal fires by gas, organising self-service breakfasts, and installing a micro-wave oven and a telephone answering system. In general, it reported that the staff were capable, helpful, and pleasant, but were organised on the basis of a five-day week – not, in other words, like hotel staff.

The notion of Wiston House as a hotel was tempting to some in the FCO. 'It is actually a hotel', wrote the Head of Finance Department on July 8, 'and the FCO should certainly not be running a hotel at a loss (or even otherwise) with public money'. Instead, it should seek conference facilities elsewhere. Apprised of this note, Information Department answered it robustly two days later, pointing out that Wiston House was not part of Government Hospitality, but a key and successful element of information policy. In any case, as the report pointed out, Wiston House's Director had not been recruited as a hotel manager. But he had excellent ideas on strategy.

Information Department also had praise for Geoffrey Denton. Reporting to Nicholas Barrington on May 27, they applauded his 'energetic and forceful leadership' and his continuing to 'shake up' Wilton Park. 'Mr Denton has his weaknesses. He is a leader by nature rather than a persuader. He has a short fuse, is impatient of the foibles of others ... [and] is inclined to try bulldozer tactics where a more sympathetic approach might have been more productive. [Nevertheless] all in all Mr Denton has proved to have been the right man for an important job.'

When Geoffrey Denton spoke to the International Advisory Council on May 21 and the Academic Council on June 20, 1986, he was able to report that the number of participants was up since last year. He himself had been making efforts to increase them, undertaking what one desk-bound FCO official later nicknamed 'Denton's World Tours'. In reality, he had travelled to Washington from May 7–10 to recruit 'multipliers' and perhaps a part-time agent, and to address a meeting of the American Friends of Wilton Park at which the UK Ambassador, Sir Oliver Wright, spoke on 'The Thatcher Revolution'. Later in that year, on September 22–24, he spoke at an Anglo-German conference in Coburg.

'Denton's World Tours', such as they were, were part of an overall, global strategy to develop Wilton Park's work in a number of key areas.

One, obviously enough, was European integration. Wilton Park had long made this a priority, but it needed to attract more non-British speakers so as to avoid any impression that the British were lecturing their continental partners. Another priority in Europe was East–West relations. The 40th Anniversary Conference in December 1986, on 'Germany in a Divided Europe in a Divided World', brought to Wilton Park the first participant and speaker from the DDR, Bishop Schonherr. The weekend after the Anniversary Conference saw a *Wiltonentreffen* or meeting of Wilton Park Associations. German participants from the earliest courses in 1946 competed for the honour of being the first at Wilton Park, and gave moving testimony to its effect on them. One even confessed: 'I was a Nazi. I came to Wilton Park and it changed my life.'

After 1986, *glasnost* and *perestroika* enabled speakers and participants from the Soviet Union to come to Wilton Park. The first was Boris Pyadishev, a Government spokesman, who took part in a conference on arms control in February 1987. The Soviet Embassy co-operated by sending interpreters – one of whom became so excited by the discussion that he burst out of his box and joined in.

In the late 1980s, Wilton Park became an important venue of dialogue with East European countries – notably Hungary and Poland – as they gradually asserted their independence from the Soviet Union. In one conference in October 1988, a Romanian speaker dramatically announced the forthcoming collapse of the communist system. To the question 'Do you mean in Romania?' he answered: 'No: everywhere.'

On security policy, Wilton Park's emphasis gradually shifted from the depressing technical discussion of cruise missiles to equally technical but also political discussion of arms control. But as the Cold War wound down, the more amorphous threat from international terrorism loomed larger; and Richard Latter organised annual conferences on its various aspects, especially with Jonah Alexander of George Washington University, but also – on chemical and biological weapons – with Graham Pearson, Director of the Porton Down Defence Establishment.

Other intractable issues faced at Wilton Park included Israel and Palestine, Kashmir, conflicts in Latin America, the aftermath of the Vietnam War, and relations between Greeks and Turks in Cyprus. A conference in 1986 included the Greek Cypriot leader and later President, Glafcos Clerides, and a senior colleague of his Turkish counterpart Rauf Denktash. The two men had not met since 1974, but by the end of the conference they were amusing participants by exchanging stories from the time when they both served in the Government of Archbishop Makarios.

Like Europe, the Third World had long been on Wilton Park's agenda, talked about rather than with. Co-operation with other institutions began to remedy this: a notable instance was the Madrid-based *Instituto de Relaciones Europeo-Latino Americanas*, backed by the European Parliament.

More ambitiously, on October 5–15, 1986, 'Denton's World Tours' included a visit to China – a follow-up of the previous year's China–US–Wilton Park conference. He went with a number of colleagues, including Valerie Seward, John Pinder, Edmund Dell, and Michael Kaser, the Oxford economist who had succeeded Peter Nailor as Chairman of the Academic Council. It was a further part of the effort to make Wilton Park's purview truly worldwide. At times, this backfired. Earlier in the year, elements in the UK and South African press had campaigned against a Wilton Park conference on 'South Africa in Crisis' (on March 23–25, 1986), with the result that some black participants had withdrawn and the proceedings had ended early. But risk had always been part of Wilton Park's remit, and hot potatoes its staple diet.

Now a new challenge was facing it, much nearer home. The MRS report had recommended reform and refurbishment at Wiston House. It proposed spending £350,000 on modernisation (Option A), and letting it out for conferences (Option B), with more budgetary flexibility, possibly with separate budgets for Wiston House and Wilton Park. It also recommended renewing the lease for at least 10–15 years.

But the report foreshadowed more. In the context of Mrs Thatcher's 'Next Steps' strategy, he also put up Option C: a private-sector partnership. To many, this looked like privatisation. The domestic staff at Wiston House, an FCO official noted on September 25, had the impression that 'privatisation was a foregone conclusion'. It was not. But it was being privately discussed. On Tuesday September 2, Nicholas Barrington had lunched with the owner of Wiston House, John Goring, at the Athenaeum. Among other things they had discussed the future rent of Wiston House. If it were privatised, Goring had warned, the rent would be much more. On October 17, Goring wrote to Barrington on behalf of the Wiston Estate Trustees. Privatisation, he thought, 'would destroy the unique environment' of the place; he 'would wish to retain the present position between my family and the Foreign Office'. He had already told Geoffrey Denton that he would like to agree on a long lease – something that the FCO Finance Department still opposed.

On November 7, Geoffrey Denton and FCO officials went through the whole of the MRS report. They agreed on almost all of it. On November 25, they made their recommendations to Nicholas Barrington: to adopt Options A and B (refurbishment and leasing out), to appoint a Marketing

Manager, and to seek a longer lease. Next day, a former head of the FCO's Information Department, Keith MacInnes, briefly returned to his old haunts. He was now an Assistant Under-Secretary of State, with a CMG. More to the point, he was the FCO's Principal Finance Officer. He had an offer to Nicholas Barrington of funds for Wiston House. To refurbish it, he said, he could find £90,000 over three years. Geoffrey Denton described the situation to the Wilton Park Academic Council when it met in London on November 27, and explained that John Goring had opposed Option C.

As that year drew to a close, Denton could look back on 1986 with some satisfaction. In the summer, there had been a further domestic problem, when the Bursar had shown signs of being tired and stressed; but once reassured that privatisation was excluded, the staff had settled down. Relations with the Koeppler Trust had been smoothed into a routine, and regular contributions were being used chiefly to support needy participants. Above all, Wiston House was to be secured with a longer lease, and smartened up physically. It would have new bathrooms and loos, better bedrooms and – in the longer term – visitors' rooms converted from the stables and cottages outside the house. All this would take time. Tim Eggar, Parliamentary Under-Secretary of State at the FCO, had his Private Secretary ask, on December 22, why the three years' works could not all be done at the same time, to save continual disruption.

It was a sensible question. But not until March 1987 did Ministers finally decide on the £350,000 package recommended by the MRS review, including letting Wilton House out (when free) as a Conference Centre, and renewing the lease for twenty years. The marketing plan, worked out later in the year, was to use the house for 300 days a year, and to reduce the cost to the Foreign Office to zero by 1991/92. On these best-laid plans, Robert Burns had long since made the aptest comment.

Almost equally ambitious were new plans to expand Wilton Park's activities overseas. In both Western and Eastern Europe, especially, the political scene was changing very rapidly. On January 1, 1986, Spain and Portugal had joined the European Community. On February 28, 1986, its member States had signed the Single European Act to transform their mutual relations as a whole into a European Union. On February 7, 1992, they signed the Treaty of Maastricht; in January 1994 they set up the European Monetary Institute to prepare for a single currency; and in January 1995 they recruited Austria, Finland and Sweden, making the European Union fifteen members strong. In the East, Mikhail Gorbachev had become Secretary-General of the Soviet Communist Party in March 1985, and had begun the process of *glasnost* and *perestroika* that were to transform and finally dissolve Eastern Europe's Communist bloc, culminating in the breaching of the Berlin Wall on November 9, 1989. In October 1990 Germany was reunified; in June 1991 Yugoslavia began to break up; in December 1991 the Soviet Union became the Commonwealth of Independent States.

Wilton Park could not fail to respond to this multiple transformation, which was replacing the rigid, divided postwar East–West Europe of Yalta by the uniting Western Europe of Brussels in the wider Europe of conflict, painful adjustment, and hazardous instability, notably in the Balkans. On January 27, 1988, Geoffrey Denton wrote to Brian Barder, the British Ambassador in Warsaw, announcing that from June 5 to 10 that year he was hoping to hold a Wilton Park conference on 'Europe into the 1990s'. What was novel about the plan was not the subject, but the venue. This was not to be Wiston House, but Haikko Manor, Porvoo, a mansion about 30 miles from Helsinki, Finland. It made some in the FCO uneasy, but it set a precedent soon followed.

Similar outreach of a different sort was in evidence that October, when Denton proposed that BBC television's 'Newsnight' programme cover part of another Wilton Park conference, this time at Wiston House, on 'Soviet Reforms in Eastern Europe'. On October 19, 1988, the new Head of the FCO's Information Department asked Tim Eggar's Private Secretary for advice on how to proceed. Given Wilton Park's 'off-the-record' rule, it was a delicate question – made all the more so by an incident a week later, when an FCO official in the Far Eastern Department reported to a colleague *and ten others* on a Wilton Park China conference, quoting participants by name. It was the third such breach in Wilton Park's history, and the second since 1985. After some discussion, Denton wrote to Charles Colville, the *Newsnight* producer, giving him the go-ahead with strict conditions about non-attributability. What mattered most was not television publicity, but – as Denton told the Academic Council on December 14 – the fact that more East European and Soviet nationals were now willing and able to come to Wilton Park.

In this way Denton had fulfilled one of the aims he had spelled out with Nicholas Barrington in their memorandum of August 1985 on 'objectives' for Wilton Park. That document had been prepared with a view to the 'Next Steps' exercise that might eventually lead to semi-autonomy and Executive Agency status. Now, with a long lease under negotiation and the refurbishment of Wiston House under way, the conditions for greater autonomy were being set in place. On October 16, 1988, FCO Ministers decided in principle to pursue plans to establish it as an Executive Agency. As a move in this direction, on November 9 the FCO's Finance

Department suggested that Wiston House accounts could have a 'net subhead'. This would cover all salary, accommodation and office costs, and be credited with total receipts, so that staff could be increased if covered by increased income. It added next day that this would be a 'major advance' pending agency status – on which, it had to admit, the Treasury still had its doubts.

Another, more personal uncertainty marked Wilton Park at that time. This was Geoffrey Denton's continued role as Director. In February 1988 he had reminded the FCO that his five-year contract was due to expire on October 9. If it were not to be renewed, he would have to look for another post, probably at a university. In order to take up any appointment in the autumn term, he ought to start looking now. His query led to no serious discussion; and although the FCO's Policy Planning Department was preparing a draft contract in August, he received it only in September, six weeks before the expiry of his current engagement. Nor was it a new five-year contract. Because Denton would be 60 in 1991, his new contract was for three years only – although Heinz Koeppler had been allowed to stay on until he was 65. Once again, a Director of Wilton Park was having trouble with FCO personnel policy – despite the fact that it had never been an embassy and was heading for a status all its own. It was with mixed feelings, therefore, that Geoffrey Denton received the congratulations of Michael Kaser, Chairman of the Academic Council, when he complimented him on the improvements at Wiston House.

His feelings were more mixed still when Tim Eggar, Parliamentary Under-Secretary of State at the FCO, paid a visit to Wilton Park in January 1989. The simultaneous interpretation system broke down. John Melser, the Manager of Wiston House, explained on February 2 that it had been renovated in 1981, but dated from 1968. Nor was this the only mechanical problem. In the previous November, a burglar had broken into the house and stolen some items of the landlord's property. The Property Services Agency (PSA), who would be responsible for Wiston House until March 1990, had written to Melser about the question of burglar alarms, but claimed to have received no reply. Meanwhile, the landlord had himself broken in, leaving a message to say so, and pressing the PSA to improve security at Wiston House.

There was, however, one major cause for satisfaction. For 38 years, because Wilton Park's future had been so uncertain, Wiston House had been rented on a series of uneconomic short leases. Now at last all were able to agree to the signing of a new 20-year lease. At the same time continuing efforts were made to put Wiston House on the 'net subhead' accountancy basis previously discussed. This would bring its finances closer to those of an Executive Agency, allowed to keep all receipts from income. But despite Finance Department's backing, the Treasury was being 'very slow' to accept such arrangements for 'organisations like Wiston House'.

Inching in that direction, Melser and Geoffrey Denton met with colleagues on April 14, 1989, to discuss new financial arrangements. They agreed to maintain and update a three-year business plan, to budget for each year and to seek annual approval for the FCO subsidy. By 1991/92 – preferably sooner – the subsidy should be no greater than the cost of (hypothetically) running Wilton Park in the FCO and renting conference venues. The Director would be allowed discretionary spending of £10,000 a year, and a 'manpower delegation' to employ clerical and ancillary staff.

By this time the improvements at Wiston House were becoming more tangible. An article in the May/June issue of *The Diplomat* announced that Wiston House now had 26 rooms in the main house, and 24 in the cottages. There were nevertheless problems with the PSA, which Denton reported to the Assistant Under-Secretary at the FCO, Rosemary Spencer, on July 19, 1989. No action had been taken to improve fire precautions or health conditions in the kitchens; and the PSA's charges seemed unduly high. Still, the gradual improvements had helped improve attendance figures. At the Academic Council meeting on June 16, Denton reported that numbers of participants had risen despite an increase of fees from £320 to £390, so that financial targets had been exceeded by £86,000.

As for Executive Agency status, the FCO told the Council they could expect this within six months. Council members had no objections; but Valerie Seward, who was at the meeting, confided her anxieties to her union, the Institute of Professional Civil Servants. In response, an official from the FCO's Information Department met with Valerie Seward and her colleagues at Wiston House. At that time there were five Academic Staff: Denton, Seward, Nicholas Hopkinson, Richard Latter, and John Dunn. Their anxieties were not political. They were concerned about individual terms and conditions of service, including their status as civil servants, their pension rights, and the power and status of the Director. The official agreed to consult with them all the way. He reported back that there was a *de facto* division between the Academic Staff and what might be termed the 'hotel' staff – John Melser had said a year earlier that 'Wiston House is now an Hotel' as recognised by the MRS report.

Talking with Rosemary Spencer on July 19, 1989, Denton stressed that staffing was the greatest problem. Two days later, on Friday July 21, they had lunch together, and he explained his own difficulties. Recalling the manner of his reappointment a year ago, he said he thought that Academic

Staff should be told a year before their contracts expired whether or not they would be invited to renew them. Rosemary Spencer noted afterwards: 'He clearly felt sore.' He did. He raised the subject with her again some months later, on December 11. From July 1984 onwards, having decided to relinquish the post of Deputy Director, he had done all the administration, as well as taking part in virtually every conference. There had been four Academic Staff, then three, then for a time only two. In 1987 he had himself organised eight conferences – double the workload of each conference organiser on the Academic Staff. The only financial recognition he had received had been one performance point on his salary, earned as from September 1987 but not notified and paid until October 1989. He had never been informed of any personal report or invited to a job appraisal interview. In 1988, having raised the question of his contract's renewal in February, he had been offered a new contract only six weeks before the expiry of the old. Rosemary Spencer duly reported these grievances. But she also reported, from the earlier conversation, that when Wilton Park acquired agency status, Denton would welcome an FCO Board to help it generate conference ideas and drum up participants.

Another source of dissatisfaction was the PSA. On July 26 Denton wrote to the FCO repeating what he had reported a week earlier to Rosemary Spencer. In 1986/87, the PSA had charged £36,108 for work on Wiston House: Denton and his staff had estimated that the true cost should have been £32,762. In 1987/88, the respective figures had been £42,478 and £35,302; in 1988/89, £66,391 and £23,880. Moreover, if Wilton Park were to be an agency from April 1990, 'we cannot start with a large backlog of maintenance work, which should have been carried out by the PSA during previous financial years'. This would be 'an intolerable situation'. The FCO replied, on August 4, that after 1990 the PSA's present charging policy, which was based on the square metrage of the property, would be scrapped. It would then work on a 'job-cost' basis – and clients would be able to go to another contractor. For the time being, they must bide their time.

Meanwhile, on August 9, the FCO and Denton went over the first draft of an Executive Agency Framework Agreement. This revealed two unexpected minor hurdles: charitable status and exemption from Value Added Tax or VAT. Denton had couched it, moreover, as an official alleged on October 25, 'in terms of complete independence from the FCO' – a charge Denton strongly denied. Nor was this the sole bone of contention. On October 30, the FCO reported that Denton not only wanted more autonomy: he also wanted to continue as Director of Wilton Park after reaching the age of 60 on June 10, 1991. Two months before, however, officials had seemed to rule this out, writing that: 'we do not at present expect to renew the contract beyond that'. If Wilton Park became an Executive Agency, Denton could argue for more pay. This time at least, the FCO was prompt in raising the question of retirement: it put it forward on October 18.

Geoffrey Denton had seen Agency status as providing greater operational independence, in line with Wilton Park's academic independence from the FCO. At the same time, he welcomed the proposed FCO Departmental Board as broadening administrative contacts. The Wiston House Manager John Melser had more radical ideas. On October 27, 1989, he suggested that the place be fully privatised, and he proposed to take over the new lease that was to be signed on November 7. When Denton heard of this démarche, his reaction was predictable. 'Geoffrey Denton is not a happy man', Melser told the FCO on November 8. Indeed he was not. On the same day he wrote to Rosemary Spencer: 'I take strong exception to a member of Wilton Park staff having conversations on such a sensitive subject with a junior member of Information Department without informing me.' Others on the Academic Staff agreed. So did the FCO. On November 10 Melser told Information Department that he was withdrawing the plan. Nothing more was heard of it until November 24, when an official reported that John Goring had been 'taken aback' by it and hoped the FCO would squash it. It had been a minor affair: as Melser himself admitted, it had changed his relations with Geoffrey Denton, but there was still mutual respect and support, and the incident was soon forgotten.

Two further distractions marked the end of that year. On November 2, an official from the Policy Planning Staff committed a fourth breach of Wilton Park rules by circulating a record of a trilateral conference on 'Europe in the Nineties' held on October 28 and 29. This bad example was followed on December 28 by a fifth breach of the rules, when an official from the FCO's Soviet Department wrote a detailed report to a colleague and to three others about a Wilton Park conference devoted to 'Socialist Reform and East–West Relations' on December 11–15. Both indiscretions were all the more galling in that, only a few weeks before, on September 25, an official from the Security Policy Department had quoted a Danish conference member as saying: 'They would not have been ready to be so frank about each other had the conference been anywhere in Scandinavia.'

So Wilton Park could still work its magic. On another occasion, Geoffrey Denton recalled, one black South African, who bitterly resented the presence of a Nationalist MP (not a Government official), said at the end of the conference he had come to realise that the man in question was a human being.

When Denton made his end-of-year report to the Academic Council on December 15, 1989, he looked back at least to twelve months of stability in the Academic Staff. Not only this, but the numbers of participants had increased, from 717 in 1987/88 to 770 in 1988/89. Above all, whatever the shortcomings of the PSA, the physical amenities at Wiston House were being improved. At last, after many wrangles, the tennis courts had been resurfaced. At last, after much noise and dust, it had new bathrooms. Compared with Koeppler's day, all this was luxury. But it was a necessity for the 1990s, if Wilton Park was to succeed in its new role.

CHAPTER 26

New Status

'There is no easy walk-over to freedom anywhere.'
Jawaharlal Nehru, 'From Lucknow to Tripuri' (1939)

To prepare Wilton Park for its possible future as an Executive Agency, its ideals and purposes had to be reaffirmed. This *credo* was known in Whitehall, uninspiringly, as 'The Framework Document'. Heinz Koeppler might have found another title for it: he would certainly have infused it with his own ringing rhetoric. The version drafted in August 1985 by Geoffrey Denton and Nicholas Barrington had been both schematic and laboured. By November 1989 it had been pummelled into rather different shape:

Aims and objectives:
Wilton Park's aim as an Executive Agency will be to operate conferences in international affairs of a high quality, intended to attract senior politicians, officials, businessmen, academics, and other professionals from many countries and international organisations to the UK; and to serve the interests of HMG by presenting the UK as a country which aims to promote the solution of international problems by improving international understanding through dialogue.
     Wilton Park's more specific objectives are:
(a) to raise progressively the international renown of its conferences and the prestige of Wilton Park.
(b) to ensure that its conferences remain relevant to the most important issues of international affairs and especially to regions and subjects where dialogue can contribute to finding solutions to international problems.
(c) to keep the content and style of its conferences up to date with changes in the international operational environment.

(d) to achieve the highest utilisation of Wilton House Conference Centre consistent with maintaining the quality of the Wilton Park conferences.

(e) to recover not less than the prime cost of the Wiston House Conference Centre, and as far as possible to contribute to the cost of Wilton Park conferences.

(f) to achieve such financial and other performance targets as Foreign and Commonwealth Office Ministers may from time to time determine, in agreement with the Director and the Academic Council.

In order to achieve these objectives, Wilton Park will undertake to:

(a) publish conference reports promptly and ensure their wide dissemination;

(b) follow conferences up by maintaining contacts with participants and their sponsoring organisations;

(c) build the recruitment network up so as to ensure a steady improvement in the international and professional balance of participation.

Already, this lumpish, repetitive prose omitted three important elements in the document discussed by Denton and Barrington in 1985. They had spoken of 'free and unattributable discussion': the new version mentioned only 'dialogue'. Secondly, they had stressed 'Wilton Park's ... academic independence': for the moment, the new version did not. Thirdly, it omitted what Denton and Barrington had called 'the very special 'atmosphere' engendered by Wiston House'. Later hands made further adjustments still. Most were minor matters of style. But by March 27, 1991 two unobtrusive changes had slightly skewed the text even more. In (e), 'contribute' had become 'secure an increasing contribution', and in (f) 'in agreement with the Director and the Academic Council' had been deleted. Presumably, someone in the FCO hankered after more money and more control.

The former – making Wiston House pay its way better – was already in prospect. On January 16, 1990, the FCO noted that it was now occupied for 80 per cent of the year. The latter – keeping a grip on the Director's plans – had always caused creative tension, and always would. But at least Wilton Park went on retaining and proclaiming its much-prized academic independence. As late as June 18, 1991, less than three months before Wiston House acquired Agency status, Information Department was still at pains to describe to the Treasury what this meant:

Academic independence is difficult to explain in a document such as this [the Framework Document]. We do not stipulate:

– who should participate in conferences
– what should be said or done by Wilton Park staff at conferences, e.g. promote HMG's views

390

- what the conclusions of a conference should be
- what the contents of the annual programme is (although we naturally have the chance to make our views known on what goes in).

Essentially, once the FCO has indicated the nature of the conferences it would like Wilton Park to organise and has approved the programme of conferences, the Director has the freedom to take arrangements forward in his own way.

In other words, what Heinz Koeppler had called the FCO's 'self-denying ordinance' was still largely inviolate.

Over the Christmas and New Year break of 1989–90, Geoffrey Denton visited Budapest, behind the now vanished 'Iron Curtain'. As always, he was seeking contact with likely participants and likely recruiters. Returning on Sunday January 7, he wrote a confidential report a week later for the Assistant Head of the FCO's Eastern Europe Department.

But it was on January 25 that the FCO took the decisive step, when the Parliamentary Under-Secretary of State, Timothy Sainsbury, MP for nearby Hove, wrote formally to Norman Lamont, Chief Secretary to the Treasury, asking for Wilton Park to be turned into an Executive Agency, with all that this implied. Mrs Thatcher herself, in a footnote to her memoirs *The Downing Street Years*, spelled out 'the radical reforms of the civil service which were contained in the "Next Steps" programme':

Under this programme much of the administrative – as opposed to the policy-making – work of government departments is being transferred to agencies, staffed by civil servants and headed by chief executives appointed by open competition. The agencies operate within frameworks set by the departments, but are free of detailed departmental control.

In some degree, this described the status already enjoyed in practice by Wilton Park. So it took quite a short time for the Permanent Secretary at the Treasury to agree in principle, on February 14, stipulating only that the FCO must work out costs with advice from the Central Office of Information. Five days later, however, Norman Lamont sent a rather more cautious official reply. He wanted to discuss the question before giving formal consent.

Not until the autumn was it discussed at the Treasury with Geoffrey Denton. On October 26 he reported a meeting there three days earlier:

They insisted on going back to fundamentals and asking first: 'Why should there be Wilton Park conferences?' Then: 'Why should Wilton Park conferences be held at Wiston House?' The Treasury and OCMS [the

Office of the Minister for the Civil Service] showed considerable ignorance
and lack of understanding of the financial situation.

They wondered whether Wilton Park might not simply be privatised or
become a charitable foundation. In fact, it took several more meetings and
many more months before all these questions were answered and related
questions were resolved.

Meanwhile, Wilton Park's work was continuing as before, but feeling
the impact of events in the outside world. On May 16, 1990, Denton
confessed to the International Advisory Council that two projected conferences had had to be cancelled, at a loss of 85 participants. One conference
had been designed to bring together black and white South Africans, but
had been overtaken by the rapidity of events in the Republic: now, they
were talking anyway. The other, on UK relations with the USSR, had
fallen victim to tensions among the Soviet republics, which had detained
the USSR parliamentary delegation in Moscow when it had been expected
at Wilton Park. However, as Denton told the Academic Council when it
met on June 15, the number of participants from Eastern Europe in
general had gone up from 25 in 1988/89 to 38 in 1989/90. Total numbers
were down, from a peak of 770 in 1988/89 to 729 in 1989/90, but there
were now a manageable 40 on each conference. Events in China had also
affected Wilton Park: just after the Tiananmen Square assault on protesting students, the Chinese had not replied to an invitation to a conference
on South-East Asia.

One unusual event broke the routine at Wiston House on August 18,
1990. This was its use for a wedding reception. The event sharply illustrated the Manager, John Melser's, view of the premises as an 'hotel', but
it also gave rise to complications with which hoteliers are sadly familiar. By
the following January the clients had still not paid their bill of £1,584, and
had to be pursued in the County Court.

Another, graver piece of unfinished business was the question of when
Geoffrey Denton should retire and be replaced. This had been left unresolved at the end of last year; but with Executive Agency status in the
offing, there had since been general agreement not to change Directors in
mid-stream. So the FCO had extended Denton's contract by an extra year,
until October 1992. That broke with the normal practice of retirement at
60; but, as Denton himself had pointed out, Heinz Koeppler had not
retired until he was 65.

Some feared that the extension of Denton's contract for just one year
might make him, like a departing US President, a 'lame duck'. Denton
himself, as an observer noted after visiting Wilton Park on February

26–27, was 'clearly unhappy at having to go'. The Treasury had different objections. It failed to see the need, stressed long ago by Denton and now accepted by the FCO, to look for academic staff in good time. One senior Treasury official wrote on April 17:

> I am concerned that it was planned to undertake recruitment before a final decision had been made about the Wiston House Conference Centre becoming a Next Steps Agency ... Also, I was perplexed by the apparent need to start recruiting now when the existing Director's contract does not expire until October 1992.

Despite these misgivings, the FCO advertised the Director's post in *The Guardian* on April 25, 1991, offering an annual salary of between £32,000 and £37,000. It hoped to hold a Selection Board on June 12. By May 10 there had been eight applications; by May 23 there had been twenty in full and three in outline. In the end, the Board was postponed.

This process did not altogether please the Wilton Park Academic Council. On May 11, Ernest Wistrich wrote to its Chairman, Michael Kaser, complaining that members had not been adequately consulted. On June 6, John Pinder urged Kaser to press for Denton to be kept on. When the Council met on June 14, Geoffrey Denton himself declared that he would like to stay until he was 65 – as Koeppler had, and as did the head of Ditchley Park. This would extend his tenure until June 1996. The majority of the Council strongly supported this plea, as Rosemary Spencer noted on June 18. In Denton's absence, Michael Kaser put on record that: 'The Academic Council had been tremendously satisfied with the work Geoffrey Denton had done. He had revivified Wilton Park and guided the conferences outstandingly well.' It also noted that 66 per cent of Wiston House's running costs were now met from income. For 1991/92, the FCO contribution was expected to be in the region of £10,000.

On July 1, 1991, Rosemary Spencer told Information Department that the selection process had failed to produce a good enough successor to Geoffrey Denton. The FCO's Personnel Policy Division later admitted that the trawl had had several handicaps: too early a start, too few advisers, too small and specialised a choice of media, and no use of professional head-hunters. With no new Director in sight, therefore, Rosemary Spencer recommended that Denton be given one more year, until October 1993, completing ten years in the job. A few days later, Michael Kaser discussed this idea with him. Denton said he was 'reasonably content'. On July 19, when he was just going on leave, the FCO made an informal offer of the extra year. He said he would decide 'soon'; and on September 12 he

provisionally agreed. The formal offer, at a salary higher than that advertised, was made on October 14.

Even so, Denton hesitated. On November 21, he told the Academic
Council that he would accept only on certain conditions. He wanted, first,
the completion of his annual report and a Job Appraisal interview;
secondly, a decision about performance pay; thirdly, clarification of Wilton
Park's policy and objectives; and fourthly, some assurance of being
consulted over the selection and appointment of his successor. At a
meeting with FCO officials on December 13, it was agreed that he would
assist the Departmental Board with its choice of a new Director, and that
meanwhile it would be sensible for Dr Richard Latter, who had been at
Wilton Park since November 1987, to be made Deputy Director. On the
one-year contract offer the FCO was firm: there would be no further
extension after 1993. Denton responded that he would think about it over
Christmas.

The New Year brought little light on the subject and some heat. On
January 31, 1992, Geoffrey Denton talked with Information Department.
He was 'fairly aggrieved', an official reported, about not knowing whether
he had been awarded a performance point, about having had to wait until
September before knowing what salary he would be offered, and about
being in effect downgraded by the change to Agency status: his case, he
said, had been 'badly handled over a long period'. Some weeks later,
Denton talked with the Head of Information Department, and some sharp
words were exchanged. 'I said it was not in our culture', the FCO official
reported on March 18, 1992, 'to bargain with our employers in the way he
was now doing.' At length, faced with this culture clash, Denton accepted
his final one-year contract extension on May 21, 1992.

Mutual irritation had been growing for some time. An FCO official had
complained about Denton on July 10, 1991: 'His performance in Agency
arrangements has been infuriating.' Denton was equally cross. 'It seems
remarkable', he wrote on October 7, 'that as an Executive Agency we still
have no freedom whatsoever in respect of such obvious internal management decisions' – by which he meant the hiring and firing of domestic
staff. On November 21, he received a query – 'I am concerned' – from the
FCO because he was planning as many as eight special conferences for
1992. On December 3, he wrote:

> As I mentioned to you on 21 November, I am keen not to become involved
> in detailed discussion and obtaining permission from Information
> Department to go ahead, especially in cases where we need to give quick
> responses. I am also keen to avoid anything which will reduce the enthusi-

asm of my colleagues and cause them to take a negative attitude towards suggestions we receive. Wilton Park has made progress over the years by having an innovative and enterprising attitude, and this must be maintained especially now that we are an Executive Agency.

By then, Wilton Park had been an Executive Agency for just over three months. Denton had hoped that the change would simplify his tasks as Director. But, as he wrote to the FCO on December 16, 1991: 'So far, Agency Status has only added to our problems.'

It was not simply that the Foreign and Commonwealth Office, needing to justify itself to the Treasury, still hankered after exerting political influence on Wilton Park. The need to go on fighting for academic independence was a permanent feature of life. What was new, and unwelcome, was the multiplication of paperwork.

Executive Agency status, that is, codified relations with the FCO. The Director and his staff, reconstituted as a Management Board under his chairmanship as 'Director and Chief Executive', were still to work out and run Wilton Park's programmes. The International Advisory Council was to go on monitoring their international relevance, while the Academic Council monitored their academic standards. But from now on, Wilton Park's work would be overseen by an FCO Departmental Board of up to a dozen people. Its job would be to set annual financial and quality targets, and like the two Councils, it would clearly expect to receive regular reports.

That was one new task for management. But there was also additional auditing. Suddenly, Wilton Park seemed to need not one audit, but three. On May 21, 1992 – the same day as he accepted his final one-year contract – Denton broached the subject with the Head of the FCO's Internal Audit Unit:

> Internal audit is only one of the bureaucratic burdens which appear to have followed from Agency status. Another is annual audit by the National Audit Office. A further one is audit by the Inland Revenue. Together with the requirement to report to the Departmental Board, in addition to our previous reports which went to our International Advisory Council and our Academic Council, we fear that too much of our limited management time will be taken up.

Internal audit, he added, would cost £18,500 over the next 5 years, so why not hire outside auditors? This was an idea that the Unit rather liked.

The complications of life as an Executive Agency arose again when it was suggested that a link might be formed between Wilton Park and the

Royal Institute of International Affairs at Chatham House. On July 17, 1992, the Head of Information Department proposed that the Permanent Under-Secretary at the Treasury should discuss this with Professor Laurence Martin, the Institute's Director. Commenting on the idea a few months later, a member of the Policy Planning Staff remarked: 'If Chatham House saw the burden of administration imposed by the Treasury they would run a mile.'

The Departmental Board, chaired by Rosemary Spencer, met for the first time on Friday October 23, 1992. Geoffrey Denton reported that commercial bookings of Wiston House were down, owing to the current recession, but that Wilton Park operations had more than offset the decline. Over sixty Reports on conferences, he added, had now been produced by Her Majesty's Stationery Office, with a print run of about 1,000 each. He swallowed his indignation about another report, in April, when an official of the CSCE [Conference on Security and Co-operation in Europe] Unit had committed the sixth breach of Wilton Park's rules. He had sent to seven other departments his account of a panel discussion on the Commonwealth of Independent States (CIS) during a conference on 'Building a European–Atlantic Community: Co-operation in Promoting Security and Economic Stability in Eastern Europe and the former Soviet Union'.

One idea from a Wilton Park Conference on the CIS and Eastern Europe, however, had borne unexpected fruit. This was a programme to advise the Russians on resettling ex-servicemen. At the Academic Council meeting on November 26, Denton was able to report that it had actually become Government policy. He was also pleased to announce that this year had seen an all-time high of 951 participants at Wilton Park, some of them assisted by the £10,000 a year or so donated by the Sir Heinz Koeppler Trust.

Pace the Treasury, the autumn of 1992 was high time for the FCO to start looking for Denton's successor a year later. The first advertisements appeared in October. By late November there were no fewer than 94 candidates, including Richard Latter from Wilton Park, a Group Captain, and an Air Commodore. Only Dr Latter no doubt realised the administrative maze that might lie ahead. Fortunately, however, Denton's complaints had not gone unheard. On January 6, 1993, the new Permanent Under-Secretary learned that FCO officials were urgently concerned about the multiple auditing and other problems imposed on Wilton Park, and he decided to go there and see for himself. The upshot was a measure of simplification, especially on the question of audits. On Friday January 22 Geoffrey Denton drew up a 'balance sheet' of the advantages and drawbacks that Executive Agency status had brought.

The two major improvements, he thought, were the Departmental Board and greater flexibility in staffing and recruitment. But there were four disadvantages: accountancy, spending limits, auditing, and reporting. Part of the difficulty sprang from the fact that Wilton Park was the smallest of all the Executive Agencies, half the size of the Queen Elizabeth Conference Centre; and the rules had been tailored to fit entities on a larger scale.

The first question was a technical, accounting matter. Agency status should make it possible to move from cash to accruals accountancy. Wilton Park already used the latter – but to satisfy the FCO Finance Department was now having to do cash accounting as well, and manually at that, because the software could not do both. Denton had had to appoint an accounts assistant to cope with the work.

Spending limits posed a second problem. He was not allowed to exceed them without permission, even if the extra expenditure would bring in more revenue.

Thirdly, there was the matter of auditing. Denton had already raised this, and as a result the Internal Audit Unit had already agreed to reduce its charges in 1993/94.

Finally, there was the demand for multiple reports. The Director had to report twice a year to the Departmental Board, twice a year to the Academic Council, and once a year to the International Advisory Council. He had to present monthly accounts, quarterly financial reports, and a report for the Annual Review of Executive Agencies. He was also bombarded with questionnaires, and inundated with copies of letters to all Agencies from the Treasury and the Office of Public Service and Science (OPSS) in the Cabinet Office. The Treasury, incidentally, had still not quite abandoned its distaste for having Wilton Park on its books. On January 18, the Financial Secretary Stephen Dorrell wrote to the Foreign Secretary Douglas Hurd suggesting that it move further towards full privatisation.

Denton's complaints were not well received by the OPSS. Its Permanent Secretary disliked what he described on October 22 as their 'carping and self-pitying tone' – particularly when they were widely circulated. But, despite these travails, Wilton Park continued to meet most of its targets. Wilton Park had exceeded four of its 1992/93 targets, and only narrowly failed (by 1 per cent) to recover the planned percentage of its costs. As Geoffrey Denton reported June 18, 1993, to the Academic Council, Wilton Park had met all its targets; total participant numbers had reached 1047 in 1992/93 compared with 916 in 1991/92; and, as a result, he needed two extra staff.

This was Geoffrey Denton's last report to the Academic Council before his retirement in October 1993. When inviting members to the Council meeting, the FCO had announced that on October 1 Denton would be succeeded by Richard Langhorne, Director of the Centre for International Studies at the University of Cambridge.

Born on May 6, 1940, and hence some ten years younger than Geoffrey Denton, Richard Langhorne had been a Fellow and Junior Bursar of St John's College, Cambridge, since 1974. A Fellow of the Royal Historical Society, he had taught at the Universities of Exeter and Kent at Canterbury, and been a Visiting Professor at the University of Southern California. His speciality was twentieth-century diplomatic history. In *Who's Who* he described his recreations as 'music, railways'. But his qualifications were more specifically academic than those of any previous incumbent at Wilton Park. Perhaps for this reason, Liliana Archibald, the new chairman of the Academic Council, suggested on October 7 to the new Head of Information Department, that Langhorne might welcome management training now that he had taken on so managerial a job.

His academic responsibilities overlapped with his early months at Wilton Park – and led to unfounded suspicions of 'moonlighting'. Before he left Cambridge, Langhorne had agreed with Dr March of the Spanish Centre of International Studies at Barcelona to run a trainee diplomats' course in Cambridge in conjunction with Geoffrey Edwards of the Centre for International Studies. The original plan had been for the whole course to take place in Cambridge. When Langhorne was appointed to Wilton Park, he envisaged spending the relevant time in Cambridge by using part of his annual leave. Then, with Wiston House vacant for a week, he offered to split the venues between Cambridge and Wilton Park. The total cost to Barcelona was to be £300 per head plus a £1,000 'facilities fee' (for organisation, travel, and administration). Though apparently costly, the facilities fee was normal practice, accepted by both sides. March paid the resultant total of £7,060 into a 'Cambridge Account', with £3,360 earmarked for Cambridge and £3,700 for Wilton Park. The facilities fee was deducted from this second sum, so that Wilton Park banked £2,700. This, thought suspicious minds in the FCO Finance Department, was '*prima facie* evidence of misappropriation'. In reality, the splitting of venues (and costs) had brought custom to Wilton Park which would otherwise have gone only to Cambridge; and Langhorne's teaching on the course, which he would otherwise have done in Cambridge, took place in Wilton Park but still as part of his annual leave.

The ensuing storm, though of teacup proportions, took several months to clear, between June and October 1994. In other respects, according to one Information Department official, Richard Langhorne had 'a more harmonious relationship with OPSS' than Denton had had. He certainly shared Denton's outward-looking concerns. Soon after taking his post, on October 27, 1993, he had surveyed Wilton Park's overseas associations: they were flourishing, he found, in Austria, Belgium and France, Canada, Finland, Germany, Gibraltar, Greece, Italy, Portugal, the United States, and Switzerland, where the two existing organisations – the Friends of Wilton Park and the Wilton Park Committee – decided to merge on November 6, 1993, as the Swiss Association for Wilton Park. In May 1994 Langhorne visited Los Angeles, and at a reception at the residence of the British Consul-General he spoke to the Southern California Friends of Wilton Park. Their *Newsletter*, Vol. 7 (Winter 1994–95) summarised his speech:

> The end of the Cold War, he said, had not simplified the international situation, nor had it resulted in a reduction of the number of topics and conferences at Wilton Park. Some 28 conferences were held in 1994, and 32 were planned for 1995 with a total of approximately 1,200 participants expected to attend (compared to 1,055 in 1993).
>
> The week-long conference format was now firmly established, as longer conferences were just not sustainable due to the time pressure on participants.
>
> Major topics included European integration, international security, arms control, and the reform process in the former Soviet Union and Eastern Europe. Among the new subjects discussed at Wilton Park would be the role of world communications and the media in the conduct of foreign policy. Professor Langhorne said that he planned to increase the number of conferences devoted to South-East Asia and the Pacific Basin. Asia was now an important center of gravity in the international system and it was right to take account of this development.
>
> In 1995 there would be 5 conferences on Asian topics. These would include both geographically-based subjects – for example, a conference in September on the Indian sub-continent and Sri Lanka – as well as thematic conferences (for example, one on what he described as political stultification in South-East Asia). [This was presumably No. 447, more tactfully entitled 'Prospects for Regional Security and Prosperity in South-East Asia: Indonesia at 50 and her Neighbours': it was held on September 4–8, 1995, following a visit to the region by Langhorne in 1994.]
>
> In order to raise funds to help bring over participants from the former Soviet bloc and the third world, Wiston House would be let for private use when the conference center was not in use. Also a tax-exempt branch of the Heinz Koeppler Trust would be established in the United States ...
>
> The responsibilities of the Wilton Park Staff had been rearranged.

Professor Langhorne himself dealt with the evolution and present-day machinery of diplomacy. His deputy, Richard Latter, dealt with international security, terrorism and arms control.

The four conference organizers divided their energies as follows: Nicholas Hopkinson – *international economics, trade and the European Union*; Claire Spencer – *north Africa, southern Europe, the Mediterranean, and the rise of Islam and its consequences*; David Cairncross – Japan and Asia; and Jenny Little (a new addition who had previously been a Foreign Office research cadre and International Secretary of the Labour Party) – *former Yugoslavia and Eastern Europe*.

Wilton Park, Professor Langhorne concluded, could now offer 50 rooms for each conference with en suite bathrooms and central heating. Exercise equipment was soon to be installed. The standard was that of a luxury hotel, and Wiston House was really a 'small palace' or great house in the best English tradition, with a park and gardens.

This assurance was no doubt in answer to a comment earlier that year by the British Information Services in New York, who on January 18 had repeated to Langhorne what he had said of Geoffrey Denton's policy as long ago as November 1992: that Wilton Park's high fees tended to put off US visitors.

As Langhorne said in Los Angeles, he was casting his net wide. Geoffrey Denton had set a precedent by holding the first Wilton Park conference outside the United Kingdom. Langhorne determined to follow it. He told the International Advisory Council on May 18 that he had tentative plans to run a conference in Poland later in 1994; in 1995, there might be one in the Caribbean. His hope was to hold one overseas conference every year. It was ambitious, but Wiston House was more and more paying its way.

The Caribbean conference did not figure on the 1995 calendar: but the Polish conference took place from September 12–16, 1994. It was held at Natolin, near Warsaw, in association with the Council of Ministers, Warsaw. Its subject was 'The European Union and Central Europe: From Association to Membership?' There were 92 participants, 24 of them Polish; others came from Austria, Belgium, Bulgaria, the College of Europe, Denmark, Estonia, the European Union institutions, Finland, France, Germany, Hungary, Italy, Latvia, Lithuania, the Netherlands, New Zealand, Romania, Russia, Slovakia, Spain, Sweden, Switzerland, the UK and the USA.

Afterwards, Nicholas Hopkinson's contribution on 'The Eastern Enlargement of the European Union' was published as a 48-page *Wilton Park Paper*. It concluded, among other things, that 'EU membership would effectively be today's equivalent of the Marshall Plan'. It argued that 'the best way the CEECs [Central and East European Countries] can prepare themselves for EMU [Economic and Monetary Union] and membership is by speeding up their market reforms'. It acknowledged that 'an EU [European Union] with more than 15 members will be unable to function unless its institutions and procedures are reformed'. It reported that 'the CEECs believe that it is vital for the EU to conclude a clear timetable of the essential requirements for eventual CEEC membership'. It argued that 'the eventual accession of CEECs to the EU, and possibly NATO, should not isolate the Russian Federation'. It declared that 'political and economic agreements must be reached in order to ensure that the Russian reform process is both encouraged and reinforced'. And it warned that 'to encompass the CEECs whilst isolating Russia would be a mistake that risks jeopardising not only the enlargement process but also the future stability and prosperity of the entire continent'.

This large, timely, and very successful conference was the precursor of many similar ventures, usually with co-sponsorship, in such venues as Vienna, Helsinki, Brdo Castle in Slovenia, Tallinn, Natolin again, Dubrovnik, and Bratislava.

Having launched the first of this series in September 1994, Richard Langhorne had disconcerting news for the Foreign and Commonwealth Office. On December 2, 1994, he told the Head of Information Department, that he had been offered a possible job in the United States, at Rutgers University, Newark. He would not leave, he said, before October 1995, and would give at least six months' notice.

Langhorne's last year of office at Wilton Park was marked by a series of encouraging reports. The first, on January 24, 1995, was prompted by a mischievous Parliamentary Question tabled by the Labour MP Gerald Kaufman. Langhorne prepared the deadpan answer. Wiston House had been leased since 1951. It had recruited three more support staff since acquiring Agency status, to deal with a 60 per cent increase in the programme of work. It published no periodical journal. It had no executive cars. There was no corporate clothing, though the trade union side was pressing for some kind of staff uniform. It had always had Wilton Park stationery, and there was no extra cost in that respect now that it was an Executive Agency.

July 10, 1995, brought another Parliamentary Question, this time inspired. The answer revealed that in 1994/95 Wilton Park had exceeded all four of its agreed targets – in number of participants, income, cost recovery, and overall cost per head to the FCO.

Richard Langhorne confirmed Wilton Park's continuing success in the

Annual Report and Accounts for 1994/95, published on July 12, 1995. This revealed that, on the basis of voluntary questionnaires, 56.4 per cent of all respondents judged the programmes to be 'excellent' and 36.9 per cent 'above average', with 50.3 per cent and 41.2 per cent giving the same rating to the quality of discussion. The administration of the conferences was judged 'excellent' by 79.6 per cent and 'above average' by 18.4 per cent. Rooms, meals, and service respectively were rated 'excellent' by 55.9 per cent, 58.7 per cent, and 82.2 per cent. Langhorne concluded:

> Wilton Park has now reached its maximum planned level of activity and neither in Wilton Park conferences themselves, nor in private sector letting is there space or time for further expansion. The number of calendar conferences will therefore remain at 32, with the possibility of a small rise to 35, depending on international events and the desire of sponsors to arrange special meetings ... Another important factor ... will continue to operate in 1995/96. Wilton Park deals with the most difficult international issues of the day, and those issues tend to arise in areas of the world where these very difficulties create a shortage of domestic resources. Some of the most significant conferences therefore also bring greater costs and may be smaller in number than others ... Despite uncertainties of this kind, however, Wilton Park's prospects for 1995/96 look both busy and financially successful.
>
> Wilton Park is willing to consider holding meetings abroad once a year, provided that the resources on offer are fully suitable, and recent successful conferences in Finland and Poland have been the result. In 1996, there will be a conference in Zürich, held in association with the Europa Institute of Zürich University, to mark the fiftieth anniversary of Sir Winston Churchill's speech on the possibility of future European integration given at Zürich University in September, 1946.

Later that year, on November 2, 1995, the 'Next Steps Team' of the Office of Public Service (formerly the OPSS) in the Cabinet Office produced its rather ominously entitled 'Prior Options Review' of Wilton Park. This recognised a steady growth in the annual number of participants, from 914 in 1991/92 to 1,260 in 1994/95, and a fall in the average number on each course, from 48.1 to about 42. It recommended that Wilton Park should continue, but noted that a university or a foundation could perform its task if any were willing to take it on. Wiston House, however, was 'tailor made for Wilton Park conferences'. Should Wilton Park be abolished? No. Should it be wholly privatised? No. Would a university take it on? No. Should it be reabsorbed into the Foreign Office? No again.

All this was a great advance on Wilton Park's long, precarious years of hand-to-mouth existence, drastic cuts, and Treasury threats of extinction.

However, security had a price-tag. The Prior Options Review insisted that Wilton Park should break even, charge full commercial fees to all those who could afford them, and not only test the market, but actively market itself. That made good commercial sense. More questionable, however, was the Prior Option Review's slant on Wilton Park's relations with the Foreign and Commonwealth Office. The FCO, it suggested, should sponsor individual conferences. There seemed no harm in that, provided that Wilton Park could go on running its own. FCO departments, the Review continued, should contribute ideas for Wilton Park programmes. Again, this presented no problem: everyone could usefully offer suggestions and expertise. It was the Review's culminating recommendation that raised eyebrows. This was that Wilton Park should adjust its programmes if FCO departments failed to endorse them.

Richard Langhorne had left Wilton Park by the time the Prior Options Review was completed; but he had sensed its possible drift. At worst, the FCO might increasingly control Wilton Park just as it gradually ceased financing it – a seemingly splendid bargain for Whitehall, but a potential erosion of academic independence and, in the long run, of Britain's own interest in showing itself open to free debate. Fear of future lengthy battles, coupled with a tempting US job offer, helped convince Langhorne that his place lay elsewhere. He duly left, to become Director of the Center for Global Change and Governance at Rutgers University. But like many Old Wiltonians, he was still drawn back to Wiston House. In January 2001 he was one of the participants at a Special Conference to celebrate 50 years of Wilton Park in its Sussex home. Another participant on that occasion was Rainer Barzel, a highly distinguished Old Wiltonian from the very early days.

Richard Langhorne's successor was Colin Jennings, who replaced him as Chief Executive and Director in May 1996. After Leicester University, where he had taken an MA with Distinction, Jennings had worked for the UK Ministry of Defence from 1976 to 1983, primarily on NATO conventional and nuclear defence weapons policy, including a secondment to the UK Delegation to NATO, and on defence commitments in the Falkland Islands and Belize. In 1983 he had transferred to the Foreign and Commonwealth Office. Here he had a varied career. He first worked in Policy Planning Staff on security issues and the Americas, then from 1986 to 1989 was First Secretary (Economic) in Lagos, concentrating on international debt issues and the oil industry. From 1990 to 1992 he was Assistant Head of the FCO's Central and Southern Africa Department, and finally from 1992 to 1996 Deputy High Commissioner in Nicosia.

Jennings's arrival at Wilton Park was followed – and marked – by a spate of anniversary conferences. The first took place on Friday June 14 1996, and commemorated the foundation of Wilton Park fifty years before. Two former Directors were present – Tim Slack and Geoffrey Denton; so were former and present Associate Directors, members of the Academic and International Councils, and other eminent friends of Wilton Park. Colin Jennings introduced the conference: he was followed by Dr Jürgen Oesterhelt, the German Ambassador, by Geoffrey Denton and by Lawrence Freedman of King's College, London. Jeremy Hanley, MP, Minister of State at the FCO, spoke at the lunch.

That September, in Zürich, Wilton Park fêted the fiftieth anniversary of Winston Churchill's speech there envisaging a United States of Europe. Hundreds of people gathered in the same hall at the University of Zürich to hear keynote addresses from Federal Councillor Flavio Cotti and the UK Foreign Secretary Malcolm Rifkind, as well as reflections on Churchill's speech by his grandson Nicholas Soames and by Robert Rhodes James. Ninety-eight of those present, from a dozen countries, took part in the Wilton Park Conference that followed, to discuss the future of Europe.

In December, again celebrating its fiftieth anniversary, Wilton Park hosted a meeting of some seventy distinguished visitors, Muslim, Jewish and Christian, to discuss 'A Sense of the Sacred: Building Bridges between Islam and the West'. After introductions by Colin Jennings and by Sir John Coles, Permanent Under-Secretary at the FCO, the opening speaker was His Royal Highness the Prince of Wales. It was a further august welcome to the new hand on the Wilton Park helm.

Colin Jennings was the first veteran of the FCO to head Wilton Park. His appointment, as a senior official noted in a Five-Year Review of Wilton Park (1995–2000), had two consequences:

> Mr Jennings's FCO background and good working knowledge of senior FCO personnel and methods of operation have led to a more harmonious and productive relationship than was previously the case and have enhanced Wilton Park's profile and range of direct contacts within the FCO. The relationship has been further assisted by FCO confidence in Mr Jennings's proactive and competent management and commitment to raising the value for money efficiency of Wilton Park.

In practice, proposals for conference themes continued to emanate from the Academic Council, now strengthened to include wider NGO, ethnic, and business participation, and from Wilton Park itself. Wilton Park then sent an annual list of 30 to the relevant parts of the FCO, which had then to assess priorities and discuss their validity. The Chief Executive would follow this up in person, partly to get backing for participants, speakers, publicity through diplomatic posts, sponsorship, and contributions to costs.

At the same time, it was vital to maintain Wilton Park's academic independence. Colin Jennings had to make clear that his determination to shed old attachments and devote his energies wholly and loyally to Wilton Park and Wiston House. He spelled out Wilton Park's continuing aims, and his own, in the statement with which he prefaced the Annual Report and Accounts:

> Wilton Park was established in 1946 ... to help re-establish peace and democracy in Europe. Since then it has developed a unique status as an academically independent and non-profit making Executive Agency of the Foreign and Commonwealth Office (FCO), and has become one of the world's leading institutions for discussion of international issues ...
>
> In a fast-moving world, Wilton Park's conferences provide an opportunity for people of influence from within and outside government to share experience on the best ways of dealing with major international and domestic challenges ...
>
> The participants comprise a wide range of nationalities and professional disciplines. Most are in a position to make a direct impact on future policy (on average over 60% are officials working on the issues concerned) ...
>
> Discussions are confidential and unattributable to encourage frank exchanges ...
>
> Wilton Park is underwritten financially by the FCO, which also provides invaluable advice and contacts ... Its academic independence is guaranteed by an Academic Council of distinguished figures from a range of professions in Britain and by an International Advisory Council of the OECD Ambassadors and High Commissioners based in London.

Under Jennings's stewardship, as the 2000 report noted, the number of Wilton Park and Special Conferences rose from 32 in 1994/95 to 44 in 1998/99, with participation increasing from 1,363 to 2,194, and average attendance per conference rising from 42 to 50. To handle these volumes, staff had to be increased from 32 to 45, eight of them part-time. This involved adding one Associate Director, and creating seven teams comprising a Conference Administrator and a Secretary working to a member of the Academic staff. The Five-Year Review commented:

> Staff management, since the appointment of the present Chief Executive in 1996, has been a clear success story. Longer serving staff stress the transformation which Mr Jennings's firm and sensitive management has achieved over the past four years in developing a strong corporate spirit, in

giving staff a clear sense of direction and in bridging the previous divisions between academic and administrative personnel. Internal communication and team building have been greatly improved ... Greater responsibility has been delegated to Associate Directors with clear management lines and objectives for the academic teams ... Training has been stepped up internally, by more use of FCO management courses and for IT [Information Technology]. The management of Wiston House is in similar good order, with the Associate Director (Finance and Management), Mr [Roger] Barr, providing good leadership in running a committed and hardworking team. No visitor to Wilton Park can fail to be impressed by the high morale and strong motivation of the staff; and Mr Jennings and his team are to be congratulated on obtaining for Wilton Park the award of the Investors in People standard at the first attempt in 1998.

The Academic staff had come from many backgrounds. In 2001, as well as Richard Latter and Nicholas Hopkinson, it included Virginia Crowe, who was on the staff from 1995 to her retirement at the end of the year. She presided over conferences on a particularly wide range of subjects, from cultural policy to the environment. She had followed a research post in the House of Commons Library with relevant work in a variety of international contexts, and brought with her useful skills, contacts and experience from the diplomatic world. Ironically, her husband, when Head of FCO Policy Planning Staff, had advocated the closure of Wilton Park in 1976 to save costs.

Robin Hart joined in 1996 from the Ministry of Defence, and transformed the programme of conferences on China and East Asia, and following the spirit of Koeppler, ran the annual British German Forum, which gathered people under 35 from both countries for what was often, by common consent, one of the most lively events of the year.

Chris Langdon moved from the TV newsroom to Wilton Park when he joined in 1997 running events, based on his experience as a news producer, on the new electronic agenda. True to the ethos of Wilton Park, he also ran many conferences on post-conflict reconciliation in former Yugoslavia held both at Wilton Park and in South East Europe.

In 1999 Roger Williamson enriched Wilton Park's Third World agenda with his experience of working for the Church of England and Christian Aid. Both he and Isobelle Jaques, who joined in 2001, with a background in human rights at the Council of Europe and Amnesty International, also covered the conflict and post-conflict agenda, and the role of the UN institutions. The Ukraine, the Middle East, including Iran, were among the difficult themes that Isobelle Jaques took on.

David Pinder, who came in 2001 after a varied career in business and the forces, further developed long-established contacts with the Russian military and the Russian political scene.

After the departure of Roger Barr, the commercial running of Wiston House was split into two. Nick Beard, a former army officer who had managed the royal palaces of King Hussein of Jordan until the King's death, and who joined Wiston House in 2000, took over the management side. And Tim Willows, who was seconded from the Inland Revenue and had close family connections with the Wiston Estate, supervised the finances from 2001 onwards.

By the summer of 2001, total staff numbers had risen to 57 (including 15 part-timers), of whom 23 organised Wilton Park Conferences and 34 dealt with commercial events and provided 'hotel' services.

The reason was the increasing burden of work which the Five-Year Review had already highlighted. The number of conferences had increased from 32 in 1994/95 to 44 in 1998/99; in 2000/01, there were 46. Even before this last record number, the Review had remarked:

> Conferences have been delivered without apparent loss of quality. Staff however are certainly very stretched and the view of both the FCO and the Academic Council is that, without a further increase in staff resources, the number of Conferences is at or very near the limit, if quality is not to be prejudiced.

This, then, was not an option for increasing revenue. Further raising fees was possible: but here too the Review was cautious: 'There is as yet no solid evidence of customer resistance, though the fact that a European Foreign Ministry is currently seeking reduced rates gives an amber light.'

There remained the possibility of increasing conference sponsorship. Already, this was playing an important and growing role. By the time of the report, it had increased from £100,000 in 1995/96 to £494,000 in 1998/99; by 2000/01 it had reached £1,278,000. In that year, those involved in co-sponsorship of conferences included 45 public and private institutions throughout the world. They ranged from Beijing to Los Alamos, from Hong Kong to the West Indies; from UK Government Departments (including the FCO) to the European Parliament, from the International Committee of the Red Cross to NATO, from Cisco Systems to De la Rue Currency, from the Carnegie Foundation to the Media Centre, Belgrade, from Barclays Bank to the Swedish Ministry for Foreign Affairs. In July 2001, Wilton Park even returned to its Anglo-German roots by replacing the British Council as the Bavarian Government's partner in the British-Bavarian Seminar at the Akademie Schloss Hohenkammer.

As well as co-sponsorship, Wilton Park continued to earn some 20 per cent of its revenue from commercial business. Social affairs such as weddings were now less frequent; but when Wilton Park conferences were not in session, the house accommodated such paying customers as American Express, the British Council, the European Commission, the Export and Credit Guarantee Department, and the University of Sussex.

In both sponsorship and to a lesser extent commercial letting, there was scope for further expansion. Already, Wilton Park had been developing and adapting its marketing to new technology and new needs. That meant not only new and smarter publications, but also a video, narrated by the BBC's Nik Gowing, a member of the Academic Council, and a website (www.wiltonpark.org.uk), opened in 1998. This last not only gave Wilton Park greater publicity, but was developed to lighten the administrative workload, by offering documentation and a registration pack for conferences.

Even so, marketing and fund-raising remained labour-intensive tasks. Fearn reported:

> The option of appointing a specialist fund raiser at Associate Director level has been considered. Such a post, detached from Conference management and knowledge of conference themes would however seem unlikely to work well or to provide value for money.

Given this judgement, the report recommended separating Colin Jennings's two jobs of Chief Executive and Director. Accordingly, in 2001, Jennings was reappointed for another five years as Chief Executive of Wilton Park, while Dr Richard Latter became its Director. Latter was a familiar face at Wiston House. A graduate of Liverpool University and the London School of Economics, who had been a lecturer at Leiden, he had been on the Academic Staff at Wilton Park since November 1987, most recently as Deputy Director.

There was now a duumvirate at the top. Essentially, this meant changes of title, task and status, not of teamwork. The Chief Executive retained the main responsibility for strengthening the dialogue with FCO and other Government departments, with the business community, and overseas, but now had more time for promotion, marketing, and sponsorship fund-raising. The Director, under the Chief Executive and supporting him in his sponsorship and marketing work, was responsible for conference management and for co-ordinating the core Conference agenda.

Wilton Park's conference programme was, of course, its *raison d'être*. Its scope, once Anglo–German, had become West European, pan-European,

Atlantic, and finally global. In the early 1990s, Europe had still been predominant. In 1993, for instance, out of 24 conferences, a good half had mainly concerned Europe, although China, Russia, South Asia, and South Africa had also played their part. A similar pattern emerged in the following year, but with two Middle-Eastern subjects and emphasis on ecology, demography, law enforcement, the media, and biological weapons appearing alongside more traditional general topics such as trade, security and arms control. This broad balance continued, varying debates on 'hot spots' with longer-term consideration of technology, communications, religion, the environment, aid, and diplomacy in general. 'Britain and Ireland: a New Relationship within Europe?' was a 'hot' topic broached in 1996. On the first day of the Conference the Canary Wharf bomb went off. Other conferences that year covered India, the Caribbean, and the CIS. Novel subjects for 1997 included the marine environment, drugs, New Zealand, and media coverage of election campaigns. The 1998 programme included two France/Russia/UK military symposia and discussions of equity markets, race, human rights, and Islam and the West. The prospects for small states, transnational organised crime, press freedom in the Commonwealth, CBW (chemical and biological weapons) terrorism, the privatisation of security, the digital economy, Antarctica, oil and gas, the Caspian, and Global Corporate Citizenship – all these were issues well beyond the ordinary pabulum of international debate. But they co-existed with work on tried and true topics, as well as those in the news at the time.

The balance was not always easy to maintain. The 2000 Review had made this clear:

> The length of the agenda setting process, the time needed to research, prepare and market Conferences, and Wilton Park's traditional view of its role as focussing on the medium term, combine to dictate an emphasis on the durable 'bigger issues' on the international agenda. Such Conferences also tend to guarantee greater participation (if, as a generalisation, at more middle than senior levels). The need to maintain flexibility to respond to FCO, OGD [other Government Departments] and overseas initiatives for Conferences on more short-term 'cutting edge' problems is recognised and current policy is to leave sufficient gaps in the agenda to accommodate these. However, holding such Conferences depends on financial resources through sponsorship. The requirement to meet financial targets by maximising occupancy also limits the ability to keep such gaps open into the Conference year.

'Cutting edge' *versus* 'bigger issues' was a dichotomy that Colin Jennings thought overdone. Virtually all the subjects addressed by Wilton

Park were 'cutting edge'. What the author of the Review had in mind were matters of urgent current policy yielding short-term practical results. He admitted that 'specific outcomes from Wilton Park Conferences are inevitably ... difficult to define'. In his report he gave one instance: 'the FCO sponsored post-Kosovo Conference in (September) 1999 which generated specific new policy initiatives'.

Such policy innovation comes most notably from top decision-makers; and Wilton Park certainly continued to attract them. They included Heads of State, premiers, departmental ministers, speakers of parliaments, party leaders, ambassadors, heads of international organisations both public and private, chairmen and presidents of corporations, university professors, media editors, and many younger high-flyers from all over the world. It would be tempting to quote their words. But the fact that discussions at Wilton Park remain unattributable makes it rarely possible to do so, and hard to identify all but a handful of 'specific outcomes'.

A few examples must stand for many. In May 1997, a Scandinavian diplomat said that Conference No 499 on European Union Enlargement had been 'instrumental in putting Estonia in the front rank of applicants for the EU. Discussions during the conference had convinced Finnish, German and other officials that Estonia was significantly ahead ... in its political and economic development.' In October 1997, the Greece–Turkey conference 'produced sustained follow-up dialogue between senior politicians and former officials from both countries ... This ... was regarded by the FCO with great favour as virtually the only productive dialogue in that difficult bilateral relationship.' A conference on Welfare Reform in July 1998 had spawned 'important policy initiatives through further dialogue between US and UK researchers and policy makers'. In the same year, when Israeli–Palestinian contacts were interrupted, Wilton Park helped to maintain communication. 'As an Israeli', wrote a senior diplomat, 'Wilton Park has provided my colleagues and me with the unique opportunity to exchange views with our counterparts from Syria, Lebanon, Iran, Saudi Arabia, and Kuwait.' After an invitation-only conference in March 1999, on supporting the independent media in Serbia and Kosovo, 'an Albanian said how incredible it was for him to sit down and talk with the leader of the Serbian opposition – impossible anywhere else'. At the France/ Russia/UK Defence Symposium in October 1999, the head of the Russian Delegation, General Manilov, First Deputy Chief of the Russian General Staff, said that 'he had persuaded the Russian National Security Council that Russia must participate in this third trilateral. He did so at a time when Russian contacts with the West and NATO were frosty post-Kosovo. The event thus marked the beginning of efforts

to re-open bridge-building between the Russian military and the West.'
After the Dubrovnik conference in May 2001 which continued while
fighting in Macedonia grew more intense, Gordon Brett of NATO's Crisis
Management Section wrote: 'Some of the ideas we were discussing on the
last day to encourage the authorities in Skopje to bridge the gap between
themselves and the ethnic-Albanian extremists/terrorists are being
actively followed up by NATO and the EU at the moment.'

The paucity of quotable 'specific outcomes' was a dilemma long
acknowledged by Heinz Koeppler. When he and others sought to 'prove'
the value of their work, they were reduced to citing participants' praise,
either in bald evaluation forms, or in often glowing *lettres de château*.

The author of the 2000 Review faced the same problem. As he
admitted: 'The value of the majority of Conferences is cumulative in terms
of new insights and greater comparative knowledge and understanding,
which feed into policy making in the medium rather than the short term.'
He therefore relied on seeking 'the views of some 30 main users ... and
members of the Academic and Advisory Councils'.

> These soundings confirm the highly positive, indeed warm and enthusi-
> astic, level of customer appreciation. Comments focus on:
> * the unique status internationally of Wilton Park in providing a high
>   quality forum for expert, informed and objective discussion on a very
>   wide range of issues relevant to the needs of foreign policy profession-
>   als and contributing to solutions
> * the high quality of Conference preparation, organisation and discus-
>   sion with particular praise for the structure of Conferences, for the skill
>   shown in focussing on topical aspects of foreign policy problems, and
>   for effective chairmanship
> * the value of exposure to a wide diversity of approaches and views
> * the short and longer term benefits of Wilton Park's facilitation of
>   informal 'corridor' discussion and interaction with other participants
>   (particularly those on the other side of a political fence): the develop-
>   ment of personal relationships and future networks
> * the high standard of administration.

With the slightly dutiful air of covering well-trodden ground, the
Review surveyed theoretical alternative options for Wilton Park at the
beginning of the 21st century. One, as always, was abolition:

> Wilton Park and its function of organising high quality Conferences on
> international problems are not essential to the operations of the FCO.
> Wilton Park is however seen as an important asset contributing to key FCO
> objectives and doing so at a modest cost to the FCO budget and to the

taxpayer. It enjoys a high reputation internationally. Customer demand remains at a solid level with overall participation increasing and participation per Conference being maintained.

Abolition would involve significant short term costs in staff redundancy payments. Wiston House is leased so that there would be few assets to realise: and there would be no return on the capital invested in refurbishment.

Abolition would also be likely to give rise to domestic and international criticism. It would be seen as the loss of a unique asset for raising the UK profile internationally and for contributing to foreign policy problem solving. It would be viewed as representing a withdrawal by HMG from its stated policy of maximising its global influence.

This was a far cry from the years of Treasury threats, last-ditch battles for survival, and uneconomic, short-term renewals of the Wiston House lease. The Review even recommended that negotiations to replace the current lease, due to expire in 2007, should begin 'sooner rather than later'.

It also considered, and dismissed, the notions of privatisation, merger, or contracting out. Privatisation, it thought, was unlikely to find takers, make adequate commercial profits, provide the same benefits, or enjoy the same prestige: 'A privatised Wilton Park would ... soon come under pressure to use the Conference Centre for more commercially saleable conferences and activities with progressive dilution of the purpose of Wilton Park.' Merger, the Review concluded, was equally unrealistic. The only conceivable partner was the Civil Service College, whose focus was national and on training. Contracting out – to Ditchley Park, for instance, or Chatham House – seemed no less unlikely and undesirable.

That left the preferred alternative: continued agency status:

The combination, which Wilton Park provides and which Agency status assists, of a wide measure of devolved responsibility, academic independence and continued links to and support from Government gives it a unique status internationally. The FCO connection is important to its success. It is valued by participants who see it as adding weight and legitimacy to Wilton Park Conferences. Without FCO involvement, it is at least questionable whether Wilton Park Conferences would attract current levels of foreign government participation.

For the FCO, Agency status provides an effective interface, requiring minimal management oversight, at a declining and modest cost (particularly if compared with other FCO Programme Budget subventions in the public diplomacy field), while retaining final control over Wilton Park's operations. This semi-detached relationship also allows the FCO to continue to maximise the benefits in terms of influencing Conference agendas, drawing credit from the Conferences' contributions to under-standing and problem solving, and developing influence, insights and contacts.

In short, Agency status suits both the FCO and Wilton Park well.

And yet, in nationalist eyes, there must surely be a contradiction between Wilton Park's ideal of dispassionate inquiry, in which Britain's policies would be criticised as searchingly as any, and the fact of its being backed by the UK Government through the FCO. True, the FCO's strategic support for Wilton Park is now less than 5 per cent of its running costs: the rest is met by conference charges, sponsorship of individual conferences by the FCO and other bodies, and commercial revenue. But it remains nonetheless an Executive Agency of the Foreign and Commonwealth Office. How then can the circle be squared?

The answer is the same as it has been from the very beginning: enlightened creative tension. In the 21st century, Koeppler's 'self-denying ordinance' still holds good. The long-term interests of Britain are best served by free, off-the-record discussion. This might find fault with the actions of Britain, her European partners, or her transatlantic allies. But, as Socrates said, 'the unexamined life is not worth living'. Only radical scrutiny can identify flaws and look for remedies. Only unfettered debate can prove that short-term, short-sighted policies harm the national interest. Only collective effort can devise long-term solutions to problems of common concern.

It was a lesson that Jean Monnet had applied in the European Community. Thanks to Heinz Koeppler and his successors, it is still being taught and demonstrated at Wilton Park.

CHAPTER 27

Continuity

'Institutions live longer than people. If they are well constructed, they can accumulate and pass on the wisdom of successive generations.'
Jean Monnet, *Les États-unis d'Europe ont commencé* (1955)

Revolutions that fail may afterwards look heroic. Those that succeed may become institutions, eclipsing their heroic past. By any standard, Wilton Park began as a revolution. At a time of bitter hatred, recrimination, justice and revenge, it sought out the roots of evil, confronted deceitful ideologies, and began to reconcile former enemies at a level of common humanity deeper than divisive stereotypes. It turned then to the task of civic education, preparing leaders for the duties of democracy in a country of physical ruin, moral bewilderment, and near-despair. Broadening its range and ambition, it brought together people of many countries, creeds, professions and political persuasions to discuss not only their shared problems but also their mutual conflicts, again to curb antagonism and encourage goodwill. Latterly, Wilton Park has focussed attention on countries newly emerged from dictatorship in Eastern Europe or struggling to escape poverty in the Third World.

In pursuing its aims, Wilton Park enjoys three advantages. Its setting and atmosphere maroon its visitors in a kind of political quarantine, away from daily routines and habits, including habits of thought. Its blend of nationalities and callings obliges them to seek mutual contact in areas beyond the familiar hierarchies of rank or expertise. The fact that they meet, speak, listen, and reflect in private and off the record, with no official statements and no verbatim reports, gives them the chance of dispassionate discussion, not partisan debate. The Academic Staff, all experienced 'moderators' in such discussion, help precisely to moderate their tone and

414

enhance their impartiality. And the Advisory and Academic Councils, the guardians of Wilton Park's independence, are the final guarantors that it is not, despite some newcomers' suspicions, a propaganda outfit or brain-washing machine.

Over fifty years and more, Wilton Park has obviously changed. Even its nomenclature has altered. Heinz Koeppler was its only *Warden*: since then it has been headed by a *Director*, and now by a *Chief Executive*. In Koeppler's day, meetings were known as *Courses*; today, they are *Conferences* – less didactic, but less purposeful in apparent intent. *Wilton Park*, the name borrowed from Beaconsfield, remains a proud, time-honoured title: but Whitehall's later written records increasingly refer to *Wiston House* or the *Wiston House Conference Centre* – less arresting and less distinctive from other centres elsewhere.

Over the years, too, Wilton Park has attracted its share of hostility. On at least a dozen occasions, the Treasury tried to close it down. Ostensibly, the reason was hard-headed economics. As costs mounted, Treasury officials understandably asked whether foreigners and others should enjoy free board and lodging and discussion, partly or wholly at taxpayers' expense. If this was part of Britain's information or propaganda effort, it was just about acceptable to Treasury housekeepers; but Wilton Park encouraged open discussion, including criticism of HMG. The Treasury's objection, of course, reflected a narrow conception of the information effort, ignoring the subtle benefits of Koeppler's 'self-denying ordinance' as it ignored those of the BBC World Service, projecting Britain's reputation as a champion of free speech. But the persistence and intensity of Wilton Park's critics, some in the FCO as well as the Treasury, smacked of more than a desire to save money. It seemed to be fuelled by resentment, envying a life of luxury in a venerable stately home.

Wilton Park's survival against these onslaughts is remarkable in itself. It owes much to the efforts, intellectual and political, of individuals who have led, championed, defended, and adapted the institution that Heinz Koeppler virtually invented. They have ensured not only that Wilton Park resisted attempts to abolish it, but that its essential qualities have been preserved.

Some early elements it has had to modify. In a busy world, few can now afford to spend several weeks away from their official duties. This is a loss, but unavoidable: Heinz Koeppler himself would have accepted that. More participants, likewise, are specialists than in Koeppler's day. This is partly because Koeppler's political task was to tackle first principles, and partly because life itself now requires more expertise. It has not meant that first principles are neglected: Geoffrey Denton's debate with the Chinese is a case in point. The Foreign and Commonwealth Office may now seem to exercise a greater *droit de regard* on Wilton Park's programmes; but even Koeppler discussed them with it, and how much notice the Chief Executive takes of its suggestions is still up to him. Finally, as an Executive Agency, Wilton Park is obliged to move ever closer towards balancing its books. Accountancy might conceivably taint academic independence; but financial independence from the FCO and the Treasury would surely enhance academic freedom too.

So Wilton Park endures and flourishes, outliving its founder and outlasting its detractors. Certainly, it is now an institution. Its heroic battles are history. But its purpose remains revolutionary – simple to state and immensely hard to achieve. Its task is what it has always been: to turn ignorance into understanding, prejudice into appreciation, suspicion and hatred into respect and trust.

Index